"WAS SHE A FAIR WOMAN—OR DARK, LIKE ME?"

—Frontispiece, Vol. Eight, page 44.

# THE WORKS OF

# WILKIE COLLINS

## VOLUME EIGHT

### *WITH EIGHT ILLUSTRATIONS*

# ARMADALE

## (PART ONE)

———

NEW YORK
PETER FENELON COLLIER, PUBLISHER

# LIST OF ILLUSTRATIONS.

## VOLUME EIGHT.

---

## ARMADALE.

READERS in general—on whose friendly reception experience has given me some reason to rely—will, I venture to hope, appreciate whatever merit there may be in this story without any prefatory pleading for it on my part. They will, I think, see that it has not been hastily meditated or idly wrought out. They will judge it accordingly, and I ask no more.

Readers in particular will, I have some reason to suppose, be here and there disturbed, perhaps even offended, by finding that "Armadale" oversteps, in more than one direction, the narrow limits within which they are disposed to restrict the development of modern fiction—if they can.

Nothing that I could say to these persons here would help me with them as Time will help me if my work lasts. I am not afraid of my design being permanently misunderstood, provided the execution has done it any sort of justice. Estimated by the clap-trap morality of the present day, this may be a very daring book. Judged by the Christian morality which is of all time, it is only a book that is daring enough to speak the truth.

LONDON, *April, 1866.*

# ARMADALE.

## PROLOGUE.

### CHAPTER I.

#### THE TRAVELERS.

It was the opening of the season of eighteen hundred and thirty-two, at the Baths of WILD-BAD.

The evening shadows were beginning to gather over the quiet little German town, and the diligence was expected every minute. Before the door of the principal inn, waiting the arrival of the first visitors of the year, were assembled the three notable personages of Wildbad, accompanied by their wives—the mayor, representing the inhabitants; the doctor, representing the waters; the landlord, representing his own establishment. Beyond this select circle, grouped snugly about the trim little square in front of the inn, appeared the towns-people in general, mixed here and there with the country people, in their quaint German costume, placidly expectant of the diligence—the men in short black jackets, tight black breeches, and three-cornered

(5)

beaver hats; the women with their long light
hair hanging in one thickly plaited tail behind
them, and the waists of their short woolen gowns
inserted modestly in the region of their shoulder-
blades. Round the outer edge of the assemblage
thus formed, flying detachments of plump white-
headed children careered in perpetual motion;
while, mysteriously apart from the rest of the
inhabitants, the musicians of the Baths stood
collected in one lost corner, waiting the appearance of the first visitors to play the first tune of
the season in the form of a serenade. The light
of a May evening was still bright on the tops
of the great wooded hills watching high over
the town on the right hand and the left; and the
cool breeze that comes before sunset came keenly
fragrant here with the balsamic odor of the first
of the Black Forest.

"Mr. Landlord," said the mayor's wife (giving the landlord his title), "have you any foreign guests coming on this first day of the
season?"

"Madame Mayoress," replied the landlord (returning the compliment), "I have two. They
have written—the one by the hand of his servant, the other by his own hand apparently—to
order their rooms; and they are from England
both, as I think by their names. If you ask
me to pronounce those names, my tongue hesi-
tates; if you ask me to spell them, here they
are, letter by letter, first and second in their
order as they come. First, a high-born stranger (by title Mister) who introduces himself in

eight letters—A, r, m, a, d, a, l, e—and comes ill in his own carriage. Second, a high-born stranger (by title Mister also), who introduces himself in four letters—N, e, a, l—and comes ill in the diligence. His excellency of the eight letters writes to me (by his servant) in French; his excellency of the four letters writes to me in German. The rooms of both are ready. I know no more."

"Perhaps," suggested the mayor's wife, "Mr. Doctor has heard from one or both of these illustrious strangers?"

"From one only, Madam Mayoress; but not, strictly speaking, from the person himself. I have received a medical report of his excellency of the eight letters, and his case seems a bad one. God help him!"

"The diligence!" cried a child from the outskirts of the crowd.

The musicians seized their instruments, and silence fell on the whole community. From far away in the windings of the forest gorge, the ring of horses' bells came faintly clear through the evening stillness. Which carriage was approaching—the private carriage with Mr. Armadale, or the public carriage with Mr. Neal?

"Play, my friends!" cried the mayor to the musicians. "Public or private, here are the first sick people of the season. Let them find us cheerful."

The band played a lively dance tune, and the children in the square footed it merrily to the music. At the same moment, their elders near

the inn door drew aside, and disclosed the first
shadow of gloom that fell over the gayety and
beauty of the scene. Through the opening made
on either hand, a little procession of stout country girls advanced, each drawing after her an
empty chair on wheels; each in waiting (and
knitting while she waited) for the paralyzed
wretches who came helpless by hundreds then
—who come helpless by thousands now—to the
waters of Wildbad for relief.

While the band played, while the children
danced, while the buzz of many talkers deepened, while the strong young nurses of the
coming cripples knitted impenetrably, a woman's insatiable curiosity about other women
asserted itself in the mayor's wife. She drew
the landlady aside, and whispered a question
to her on the spot.

"A word more, ma'am," said the mayor's
wife, "about the two strangers from England.
Are their letters explicit? Have they got any
ladies with them?"

"The one by the diligence—no," replied the
landlady. "But the one by the private carriage
—yes. He comes with a child; he comes with
a nurse; and," concluded the landlady, skillfully
keeping the main point of interest till the last,
"he comes with a Wife."

The mayoress brightened; the doctoress (assisting at the conference) brightened; the landlady
nodded significantly. In the minds of all three
the same thought started into life at the same
moment—"We shall see the Fashions!"

In a minute more, there was a sudden movement in the crowd; and a chorus of voices proclaimed that the travelers were at hand.

By this time the coming vehicle was in sight, and all further doubt was at an end. It was the diligence that now approached by the long street leading into the square—the diligence (in a dazzling new coat of yellow paint) that delivered the first visitors of the season at the inn door. Of the ten travelers released from the middle compartment and the back compartment of the carriage—all from various parts of Germany— three were lifted out helpless, and were placed in the chairs on wheels to be drawn to their lodgings in the town. The front compartment contained two passengers only—Mr. Neal and his traveling servant. With an arm on either side to assist him, the stranger (whose malady appeared to be locally confined to a lameness in one of his feet) succeeded in descending the steps of the carriage easily enough. While he steadied himself on the pavement by the help of his stick —looking not over-patiently toward the musicians who were serenading him with the waltz in "Der Freischütz" — his personal appearance rather damped the enthusiasm of the friendly little circle assembled to welcome him. He was a lean, tall, serious, middle - aged man, with a cold gray eye and a long upper lip, with overhanging eyebrows and high cheek-bones; a man who looked what he was—every inch a Scotchman.

"Where is the proprietor of this hotel?" he

asked, speaking in the German language, with a fluent readiness of expression, and an icy coldness of manner. "Fetch the doctor," he continued, when the landlord had presented himself, "I want to see him immediately."

"I am here already, sir," said the doctor, advancing from the circle of friends, "and my services are entirely at your disposal."

"Thank you," said Mr. Neal, looking at the doctor, as the rest of us look at a dog when we have whistled and the dog has come. "I shall be glad to consult you to-morrow morning, at ten o'clock, about my own case. I only want to trouble you now with a message which I have undertaken to deliver. We overtook a traveling-carriage on the road here with a gentleman in it—an Englishman, I believe—who appeared to be seriously ill. A lady who was with him begged me to see you immediately on my arrival, and to secure your professional assistance in removing the patient from the carriage. Their courier has met with an accident, and has been left behind on the road, and they are obliged to travel very slowly. If you are here in an hour, you will be here in time to receive them. That is the message. Who is this gentleman who appears to be anxious to speak to me? The mayor? If you wish to see my passport, sir, my servant will show it to you. No? You wish to welcome me to the place, and to offer your services? I am infinitely flattered. If you have any authority to shorten the performances of your town band, you would be doing me a kindness to exert it.

My nerves are irritable, and I dislike music. Where is the landlord? No; I want to see my rooms. I don't want your arm; I can get upstairs with the help of my stick. Mr. Mayor and Mr. Doctor, we need not detain one another any longer. I wish you good-night."

Both mayor and doctor looked after the Scotchman as he limped upstairs, and shook their heads together in mute disapproval of him. The ladies, as usual, went a step further, and expressed their opinions openly in the plainest words. The case under consideration (so far as *they* were concerned) was the scandalous case of a man who had passed them over entirely without notice. Mrs. Mayor could only attribute such an outrage to the native ferocity of a savage. Mrs. Doctor took a stronger view still, and considered it as proceeding from the inbred brutality of a hog.

The hour of waiting for the traveling-carriage wore on, and the creeping night stole up the hillsides softly. One by one the stars appeared, and the first lights twinkled in the windows of the inn. As the darkness came, the last idlers deserted the square; as the darkness came, the mighty silence of the forest above flowed in on the valley, and strangely and suddenly hushed the lonely little town.

The hour of waiting wore out, and the figure of the doctor, walking backward and forward anxiously, was still the only living figure left in the square. Five minutes, ten minutes, twenty minutes, were counted out by the doctor's watch, before the first sound came through

the night silence to warn him of the approaching
carriage. Slowly it emerged into the square, at
the walking pace of the horses, and drew up, as
a hearse might have drawn up, at the door of the
inn.

"Is the doctor here?" asked a woman's voice,
speaking, out of the darkness of the carriage, in
the French language.

"I am here, madam," replied the doctor, taking a light from the landlord's hand and opening
the carriage door.

The first face that the light fell on was the
face of the lady who had just spoken—a young,
darkly beautiful woman, with the tears standing
thick and bright in her eager black eyes. The
second face revealed was the face of a shriveled
old negress, sitting opposite the lady on the back
seat. The third was the face of a little sleeping
child in the negress's lap. With a quick gesture
of impatience, the lady signed to the nurse to
leave the carriage first with the child. "Pray
take them out of the way," she said to the landlady; "pray take them to their room." She got
out herself when her request had been complied
with. Then the light fell clear for the first time
on the further side of the carriage, and the fourth
traveler was disclosed to view.

He lay helpless on a mattress, supported by
a stretcher; his hair, long and disordered, under
a black skull-cap; his eyes wide open, rolling
to and fro ceaselessly anxious; the rest of his
face as void of all expression of the character
within him, and the thought within him, as

if he had been dead. There was no looking
at him now, and guessing what he might once
have been. The leaden blank of his face met
every question as to his age, his rank, his
temper, and his looks which that face might
once have answered, in impenetrable silence.
Nothing spoke for him now but the shock that
had struck him with the death-in-life of paralysis. The doctor's eye questioned his lower
limbs, and Death-in-Life answered, *I am here.*
The doctor's eye, rising attentively by way of
his hands and arms, questioned upward and
upward to the muscles round his mouth, and
Death-in-Life answered, *I am coming.*

In the face of a calamity so unsparing and so
dreadful, there was nothing to be said. The silent sympathy of help was all that could be
offered to the woman who stood weeping at the
carriage door.

As they bore him on his bed across the hall of
the hotel, his wandering eyes encountered the
face of his wife. They rested on her for a moment, and in that moment he spoke.

"The child?" he said in English, with a slow,
thick, laboring articulation.

"The child is safe upstairs," she answered,
faintly.

"My desk?"

"It is in my hands. Look! I won't trust it
to anybody; I am taking care of it for you myself."

He closed his eyes for the first time after that
answer, and said no more. Tenderly and skill-

fully he was carried up the stairs, with his wife on one side of him, and the doctor (ominously silent) on the other. The landlord and the servants following saw the door of his room open and close on him; heard the lady burst out crying hysterically as soon as she was alone with the doctor and the sick man; saw the doctor come out, half an hour later, with his ruddy face a shade paler than usual; pressed him eagerly for information, and received but one answer to all their inquiries—"Wait till I have seen him to-morrow. Ask me nothing to-night." They all knew the doctor's ways, and they augured ill when he left them hurriedly with that reply.

So the two first English visitors of the year came to the Baths of Wildbad in the season of eighteen hundred and thirty-two.

## CHAPTER II.

### THE SOLID SIDE OF THE SCOTCH CHARACTER.

At ten o'clock the next morning, Mr. Neal—waiting for the medical visit which he had himself appointed for that hour—looked at his watch, and discovered, to his amazement, that he was waiting in vain. It was close on eleven when the door opened at last, and the doctor entered the room.

"I appointed ten o'clock for your visit," said Mr. Neal. "In my country, a medical man is a punctual man."

"In my country," returned the doctor, without the least ill-humor, "a medical man is exactly like other men—he is at the mercy of accidents. Pray grant me your pardon, sir, for being so long after my time; I have been detained by a very distressing case—the case of Mr. Armadale, whose traveling-carriage you passed on the road yesterday."

Mr. Neal looked at his medical attendant with a sour surprise. There was a latent anxiety in the doctor's eye, a latent preoccupation in the doctor's manner, which he was at a loss to account for. For a moment the two faces confronted each other silently, in marked national contrast—the Scotchman's, long and lean, hard and regular; the German's, plump and florid, soft and shapeless. One face looked as if it had never been young; the other, as if it would never grow old.

"Might I venture to remind you," said Mr. Neal, "that the case now under consideration is MY case, and not Mr. Armadale's?"

"Certainly," replied the doctor, still vacillating between the case he had come to see and the case he had just left. "You appear to be suffering from lameness; let me look at your foot."

Mr. Neal's malady, however serious it might be in his own estimation, was of no extraordinary importance in a medical point of view. He was suffering from a rheumatic affection of the ankle-joint. The necessary questions were asked and answered, and the necessary baths were prescribed. In ten minutes the consultation was at an end, and the patient was waiting in significant silence for the medical adviser to take his leave.

"I cannot conceal from myself," said the doctor, rising, and hesitating a little, "that I am intruding on you. But I am compelled to beg your indulgence if I return to the subject of Mr. Armadale."

"May I ask what compels you?"

"The duty which I owe as a Christian," answered the doctor, "to a dying man."

Mr. Neal started. Those who touched his sense of religious duty touched the quickest sense in his nature.

"You have established your claim on my attention," he said, gravely. "My time is yours."

"I will not abuse your kindness," replied the doctor, resuming his chair. "I will be as short as I can. Mr. Armadale's case is briefly this: He has passed the greater part of his life in the West Indies—a wild life, and a vicious life, by his own confession. Shortly after his marriage —now some three years since—the first symptoms of an approaching paralytic affection began to show themselves, and his medical advisers ordered him away to try the climate of Europe. Since leaving the West Indies he has lived principally in Italy, with no benefit to his health. From Italy, before the last seizure attacked him, he removed to Switzerland, and from Switzerland he has been sent to this place. So much I know from his doctor's report; the

rest I can tell you from my own personal experience. Mr. Armadale has been sent to Wildbad too late: he is virtually a dead man. The
paralysis is fast spreading upward, and disease
of the lower part of the spine has already taken
place. He can still move his hands a little, but
he can hold nothing in his fingers. He can still
articulate, but he may wake speechless to-morrow or next day. If I give him a week more
to live, I give him what I honestly believe to
be the utmost length of his span. At his own
request I told him, as carefully and as tenderly
as I could, what I have just told you. The result was very distressing; the violence of the
patient's agitation was a violence which I despair of describing to you. I took the liberty
of asking him whether his affairs were unsettled.
Nothing of the sort. His will is in the hands of
his executor in London, and he leaves his wife
and child well provided for. My next question
succeeded better; it hit the mark: 'Have you
something on your mind to do before you die
which is not done yet?' He gave a great gasp
of relief, which said, as no words could have
said it, Yes. 'Can I help you?' 'Yes. I have
something to write that I *must* write; can you
make me hold a pen?'

"He might as well have asked me if I could
perform a miracle. I could only say No. 'If
I dictate the words,' he went on, 'can you write
what I tell you to write?' Once more I could
only say No. I understand a little English, but
I can neither speak it nor write it. Mr. Arma-

dale understands French when it is spoken (as
I speak it to him) slowly, but he cannot express
himself in that language; and of German he is
totally ignorant. In this difficulty, I said, what
any one else in my situation would have said:
'Why ask *me?* there is Mrs. Armadale at your
service in the next room.' Before I could get
up from my chair to fetch her, he stopped me—
not by words, but by a look of horror which fixed
me, by main force of astonishment, in my place.
'Surely,' I said, 'your wife is the fittest person
to write for you as you desire?' 'The last person. under heaven!' he answered. 'What!' I
said, 'you ask me, a foreigner and a stranger,
to write words at your dictation which you keep
a secret from your wife!' Conceive my astonishment when he answered me, without a moment's hesitation, 'Yes!' I sat lost; I sat silent.
'If *you* can't write English,' he said, 'find somebody who can.' I tried to remonstrate. He
burst into a dreadful moaning cry—a dumb entreaty, like the entreaty of a dog. 'Hush! hush!'
I said, 'I will find somebody.' 'To-day!' he broke
out, 'before my speech fails me, like my hand.'
'To-day, in an hour's time.' He shut his eyes; he
quieted himself instantly. 'While I am waiting
for you,' he said, 'let me see my little boy.' He
had shown no tenderness when he spoke of his
wife, but I saw the tears on his cheeks when
he asked for his child. My profession, sir, has
not made me so hard a man as you might think;
and my doctor's heart was as heavy, when I
went out to fetch the child, as if I had not been

a doctor at all. I am afraid you think this rather weak on my part?"

The doctor looked appealingly at Mr. Neal. He might as well have looked at a rock in the Black Forest. Mr. Neal entirely declined to be drawn by any doctor in Christendom out of the regions of plain fact.

"Go on," he said. "I presume you have not told me all that you have to tell me, yet?"

"Surely you understand my object in coming here, now?" returned the other.

"Your object is plain enough, at last. You invite me to connect myself blindfold with a matter which is in the last degree suspicious, so far. I decline giving you any answer until I know more than I know now. Did you think it necessary to inform this man's wife of what had passed between you, and to ask her for an explanation?"

"Of course I thought it necessary!" said the doctor, indignant at the reflection on his humanity which the question seemed to imply. "If ever I saw a woman fond of her husband, and sorry for her husband, it is this unhappy Mrs. Armadale. As soon as we were left alone together, I sat down by her side, and I took her hand in mine. Why not? I am an ugly old man, and I may allow myself such liberties as these!"

"Excuse me," said the impenetrable Scotchman. "I beg to suggest that you are losing the thread of the narrative."

"Nothing more likely," returned the doctor,

recovering his good humor. "It is in the habit of my nation to be perpetually losing the thread; and it is evidently in the habit of yours, sir, to be perpetually finding it. What an example here of the order of the universe, and the everlasting fitness of things!"

"Will you oblige me, once for all, by confining yourself to the facts," persisted Mr. Neal, frowning impatiently. 'May I inquire, for my own information, whether Mrs. Armadale could tell you what it is her husband wishes me to write, and why it is that he refuses to let her write for him?"

"There is my thread found—and thank you for finding it!" said the doctor. "You shall hear what Mrs. Armadale had to tell me, in Mrs. Armadale's own words. 'The cause that now shuts me out of his confidence,' she said, 'is, I firmly believe, the same cause that has always shut me out of his heart. I am the wife he has wedded, but I am not the woman he loves. I knew when he married me that another man had won from him the woman he loved. I thought I could make him forget her. I hoped when I married him; I hoped again when I bore him a son. Need I tell you the end of my hopes—you have seen it for yourself.' (Wait, sir, I entreat you! I have not lost the thread again; I am following it inch by inch.) 'Is this all you know?' I asked. 'All I knew,' she said, 'till a short time since. It was when we were in Switzerland, and when his illness was nearly at its worst, that news came to him by accident of

that other woman who has been the shadow and
the poison of my life—news that she (like me)
had borne her husband a son. On the instant of
his making that discovery—a trifling discovery,
if ever there was one yet—a mortal fear seized
on him: not for me, not for himself; a fear for
his own child. The same day (without a word
to me) he sent for the doctor. I was mean,
wicked, what you please—I listened at the door.
I heard him say: *I have something to tell my
son, when my son grows old enough to understand me. Shall I live to tell it?* The
doctor would say nothing certain. The same
night (still without a word to me) he locked
himself into his room. What would any woman, treated as I was, have done in my place?
She would have done as I did—she would have
listened again. I heard him say to himself: *I
shall not live to tell it: I must write it before
I die.* I heard his pen scrape, scrape, scrape
over the paper; I heard him groaning and sobbing as he wrote; I implored him for God's sake
to let me in. The cruel pen went scrape, scrape,
scrape; the cruel pen was all the answer he gave
me. I waited at the door—hours—I don't know
how long. On a sudden, the pen stopped; and
I heard no more. I whispered through the key-
hole softly; I said I was cold and weary with
waiting; I said, Oh, my love, let me in! Not
even the cruel pen answered me now: silence answered me. With all the strength of my miserable hands I beat at the door. The servants came
up and broke it in. We were too late; the harm

was done. Over that fatal letter, the stroke had struck him—over that fatal letter, we found him, paralyzed as you see him now. Those words which he wants you to write are the words he would have written himself if the stroke had spared him till the morning. From that time to this there has been a blank place left in the letter; and it is that blank place which he has just asked you to fill up.'—In those words Mrs. Armadale spoke to me; in those words you have the sum and substance of all the information I can give. Say, if you please, sir, have I kept the thread at last? Have I shown you the necessity which brings me here from your countryman's death-bed?''

"Thus far," said Mr. Neal, "you merely show me that you are exciting yourself. This is too serious a matter to be treated as you are treating it now. You have involved Me in the business, and I insist on seeing my way plainly. Don't raise your hands; your hands are not a part of the question. If I am to be concerned in the completion of this mysterious letter, it is only an act of justifiable prudence on my part to inquire what the letter is about. Mrs. Armadale appears to have favored you with an infinite number of domestic particulars—in return, I presume, for your polite attention in taking her by the hand. May I ask what she could tell you about her husband's letter, so far as her husband has written it?"

"Mrs. Armadale could tell me nothing," replied the doctor, with a sudden formality in his manner, which showed that his forbearance was at last failing him. "Before she was composed enough to think of the letter, her husband had asked for it, and had caused it to be locked up in his desk. She knows that he has since, time after time, tried to finish it, and that, time after time, the pen has dropped from his fingers. She knows, when all other hope of his restoration was at an end, that his medical advisers encouraged him to hope in the famous waters of this place. And last, she knows how that hope has ended; for she knows what I told her husband this morning."

The frown which had been gathering latterly on Mr. Neal's face deepened and darkened. He looked at the doctor as if the doctor had personally offended him.

"The more I think of the position you are asking me to take," he said, "the less I like it. Can you undertake to say positively that Mr. Armadale is in his right mind?"

"Yes; as positively as words can say it."

"Does his wife sanction your coming here to request my interference?"

"His wife sends me to you—the only Englishman in Wildbad—to write for your dying countryman what he cannot write for himself; and what no one else in this place but you can write for him."

That answer drove Mr. Neal back to the last inch of ground left him to stand on. Even on that inch the Scotchman resisted still.

"Wait a little!" he said. "You put it strongly;

let us be quite sure you put it correctly as well.
Let us be quite sure there is nobody to take this
responsibility but myself. There is a mayor in
Wildbad, to begin with—a man who possesses
an official character to justify his interference."

"A man of a thousand," said the doctor.
"With one fault—he knows no language but
his own."

"There is an English legation at Stuttgart,"
persisted Mr. Neal.

"And there are miles on miles of the forest
between this and Stuttgart," rejoined the doctor. "If we sent this moment, we could get no
help from the legation before to-morrow; and it
is as likely as not, in the state of this dying
man's articulation, that to-morrow may find
him speechless. I don't know whether his last
wishes are wishes harmless to his child and to
others, or wishes hurtful to his child and to others; but I *do* know that they must be fulfilled at
once or never, and that you are the only man
that can help him."

That open declaration brought the discussion
to a close. It fixed Mr. Neal fast between the
two alternatives of saying Yes, and committing
an act of imprudence, or of saying No, and committing an act of inhumanity. There was a
silence of some minutes. The Scotchman steadily
reflected; and the German steadily watched him.

The responsibility of saying the next words
rested on Mr. Neal, and in course of time Mr.
Neal took it. He rose from his chair with a
sullen sense of injury lowering on his heavy

eyebrows, and working sourly in the lines at the corners of his mouth.

"My position is forced on me," he said. "I have no choice but to accept it."

The doctor's impulsive nature rose in revolt against the merciless brevity and gracelessness of that reply. "I wish to God," he broke out fervently, "I knew English enough to take your place at Mr. Armadale's bedside!"

"Bating your taking the name of the Almighty in vain," answered the Scotchman, "I entirely agree with you. I wish you did."

Without another word on either side, they left the room together—the doctor leading the way.

## CHAPTER III.

### THE WRECK OF THE TIMBER SHIP.

No one answered the doctor's knock when he and his companion reached the antechamber door of Mr. Armadale's apartments. They entered unannounced; and when they looked into the sitting-room, the sitting-room was empty.

"I must see Mrs. Armadale," said Mr. Neal. "I decline acting in the matter unless Mrs. Armadale authorizes my interference with her own lips."

"Mrs. Armadale is probably with her husband," replied the doctor. He approached a door at the inner end of the sitting-room while he spoke—hesitated—and, turning round again,

Vol. 8                                      -B

looked at his sour companion anxiously. "I am afraid I spoke a little harshly, sir, when we were leaving your room," he said. "I beg your pardon for it, with all my heart. Before this poor afflicted lady comes in, will you—will you excuse my asking your utmost gentleness and consideration for her?"

"No, sir," retorted the other harshly; "I won't excuse you. What right have I given you to think me wanting in gentleness and consideration toward anybody?"

The doctor saw it was useless. "I beg your pardon again," he said, resignedly, and left the unapproachable stranger to himself.

Mr. Neal walked to the window, and stood there, with his eyes mechanically fixed on the prospect, composing his mind for the coming interview.

It was midday; the sun shone bright and warm; and all the little world of Wildbad was alive and merry in the genial springtime. Now and again heavy wagons, with black-faced carters in charge, rolled by the window, bearing their precious lading of charcoal from the forest. Now and again, hurled over the headlong current of the stream that runs through the town, great lengths of timber, loosely strung together in interminable series—with the booted raftsmen, pole in hand, poised watchful at either end— shot swift and serpent-like past the houses on their course to the distant Rhine. High and steep above the gabled wooden buildings on the river-bank, the great hillsides, crested black

with firs, shone to the shining heavens in a
glory of lustrous green. In and out, where the
forest foot-paths wound from the grass through
the trees, from the trees over the grass, the bright
spring dresses of women and children, on the
search for wild flowers, traveled to and fro in
the lofty distance like spots of moving light.
Below, on the walk by the stream side, the
booths of the little bazar that had opened punctually with the opening season showed all their
glittering trinkets, and fluttered in the balmy air
their splendor of many-colored flags. Longingly,
here the children looked at the show; patiently
the sunburned lasses plied their knitting as they
paced the walk; courteously the passing towns-
people, by fours and fives, and the passing visitors, by ones and twos, greeted each other, hat
in hand; and slowly, slowly, the crippled and
the helpless in their chairs on wheels came out
in the cheerful noontide with the rest, and took
their share of the blessed light that cheers, of the
blessed sun that shines for all.

On this scene the Scotchman looked, with eyes
that never noted its beauty, with a mind far
away from every lesson that it taught. One by
one he meditated the words he should say when
the wife came in. One by one he pondered
over the conditions he might impose before
he took the pen in hand at the husband's bedside.

"Mrs. Armadale is here," said the doctor's
voice, interposing suddenly between his reflections and himself.

He turned on the instant, and saw before him, with the pure midday light shining full on her, a woman of the mixed blood of the European and the African race, with the Northern delicacy in the shape of her face, and the Southern richness in its color—a woman in the prime of her beauty, who moved with an inbred grace, who looked with an inbred fascination, whose large, languid black eyes rested on him gratefully, whose little dusky hand offered itself to him in mute expression of her thanks, with the welcome that is given to the coming of a friend. For the first time in his life the Scotchman was taken by surprise. Every self-preservative word that he had been meditating but an instant since dropped out of his memory. His thrice impenetrable armor of habitual suspicion, habitual self-discipline, and habitual reserve, which had never fallen from him in a woman's presence before, fell from him in this woman's presence, and brought him to his knees, a conquered man. He took the hand she offered him, and bowed over it his first honest homage to the sex, in silence.

She hesitated on her side. The quick feminine perception which, in happier circumstances, would have pounced on the secret of his embarrassment in an instant, failed her now. She attributed his strange reception of her to pride, to reluctance—to any cause but the unexpected revelation of her own beauty. "I have no words to thank you," she said, faintly, trying to propitiate him. "I should only distress you if I tried to speak." Her lip began to tremble, she drew back a little, and turned away her head in silence.

The doctor, who had been standing apart, quietly observant in a cornèr, advanced before Mr. Neal could interfere, and led Mrs. Armadale to a chair. "Don't be afraid of him," whispered the good man, patting her gently on the shoulder. "He was hard as iron in my hands, but I think, by the look of him, he will be soft as wax in yours. Say the words I told you to say, and let us take him to your husband's room, before those sharp wits of his have time to recover themselves."

She roused her sinking resolution, and advanced half-way to the window to meet Mr. Neal. "My kind friend, the doctor, has told me, sir, that your only hesitation in coming here is a hesitation on my account," she said, her head drooping a little, and her rich color fading away while she spoke. "I am deeply grateful, but I entreat you not to think of *me*. What my husband wishes—" Her voice faltered; she waited resolutely, and recovered herself. "What my husband wishes in his last moments, I wish too."

This time Mr. Neal was composed enough to answer her. In low, earnest tones, he entreated her to say no more. "I was only anxious to show you every consideration," he said. "I am only anxious now to spare you every distress." As he spoke, something like a glow of color rose slowly on his sallow face. Her eyes were looking at him, softly attentive; and he thought guiltily of his meditations at the window before she came in.

The doctor saw his opportunity. He opened the door that led into Mr. Armadale's room, and stood by it, waiting silently. Mrs. Armadale entered first. In a minute more the door was closed again; and Mr. Neal stood committed to the responsibility that had been forced on him— committed beyond recall.

The room was decorated in the gaudy continental fashion, and the warm sunlight was shining in joyously. Cupids and flowers were painted on the ceiling; bright ribbons looped up the white window-curtains; a smart gilt clock ticked on a velvet-covered mantelpiece; mirrors gleamed on the walls, and flowers in all the colors of the rainbow speckled the carpet. In the midst of the finery, and the glitter, and the light, lay the paralyzed man, with his wandering eyes, and his lifeless lower face—his head propped high with many pillows; his helpless hands laid out over the bed-clothes like the hands of a corpse. By the bed head stood, grim, and old, and silent, the shriveled black nurse; and on the counterpane, between his father's outspread hands, lay the child, in his little white frock, absorbed in the enjoyment of a new toy. When the door opened, and Mrs. Armadale led the way in, the boy was tossing his plaything—a soldier on horseback—backward and forward over the helpless hands on either side of him; and the father's wandering eyes were following the toy to and fro, with a stealthy and ceaseless vigilance—

a vigilance as of a wild animal, terrible to
see.

The moment Mr. Neal appeared in the doorway, those restless eyes stopped, looked up, and
fastened on the stranger with a fierce eagerness
of inquiry. Slowly the motionless lips struggled
into movement. With thick, hesitating articulation, they put the question which the eyes asked
mutely, into words: "Are you the man?"

Mr. Neal advanced to the bedside, Mrs. Armadale drawing back from it as he approached, and
waiting with the doctor at the further end of the
room. The child looked up, toy in hand, as the
stranger came near, opened his bright brown eyes
in momentary astonishment, and then went on
with his game.

"I have been made acquainted with your sad
situation, sir," said Mr. Neal; "and I have come
here to place my services at your disposal—services which no one but myself, as your medical
attendant informs me, is in a position to render
you in this strange place. My name is Neal. I
am a writer to the signet in Edinburgh; and I
may presume to say for myself that any confidence you wish to place in me will be confidence
not improperly bestowed."

The eyes of the beautiful wife were not confusing him now. He spoke to the helpless husband
quietly and seriously, without his customary
harshness, and with a grave compassion in his
manner which presented him at his best. The
sight of the death-bed had steadied him.

"You wish me to write something for you?"

he resumed, after waiting for a reply, and waiting in vain.

"Yes!" said the dying man, with the all-mastering impatience which his tongue was powerless to express, glittering angrily in his eye. "My hand is gone, and my speech is going. Write!"

Before there was time to speak again, Mr. Neal heard the rustling of a woman's dress, and the quick creaking of casters on the carpet behind him. Mrs. Armadale was moving the writing-table across the room to the foot of the bed. If he was to set up those safeguards of his own devising that were to bear him harmless through all results to come, now was the time, or never. He kept his back turned on Mrs. Armadale, and put his precautionary question at once in the plainest terms.

"May I ask, sir, before I take the pen in hand, what it is you wish me to write?"

The angry eyes of the paralyzed man glittered brighter and brighter. His lips opened and closed again. He made no reply.

Mr. Neal tried another precautionary question, in a new direction.

"When I have written what you wish me to write," he asked, "what is to be done with it?"

This time the answer came:

"Seal it up in my presence, and post it to my ex—"

His laboring articulation suddenly stopped, and he looked piteously in the questioner's face for the next word.

ARMADALE.                    33

"Do you mean your executor?"

"Yes."

"It is a letter, I suppose, that I am to post?" There was no answer. "May I ask if it is a letter altering your will?"

"Nothing of the sort."

Mr. Neal considered a little. The mystery was thickening. The one way out of it, so far, was the way traced faintly through that strange story of the unfinished letter which the doctor had repeated to him in Mrs. Armadale's words. The nearer he approached his unknown responsibility, the more ominous it seemed of something serious to come. Should he risk another question before he pledged himself irrevocably? As the doubt crossed his mind, he felt Mrs. Armadale's silk dress touch him on the side furthest from her husband. Her delicate dark hand was laid gently on his arm; her full deep African eyes looked at him in submissive entreaty. "My husband is very anxious," she whispered. "Will you quiet his anxiety, sir, by taking your place at the writing-table?"

It was from *her* lips that the request came— from the lips of the person who had the best right to hesitate, the wife who was excluded from the secret! Most men in Mr. Neal's position would have given up all their safeguards on the spot. The Scotchman gave them all up but one.

"I will write what you wish me to write," he said, addressing Mr. Armadale. "I will seal it in your presence; and I will post it to your executor myself. But, in engaging to do this, I must

beg you to remember that I am acting entirely
in the dark; and I must ask you to excuse me,
if I reserve my own entire freedom of action,
when your wishes in relation to the writing and
the posting of the letter have been fulfilled.''

"Do you give me your promise?''

"If you want my promise, sir, I will give it
—subject to the condition I have just named.''

"Take your condition, and keep your promise.
My desk,'' he added, looking at his wife for the
first time.

She crossed the room eagerly to fetch the desk
from a chair in a corner. Returning with it,
she made a passing sign to the negress, who still
stood, grim and silent, in the place that she had
occupied from the first. The woman advanced,
obedient to the sign, to take the child from the
bed. At the instant when she touched him, the
father's eyes — fixed previously on the desk—
turned on her with the stealthy quickness of a
cat. "No!'' he said. "No!'' echoed the fresh
voice of the boy, still charmed with his plaything, and still liking his place on the bed. The
negress left the room, and the child, in high
triumph, trotted his toy soldier up and down on
the bedclothes that lay rumpled over his father's
breast. His mother's lovely face contracted with
a pang of jealousy as she looked at him.

"Shall I open your desk?'' she asked, pushing back the child's plaything sharply while she
spoke. An answering look from her husband
guided her hand to the place under his pillow
where the key was hidden. She opened the

desk, and disclosed inside some small sheets of manuscript pinned together. "These?" she inquired, producing them.

"Yes," he said. "You can go now."

The Scotchman sitting at the writing-table, the doctor stirring a stimulant mixture in a corner, looked at each other with an anxiety in both their faces which they could neither of them control. The words that banished the wife from the room were spoken. The moment had come.

"You can go now," said Mr. Armadale, for the second time.

She looked at the child, established comfortably on the bed, and an ashy paleness spread slowly over her face. She looked at the fatal letter which was a sealed secret to her, and a torture of jealous suspicion—suspicion of that other woman who had been the shadow and the poison of her life—wrung her to the heart. After moving a few steps from the bedside, she stopped, and came back again. Armed with the double courage of her love and her despair, she pressed her lips on her dying husband's cheek, and pleaded with him for the last time. Her burning tears dropped on his face as she whispered to him: "Oh, Allan, think how I have loved you! think how hard I have tried to make you happy! think how soon I shall lose you! Oh, my own love! don't, don't send me away!"

The words pleaded for her; the kiss pleaded for her; the recollection of the love that had been given to him, and never returned, touched the heart of the fast-sinking man as nothing had touched it since the day of his marriage. A heavy sigh broke from him. He looked at her, and hesitated.

"Let me stay," she whispered, pressing her face closer to his.

"It will only distress you," he whispered back.

"Nothing distresses me, but being sent away from *you!*"

He waited. She saw that he was thinking, and waited too.

"If I let you stay a little—?"

"Yes! yes!"

"Will you go when I tell you?"

"I will."

"On your oath?"

The fetters that bound his tongue seemed to be loosened for a moment in the great outburst of anxiety which forced that question to his lips. He spoke those startling words as he had spoken no words yet.

"On my oath!" she repeated, and, dropping on her knees at the bedside, passionately kissed his hand. The two strangers in the room turned their heads away by common consent. In the silence that followed, the one sound stirring was the small sound of the child's toy, as he moved it hither and thither on the bed.

The doctor was the first who broke the spell of stillness which had fallen on all the persons present. He approached the patient, and examined him anxiously. Mrs. Armadale rose from her knees; and, first waiting for her husband's permission, carried the sheets of manuscript which she had taken out of the desk to the table at which Mr. Neal was waiting. Flushed and eager, more beautiful than ever in the vehement agitation which still possessed her, she stooped over him as she put the letter into his hands, and, seizing on the means to her end with a woman's headlong self-abandonment to her own impulses, whispered to him, "Read it out from the beginning. I must and will hear it!" Her eyes flashed their burning light into his; her breath beat on his cheek. Before he could answer, before he could think, she was back with her husband. In an instant she had spoken, and in that instant her beauty had bent the Scotchman to her will. Frowning in reluctant acknowledgment of his own inability to resist her, he turned over the leaves of the letter; looked at the blank place where the pen had dropped from the writer's hand and had left a blot on the paper; turned back again to the beginning, and said the words, in the wife's interest, which the wife herself had put into his lips.

"Perhaps, sir, you may wish to make some corrections," he began, with all his attention apparently fixed on the letter, and with every outward appearance of letting his sour temper again get the better of him. "Shall I read over to you what you have already written?"

Mrs. Armadale, sitting at the bed head on one side, and the doctor, with his fingers on the patient's pulse, sitting on the other, waited with widely different anxieties for the answer to Mr. Neal's question. Mr. Armadale's eyes turned searchingly from his child to his wife.

"You *will* hear it?" he said. Her breath came and went quickly; her hand stole up and took his; she bowed her head in silence. Her husband paused, taking secret counsel with his thoughts, and keeping his eyes fixed on his wife. At last he decided, and gave the answer. "Read it," he said, "and stop when I tell you."

It was close on one o'clock, and the bell was ringing which summoned the visitors to their early dinner at the inn. The quick beat of footsteps, and the gathering hum of voices outside, penetrated gayly into the room, as Mr. Neal spread the manuscript before him on the table, and read the opening sentences in these words:

"I address this letter to my son, when my son is of an age to understand it. Having lost all hope of living to see my boy grow up to manhood, I have no choice but to write here what I would fain have said to him at a future time with my own lips.

"I have three objects in writing. First, to reveal the circumstances which attended the marriage of an English lady of my acquaintance, in the island of Madeira. Secondly, to throw the true light on the death of her husband a short time afterward, on board the French timber ship *La Grâce de Dieu*. Thirdly, to warn my son of a danger that lies in wait for him—a danger that will rise from his father's grave when the earth has closed over his father's ashes.

"The story of the English lady's marriage begins with my inheriting the great Armadale property, and my taking the fatal Armadale name.

"I am the only surviving son of the late Mathew Wrentmore, of Barbadoes. I was born on our family estate in that island, and I lost my father when I was still a child. My mother was blindly fond of me; she denied me nothing; she let me live as I pleased. My boyhood and youth were passed in idleness and self-indulgence, among people—slaves and half-castes mostly—to whom my will was law. I doubt if there is a gentleman of my birth and station in all England as ignorant as I am at this moment. I doubt if there was ever a young man in this world whose passions were left so entirely without control of any knd as mine were in those early days.

"My mother had a woman's romantic objection to my father's homely Christian name. I was christened Allan, after the name of a wealthy cousin of my father's—the late Allan Armadale—who possessed estates in our neighborhood, the largest and most productive in the island, and who consented to be my godfather by proxy. Mr. Armadale had never seen his West Indian property. He lived in England; and, after sending me the customary godfather's present, he held no further communication with my parents for years afterward. I was just twenty-one before we heard again from Mr. Armadale. On that occasion my mother received a letter from him asking if I was still alive, and offering no less (if I was) than to make me the heir to his West Indian property.

"This piece of good fortune fell to me entirely through the misconduct of Mr. Armadale's son, an only child. The young man had disgraced himself beyond all redemption; had left his home an outlaw; and had been thereupon renounced by his father at once and forever. Having no other near male relative to succeed him, Mr. Armadale thought of his cousin's son, and his own godson; and he offered the West Indian estate to me, and my heirs after me, on one condition—that I and my heirs should take his name. The proposal was gratefully accepted, and the proper legal measures were adopted for changing my name in the colony and in the mother country. By the next mail information reached Mr. Armadale that his condition had been complied with. The return mail brought news from the lawyers. The will had been altered in my favor, and in a week afterward the death of my benefactor had made me the largest proprietor and the richest man in Barbadoes.

"This was the first event in the chain. The second event followed it six weeks afterward.

"At that time there happened to be a vacancy in the clerk's office on the estate, and there came to fill it a young man about my own age who had recently arrived in the island. He announced himself by the name of Fergus Ingleby. My impulses governed me in everything; I knew no law but the law of my own caprice, and I took a fancy to the stranger the moment I set eyes on him. He had the manners of a gentleman, and he possessed the most attractive social qualities which, in my small experience, I had ever met with. When I heard that the written references to character which he had brought with him were pronounced to be unsatisfactory, I interfered, and insisted that he should have the place. My will was law, and he had it.

"My mother disliked and distrusted Ingleby from the first. When she found the intimacy between us rapidly ripening; when she found me admitting this inferior to the closest companionship and confidence (I had lived with my inferiors all my life, and I liked it), she made effort after effort to part us, and failed in one and all. Driven to her last resources, she resolved to try the one chance left—the chance of persuading me to take a voyage which I had often thought of—a voyage to England.

"Before she spoke to me on the subject, she resolved to interest me in the idea of seeing England, as I had never been interested yet. She wrote to an old friend and an old admirer of hers, the late Stephen Blanchard, of Thorpe Ambrose, in Norfolk—a gentleman of landed estate, and a widower with a grown-up family. After-discoveries informed me that she must have alluded to their former attachment (which was checked, I believe, by the parents on either side); and that, in asking Mr. Blanchard's welcome for her son when he came to England, she made inquiries about his daughter, which hinted at the chance of a marriage uniting the two families, if the young lady and I met and liked one another. We were equally matched in every respect, and my mother's recollection of her girlish attachment to Mr. Blanchard made the prospect of my marrying her old admirer's daughter the brightest and happiest prospect that her eyes could see. Of all this I knew nothing until Mr. Blanchard's answer arrived at Barbadoes. Then my mother showed me the letter, and put the temptation which was to separate me from Fergus Ingleby openly in my way.

"Mr. Blanchard's letter was dated from the Island of Madeira. He was out of health, and he had been ordered there by the doctors to try the climate. His daughter was with him. After heartily reciprocating all my mother's hopes and wishes, he proposed (if I intended leaving Barbadoes shortly) that I should take Madeira on my way to England, and pay him a visit at his temporary residence in the island. If this could not be, he mentioned the time at which he expected to be back in England, when I might be sure of finding a welcome at his own house of Thorpe Ambrose. In conclusion, he apologized for not writing at greater length; explaining that his sight was affected, and that he had disobeyed the doctor's orders by yielding to the temptation of writing to his old friend with his own hand.

"Kindly as it was expressed, the letter itself might have had little influence on me. But there was something else besides the letter; there was inclosed in it a miniature portrait of Miss Blanchard. At the back of the portrait, her father had written, half-jestingly, half-tenderly, 'I can't ask my daughter to spare my eyes as usual, without telling her of your inquiries, and putting a young lady's diffidence to the blush. So I send her in effigy (without her knowledge) to answer for herself. It is a good likeness of a good girl. If she likes your son—and if I like him, which I am sure I shall—we may yet live, my good friend, to see our children what we might once have been ourselves—man and wife.' My mother gave me the miniature with the letter. The portrait at once struck me—I can't say why, I can't say how—as nothing of the kind had ever struck me before.

"Harder intellects than mine might have attributed the extraordinary impression produced on me to the disordered condition of my mind at that time; to the weariness of my own base pleasures which had been gaining on me for months past; to the undefined longing which that weariness implied for newer interests and fresher hopes than any that had possessed me yet. I attempted no such sober self-examination as this: I believed in destiny then, I believe in destiny now. It was enough for me to know

—as I did know—that the first sense I had ever
felt of something better in my nature than my
animal self was roused by that girl's face looking at me from her picture as no woman's face
had ever looked at me yet. In those tender eyes
—in the chance of making that gentle creature
my wife—I saw my destiny written. The portrait which had come into my hands so strangely
and so unexpectedly was the silent messenger of
happiness close at hand, sent to warn, to encourage, to rouse me before it was too late. I
put the miniature under my pillow at night;
I looked at it again the next morning. My conviction of the day before remained as strong as
ever; my superstition (if you please to call it
so) pointed out to me irresistibly the way on
which I should go. There was a ship in port
which was to sail for England in a fortnight,
touching at Madeira. In that ship I took my
passage."

Thus far the reader had advanced with no interruption to disturb him. But at the last words
the tones of another voice, low and broken,
mingled with his own.

"Was she a fair woman," asked the voice, "or
dark, like me?"

Mr. Neal paused, and looked up. The doctor
was still at the bed head, with his fingers mechanically on the patient's pulse. The child,
missing his midday sleep, was beginning to play
languidly with his new toy. The father's eyes
were watching him with a rapt and ceaseless

attention. But one great change was visible
in the listeners since the narrative had begun.
Mrs. Armadale had dropped her hold of her husband's hand, and sat with her face steadily
turned away from him. The hot African blood
burned red in her dusky cheeks as she obstinately
repeated the question: "Was she a fair woman,
or dark, like me?"

"Fair," said her husband, without looking at
her.

Her hands, lying clasped together in her lap,
wrung each other hard—she said no more. Mr.
Neal's overhanging eyebrows lowered ominously
as he returned to the narrative. He had incurred his own severe displeasure—he had caught
himself in the act of secretly pitying her.

"I have said"—the letter proceeded—"that
Ingleby was admitted to my closest confidence.
I was sorry to leave him; and I was distressed
by his evident surprise and mortification when
he heard that I was going away. In my own
justification, I showed him the letter and the
likeness, and told him the truth. His interest
in the portrait seemed to be hardly inferior to
my own. He asked me about Miss Blanchard's
family and Miss Blanchard's fortune with the
sympathy of a true friend; and he strengthened
my regard for him, and my belief in him, by
putting himself out of the question, and by generously encouraging me to persist in my new
purpose. When we parted, I was in high health
and spirits. Before we met again the next day,

I was suddenly struck by an illness which threatened both my reason and my life.

"I have no proof against Ingleby. There was more than one woman on the island whom I had wronged beyond all forgiveness, and whose vengeance might well have reached me at that time. I can accuse nobody. I can only say that my life was saved by my old black nurse; and that the woman afterward acknowledged having used the known negro antidote to a known negro poison in those parts. When my first days of convalescence came, the ship in which my passage had been taken had long since sailed. When I asked for Ingleby, he was gone. Proofs of his unpardonable misconduct in his situation were placed before me, which not even my partiality for him could resist. He had been turned out of the office in the first days of my illness, and nothing more was known of him but that he had left the island.

"All through my sufferings the portrait had been under my pillow. All through my convalescence it was my one consolation when I remembered the past, and my one encouragement when I thought of the future. No words can describe the hold that first fancy had now taken of me—with time and solitude and suffering to help it. My mother, with all her interest in the match, was startled by the unexpected success of her own project. She had written to tell Mr. Blanchard of my illness, but had received no reply. She now offered to write again, if I would promise not to leave her be-

fore my recovery was complete.   My impatience
acknowledged no restraint.   Another ship in port
gave me another chance of leaving for Madeira.
Another examination of Mr. Blanchard's letter
of invitation assured me that I should find him
still in the island, if I seized my opportunity on
the spot.   In defiance of my mother's entreaties,
I insisted on taking my passage in the second
ship—and this time, when the ship sailed, I was
on board.

"The change did me good; the sea-air made
a man of me again.   After an unusually rapid
voyage, I found myself at the end of my pil-
grimage.   On a fine, still evening which I can
never forget, I stood alone on the shore, with
her likeness in my bosom, and saw the white
walls of the house where I knew that she lived.

"I strolled round the outer limits of the
grounds to compose myself before I went in.
Venturing through a gate and a shrubbery, I
looked into the garden, and saw a lady there,
loitering alone on the lawn.   She turned her
face toward me—and I beheld the original of
my portrait, the fulfillment of my dream!   It is
useless, and worse than useless, to write of it
now.   Let me only say that every promise which
the likeness had made to my fancy the living
woman kept to my eyes in the moment when
they first looked on her.   Let me say this—and
no more.

"I was too violently agitated to trust myself
in her presence.   I drew back undiscovered, and,
making my way to the front door of the house,

asked for her father first. Mr. Blanchard had
retired to his room, and could see nobody. Upon
that I took courage, and asked for Miss Blanchard. The servant smiled. 'My young lady is
not Miss Blanchard any longer, sir,' he said.
'She is married.' Those words would have
struck some men, in my position, to the earth.
They fired my hot blood, and I seized the servant by the throat, in a frenzy of rage. 'It's a
lie!' I broke out, speaking to him as if he had
been one of the slaves on my own estate. 'It's
the truth,' said the man, struggling with me;
'her husband is in the house at this moment.'
'Who is he, you scoundrel?' The servant answered by repeating my own name, to my own
face: '*Allan Armadale.*'

"You can now guess the truth. Fergus Ingleby was the outlawed son whose name and whose
inheritance I had taken. And Fergus Ingleby
was even with me for depriving him of his birth-
right.

"Some account of the manner in which the
deception had been carried out is necessary to
explain — I don't say to justify — the share I
took in the events that followed my arrival at
Madeira.

"By Ingleby's own confession, he had come
to Barbadoes — knowing of his father's death
and of my succession to the estates—with the
settled purpose of plundering and injuring me.
My rash confidence put such an opportunity into
his hands as he could never have hoped for. He
had waited to possess himself of the letter which

my mother wrote to Mr. Blanchard at the outset
of my illness—had then caused his own dismissal
from his situation—and had sailed for Madeira
in the very ship that was to have sailed with
me.   Arrived at the island, he had waited again
till the vessel was away once more on her voyage,
and had then presented himself at Mr. Blanchard's—not in the assumed name by which I shall
continue to speak of him here, but in the name
which was as certainly his as mine, 'Allan Armadale.'  The fraud at the outset presented few
difficulties.  He had only an ailing old man
(who had not seen my mother for half a lifetime) and an innocent, unsuspicious girl (who
had never seen her at all) to deal with; and he
had learned enough in my service to answer the
few questions that were put to him as readily as
I might have answered them myself.  His looks
and manners, his winning ways with women,
his quickness and cunning, did the rest.  While
I was still on my sick-bed, he had won Miss
Blanchard's affections.  While I was dreaming
over the likeness in the first days of my convalescence, he had secured Mr. Blanchard's consent
to the celebration of the marriage before he and
his daughter left the island.

"Thus far Mr. Blanchard's infirmity of sight
had helped the deception.  He had been content
to send messages to my mother, and to receive
the messages which were duly invented in return.  But when the suitor was accepted, and
the wedding-day was appointed, he felt it due
to his old friend to write to her, asking her

formal consent, and inviting her to the marriage. He could only complete part of the letter himself; the rest was finished, under his dictation, by Miss Blanchard. There was no chance of being beforehand with the post-office this time; and Ingleby, sure of his place in the heart of his victim, waylaid her as she came out of her father's room with the letter, and privately told her the truth. She was still under age, and the position was a serious one. If the letter was posted, no resource would be left but to wait and be parted forever, or to elope under circumstances which made detection almost a certainty. The destination of any ship which took them away would be known beforehand; and the fast-sailing yacht in which Mr. Blanchard had come to Madeira was waiting in the harbor to take him back to England. The only other alternative was to continue the deception by suppressing the letter, and to confess the truth when they were securely married. What arts of persuasion Ingleby used—what base advantage he might previously have taken of her love and her trust in him to degrade Miss Blanchard to his own level—I cannot say. He did degrade her. The letter never went to its destination; and, with the daughter's privity and consent, the father's confidence was abused to the very last.

"The one precaution now left to take was to fabricate the answer from my mother which Mr. Blanchard expected, and which would arrive in due course of post before the day appointed for the marriage. Ingleby had my mother's stolen letter with him; but he was without the imitative dexterity which would have enabled him to make use of it for a forgery of her handwriting. Miss Blanchard, who had consented passively to the deception, refused to take any active share in the fraud practiced on her father. In this difficulty, Ingleby found an instrument ready to his hand in an orphan girl of barely twelve years old, a marvel of precocious ability, whom Miss Blanchard had taken a romantic fancy to befriend, and whom she had brought away with her from England to be trained as her maid. That girl's wicked dexterity removed the one serious obstacle left to the success of the fraud. I saw the imitation of my mother's writing which she had produced under Ingleby's instructions, and (if the shameful truth must be told) with her young mistress's knowledge— and I believe I should have been deceived by it myself. I saw the girl afterward—and my blood curdled at the sight of her. If she is alive now, woe to the people who trust her! No creature more innately deceitful and more innately pitiless ever walked this earth.

"The forged letter paved the way securely for the marriage; and when I reached the house, they were (as the servant had truly told me) man and wife. My arrival on the scene simply precipitated the confession which they had both agreed to make. Ingleby's own lips shamelessly acknowledged the truth. He had nothing to lose by speaking out—he was married, and his wife's fortune was beyond her father's control. I pass over all that followed—my interview with the daughter, and my interview with the father—to come to results. For two days the efforts of the wife, and the efforts of the clergyman who had celebrated the marriage, were successful in keeping Ingleby and myself apart. On the third day I set my trap more successfully, and I and the man who had mortally injured me met together alone, face to face.

"Remember how my confidence had been abused; remember how the one good purpose of my life had been thwarted; remember the violent passions rooted deep in my nature, and never yet controlled—and then imagine for yourself what passed between us. All I need tell here is the end. He was a taller and a stronger man than I, and he took his brute's advantage with a brute's ferocity. He struck me.

"Think of the injuries I had received at that man's hands, and then think of his setting his mark on my face by a blow!

"I went to an English officer who had been my fellow-passenger on the voyage from Barbadoes. I told him the truth, and he agreed with me that a meeting was inevitable. Dueling had its received formalities and its established laws in those days; and he began to speak of them. I stopped him. 'I will take a pistol in my right hand,' I said, 'and he shall take a pistol in his: I will take one end of a handkerchief in my left hand, and he shall take the other end in his; and across that handkerchief the duel shall be fought.' The officer got up, and looked at me as if I had personally insulted him. 'You are asking me to be present at a murder and a suicide,' he said; 'I decline to serve you.' He left the room. As soon as he was gone I wrote down the words I had said to the officer and sent them by a messenger to Ingleby. While I was waiting for an answer, I sat down before the glass, and looked at his mark on my face. 'Many a man has had blood on his hands and blood on his conscience,' I thought, 'for less than this.'

"The messenger came back with Ingleby's answer. It appointed a meeting for three o'clock the next day, at a lonely place in the interior of the island. I had resolved what to do if he refused; his letter released me from the horror of my own resolution. I felt grateful to him—yes, absolutely grateful to him—for writing it.

"The next day I went to the place. He was not there. I waited two hours, and he never came. At last the truth dawned on me. 'Once a coward, always a coward,' I thought. I went back to Mr. Blanchard's house. Before I got there, a sudden misgiving seized me, and I turned aside to the harbor. I was right; the harbor was the place to go to. A ship sailing for Lisbon that afternoon had offered him the opportunity of taking a passage for himself and his wife, and escaping me. His answer to my challenge had served its purpose of sending me out of the way into the interior of the island. Once more I had trusted in Fergus Ingleby, and once more those sharp wits of his had been too much for me.

"I asked my informant if Mr. Blanchard was aware as yet of his daughter's departure. He had discovered it, but not until the ship had sailed. This time I took a lesson in cunning from Ingleby. Instead •of showing myself at Mr. Blanchard's house, I went first and looked at Mr. Blanchard's yacht.

"The vessel told me what the vessel's master might have concealed—the truth. I found her in the confusion of a sudden preparation for sea. All the crew were on board, with the exception of some few who had been allowed their leave on shore, and who were away in the interior of the island, nobody knew where. When I discovered that the sailing-master was trying to supply their places with the best men he could pick up at a moment's notice, my resolution was instantly taken. I knew the duties on board a yacht well enough, having had a vessel of my own, and having sailed her myself. Hurrying into the town, I changed my dress for a sailor's coat and hat, and, returning to the harbor, I offered myself as one of the volunteer crew. I don't know what the sailing-master saw in my face. My answers to his questions satisfied him, and yet he looked at me and hesitated. But hands were scarce, and it ended in my being taken on board. An hour later Mr. Blanchard joined us, and was assisted into the cabin, suffering pitiably in mind and body both. An hour after that we were at sea, with a starless night overhead, and a fresh breeze behind us.

"As I had surmised, we were in pursuit of

the vessel in which Ingleby and his wife had left the island that afternoon. The ship was French, and was employed in the timber trade: her name was *La Grâce de Dieu.* Nothing more was known of her than that she was bound for Lisbon; that she had been driven out of her course; and that she had touched at Madeira, short of men and short of provisions. The last want had been supplied, but not the first. Sailors distrusted the sea-worthiness of the ship, and disliked the look of the vagabond crew. When those two serious facts had been communicated to Mr. Blanchard, the hard words he had spoken to his child in the first shock of discovering that she had helped to deceive him smote him to the heart. He instantly determined to give his daughter a refuge on board his own vessel, and to quiet her by keeping her villain of a husband out of the way of all harm at my hands. The yacht sailed three feet and more to the ship's one. There was no doubt of our overtaking *La Grâce de Dieu;* the only fear was that we might pass her in the darkness.

"After we had been some little time out, the wind suddenly dropped, and there fell on us an airless, sultry calm. When the order came to get the topmasts on deck, and to shift the large sails, we all knew what to expect. In little better than an hour more, the storm was upon us, the thunder was pealing over our heads, and the yacht was running for it. She was a powerful schooner-rigged vessel of three hundred tons, as strong as wood and iron could make her; she was handled by a sailing-master who thoroughly understood his work, and she behaved nobly. As the new morning came, the fury of the wind, blowing still from the southwest quarter, subsided a little, and the sea was less heavy. Just before daybreak we heard faintly, through the howling of the gale, the report of a gun. The men collected anxiously on deck, looked at each other, and said: 'There she is!'

"With the daybreak we saw the vessel, and the timber-ship it was. She lay wallowing in the trough of the sea, her foremast and her mainmast both gone—a water-logged wreck. The yacht carried three boats; one amidships, and two slung to davits on the quarters; and the sailing-master, seeing signs of the storm renewing its fury before long, determined on lowering the quarter-boats while the lull lasted. Few as the people were on board the wreck, they were too many for one boat, and the risk of trying two boats at once was thought less, in the critical state of the weather, than the risk of making two separate trips from the yacht to the ship. There might be time to make one trip in safety, but no man could look at the heavens and say there would be time enough for two.

"The boats were manned by volunteers from the crew, I being in the second of the two. When the first boat was got alongside of the timber ship—a service of difficulty and danger which no words can describe—all the men on board made a rush to leave the wreck together. If the boat had not been pulled off again before the whole of them had crowded in, the lives of all must have been sacrificed. As our boat approached the vessel in its turn, we arranged that four of us should get on board—two (I being one of them) to see to the safety of Mr. Blanchard's daughter, and two to beat back the cowardly remnant of the crew if they tried to crowd in first. The other three—the coxswain and two oarsmen—were left in the boat to keep her from being crushed by the ship. What the others saw when they first boarded *La Grâce de Dieu* I don't know; what *I* saw was the woman whom I had lost, the woman vilely stolen from me, lying in a swoon on the deck. We lowered her, insensible, into the boat. The remnant of the crew — five in number—were compelled by main force to follow her in an orderly manner, one by one, and minute by minute, as the chance offered for safely taking them in. I was the last who left; and, at the next roll of the ship toward us, the empty length of the deck, without a living creature on it from stem to stern, told the boat's crew that their work was done. With the louder and louder howling of the fast-rising tempest to warn them, they rowed for their lives back to the yacht.

"A succession of heavy squalls had brought round the course of the new storm that was coming, from the south to the north; and the sailing-master, watching his opportunity, had wore the yacht to be ready for it. Before the last of our men had got on board again, it burst

on us with the fury of a hurricane. Our boat
was swamped, but not a life was lost. Once
more we ran before it, due south, at the mercy
of the wind. I was on deck with the rest,
watching the one rag of sail we could venture
to set, and waiting to supply its place with another, if it blew out of the bolt-ropes, when the
mate came close to me, and shouted in my ear
through the thunder of the storm: 'She has come
to her senses in the cabin, and has asked for her
husband. Where is he?' Not a man on board
knew. The yacht was searched from one end to
another without finding him. The men were
mustered in defiance of the weather—he was not
among them. The crews of the two boats were
questioned. All the first crew could say was
that they had pulled away from the wreck when
the rush into their boat took place, and that they
knew nothing of whom they let in or whom they
kept out. All the second crew could say was that
they had brought back to the yacht every living
soul left by the first boat on the deck of the timber
ship. There was no blaming anybody; but, at
the same time, there was no resisting the fact
that the man was missing.

"All through that day the storm, raging un-
abatedly, never gave us even the shadow of a
chance of returning and searching the wreck.
The one hope for the yacht was to scud. Toward evening the gale, after having carried us to
the southward of Madeira, began at last to break—
the wind shifted again—and allowed us to bear
up for the island. Early the next morning we

got back into port. Mr. Blanchard and his
daughter were taken ashore, the sailing-master
accompanying them, and warning us that he
should have something to say on his return
which would nearly concern the whole crew.

"We were mustered on deck, and addressed
by the sailing-master as soon as he came on
board again. He had Mr. Blanchard's orders
to go back at once to the timber ship and to
search for the missing man. We were bound
to do this for his sake, and for the sake of his
wife, whose reason was despaired of by the
doctors if something was not done to quiet her.
We might be almost sure of finding the vessel
still afloat, for her lading of timber would keep
her above water as long as her hull held together.
If the man was on board—living or dead—he
must be found and brought back. And if the
weather continued to be moderate, there was
no reason why the men, with proper assistance,
should not bring the ship back, too, and (their
master being quite willing) earn their share of
the salvage with the officers of the yacht.

"Upon this the crew gave three cheers, and
set to work forthwith to get the schooner to
sea again. I was the only one of them who
drew back from the enterprise. I told them
the storm had upset me—I was ill, and wanted
rest. They all looked me in the face as I passed
through them on my way out of the yacht, but
not a man of them spoke to me.

"I waited through that day at a tavern on
the port for the first news from the wreck. It

was brought toward night-fall by one of the
pilot-boats which had taken part in the enterprise — a successful enterprise, as the event
proved—for saving the abandoned ship. *La
Grâce de Dieu* had been discovered still floating, and the body of Ingleby had been found
on board, drowned in the cabin. At dawn the
next morning the dead man was brought back
by the yacht; and on the same day the funeral
took place in the Protestant cemetery.''

''Stop!'' said the voice from the bed, before
the reader could turn to a new leaf and begin
the next paragraph.

There was a change in the room, and there
were changes in the audience, since Mr. Neal
had last looked up from the narrative. A ray
of sunshine was crossing the death-bed; and the
child, overcome by drowsiness, lay peacefully
asleep in the golden light. The father's countenance had altered visibly. Forced into action
by the tortured mind, the muscles of the lower
face, which had never moved yet, were moving
distortedly now. Warned by the damps gathering heavily on his forehead, the doctor had
risen to revive the sinking man. On the other
side of the bed the wife's chair stood empty.
At the moment when her husband had interrupted the reading, she had drawn back behind the bed head, out of his sight. Supporting
herself against the wall, she stood there in hiding, her eyes fastened in hungering suspense
on the manuscript in Mr. Neal's hand.

In a minute more the silence was broken again by Mr. Armadale.

"Where is she?" he asked, looking angrily at his wife's empty chair. The doctor pointed to the place. She had no choice but to come forward. She came slowly and stood before him.

"You promised to go when I told you," he said. "Go now."

Mr. Neal tried hard to control his hand as it kept his place between the leaves of the manuscript, but it trembled in spite of him. A suspicion which had been slowly forcing itself on his mind, while he was reading, became a certainty when he heard those words. From one revelation to another the letter had gone on, until it had now reached the brink of a last disclosure to come. At that brink the dying man had predetermined to silence the reader's voice, before he had permitted his wife to hear the narrative read. *There* was the secret which the son was to know in after years, and which the mother was never to approach. From that resolution, his wife's tenderest pleadings had never moved him an inch—and now, from his own lips, his wife knew it.

She made him no answer. She stood there and looked at him; looked her last entreaty— perhaps her last farewell. His eyes gave her back no answering glance: they wandered from her mercilessly to the sleeping boy. She turned speechless from the bed. Without a look at the child — without a word to the two strangers

breathlessly watching her—she kept the promise she had given, and in dead silence left the
room.

There was something in the manner of her departure which shook the self-possession of both
the men who witnessed it.   When the door closed
on her, they recoiled instinctively from advancing further in the dark.   The doctor's reluctance
was the first to express itself.   He attempted to
obtain the patient's permission to withdraw until
the letter was completed.   The patient refused.

Mr. Neal spoke next at greater length and to
more serious purpose.

"The doctor is accustomed in his profession,"
he began, "and I am accustomed in mine, to
have the secrets of others placed in our keeping.
But it is my duty, before we go further, to ask if
you really understand the extraordinary position
which we now occupy toward one another.   You
have just excluded Mrs. Armadale, before our
own eyes, from a place in your confidence.   And
you are now offering that same place to two men
who are total strangers to you."

"Yes," said Mr. Armadale, "*because* you are
strangers."

Few as the words were, the inference to be
drawn from them was not of a nature to set
distrust at rest.   Mr. Neal put it plainly into
words.

"You are in urgent need of my help and of
the doctor's help," he said.   "Am I to understand (so long as you secure our assistance) that
the impression which the closing passages of this

letter may produce on us is a matter of indifference to you?"

"Yes. I don't spare you. I don't spare myself. I *do* spare my wife."

"You force me to a conclusion, sir, which is a very serious one," said Mr. Neal. "If I am to finish this letter under your dictation, I must claim permission—having read aloud the greater part of it already—to read aloud what remains, in the hearing of this gentleman, as a witness."

"Read it."

Gravely doubting, the doctor resumed his chair. Gravely doubting, Mr. Neal turned the leaf, and read the next words:

"There is more to tell before I can leave the dead man to his rest. I have described the finding of his body. But I have not described the circumstances under which he met his death.

"He was known to have been on deck when the yacht's boats were seen approaching the wreck; and he was afterward missed in the confusion caused by the panic of the crew. At that time the water was five feet deep in the cabin, and was rising fast. There was little doubt of his having gone down into that water of his own accord. The discovery of his wife's jewel box, close under him, on the floor, explained his presence in the cabin. He was known to have seen help approaching, and it was quite likely that he had thereupon gone below to make an effort at saving the box. It was less probable—though it might still have

been inferred—that his death was the result of
some accident in diving, which had for the moment deprived him of his senses. But a discovery made by the yacht's crew pointed straight to
a conclusion which struck the men, one and all,
with the same horror. When the course of their
search brought them to the cabin, they found
the scuttle bolted, and the door locked on the
outside. Had some one closed the cabin, not
knowing he was there? Setting the panic-
stricken condition of the crew out of the question, there was no motive for closing the cabin
before leaving the wreck. But one other conclusion remained. Had some murderous hand
purposely locked the man in, and left him to
drown as the water rose over him?

"Yes. A murderous hand had locked him in,
and left him to drown. That hand was mine."

The Scotchman started up from the table; the
doctor shrank from the bedside. The two looked
at the dying wretch, mastered by the same loathing, chilled by the same dread. He lay there,
with his child's head on his breast; abandoned
by the sympathies of man, accursed by the justice of God—he lay there, in the isolation of
Cain, and looked back at them.

At the moment when the two men rose to
their feet, the door leading into the next room
was shaken heavily on the outer side, and a
sound like the sound of a fall, striking dull on
their ears, silenced them both. Standing nearest to the door, the doctor opened it, passed

through, and closed it instantly. Mr. Neal turned his back on the bed, and waited the event in silence. The sound, which had failed to awaken the child, had failed also to attract the father's notice. His own words had taken him far from all that was passing at his death-bed. His helpless body was back on the wreck, and the ghost of his lifeless hand was turning the lock of the cabin door.

A bell rang in the next room—eager voices talked; hurried footsteps moved in it—an inter-val passed, and the doctor returned. "Was she listening?" whispered Mr. Neal, in German. "The women are restoring her," the doctor whispered back. "She has heard it all. In God's name, what are we to do next?" Be-fore it was possible to reply, Mr. Armadale spoke. The doctor's return had roused him to a sense of present things.

"Go on," he said, as if nothing had happened.

"I refuse to meddle further with your infamous secret," returned Mr. Neal. "You are a mur-derer on your own confession. If that letter is to be finished, don't ask *me* to hold the pen for you."

"You gave me your promise," was the reply, spoken with the same immovable self-possession. "You must write for me, or break your word."

For the moment, Mr. Neal was silenced. There the man lay—sheltered from the execration of his fellow-creatures, under the shadow of Death —beyond the reach of all human condemnation, beyond the dread of all mortal laws; sensitive to nothing but his one last resolution to finish the letter addressed to his son.

Mr. Neal drew the doctor aside. "A word with you," he said, in German. "Do you persist in asserting that he may be speechless before we can send to Stuttgart?"

"Look at his lips," said the doctor, "and judge for yourself."

His lips answered for him: the reading of the narrative had left its mark on them already. A distortion at the corners of his mouth, which had been barely noticeable when Mr. Neal entered the room, was plainly visible now. His slow articulation labored more and more painfully with every word he uttered. The position was emphatically a terrible one. After a moment more of hesitation, Mr. Neal made a last attempt to withdraw from it.

"Now my eyes are open," he said, sternly, "do you dare hold me to an engagement which you forced on me blindfold?"

"No," answered Mr. Armadale. "I leave you to break your word."

The look which accompanied that reply stung the Scotchman's pride to the quick. When he spoke next, he spoke seated in his former place at the table.

"No man ever yet said of me that I broke my word," he retorted, angrily; "and not even *you* shall say it of me now. Mind this! If you hold me to my promise, I hold you to my condition. I have reserved my freedom of action, and I warn you I will use it at my own sole discretion, as soon as I am released from the sight of you."

"Remember he is dying," pleaded the doctor, gently.

"Take your place, sir," said Mr. Neal, pointing to the empty chair. "What remains to be read, I will only read in your hearing. What remains to be written, I will only write in your presence. *You* brought me here. I have a right to insist—and I do insist—on your remaining as a witness to the last."

The doctor accepted his position without remonstrance. Mr. Neal returned to the manuscript, and read what remained of it uninterruptedly to the end:

"Without a word in my own defense, I have acknowledged my guilt. Without a word in my own defense, I will reveal how the crime was committed.

"No thought of him was in my mind, when I saw his wife insensible on the deck of the timber ship. I did my part in lowering her safely into the boat. Then, and not till then, I felt the thought of him coming back. In the confusion that prevailed while the men of the yacht were forcing the men of the ship to wait their time, I had an opportunity of searching for him unobserved. I stepped back from the bulwark, not knowing whether he was away in the first boat, or whether he was still on board—I stepped back, and saw him mount the cabin stairs empty-handed, with the water dripping from him.

After looking eagerly toward the boat (without noticing me), he saw there was time to spare before the crew were taken off. 'Once more!' he said to himself — and disappeared again, to make a last effort at recovering the jewel box. The devil at my elbow whispered, 'Don't shoot him like a man: drown him like a dog!' He was under water when I bolted the scuttle. But his head rose to the surface before I could close the cabin door. I looked at him, and he looked at me—and I locked the door in his face. The next minute, I was back among the last men left on deck. The minute after, it was too late to repent. The storm was threatening us with destruction, and the boat's crew were pulling for their lives from the ship.

"My son! I have pursued you from my grave with a confession which my love might have spared you. Read on, and you will know why.

"I will say nothing of my sufferings; I will plead for no mercy to my memory. There is a strange sinking at my heart, a strange trembling in my hand, while I write these lines, which warns me to hasten to the end. I left the island without daring to look for the last time at the woman whom I had lost so miserably, whom I had injured so vilely. When I left, the whole weight of the suspicion roused by the manner of Ingleby's death rested on the crew of the French vessel. No motive for the supposed murder could be brought home to any of them; but they were known to be, for the most part, outlawed ruffians capable of any crime, and they were suspected and examined accordingly. It was not till afterward that I heard by accident of the suspicion shifting round at last to me. The widow alone recognized the vague description given of the strange man who had made one of the yacht's crew, and who had disappeared the day afterward. The widow alone knew, from that time forth, why her husband had been murdered, and who had done the deed. When she made that discovery, a false report of my death had been previously circulated in the island. Perhaps I was indebted to the report for my immunity from all legal proceedings; perhaps (no eye but Ingleby's having seen me lock the cabin door) there was not evidence enough to justify an inquiry; perhaps the widow shrank from the disclosures which must have followed a public charge against me, based on her own bare suspicion of the truth. However it might be, the crime which I had committed unseen has remained a crime unpunished from that time to this.

"I left Madeira for the West Indies in disguise. The first news that met me when the ship touched at Barbadoes was the news of my mother's death. I had no heart to return to the old scenes. The prospect of living at home in solitude, with the torment of my own guilty remembrances gnawing at me day and night, was more than I had the courage to confront. Without landing, or discovering myself to any one on shore, I went on as far as the ship would take me—to the island of Trinidad.

"At that place I first saw your mother. It was my duty to tell her the truth—and I treacherously kept my secret. It was my duty to spare her the hopeless sacrifice of her freedom and her happiness to such an existence as mine—and I did her the injury of marrying her. If she is alive when you read this, grant her the mercy of still concealing the truth. The one atonement I can make to her is to keep her unsuspicious to the last of the man she has married. Pity her, as I have pitied her. Let this letter be a sacred confidence between father and son.

"The time when you were born was the time when my health began to give way. Some months afterward, in the first days of my recovery, you were brought to me; and I was told that you had been christened during my illness. Your mother had done as other loving mothers do—she had christened her first-born by his father's name. You, too, were Allan Armadale. Even in that early time—even while I was happily ignorant of what I have discovered since—my mind misgave me when I looked at you, and thought of that fatal name.

"As soon as I could be moved, my presence was required at my estates in Barbadoes. It crossed my mind—wild as the idea may appear to you—to renounce the condition which compelled my son as well as myself to take the Armadale name, or lose the succession to the Armadale property. But, even in those days, the rumor of a contemplated emancipation of the slaves—the emancipation which is now close at hand—was spreading widely in the colony. No man could tell how the value of West Indian property might be affected if that threatened change ever took place. No man could tell— if I gave you back my own paternal name, and left you without other provision in the future than my own paternal estate—how you might one day miss the broad Armadale acres, or to what future penury I might be blindly condemning your mother and yourself. Mark how the fatalities gathered one on the other! Mark how your Christian name came to you, how your surname held to you, in spite of me!

"My health had improved in my old home— but it was for a time only. I sank again, and the doctors ordered me to Europe. Avoiding England (why, you may guess), I took my passage, with you and your mother, for France. From France we passed into Italy. We lived here; we lived there. It was useless. Death had got me, and Death followed me, go where I might. I bore it, for I had an alleviation to turn to which I had not deserved. You may shrink in horror from the very memory of me now. In those days, you comforted me. The only warmth I still felt at my heart was the warmth you brought to it. My last glimpses of happiness in this world were the glimpses given me by my infant son.

"We removed from Italy, and went next to Lausanne—the place from which I am now writing to you. The post of this morning has brought me news, later and fuller than any I had received thus far, of the widow of the murdered man. The letter lies before me while I write. It comes from a friend of my early days, who has seen her, and spoken to her—who has been the first to inform her that the report of my death in Madeira was false. He writes, at a loss to account for the violent agitation which she showed on hearing that I was still alive, that I was married, and that I had an infant son. He asks me if I can explain it. He speaks in terms of sympathy for her—a young and beautiful woman, buried in the retirement of a fishing-village on the Devonshire coast; her father dead; her family estranged from her, in merciless disapproval of her marriage. He writes words which might have cut me to the heart, but for a closing passage in his letter, which seized my whole attention the instant I came to it, and which has forced from me the narrative that these pages contain.

"I now know what never even entered my mind as a suspicion till the letter reached me. I now know that the widow of the man whose death lies at my door has borne a posthumous child. That child is a boy—a year older than my own son. Secure in her belief in my death, his mother has done what my son's mother did: she has christened her child by his father's name. Again, in the second generation, there are two Allan Armadales as there were in the first. After working its deadly mischief with the fathers, the fatal resemblance of names has descended to work its deadly mischief with the sons.

"Guiltless minds may see nothing thus far but the result of a series of events which could lead no other way. I—with that man's life to answer for—I, going down into my grave, with my crime unpunished and unatoned, see what no guiltless minds can discern. I see danger in the future, begotten of the danger in the past —treachery that is the offspring of *his* treachery, and crime that is the child of *my* crime. Is the dread that now shakes me to the soul a phantom raised by the superstition of a dying man? I look into the Book which all Christendom venerates, and the Book tells me that the sin of the father shall be visited on the child. I look out into the world, and I see the living witnesses round me to that terrible truth. I see the vices which have contaminated the father descending, and contaminating the child; I see the shame which has disgraced the father's name descending, and disgracing the child's. I look in on myself, and I see my crime ripening again for the future in the self-same circumstance which first sowed the seeds of it in the past, and descending, in inherited contamination of evil, from me to my son."

At those lines the writing ended. There the stroke had struck him, and the pen had dropped from his hand.

He knew the place; he remembered the words. At the instant when the reader's voice stopped, he looked eagerly at the doctor. "I have got what comes next in my mind," he said, with slower and slower articulation. "Help me to speak it."

The doctor administered a stimulant, and signed to Mr. Neal to give him time. After a little delay, the flame of the sinking spirit leaped up in his eyes once more. Resolutely struggling with his failing speech, he summoned the Scotchman to take the pen, and pronounced the closing sentences of the narrative, as his memory gave them back to him, one by one, in these words:

"Despise my dying conviction if you will, but grant me, I solemnly implore you, one last request. My son! the only hope I have left for you hangs on a great doubt—the doubt whether we are, or are not, the masters of our own destinies. It may be that mortal free-will can conquer mortal fate; and that going, as we all do, inevitably to death, we go inevitably to nothing that is before death. If this be so, indeed, respect — though you respect nothing else — the warning which I give you from my grave. Never, to your dying day, let any living soul approach you who is associated, directly or indirectly, with the crime which your father has committed. Avoid the widow of the man I killed—if the widow still lives. Avoid the maid whose wicked hand smoothed the way to the marriage—if the maid is still in her service. And more than all, avoid the man who bears the same name as your own. Offend your best benefactor, if that benefactor's influence has connected you one with the other. Desert the woman who loves you, if that woman is a link between you and him. Hide yourself from him under an assumed name. Put the mountains and the seas between you; be ungrateful, be unforgiving; be all that is most repellent to your own gentler nature, rather than live under the same roof, and breathe the same air, with that man. Never let the two Allan Armadales meet in this world: never, never, never!

"There lies the way by which you may escape —if any way there be. Take it, if you prize your own innocence and your own happiness, through all your life to come!

"I have done. If I could have trusted any weaker influence than the influence of this confession to incline you to my will, I would have spared you the disclosure which these pages contain. You are lying on my breast, sleeping the innocent sleep of a child, while a stranger's hand writes these words for you as they fall from my lips. Think what the strength of my conviction must be, when I can find the courage, on my death-bed, to darken all your young life at its outset with the shadow of your father's crime. Think, and be warned. Think, and forgive me if you can."

There it ended. Those were the father's last words to the son.

Inexorably faithful to his forced duty, Mr. Neal laid aside the pen, and read over aloud the lines he had just written. "Is there more to add?" he asked, with his pitilessly steady voice. There was no more to add.

Mr. Neal folded the manuscript, inclosed it in a sheet of paper, and sealed it with Mr. Armadale's own seal. "The address?" he said, with his merciless business formality. "To Allan Armadale, junior," he wrote, as the words were dictated from the bed. "Care of Godfrey Hammick, Esq., Offices of Messrs. Hammick and Ridge, Lincoln's Inn Fields, London." Having written the address, he waited, and considered for a moment. "Is your executor to open this?" he asked.

"No! he is to give it to my son when my son is of an age to understand it."

"In that case," pursued Mr. Neal, with all his wits in remorseless working order, "I will add a dated note to the address, repeating your own words as you have just spoken them, and explaining the circumstances under which my handwriting appears on the document." He wrote the note in the briefest and plainest terms, read it over aloud as he had read over what went before, signed his name and address at the end, and made the doctor sign next, as witness of the proceedings, and as medical evidence of the condition in which Mr. Armadale then lay. This done, he placed the letter in a second inclosure, sealed it as before, and directed it to Mr. Hammick, with the superscription of "private" added to the address. "Do you insist on my posting this?" he asked, rising with the letter in his hand.

"Give him time to think," said the doctor.

"For the child's sake, give him time to think! A minute may change him."

"I will give him five minutes," answered Mr. Neal, placing his watch on the table, implacably just to the very last.

They waited, both looking attentively at Mr. Armadale. The signs of change which had appeared in him already were multiplying fast. The movement which continued mental agitation had communicated to the muscles of his face was beginning, under the same dangerous influence, to spread downward. His once helpless hands lay still no longer; they struggled pitiably on the bedclothes. At sight of that warning token, the doctor turned with a gesture of alarm, and beckoned Mr. Neal to come nearer. "Put the question at once," he said; "if you let the five minutes pass, you may be too late."

Mr. Neal approached the bed. He, too, noticed the movement of the hands. "Is that a bad sign?" he asked.

The doctor bent his head gravely. "Put your question at once," he repeated, "or you may be too late."

Mr. Neal held the letter before the eyes of the dying man. "Do you know what this is?"

"My letter."

"Do you insist on my posting it?"

He mastered his failing speech for the last time, and gave the answer: "Yes!"

Mr. Neal moved to the door, with the letter in his hand. The German followed him a few steps, opened his lips to plead for a longer delay, met the Scotchman's inexorable eye, and drew back again in silence. The door closed and parted them, without a word having passed on either side.

The doctor went back to the bed and whispered to the sinking man: "Let me call him back; there is time to stop him yet!" It was useless. No answer came; nothing showed that he heeded, or even heard. His eyes wandered from the child, rested for a moment on his own struggling hand, and looked up entreatingly in the compassionate face that bent over him. The doctor lifted the hand, paused, followed the father's longing eyes back to the child, and, interpreting his last wish, moved the hand gently toward the boy's head. The hand touched it, and trembled violently. In another instant the trembling seized on the arm, and spread over the whole upper part of the body. The face turned from pale to red, from red to purple, from purple to pale again. Then the toiling hands lay still, and the shifting color changed no more.

The window of the next room was open, when the doctor entered it from the death chamber, with the child in his arms. He looked out as he passed by, and saw Mr. Neal in the street below, slowly returning to the inn.

"Where is the letter?" he asked.

Three words sufficed for the Scotchman's answer.

"In the post."

THE END OF THE PROLOGUE.

# THE STORY.

## BOOK THE FIRST.

### CHAPTER I.

#### THE MYSTERY OF OZIAS MIDWINTER.

On a warm May night, in the year eighteen hundred and fifty-one, the Reverend Decimus Brock—at that time a visitor to the Isle of Man —retired to his bedroom at Castletown, with a serious personal responsibility in close pursuit of him, and with no distinct idea of the means by which he might relieve himself from the pressure of his present circumstances.

The clergyman had reached that mature period of human life at which a sensible man learns to decline (as often as his temper will let him) all useless conflict with the tyranny of his own troubles. Abandoning any further effort to reach a decision in the emergency that now beset him, Mr. Brock sat down placidly in his shirt sleeves on the side of his bed, and applied his mind to consider next whether the emergency itself was as serious as he had hitherto been inclined to think it. Following this new way out

of his perplexities, Mr. Brock found himself unexpectedly traveling to the end in view by the
least inspiriting of all human journeys—a journey through the past years of his own life.

One by one the events of those years—all connected with the same little group of characters,
and all more or less answerable for the anxiety
which was now intruding itself between the
clergyman and his night's rest—rose, in progres-
sive series, on Mr. Brock's memory. The first
of the series took him back, through a period of
fourteen years, to his own rectory on the Somersetshire shores of the Bristol Channel, and closeted
him at a private interview with a lady who had
paid him a visit in the character of a total
stranger to the parson and the place.

The lady's complexion was fair, the lady's
figure was well preserved; she was still a young
woman, and she looked even younger than her
age. There was a shade of melancholy in her
expression, and an undertone of suffering in
her voice—enough, in each case, to indicate that
she had known trouble, but not enough to ob-
trude that trouble on the notice of others. She
brought with her a fine, fair-haired boy of eight
years old, whom she presented as her son, and
who was sent out of the way, at the beginning
of the interview, to amuse himself in the rectory
garden. Her card had preceded her entrance
into the study, and had announced her under the
name of "Mrs. Armadale." Mr. Brock began
to feel interested in her before she had opened

her lips; and when the son had been dismissed, he waited with some anxiety to hear what the mother had to say to him.

Mrs. Armadale began by informing the rector that she was a widow. Her husband had perished by shipwreck a short time after their union, on the voyage from Madeira to Lisbon. She had been brought to England, after her affliction, under her father's protection; and her child— a posthumous son—had been born on the family estate in Norfolk. Her father's death, shortly afterward, had deprived her of her only surviving parent, and had exposed her to neglect and misconstruction on the part of her remaining relatives (two brothers), which had estranged her from them, she feared, for the rest of her days. For some time past she had lived in the neighboring county of Devonshire, devoting herself to the education of her boy, who had now reached an age at which he required other than his mother's teaching. Leaving out of the question her own unwillingness to part with him, in her solitary position, she was especially anxious that he should not be thrown among strangers by being sent to school. Her darling project was to bring him up privately at home, and to keep him, as he advanced in years, from all contact with the temptations and the dangers of the world.

With these objects in view, her longer sojourn in her own locality (where the services of the resident clergyman, in the capacity of tutor, were not obtainable) must come to an end. She had made inquiries, had heard of a house that would suit her in Mr. Brock's neighborhood, and had also been told that Mr. Brock himself had formerly been in the habit of taking pupils. Possessed of this information, she had ventured to present herself, with references that vouched for her respectability, but without a formal introduction; and she had now to ask whether (in the event of her residing in the neighborhood) any terms that could be offered would induce Mr. Brock to open his doors once more to a pupil, and to allow that pupil to be her son.

If Mrs. Armadale had been a woman of no personal attractions, or if Mr. Brock had been provided with an intrenchment to fight behind in the shape of a wife, it is probable that the widow's journey might have been taken in vain. As things really were, the rector examined the references which were offered to him, and asked time for consideration. When the time had expired, he did what Mrs. Armadale wished him to do—he offered his back to the burden, and let the mother load him with the responsibility of the son.

This was the first event of the series; the date of it being the year eighteen hundred and thirty-seven. Mr. Brock's memory, traveling forward toward the present from that point, picked up the second event in its turn, and stopped next at the year eighteen hundred and forty-five.

The fishing-village on the Somersetshire coast was still the scene, and the characters were once again—Mrs. Armadale and her son.

Through the eight years that had passed, Mr. Brock's responsibility had rested on him lightly enough. The boy had given his mother and his tutor but little trouble. He was certainly slow over his books, but more from a constitutional inability to fix his attention on his tasks than from want of capacity to understand them. His temperament, it could not be denied, was heedless to the last degree: he acted recklessly on his first impulses, and rushed blindfold at all his conclusions. On the other hand, it was to be said in his favor that his disposition was open as the day; a more generous, affectionate, sweet-tempered lad it would have been hard to find anywhere. A certain quaint originality of character, and a natural healthiness in all his tastes, carried him free of most of the dangers to which his mother's system of education inevitably exposed him. He had a thoroughly English love of the sea and of all that belongs to it; and as he grew in years, there was no luring him away from the water-side, and no keeping him out of the boat-builder's yard. In course of time his mother caught him actually working there, to her infinite annoyance and surprise, as a volunteer. He acknowledged that his whole future ambition was to have a yard of his own, and that his one present object was to learn to build a boat for himself. Wisely foreseeing that such a pursuit as this for his leisure hours was exactly what was wanted to reconcile the lad to a position of isolation from companions of his own rank and age, Mr. Brock prevailed on Mrs.

Armadale, with no small difficulty, to let her son have his way. At the period of that second event in the clergyman's life with his pupil which is now to be related, young Armadale had practiced long enough in the builder's yard to have reached the summit of his wishes, by laying with his own hands the keel of his own boat.

Late on a certain summer day, not long after Allan had completed his sixteenth year, Mr. Brock left his pupil hard at work in the yard, and went to spend the evening with Mrs. Armadale, taking the *Times* newspaper with him in his hand.

The years that had passed since they had first met had long since regulated the lives of the clergyman and his neighbor. The first advances which Mr. Brock's growing admiration for the widow had led him to make in the early days of their intercourse had been met on her side by an appeal to his forbearance which had closed his lips for the future. She had satisfied him, at once and forever, that the one place in her heart which he could hope to occupy was the place of a friend. He loved her well enough to take what she would give him: friends they became, and friends they remained from that time forth. No jealous dread of another man's succeeding where he had failed imbittered the clergyman's placid relations with the woman whom he loved. Of the few resident gentlemen in the neighborhood, none were ever admitted by Mrs. Armadale to more than the merest acquaintance with her. Contentedly self-buried in her country retreat, she was proof against every social attraction that would have tempted other women in her position and at her age. Mr. Brock and his newspaper, appearing with monotonous regularity at her tea-table three times a week, told her all she knew or cared to know of the great outer world which circled round the narrow and changeless limits of her daily life.

On the evening in question Mr. Brock took the arm-chair in which he always sat, accepted the one cup of tea which he always drank, and opened the newspaper which he always read aloud to Mrs. Armadale, who invariably listened to him reclining on the same sofa, with the same sort of needle-work everlastingly in her hand.

"Bless my soul!" cried the rector, with his voice in a new octave, and his eyes fixed in astonishment on the first page of the newspaper.

No such introduction to the evening readings as this had ever happened before in all Mrs. Armadale's experience as a listener. She looked up from the sofa in a flutter of curiosity, and besought her reverend friend to favor her with an explanation.

"I can hardly believe my own eyes," said Mr. Brock. "Here is an advertisement, Mrs. Armadale, addressed to your son."

Without further preface, he read the advertisement as follows:

IF this should meet the eye of ALLAN ARMADALE, he is desired to communicate, either personally or by letter, with Messrs. Hammick and Ridge (Lincoln's Inn

Fields, London), on business of importance which seriously concerns him. Any one capable of informing Messrs.
H. and R. where the person herein advertised can be
found would confer a favor by doing the same. To prevent mistakes, it is further notified that the missing
Allan Armadale is a youth aged fifteen years, and that
this advertisement is inserted at the instance of his
family and friends.

"Another family, and other friends," said
Mrs. Armadale. "The person whose name appears in that advertisement is not my son."

The tone in which she spoke surprised Mr.
Brock. The change in her face, when he looked
up, shocked him. Her delicate complexion had
faded away to a dull white; her eyes were averted
from her visitor with a strange mixture of confusion and alarm; she looked an older woman
than she was, by ten good years at least.

"The name is so very uncommon," said Mr.
Brock, imagining he had offended her, and
trying to excuse himself. "It really seemed
impossible there could be two persons—"

"There *are* two," interposed Mrs. Armadale.
"Allan, as you know, is sixteen years old. If
you look back at the advertisement, you will
find the missing person described as being only
fifteen. Although he bears the same surname
and the same Christian name, he is, I thank
God, in no way whatever related to my son.
As long as I live, it will be the object of my
hopes and prayers that Allan may never see
him, may never even hear of him. My kind
friend, I see I surprise you: will you bear with
me if I leave these strange circumstances unex-

plained? There is past misfortune and misery in my early life too painful for me to speak of, even to *you*. Will you help me to bear the remembrance of it, by never referring to this again? Will you do even more—will you promise not to speak of it to Allan, and not to let that newspaper fall in his way?"

Mr. Brock gave the pledge required of him, and considerately left her to herself.

The rector had been too long and too truly attached to Mrs. Armadale to be capable of regarding her with any unworthy distrust. But it would be idle to deny that he felt disappointed by her want of confidence in him, and that he looked inquisitively at the advertisement more than once on his way back to his own house.

It was clear enough, now, that Mrs. Armadale's motives for burying her son as well as herself in the seclusion of a remote country village was not so much to keep him under her own eye as to keep him from discovery by his namesake. Why did she dread the idea of their ever meeting? Was it a dread for herself, or a dread for her son? Mr. Brock's loyal belief in his friend rejected any solution of the difficulty which pointed at some past misconduct of Mrs. Armadale's. That night he destroyed the advertisement with his own hand; that night he resolved that the subject should never be suffered to enter his mind again. There was another Allan Armadale about the world, a stranger to his pupil's blood, and a vagabond advertised in the public newspapers. So much accident had revealed to him. More, for Mrs. Armadale's sake, he had no wish to discover—and more he would never seek to know.

This was the second in the series of events which dated from the rector's connection with Mrs. Armadale and her son. Mr. Brock's memory, traveling on nearer and nearer to present circumstances, reached the third stage of its journey through the by-gone time, and stopped at the year eighteen hundred and fifty, next.

The five years that had passed had made little if any change in Allan's character. He had simply developed (to use his tutor's own expression) from a boy of sixteen to a boy of twenty-one. He was just as easy and open in his disposition as ever; just as quaintly and inveterately good-humored; just as heedless in following his own impulses, lead him where they might. His bias toward the sea had strengthened with his advance to the years of manhood. From building a boat, he had now got on — with two journeymen at work under him — to building a decked vessel of five-and-thirty tons. Mr. Brock had conscientiously tried to divert him to higher aspirations; had taken him to Oxford, to see what college life was like; had taken him to London, to expand his mind by the spectacle of the great metropolis. The change had diverted Allan, but had not altered him in the least. He was as impenetrably superior to all worldly ambition as Diogenes himself. "Which is best," asked this unconscious philosopher, "to find out the way to be happy for yourself, or to let other people try if they can find it out for you?" From that moment Mr. Brock permitted his pupil's character to grow at its own rate of development, and Allan went on uninterruptedly with the work of his yacht.

Time, which had wrought so little change in the son, had not passed harmless over the mother.

Mrs. Armadale's health was breaking fast. As her strength failed, her temper altered for the worse: she grew more and more fretful, more and more subject to morbid fears and fancies, more and more reluctant to leave her own room. Since the appearance of the advertisement five years since, nothing had happened to force her memory back to the painful associations connected with her early life. No word more on the forbidden topic had passed between the rector and herself; no suspicion had ever been raised in Allan's mind of the existence of his namesake; and yet, without the shadow of a reason for any special anxiety, Mrs. Armadale had become, of late years, obstinately and fretfully uneasy on the subject of her son. More than once Mr. Brock dreaded a serious disagreement between them; but Allan's natural sweetness of temper, fortified by his love for his mother, carried him triumphantly through all trials. Not a hard word or a harsh look ever escaped him in her presence; he was unchangeably loving and forbearing with her to the very last.

Such were the positions of the son, the mother, and the friend, when the next notable event hap-

pened in the lives of the three. On a dreary
afternoon, early in the month of November, Mr.
Brock was disturbed over the composition of his
sermon by a visit from the landlord of the village inn.

After making his introductory apologies, the
landlord stated the urgent business on which
he had come to the rectory clearly enough.

A few hours since a young man had been
brought to the inn by some farm laborers in the
neighborhood, who had found him wandering
about one of their master's fields in a disordered
state of mind, which looked to their eyes like
downright madness. The landlord had given
the poor creature shelter while he sent for medical help; and the doctor, on seeing him, had
pronounced that he was suffering from fever
on the brain, and that his removal to the nearest town at which a hospital or a work-house
infirmary could be found to receive him would
in all probability be fatal to his chances of recovery. After hearing this expression of opinion, and after observing for himself that the
stranger's only luggage consisted of a small
carpet-bag which had been found in the field
near him, the landlord had set off on the spot
to consult the rector, and to ask, in this serious
emergency, what course he was to take next.

Mr. Brock was the magistrate as well as the
clergyman of the district, and the course to be
taken, in the first instance, was to his mind clear
enough. He put on his hat, and accompanied
the landlord back to the inn.

At the inn door they were joined by Allan, who had heard the news through another channel, and who was waiting Mr. Brock's arrival, to follow in the magistrate's train, and to see what the stranger was like. The village surgeon joined them at the same moment, and the four went into the inn together.

They found the landlord's son on one side, and the hostler on the other, holding the man down in his chair. Young, slim, and undersized, he was strong enough at that moment to make it a matter of difficulty for the two to master him. His tawny complexion, his large, bright brown eyes, and his black beard gave him something of a foreign look. His dress was a little worn, but his linen was clean. His dusky hands were wiry and nervous, and were lividly discolored in more places than one by the scars of old wounds. The toes of one of his feet, off which he had kicked the shoe, grasped at the chair rail through his stocking, with the sensitive muscular action which is only seen in those who have been accustomed to go barefoot. In the frenzy that now possessed him, it was impossible to notice, to any useful purpose, more than this. After a whispered consultation with Mr. Brock, the surgeon personally superintended the patient's removal to a quiet bedroom at the back of the house. Shortly afterward his clothes and his carpet-bag were sent downstairs, and were searched, on the chance of finding a clew by which to communicate with his friends, in the magistrate's presence.

The carpet - bag contained nothing but a change of clothing, and two books—the Plays of Sophocles, in the original Greek, and the "Faust" of Goethe, in the original German. Both volumes were much worn by reading, and on the fly-leaf of each were inscribed the initials O. M. So much the bag revealed, and no more.

The clothes which the man wore when he was discovered in the field were tried next. A purse (containing a sovereign and a few shillings), a pipe, a tobacco pouch, a handkerchief, and a little drinking-cup of horn were produced in succession. The next object, and the last, was found crumpled up carelessly in the breast-pocket of the coat. It was a written testimonial to character, dated and signed, but without any address.

So far as this document could tell it, the stranger's story was a sad one indeed. He had apparently been employed for a short time as usher at a school, and had been turned adrift in the world, at the outset of his illness, from the fear that the fever might be infectious, and that the prosperity of the establishment might suffer accordingly. Not the slightest imputation of any misbehavior in his employment rested on him. On the contrary, the schoolmaster had great pleasure in testifying to his capacity and his character, and in expressing a fervent hope that he might (under Providence) succeed in recovering his health in somebody else's house.

The written testimonial which afforded this

glimpse at the man's story served one purpose more: it connected him with the initials on the books, and identified him to the magistrate and the landlord under the strangely uncouth name of Ozias Midwinter.

Mr. Brock laid aside the testimonial, suspecting that the schoolmaster had purposely abstained from writing his address on it, with the view of escaping all responsibility in the event of his usher's death. In any case, it was manifestly useless, under existing circumstances, to think of tracing the poor wretch's friends, if friends he had. To the inn he had been brought, and, as a matter of common humanity, at the inn he must remain for the present. The difficulty about expenses, if it came to the worst, might possibly be met by charitable contributions from the neighbors, or by a collection after a sermon at church. Assuring the landlord that he would consider this part of the question and would let him know the result, Mr. Brock quitted the inn, without noticing for the moment that he had left Allan there behind him.

Before he had got fifty yards from the house his pupil overtook him. Allan had been most uncharacteristically silent and serious all through the search at the inn; but he had now recovered his usual high spirits. A stranger would have set him down as wanting in common feeling.

"This is a sad business," said the rector. "I really don't know what to do for the best about that unfortunate man."

"You may make your mind quite easy, sir,"

said young Armadale, in his off-hand way. "I settled it all with the landlord a minute ago."

"You!" exclaimed Mr. Brock, in the utmost astonishment.

"I have merely given a few simple directions," pursued Allan. "Our friend the usher is to have everything he requires, and is to be treated like a prince; and when the doctor and the landlord want their money they are to come to me."

"My dear Allan," Mr. Brock gently remonstrated, "when will you learn to think before you act on those generous impulses of yours? You are spending more money already on your yacht-building than you can afford—"

"Only think! we laid the first planks of the deck the day before yesterday," said Allan, flying off to the new subject in his usual bird-witted way. "There's just enough of it done to walk on, if you don't feel giddy. I'll help you up the ladder, Mr. Brock, if you'll only come and try."

"Listen to me," persisted the rector. "I'm not talking about the yacht now; that is to say, I am only referring to the yacht as an illustration—"

"And a very pretty illustration, too," remarked the incorrigible Allan. "Find me a smarter little vessel of her size in all England, and I'll give up yacht-building to-morrow. Whereabouts were we in our conversation, sir? I'm rather afraid we have lost ourselves somehow."

"I am rather afraid one of us is in the habit

of losing himself every time he opens his lips,"
retorted Mr. Brock. "Come, come, Allan, this
is serious. You have been rendering yourself
liable for expenses which you may not be able
to pay. Mind, I am far from blaming you for
your kind feeling toward this poor friendless
man—"

"Don't be low-spirited about him, sir. He'll
get over it—he'll be all right again in a week
or so. A capital fellow, I have not the least
doubt!" continued Allan, whose habit it was to
believe in everybody and to despair of nothing.
"Suppose you ask him to dinner when he gets
well, Mr. Brock? I should like to find out (when
we are all three snug and friendly together over
our wine, you know) how he came by that extraordinary name of his. Ozias Midwinter! Upon
my life, his father ought to be ashamed of himself."

"Will you answer me one question before I
go in?" said the rector, stopping in despair at
his own gate. "This man's bill for lodging
and medical attendance may mount to twenty
or thirty pounds before he gets well again, if he
ever does get well. How are you to pay for
it?"

"What's that the Chancellor of the Exchequer
says when he finds himself in a mess with his
accounts, and doesn't see his way out again?"
asked Allan. "He always tells his honorable
friend he is quite willing to leave a something
or other—"

"A margin?" suggested Mr. Brock.

"That's it," said Allan. "I'm like the Chancellor of the Exchequer. I'm quite willing to leave a margin. The yacht (bless her heart!) doesn't eat up everything. If I'm short by a pound or two, don't be afraid, sir. There's no pride about me; I'll go round with the hat, and get the balance in the neighborhood. Deuce take the pounds, shillings, and pence! I wish they could all three get rid of themselves, like the Bedouin brothers at the show. Don't you remember the Bedouin brothers, Mr. Brock? 'Ali will take a lighted torch, and jump down the throat of his brother Muli; Muli will take a lighted torch, and jump down the throat of his brother Hassan; and Hassan, taking a third lighted torch, will conclude the performances by jumping down his own throat, and leaving the spectators in total darkness.' Wonderfully good, that — what I call real wit, with a fine strong flavor about it. Wait a minute! Where are we? We have lost ourselves again. Oh, I remember—money. What I can't beat into my thick head," concluded Allan, quite unconscious that he was preaching socialist doctrines to a clergyman, "is the meaning of the fuss that's made about giving money away. Why can't the people who have got money to spare give it to the people who haven't got money to spare, and make things pleasant and comfortable all the world over in that way? You're always telling me to cultivate ideas, Mr. Brock. There's an idea, and, upon my life, I don't think it's a bad one."

ALLAN WAS THE FIRST WHO APPEARED AT HIS BEDSIDE.
—Armadale, Vol. Eight, page 97.

Mr. Brock gave his pupil a good - humored poke with the end of his stick. "Go back to your yacht," he said. "All the little discretion you have got in that flighty head of yours is left on board in your tool-chest. How that lad will end," pursued the rector, when he was left by himself, "is more than any human being can say. I almost wish I had never taken the responsibility of him on my shoulders."

Three weeks passed before the stranger with the uncouth name was pronounced to be at last on the way to recovery.

During this period Allan had made regular inquiries at the inn, and, as soon as the sick man was allowed to see visitors, Allan was the first who appeared at his bedside. So far Mr. Brock's pupil had shown no more than a natural interest in one of the few romantic circumstances which had varied the monotony of the village life: he had committed no imprudence, and he had exposed himself to no blame. But as the days passed, young Armadale's visits to the inn began to lengthen considerably, and the surgeon (a cautious elderly man) gave the rector a private hint to bestir himself. Mr. Brock acted on the hint immediately, and discovered that Allan had followed his usual impulses in his usual headlong way. He had taken a violent fancy to the castaway usher, and had invited Ozias Midwinter to reside permanently in the neighborhood in the new and interesting character of his bosom friend.

Before Mr. Brock could make up his mind

how to act in this emergency, he received a
note from Allan's mother, begging him to use
his privilege as an old friend, and to pay her a
visit in her room.

He found Mrs. Armadale suffering under violent nervous agitation, caused entirely by a recent interview with her son. Allan had been
sitting with her all the morning, and had talked
of nothing but his new friend. The man with
the horrible name (as poor Mrs. Armadale described him) had questioned Allan, in a singularly inquisitive manner, on the subject of himself and his family, but had kept his own personal
history entirely in the dark. At some former
period of his life he had been accustomed to the
sea and to sailing. Allan had, unfortunately,
found this out, and a bond of union between
them was formed on the spot. With a merciless distrust of the stranger—simply *because* he
was a stranger—which appeared rather unreasonable to Mr. Brock, Mrs. Armadale besought
the rector to go to the inn without a moment's
loss of time, and never to rest until he had made
the man give a proper account of himself. "Find
out everything about his father and mother!"
she said, in her vehement female way. "Make
sure before you leave him that he is not a vagabond roaming the country under an assumed
name."

"My dear lady," remonstrated the rector,
obediently taking his hat, "whatever else we
may doubt, I really think we may feel sure
about the man's name! It is so remarkably

ugly that it must be genuine. No sane human being would *assume* such a name as Ozias Midwinter.''

"You may be quite right, and I may be quite wrong; but pray go and see him," persisted Mrs. Armadale. "Go, and don't spare him, Mr. Brock. How do we know that this illness of his may not have been put on for a purpose?"

It was useless to reason with her. The whole College of Physicians might have certified to the man's illness, and, in her present frame of mind, Mrs. Armadale would have disbelieved the College, one and all, from the president downward. Mr. Brock took the wise way out of the difficulty —he said no more, and he set off for the inn immediately.

Ozias Midwinter, recovering from brain-fever, was a startling object to contemplate on a first view of him. His shaven head, tied up in an old yellow silk handkerchief; his tawny, haggard cheeks; his bright brown eyes, preternaturally large and wild; his rough black beard; his long, supple, sinewy fingers, wasted by suffering till they looked like claws—all tended to discompose the rector at the outset of the interview. When the first feeling of surprise had worn off, the impression that followed it was not an agreeable one. Mr. Brock could not conceal from himself that the stranger's manner was against him. The general opinion has settled that, if a man is honest, he is bound to assert it by looking straight at his fellow - creatures when he speaks to them. If this man was honest,

his eyes showed a singular perversity in looking away and denying it. Possibly they were
affected in some degree by a nervous restlessness
in his organization, which appeared to pervade
every fiber in his lean, lithe body. The rector's
healthy Anglo-Saxon flesh crept responsively at
every casual movement of the usher's supple
brown fingers, and every passing distortion of
the usher's haggard yellow face. "God forgive
me!" thought Mr. Brock, with his mind running
on Allan and Allan's mother, "I wish I could
see my way to turning Ozias Midwinter adrift
in the world again!"

The conversation which ensued between the
two was a very guarded one. Mr. Brock felt
his way gently, and found himself, try where
he might, always kept politely, more or less, in
the dark.

From first to last, the man's real character
shrank back with a savage shyness from the
rector's touch. He started by an assertion
which it was impossible to look at him and
believe—he declared that he was only twenty
years of age. All he could be persuaded to say
on the subject of the school was that the bare
recollection of it was horrible to him. He had
only filled the usher's situation for ten days
when the first appearance of his illness caused
his dismissal. How he had reached the field
in which he had been found was more than he
could say. He remembered traveling a long distance by railway, with a purpose (if he had a
purpose) which it was now impossible to re-

call, and then wandering coastward, on foot,
all through the day, or all through the night—
he was not sure which. The sea kept running
in his mind when his mind began to give way.
He had been employed on the sea as a lad. He
had left it, and had filled a situation at a book-
seller's in a country town. He had left the book-
seller's, and had tried the school. Now the school
had turned him out, he must try something else.
It mattered little what he tried — failure (for
which nobody was ever to blame but himself)
was sure to be the end of it, sooner or later.
Friends to assist him, he had none to apply to;
and as for relations, he wished to be excused
from speaking of them. For all he knew they
might be dead, and for all *they* knew *he* might
be dead. That was a melancholy acknowledgment to make at his time of life, there was no
denying it. It might tell against him in the
opinions of others; and it did tell against him,
no doubt, in the opinion of the gentleman who
was talking to him at that moment.

These strange answers were given in a tone
and manner far removed from bitterness on the
one side, or from indifference on the other. Ozias
Midwinter at twenty spoke of his life as Ozias
Midwinter at seventy might have spoken, with
a long weariness of years on him which he had
learned to bear patiently.

Two circumstances pleaded strongly against
the distrust with which, in sheer perplexity of
mind, Mr. Brock blindly regarded him. He had
written to a savings-bank in a distant part of

England, had drawn his money, and had paid
the doctor and the landlord. A man of vulgar
mind, after acting in this manner, would have
treated his obligations lightly when he had settled
his bills. Ozias Midwinter spoke of his obligations—and especially of his obligation to Allan
—with a fervor of thankfulness which it was
not surprising only, but absolutely painful to
witness. He showed a horrible sincerity of astonishment at having been treated with common
Christian kindness in a Christian land. He spoke
of Allan's having become answerable for all the
expenses of sheltering, nursing, and curing him,
with a savage rapture of gratitude and surprise
which burst out of him like a flash of lightning.
"So help me God!" cried the castaway usher,
"I never met with the like of him: I never heard
of the like of him before!" In the next instant,
the one glimpse of light which the man had let
in on his own passionate nature was quenched
again in darkness. His wandering eyes, returning to their old trick, looked uneasily away from
Mr. Brock, and his voice dropped back once
more into its unnatural steadiness and quietness
of tone. "I beg your pardon, sir," he said. "I
have been used to be hunted, and cheated, and
starved. Everything else comes strange to me."
Half attracted by the man, half repelled by him,
Mr. Brock, on rising to take leave, impulsively offered his hand, and then, with a sudden
misgiving, confusedly drew it back again.
"You meant that kindly, sir," said Ozias Midwinter, with his own hands crossed resolutely

behind him. "I don't complain of your thinking better of it. A man who can't give a proper
account of himself is not a man for a gentleman
in your position to take by the hand."

Mr. Brock left the inn thoroughly puzzled.
Before returning to Mrs. Armadale he sent for
her son. The chances were that the guard had
been off the stranger's tongue when he spoke
to Allan, and with Allan's frankness there was
no fear of his concealing anything that had
passed between them from the rector's knowledge.

Here again Mr. Brock's diplomacy achieved
no useful results.

Once started on the subject of Ozias Midwinter, Allan rattled on about his new friend
in his usual easy, light-hearted way. But he
had really nothing of importance to tell, for
nothing of importance had been revealed to
him. They had talked about boat-building and
sailing by the hour together, and Allan had got
some valuable hints. They had discussed (with
diagrams to assist them, and with more valuable hints for Allan) the serious impending question of the launch of the yacht. On other occasions they had diverged to other subjects—to
more of them than Allan could remember, on
the spur of the moment. Had Midwinter said
nothing about his relations in the flow of all this
friendly talk? Nothing, except that they had
not behaved well to him—hang his relations!
Was he at all sensitive on the subject of his own
odd name? Not the least in the world; he had

set the example, like a sensible fellow, of laughing at it himself.

Mr. Brock still persisted. He inquired next what Allan had seen in the stranger to take such a fancy to? Allan had seen in him—what he didn't see in people in general. He wasn't like all the other fellows in the neighborhood. All the other fellows were cut out on the same pattern. Every man of them was equally healthy, muscular, loud, hard-hearted, clean-skinned, and rough; every man of them drank the same draughts of beer, smoked the same short pipes all day long, rode the best horse, shot over the best dog, and put the best bottle of wine in England on his table at night; every man of them sponged himself every morning in the same sort of tub of cold water and bragged about it in frosty weather in the same sort of way; every man of them thought getting into debt a capital joke and betting on horse-races one of the most meritorious actions that a human being can perform. They were, no doubt, excellent fellows in their way; but the worst of them was, they were all exactly alike. It was a perfect godsend to meet with a man like Midwinter—a man who was not cut out on the regular local pattern, and whose way in the world had the one great merit (in those parts) of being a way of his own.

Leaving all remonstrances for a fitter opportunity, the rector went back to Mrs. Armadale. He could not disguise from himself that Allan's mother was the person really answerable for Allan's present indiscretion. If the lad had

seen a little less of the small gentry in the
neighborhood, and a little more of the great
outside world at home and abroad, the pleasure of cultivating Ozias Midwinter's society
might have had fewer attractions for him. ·

Conscious of the unsatisfactory result of his
visit to the inn, Mr. Brock felt some anxiety
about the reception of his report when he found
himself once more in Mrs. Armadale's presence.
His forebodings were soon realized. Try as he
might to make the best of it, Mrs. Armadale
seized on the one suspicious fact of the usher's
silence about himself as justifying the strongest
measures that could be taken to separate him
from her son. If the rector refused to interfere,
she declared her intention of writing to Ozias
Midwinter with her own hand. Remonstrance
irritated her to such a pitch that she astounded
Mr. Brock by reverting to the forbidden subject
of five years since, and referring him to the
conversation which had passed between them
when the advertisement had been discovered
in the newspaper. She passionately declared
that the vagabond Armadale of that advertisement, and the vagabond Midwinter at the village inn, might, for all she knew to the contrary,
be one and the same. Foreboding a serious disagreement between the mother and son if the
mother interfered, Mr. Brock undertook to see
Midwinter again, and to tell him plainly that
he must give a proper account of himself, or
that his intimacy with Allan must cease. The
two concessions which he exacted from Mrs.

Armadale in return were that she should wait patiently until the doctor reported the man fit to travel, and that she should be careful in the interval not to mention the matter in any way to her son.

In a week's time Midwinter was able to drive out (with Allan for his coachman) in the pony chaise belonging to the inn, and in ten days the doctor privately reported him as fit to travel. Toward the close of that tenth day, Mr. Brock met Allan and his new friend enjoying the last gleams of wintry sunshine in one of the inland lanes. He waited until the two had separated, and then followed the usher on his way back to the inn.

The rector's resolution to speak pitilessly to the purpose was in some danger of failing him as he drew nearer and nearer to the friendless man, and saw how feebly he still walked, how loosely his worn coat hung about him, and how heavily he leaned on his cheap, clumsy stick. Humanely reluctant to say the decisive words too precipitately, Mr. Brock tried him first with a little compliment on the range of his reading, as shown by the volume of Sophocles and the volume of Goethe which had been found in his bag, and asked how long he had been acquainted with German and Greek. The quick ear of Midwinter detected something wrong in the tone of Mr. Brock's voice. He turned in the darkening twilight, and looked suddenly and suspiciously in the rector's face.

"You have something to say to me," he answered; "and it is not what you are saying now."

There was no help for it but to accept the challenge. Very delicately, with many preparatory words, to which the other listened in unbroken silence, Mr. Brock came little by little nearer and nearer to the point. Long before he had really reached it—long before a man of no more than ordinary sensibility would have felt what was coming—Ozias Midwinter stood still in the lane, and told the rector that he need say no more.

"I understand you, sir," said the usher. "Mr. Armadale has an ascertained position in the world; Mr. Armadale has nothing to conceal, and nothing to be ashamed of. I agree with you that I am not a fit companion for him. The best return I can make for his kindness is to presume on it no longer. You may depend on my leaving this place to-morrow morning."

He spoke no word more; he would hear no word more. With a self-control which, at his years and with his temperament, was nothing less than marvelous, he civilly took off his hat, bowed, and returned to the inn by himself.

Mr. Brock slept badly that night. The issue of the interview in the lane had made the problem of Ozias Midwinter a harder problem to solve than ever.

Early the next morning a letter was brought to the rector from the inn, and the messenger announced that the strange gentleman had taken his departure. The letter inclosed an open note

addressed to Allan, and requested Allan's tutor
(after first reading it himself) to forward it or
not at his own sole discretion. The note was a
startlingly short one; it began and ended in a
dozen words: "Don't blame Mr. Brock; Mr.
Brock is right. Thank you, and good-by.—O.
M."

The rector forwarded the note to its proper destination, as a matter of course, and sent a few
lines to Mrs. Armadale at the same time to quiet
her anxiety by the news of the usher's departure.
This done, he waited the visit from his pupil,
which would probably follow the delivery of
the note, in no very tranquil frame of mind.
There might or might not be some deep motive
at the bottom of Midwinter's conduct; but thus
far it was impossible to deny that he had behaved
in such a manner as to rebuke the rector's distrust, and to justify Allan's good opinion of
him.

The morning wore on, and young Armadale
never appeared. After looking for him vainly
in the yard where the yacht was building, Mr.
Brock went to Mrs. Armadale's house, and there
heard news from the servant which turned his
steps in the direction of the inn. The landlord
at once acknowledged the truth: young Mr.
Armadale had come there with an open letter in
his hand, and had insisted on being informed
of the road which his friend had taken. For
the first time in the landlord's experience of
him, the young gentleman was out of temper;
and the girl who waited on the customers had

stupidly mentioned a circumstance which had added fuel to the fire. She had acknowledged having heard Mr. Midwinter lock himself into his room overnight, and burst into a violent fit of crying. That trifling particular had set Mr. Armadale's face all of a flame; he had shouted and sworn; he had rushed into the stables; and forced the hostler to saddle him a horse, and had set off full gallop on the road that Ozias Midwinter had taken before him.

After cautioning the landlord to keep Allan's conduct a secret if any of Mrs. Armadale's servants came that morning to the inn, Mr. Brock went home again, and waited anxiously to see what the day would bring forth.

To his infinite relief his pupil appeared at the rectory late in the afternoon.

Allan looked and spoke with a dogged determination which was quite new in his old friend's experience of him. Without waiting to be questioned, he told his story in his usual straightforward way. He had overtaken Midwinter on the road; and—after trying vainly first to induce him to return, then to find out where he was going to—had threatened to keep company with him for the rest of the day, and had so extorted the confession that he was going to try his luck in London. Having gained this point, Allan had asked next for his friend's address in London, had been entreated by the other not to press his request, had pressed it, nevertheless, with all his might, and had got the address at last by making an appeal to Midwinter's gratitude, for which (feeling heartily ashamed of himself) he had afterward asked Midwinter's pardon. "I like the poor fellow, and I won't give him up," concluded Allan, bringing his clinched fist down with a thump on the rectory table. "Don't be afraid of my vexing my mother; I'll leave you to speak to her, Mr. Brock, at your own time and in your own way; and I'll just say this much more by way of bringing the thing to an end. Here is the address safe in my pocket-book, and here am I, standing firm for once on a resolution of my own. I'll give you and my mother time to reconsider this; and, when the time is up, if my friend Midwinter doesn't come to *me*, I'll go to my friend Midwinter." .

So the matter rested for the present; and such was the result of turning the castaway usher adrift in the world again.

A month passed, and brought in the new year —'51. Overleaping that short lapse of time, Mr. Brock paused, with a heavy heart, at the next event; to his mind the one mournful, the one memorable event of the series—Mrs. Armadale's death.

The first warning of the affliction that was near at hand had followed close on the usher's departure in December, and had arisen out of a circumstance which dwelt painfully on the rector's memory from that time forth.

But three days after Midwinter had left for London, Mr. Brock was accosted in the village by a neatly dressed woman, wearing a gown and bonnet of black silk and a red Paisley shawl, who was a total stranger to him, and who inquired the way to Mrs. Armadale's house. She put the question without raising the thick black veil that hung over her face. Mr. Brock, in giving her the necessary directions, observed that she was a remarkably elegant and graceful woman, and looked after her as she bowed and left him, wondering who Mrs. Armadale's visitor could possibly be.

A quarter of an hour later the lady, still veiled as before, passed Mr. Brock again close to the inn. She entered the house, and spoke to the landlady. Seeing the landlord shortly afterward hurrying round to the stables, Mr. Brock asked him if the lady was going away. Yes; she had come from the railway in the omnibus, but she was going back again more creditably in a carriage of her own hiring, supplied by the inn.

The rector proceeded on his walk, rather surprised to find his thoughts running inquisitively on a woman who was a stranger to him. When he got home again, he found the village surgeon waiting his return with an urgent message from Allan's mother. About an hour since, the surgeon had been sent for in great haste to see Mrs. Armadale. He had found her suffering from an alarming nervous attack, brought on (as the servants suspected) by an unexpected, and, possibly, an unwelcome visitor, who had called that morning. The surgeon had done all that was needful, and had no apprehension of any dangerous results. Finding his patient eagerly desirous,

on recovering herself, to see Mr. Brock immediately, he had thought it important to humor
her, and had readily undertaken to call at the
rectory with a message to that effect.

Looking at Mrs. Armadale with a far deeper
interest in her than the surgeon's interest, Mr.
Brock saw enough in her face, when it turned
toward him on his entering the room, to justify
instant and serious alarm.  She allowed him no
opportunity of soothing her; she heeded none of
his inquiries.  Answers to certain questions of
her own were what she wanted, and what she
was determined to have; Had Mr. Brock seen
the woman who had presumed to visit her that
morning?  Yes.  Had Allan seen her?  No;
Allan had been at work since breakfast, and
was at work still, in his yard by the water-side.

This latter reply appeared to quiet Mrs. Armadale for the moment; she put her next question
—the most extraordinary question of the three
—more composedly: Did the rector think Allan
would object to leaving his vessel for the present,
and to accompanying his mother on a journey to
look out for a new house in some other part of
England?  In the greatest amazement Mr. Brock
asked what reason there could possibly be for
leaving her present residence?  Mrs. Armadale's
reason, when she gave it, only added to his surprise.  The woman's first visit might be followed by a second; and rather than see her
again, rather than run the risk of Allan's seeing her and speaking to her, Mrs. Armadale
would leave England if necessary, and end her

days in a foreign land. Taking counsel of his experience as a magistrate, Mr. Brock inquired if the woman had come to ask for money. Yes; respectably as she was dressed, she had described herself as being "in distress"; had asked for money, and had got it. But the money was of no importance; the one thing needful was to get away before the woman came again. More and more surprised, Mr. Brock ventured on another question: Was it long since Mrs. Armadale and her visitor had last met? Yes; longer than all Allan's lifetime—as long ago as the year before Allan was born.

At that reply, the rector shifted his ground, and took counsel next of his experience as a friend.

"Is this person," he asked, "connected in any way with the painful remembrances of your early life?"

"Yes; with the painful remembrance of the time when I was married," said Mrs. Armadale. "She was associated, as a mere child, with a circumstance which I must think of with shame and sorrow to my dying day."

Mr. Brock noticed the altered tone in which his old friend spoke, and the unwillingness with which she gave her answer.

"Can you tell me more about her without referring to yourself?" he went on. "I am sure I can protect you, if you will only help me a little. Her name, for instance—you can tell me her name?"

Mrs. Armadale shook her head. "The name

I knew her by," she said, "would be of no use to you. She has been married since then; she told me so herself."

"And without telling you her married name?"

'She refused to tell it."

"Do you know anything of her friends?"

"Only of her friends when she was a child. They called themselves her uncle and aunt. They were low people, and they deserted her at the school on my father's estate. We never heard any more of them."

"Did she remain under your father's care?"

"She remained under my care; that is to say, she traveled with us. We were leaving England, just as that time, for Madeira. I had my father's leave to take her with me, and to train the wretch to be my maid—"

At those words Mrs. Armadale stopped confusedly. Mr. Brock tried gently to lead her on. It was useless; she started up in violent agitation, and walked excitedly backward and forward in the room.

"Don't ask me any more!" she cried out, in loud, angry tones. "I parted with her when she was a girl of twelve years old. I never saw her again, I never heard of her again, from that time to this. I don't know how she has discovered me, after all the years that have passed; I only know that she *has* discovered me. She will find her way to Allan next; she will poison my son's mind against me. Help me to get away from her! help me to take Allan away before she comes back!"

The rector asked no more questions; it would have been cruel to press her further. The first necessity was to compose her by promising compliance with all that she desired. The second was to induce her to see another medical man. Mr. Brock contrived to reach his end harmlessly in this latter case by reminding her that she wanted strength to travel, and that her own medical attendant might restore her all the more speedily to herself if he were assisted by the best professional advice. Having overcome her habitual reluctance to seeing strangers by this means, the rector at once went to Allan; and, delicately concealing what Mrs. Armadale had said at the interview, broke the news to him that his mother was seriously ill. Allan would hear of no messengers being sent for assistance: he drove off on the spot to the railway, and telegraphed himself to Bristol for medical help.

On the next morning the help came, and Mr. Brock's worst fears were confirmed. The village surgeon had fatally misunderstood the case from the first, and the time was past now at which his errors of treatment might have been set right. The shock of the previous morning had completed the mischief. Mrs. Armadale's days were numbered.

The son who dearly loved her, the old friend to whom her life was precious, hoped vainly to the last. In a month from the physician's visit all hope was over; and Allan shed the first bitter tears of his life at his mother's grave.

She had died more peacefully than Mr. Brock

had dared to hope, leaving all her little fortune
to her son, and committing him solemnly to the
care of her one friend on earth. The rector had
entreated her to let him write and try to reconcile her brothers with her before it was too late.
She had only answered sadly that it was too late
already. But one reference escaped her in her
last illness to those early sorrows which had
weighed heavily on all her after-life, and which
had passed thrice already, like shadows of evil,
between the rector and herself. Even on her
deathbed she had shrunk from letting the light
fall clearly on the story of the past. She had
looked at Allan kneeling by the bedside, and
had whispered to Mr. Brock: "*Never let his
Namesake come near him! Never let that
Woman find him out!*" No word more fell
from her that touched on the misfortunes which
had tried her in the past, or on the dangers which
she dreaded in the future. The secret which she
had kept from her son and from her friend was
a secret which she carried with her to the grave.

When the last offices of affection and respect
had been performed, Mr. Brock felt it his duty,
as executor to the deceased lady, to write to her
brothers, and to give them information of her
death. Believing that he had to deal with two
men who would probably misinterpret his motives
if he left Allan's position unexplained, he was
careful to remind them that Mrs. Armadale's son
was well provided for, and that the object of his
letter was simply to communicate the news of
their sister's decease. The two letters were dis-

patched toward the middle of January, and by
return of post the answers were received. The
first which the rector opened was written not
by the elder brother, but by the elder brother's
only son. The young man had succeeded to the
estates in Norfolk on his father's death, some
little time since. He wrote in a frank and
friendly spirit, assuring Mr. Brock that, however strongly his father might have been prejudiced against Mrs. Armadale, the hostile feeling
had never extended to her son. For himself, he
had only to add that he would be sincerely happy
to welcome his cousin to Thorpe Ambrose whenever his cousin came that way.

The second letter was a far less agreeable reply
to receive than the first. The younger brother
was still alive, and still resolute neither to forget
nor forgive. He informed Mr. Brock that his
deceased sister's choice of a husband, and her
conduct to her father at the time of her marriage, had made any relations of affection or
esteem impossible, on his side, from that time
forth. Holding the opinions he did, it would
be equally painful to his nephew and himself
if any personal intercourse took place between
them. He had adverted, as generally as possible, to the nature of the differences which had
kept him apart from his late sister, in order to
satisfy Mr. Brock's mind that a personal acquaintance with young Mr. Armadale was, as
a matter of delicacy, quite out of the question,
and, having done this, he would beg leave to
close the correspondence.

Mr. Brock wisely destroyed the second letter on the spot, and, after showing Allan his cousin's invitation, suggested that he should go to Thorpe Ambrose as soon as he felt fit to present himself to strangers.

Allan listened to the advice patiently enough; but he declined to profit by it. "I will shake hands with my cousin willingly if I ever meet him," he said; "but I will visit no family, and be a guest in no house, in which my mother has been badly treated." Mr. Brock remonstrated gently, and tried to put matters in their proper light. Even at that time—even while he was still ignorant of events which were then impending—Allan's strangely isolated position in the world was a subject of serious anxiety to his old friend and tutor. The proposed visit to Thorpe Ambrose opened the very prospect of his making friends and connections suited to him in rank and age which Mr. Brock most desired to see; but Allan was not to be persuaded; he was obstinate and unreasonable; and the rector had no alternative but to drop the subject.

One on another the weeks passed monotonously, and Allan showed but little of the elasticity of his age and character in bearing the affliction that had made him motherless. He finished and launched his yacht; but his own journeymen remarked that the work seemed to have lost its interest for him. It was not natural to the young man to brood over his solitude and his grief as he was brooding now. As the spring advanced,

Mr. Brock began to feel uneasy about the future, if Allan was not roused at once by change of scene. After much pondering, the rector decided on trying a trip to Paris, and on extending the journey southward if his companion showed an interest in Continental traveling. Allan's reception of the proposal made atonement for his obstinacy in refusing to cultivate his cousin's acquaintance; he was willing to go with Mr. Brock wherever Mr. Brock pleased. The rector took him at his word, and in the middle of March the two strangely assorted companions left for London on their way to Paris.

Arrived in London, Mr. Brock found himself unexpectedly face to face with a new anxiety. The unwelcome subject of Ozias Midwinter, which had been buried in peace since the beginning of December, rose to the surface again, and confronted the rector at the very outset of his travels, more unmanageably than ever.

Mr. Brock's position in dealing with this difficult matter had been hard enough to maintain when he had first meddled with it. He now found himself with no vantage-ground left to stand on. Events had so ordered it that the difference of opinion between Allan and his mother on the subject of the usher was entirely disassociated with the agitation which had hastened Mrs. Armadale's death. Allan's resolution to say no irritating words, and Mr. Brock's reluctance to touch on a disagreeable topic, had kept them both silent about Midwinter in Mrs. Armadale's presence during the three days which had intervened between that person's departure and the appearance of the strange woman in the village. In the period of suspense and suffering that had followed no recurrence to the subject of the usher had been possible, and none had taken place. Free from all mental disquietude on this score, Allan had stoutly preserved his perverse interest in his new friend. He had written to tell Midwinter of his affliction, and he now proposed (unless the rector formally objected to it) paying a visit to his friend before he started for Paris the next morning.

What was Mr. Brock to do? There was no denying that Midwinter's conduct had pleaded unanswerably against poor Mrs. Armadale's unfounded distrust of him. If the rector, with no convincing reason to allege against it, and with no right to interfere but the right which Allan's courtesy gave him, declined to sanction the proposed visit, then farewell to all the old sociability and confidence between tutor and pupil on the contemplated tour. Environed by difficulties, which might have been possibly worsted by a less just and a less kind-hearted man, Mr. Brock said a cautious word or two at parting, and (with more confidence in Midwinter's discretion and self-denial than he quite liked to acknowledge, even to himself) left Allan free to take his own way.

After whiling away an hour, during the interval of his pupil's absence, by a walk in the streets, the rector returned to his hotel, and, finding the newspaper disengaged in the coffee-room, sat down absently to look over it. His eye, rest-ing idly on the title-page, was startled into in-stant attention by the very first advertisement that it chanced to light on at the head of the column. There was Allan's mysterious name-sake again, figuring in capital letters, and asso-ciated this time (in the character of a dead man) with the offer of a pecuniary reward. Thus it ran:

SUPPOSED TO BE DEAD.—To parish clerks, sextons, and others. Twenty Pounds reward will be paid to any person who can produce evidence of the death of ALLAN ARMADALE, only son of the late Allan Armadale, of Barbadoes, and born in Trinidad in the year 1830. Further particulars, on application to Messrs. Hammick and Ridge, Lincoln's Inn Fields, London.

Even Mr. Brock's essentially unimaginative mind began to stagger superstitiously in the dark as he laid the newspaper down again. Little by little a vague suspicion took posses-sion of him that the whole series of events which had followed the first appearance of Allan's namesake in the newspaper six years since was held together by some mysterious connection, and was tending steadily to some unimaginable end. Without knowing why, he began to feel uneasy at Allan's absence. Without knowing why, he became impatient to get his pupil away from England before anything else happened between night and morning.

In an hour more the rector was relieved of all immediate anxiety by Allan's return to the hotel. The young man was vexed and out of spirits.

He had discovered Midwinter's lodgings, but he had failed to find Midwinter himself. The only account his landlady could give of him was that he had gone out at his customary time to get his dinner at the nearest eating-house, and that he had not returned, in accordance with his usual regular habits, at his usual regular hour. Allan had therefore gone to inquire at the eating-house, and had found, on describing him, that Midwinter was well known there. It was his custom, on other days, to take a frugal dinner, and to sit half an hour afterward reading the newspaper. On this occasion, after dining, he had taken up the paper as usual, had suddenly thrown it aside again, and had gone, nobody knew where, in a violent hurry. No further information being attainable, Allan had left a note at the lodgings, giving his address at the hotel, and begging Midwinter to come and say good-by before his departure for Paris.

The evening passed, and Allan's invisible friend never appeared. The morning came, bringing no obstacles with it, and Mr. Brock and his pupil left London. So far Fortune had declared herself at last on the rector's side. Ozias Midwinter, after intrusively rising to the surface, had conveniently dropped out of sight again. What was to happen next?

———

Advancing once more, by three weeks only, from past to present, Mr. Brock's memory took up the next event on the seventh of April. To all appearance, the chain was now broken at last. The new event had no recognizable connection (either to his mind or to Allan's) with any of the persons who had appeared, or any of the circumstances that had happened, in the by-gone time.

The travelers had as yet got no further than Paris. Allan's spirits had risen with the change; and he had been made all the readier to enjoy the novelty of the scene around him by receiving a letter from Midwinter, containing news which Mr. Brock himself acknowledged promised fairly for the future. The ex-usher had been away on business when Allan had called at his lodgings, having been led by an accidental circumstance to open communications with his relatives on that day. The result had taken him entirely by surprise: it had unexpectedly secured to him a little income of his own for the rest of his life. His future plans, now that this piece of good fortune had fallen to his share, were still unsettled. But if Allan wished to hear what he ultimately decided on, his agent in London (whose direction he inclosed) would receive communications for him, and would furnish Mr. Armadale at all future times with his address.

On receipt of this letter, Allan had seized the pen in his usual headlong way, and had insisted on Midwinter's immediately joining Mr. Brock and himself on their travels. The last days of March passed, and no answer to the proposal was received. The first days of April came, and on the seventh of the month there was a letter for Allan at last on the breakfast-table. He snatched it up, looked at the address, and threw the letter down again impatiently. The handwriting was not Midwinter's. Allan finished his breakfast before he cared to read what his correspondent had to say to him.

The meal over, young Armadale lazily opened the letter. He began it with an expression of supreme indifference. He finished it with a sudden leap out of his chair, and a loud shout of astonishment. Wondering, as he well might, at this extraordinary outbreak, Mr. Brock took up the letter which Allan had tossed across the table to him. Before he had come to the end of it, his hands dropped helplessly on his knees, and the blank bewilderment of his pupil's expression was accurately reflected on his own face.

If ever two men had good cause for being thrown completely off their balance, Allan and the rector were those two. The letter which had struck them both with the same shock of astonishment did, beyond all question, contain an announcement which, on a first discovery of it, was simply incredible. The news was from Norfolk, and was to this effect. In little more than one week's time death had mown down no less than three lives in the family at Thorpe Ambrose, and Allan Armadale was at that moment heir to an estate of eight thousand a year!

A second perusal of the letter enabled the rector and his companion to master the details which had escaped them on a first reading.

The writer was the family lawyer at Thorpe

Ambrose. After announcing to Allan the deaths of his cousin Arthur at the age of twenty-five, of his uncle Henry at the age of forty-eight, and of his cousin John at the age of twenty-one, the lawyer proceeded to give a brief abstract of the terms of the elder Mr. Blanchard's will. The claims of male issue were, as is not unusual in such cases, preferred to the claims of female issue. Failing Arthur and his issue male, the estate was left to Henry and his issue male. Failing them, it went to the issue male of Henry's sister; and, in default of such issue, to the next heir male. As events had happened, the two young men, Arthur and John, had died unmarried, and Henry Blanchard had died, leaving no surviving child but a daughter. Under these circumstances, Allan was the next heir male pointed at by the will, and was now legally successor to the Thorpe Ambrose estate. Having made this extraordinary announcement, the lawyer requested to be favored with Mr. Armadale's instructions, and added, in conclusion, that he would be happy to furnish any further particulars that were desired.

It was useless to waste time in wondering at an event which neither Allan nor his mother had ever thought of as even remotely possible. The only thing to be done was to go back to England at once. The next day found the travelers installed once more in their London hotel, and the day after the affair was placed in the proper professional hands. The inevitable corresponding and consulting ensued, and one by one the all - important particulars flowed in, until the measure of information was pronounced to be full.

This was the strange story of the three deaths:

At the time when Mr. Brock had written to Mrs. Armadale's relatives to announce the news of her decease (that is to say, in the middle of the month of January), the family at Thorpe Ambrose numbered five persons—Arthur Blanchard (in possession of the estate), living in the great house with his mother; and Henry Blanchard, the uncle, living in the neighborhood, a widower with two children, a son and a daughter. To cement the family connection still more closely, Arthur Blanchard was engaged to be married to his cousin. The wedding was to be celebrated with great local rejoicings in the coming summer, when the young lady had completed her twentieth year.

The month of February had brought changes with it in the family position. Observing signs of delicacy in the health of his son, Mr. Henry Blanchard left Norfolk, taking the young man with him, under medical advice, to try the climate of Italy. Early in the ensuing month of March, Arthur Blanchard also left Thorpe Ambrose, for a few days only, on business which required his presence in London. The business took him into the City. Annoyed by the endless impediments in the streets, he returned westward by one of the river steamers, and, so returning, met his death.

As the steamer left the wharf, he noticed a

woman near him who had shown a singular hesitation in embarking, and who had been the last of the passengers to take her place in the vessel. She was neatly dressed in black silk, with a red Paisley shawl over her shoulders, and she kept her face hidden behind a thick veil. Arthur Blanchard was struck by the rare grace and elegance of her figure, and he felt a young man's passing curiosity to see her face. She neither lifted her veil nor turned her head his way. After taking a few steps hesitatingly backward and forward on the deck, she walked away on a sudden to the stern of the vessel. In a minute more there was a cry of alarm from the man at the helm, and the engines were stopped immediately. The woman had thrown herself overboard.

The passengers all rushed to the side of the vessel to look. Arthur Blanchard alone, without an instant's hesitation, jumped into the river. He was an excellent swimmer, and he reached the woman as she rose again to the surface, after sinking for the first time. Help was at hand, and they were both brought safely ashore. The woman was taken to the nearest police station, and was soon restored to her senses, her preserver giving his name and address, as usual in such cases, to the inspector on duty, who wisely recommended him to get into a warm bath, and to send to his lodgings for dry clothes. Arthur Blanchard, who had never known an hour's illness since he was a child, laughed at the caution, and went back in a cab. The next day he was too ill to attend the examination before the magistrate. A fortnight afterward he was a dead man.

The news of the calamity reached Henry Blanchard and his son at Milan, and within an hour of the time when they received it they were on their way back to England. The snow on the Alps had loosened earlier than usual that year, and the passes were notoriously dangerous. The father and son, traveling in their own carriage, were met on the mountain by the mail returning, after sending the letters on by hand. Warnings which would have produced their effect under any ordinary circumstances were now vainly addressed to the two Englishmen. Their impatience to be at home again, after the catastrophe which had befallen their family, brooked no delay. Bribes lavishly offered to the postilions, tempted them to go on. The carriage pursued its way, and was lost to view in the mist. When it was seen again, it was disinterred from the bottom of a precipice—the men, the horses, and the vehicle all crushed together under the wreck and ruin of an avalanche.

So the three lives were mown down by death. So, in a clear sequence of events, a woman's suicide-leap into a river had opened to Allan Armadale the succession to the Thorpe Ambrose estates.

Who was the woman? The man who saved her life never knew. The magistrate who remanded her, the chaplain who exhorted her, the reporter who exhibited her in print, never knew. It was recorded of her with surprise that, though most respectably dressed, she had nevertheless described herself as being "in distress." She had expressed the deepest contrition, but had persisted in giving a name which was on the face of it a false one; in telling a commonplace story, which was manifestly an invention; and in refusing to the last to furnish any clew to her friends. A lady connected with a charitable institution ("interested by her extreme elegance and beauty") had volunteered to take charge of her, and to bring her into a better frame of mind. The first day's experience of the penitent had been far from cheering, and the second day's experience had been conclusive. She had left the institution by stealth; and—though the visiting clergyman, taking a special interest in the case, had caused special efforts to be made—all search after her, from that time forth, had proved fruitless.

While this useless investigation (undertaken at Allan's express desire) was in progress, the lawyers had settled the preliminary formalities connected with the succession to the property. All that remained was for the new master of Thorpe Ambrose to decide when he would personally establish himself on the estate of which he was now the legal possessor.

Left necessarily to his own guidance in this matter, Allan settled it for himself in his usual hot-headed, generous way. He positively declined to take possession until Mrs. Blanchard and her niece (who had been permitted thus far, as a matter of courtesy, to remain in their old

home) had recovered from the calamity that had
befallen them, and were fit to decide for themselves what their future proceedings should be.
A private correspondence followed this resolution, comprehending, on Allan's side, unlimited
offers of everything he had to give (in a house
which he had not yet seen), and, on the ladies'
side, a discreetly reluctant readiness to profit by
the young gentleman's generosity in the matter
of time.  To the astonishment of his legal advisers, Allan entered their office one morning,
accompanied by Mr. Brock, and announced, with
perfect composure, that the ladies had been good
enough to take his own arrangements off his
hands, and that, in deference to their convenience, he meant to defer establishing himself at
Thorpe Ambrose till that day two months.  The
lawyers stared at Allan, and Allan, returning
the compliment, stared at the lawyers.

"What on earth are you wondering at, gentlemen?" he inquired, with a boyish bewilderment
in his good-humored blue eyes.  "Why shouldn't
I give the ladies their two months, if the ladies
want them?  Let the poor things take their own
time, and welcome.  My rights? and my position?  Oh, pooh! pooh!  I'm in no hurry to be
squire of the parish; it's not in my way.  What
do I mean to do for the two months?  What I
should have done anyhow, whether the ladies
had stayed or not; I mean to go cruising at sea.
That's what *I* like!  I've got a new yacht at home
in Somersetshire—a yacht of my own building.
And I'll tell you what, sir," continued Allan,

seizing the head partner by the arm in the fervor
of his friendly intentions, "you look sadly in want
of a holiday in the fresh air, and you shall come
along with me on the trial trip of my new vessel.
And your partners, too, if they like. And the
head clerk, who is the best fellow I ever met
with in my life. Plenty of room — we'll all
shake down together on the floor, and we'll give
Mr. Brock a rug on the cabin table. Thorpe
Ambrose be hanged! Do you mean to say, if
you had built a vessel yourself (as I have), you
would go to any estate in the three kingdoms,
while your own little beauty was sitting like a
duck on the water at home, and waiting for you
to try her? You legal gentlemen are great hands
at argument. What do you think of *that* argument? I think it's unanswerable—and I'm off
to Somersetshire to-morrow."

With those words, the new possessor of eight
thousand a year dashed into the head clerk's
office, and invited that functionary to a cruise
on the high seas, with a smack on the shoulder
which was heard distinctly by his masters in the
next room. The firm looked in interrogative
wonder at Mr. Brock. A client who could see
a position among the landed gentry of England
waiting for him, without being in a hurry to
occupy it at the earliest possible opportunity,
was a client of whom they possessed no previous
experience.

"He must have been very oddly brought up,"
said the lawyers to the rector.

"Very oddly," said the rector to the lawyers.

A last leap over one month more brought Mr.
Brock to the present time—to the bedroom at
Castletown, in which he was sitting thinking,
and to the anxiety which was obstinately intruding itself between him and his night's rest. That
anxiety was no unfamiliar enemy to the rector's
peace of mind. It had first found him out in
Somersetshire six months since, and it had now
followed him to the Isle of Man under the inveterately obtrusive form of Ozias Midwinter.

The change in Allan's future prospects had
worked no corresponding alteration in his perverse fancy for the castaway at the village inn.
In the midst of the consultations with the lawyers he had found time to visit Midwinter, and
on the journey back with the rector there was
Allan's friend in the carriage, returning with
them to Somersetshire by Allan's own invitation.

The ex-usher's hair had grown again on his
shaven skull, and his dress showed the renovat-
ing influence of an accession of pecuniary means;
but in all other respects the man was unchanged.
He met Mr. Brock's distrust with the old uncom-
plaining resignation to it; he maintained the same
suspicious silence on the subject of his relatives
and his early life; he spoke of Allan's kindness
to him with the same undisciplined fervor of
gratitude and surprise. "I have done what I
could, sir," he said to Mr. Brock, while Allan
was asleep in the railway carriage. "I have
kept out of Mr. Armadale's way, and I have not
even answered his last letter to me. More than
that is more than I can do. I don't ask you to

consider my own feeling toward the only human creature who has never suspected and never ill-treated me. I can resist my own feeling, but I can't resist the young gentleman himself. There's not another like him in the world. If we are to be parted again, it must be his doing or yours—not mine. The dog's master has whistled," said this strange man, with a momentary outburst of the hidden passion in him, and a sudden springing of angry tears in his wild brown eyes, "and it is hard, sir, to blame the dog when the dog comes."

Once more Mr. Brock's humanity got the better of Mr. Brock's caution. He determined to wait, and see what the coming days of social intercourse might bring forth.

The days passed; the yacht was rigged and fitted for sea; a cruise was arranged to the Welsh coast — and Midwinter the Secret was the same Midwinter still. Confinement on board a little vessel of five-and-thirty tons offered no great attraction to a man of Mr. Brock's time of life. But he sailed on the trial trip of the yacht nevertheless, rather than trust Allan alone with his new friend.

Would the close companionship of the three on their cruise tempt the man into talking of his own affairs? No; he was ready enough on other subjects, especially if Allan led the way to them. But not a word escaped him about himself. Mr. Brock tried him with questions about his recent inheritance, and was answered as he had been answered once already at the Somersetshire inn.

It was a curious coincidence, Midwinter admitted, that Mr. Armadale's prospects and his own prospects should both have unexpectedly changed for the better about the same time. But there the resemblance ended. It was no large fortune that had fallen into his lap, though it was enough for his wants. It had not reconciled him with his relations, for the money had not come to him as a matter of kindness, but as a matter of right. As for the circumstance which had led to his communicating with his family, it was not worth mentioning, seeing that the temporary renewal of intercourse which had followed had produced no friendly results. Nothing had come of it but the money —and, with the money, an anxiety which troubled him sometimes, when he work in the small hours of the morning.

At those last words he became suddenly silent, as if for once his well-guarded tongue had betrayed him.

Mr. Brock seized the opportunity, and bluntly asked him what the nature of the anxiety might be. Did it relate to money? No; it related to a Letter which had been waiting for him for many years. Had he received the letter? Not yet; it had been left under charge of one of the partners in the firm which had managed the business of his inheritance for him; the partner had been absent from England; and the letter, locked up among his own private papers, could not be got at till he returned. He was expected back toward the latter part of that present May, and, if Midwinter could be sure where the cruise would take them to at the close of the month, he thought he would write and have the letter forwarded. Had he any family reasons to be anxious about it? None that he knew of; he was curious to see what had been waiting for him for many years, and that was all. So he answered the rector's questions, with his tawny face turned away over the low bulwark of the yacht, and his fishing-line dragging in his supple brown hands.

Favored by wind and weather, the little vessel had done wonders on her trial trip. Before the period fixed for the duration of the cruise had half expired, the yacht was as high up on the Welsh coast as Holyhead; and Allan, eager for adventure in unknown regions, had declared boldly for an extension of the voyage northward to the Isle of Man. Having ascertained from reliable authority that the weather really promised well for a cruise in that quarter, and that, in the event of any unforeseen necessity for return, the railway was accessible by the steamer from Douglas to Liverpool, Mr. Brock agreed to his pupil's proposal. By that night's post he wrote to Allan's lawyers and to his own rectory, indicating Douglas in the Isle of Man as the next address to which letters might be forwarded. At the post-office he met Midwinter, who had just dropped a letter into the box. Remembering what he had said on board the yacht, Mr. Brock concluded that they had both taken the same precaution, and had ordered their correspondence to be forwarded to the same place.

Late the next day they set sail for the Isle of Man.

For a few hours all went well; but sunset brought with it the signs of a coming change. With the darkness the wind rose to a gale, and the question whether Allan and his journeymen had or had not built a stout sea-boat was seriously tested for the first time. All that night, after trying vainly to bear up for Holyhead, the little vessel kept the sea, and stood her trial bravely. The next morning the Isle of Man was in view, and the yacht was safe at Castletown. A survey by daylight of hull and rigging showed that all the damage done might be set right again in a week's time. The cruising party had accordingly remained at Castletown, Allan being occupied in superintending the repairs, Mr. Brock in exploring the neighborhood, and Midwinter in making daily pilgrimages on foot to Douglas and back to inquire for letters.

The first of the cruising party who received a letter was Allan. "More worries from those everlasting lawyers," was all he said, when he had read the letter, and had crumpled it up in his pocket. The rector's turn came next, before the week's sojourn at Castletown had expired. On the fifth day he found a letter from Somersetshire waiting for him at the hotel. It had been brought there by Midwinter, and it contained news which entirely overthrew all Mr. Brock's holiday plans. The clergyman who had undertaken to do duty for him in his absence had been unexpectedly summoned home again; and Mr. Brock had no choice (the day of the week being Friday) but to cross the next morning from Douglass to Liverpool, and get back by railway on Saturday night in time for Sunday's service.

Having read his letter, and resigned himself to his altered circumstances as patiently as he might, the rector passed next to a question that pressed for serious consideration in its turn. Burdened with his heavy responsibility toward Allan, and conscious of his own undiminished distrust of Allan's new friend, how was he to act, in the emergency that now beset him, toward the two young men who had been his companions on the cruise?

Mr. Brock had first asked himself that awkward question on the Friday afternoon, and he was still trying vainly to answer it, alone in his own room, at one o'clock on the Saturday morning. It was then only the end of May, and the residence of the ladies at Thorpe Ambrose (unless they chose to shorten it of their own accord) would not expire till the middle of June. Even if the repairs of the yacht had been completed (which was not the case), there was no possible pretense for hurrying Allan back to Somersetshire. But one other alternative remained—to leave him where he was. In other words, to leave him, at the turning-point of his life, under the sole influence of a man whom he had first met with as a castaway at a village inn, and who was still, to all practical purposes, a total stranger to him.

In despair of obtaining any better means of
enlightenment to guide his decision, Mr. Brock
reverted to the impression which Midwinter had
produced on his own mind in the familiarity of
the cruise.

Young as he was, the ex-usher had evidently
lived a varied life.   He could speak of books like
a man who had really enjoyed them; he could
take his turn at the helm like a sailor who knew
his duty; he could cook, and climb the rigging,
and lay the cloth for dinner, with an odd delight
in the exhibition of his own dexterity.   The dis-
play of these, and other qualities like them, as
his spirits rose with the cruise, had revealed the
secret of his attraction for Allan plainly enough.
But had all disclosures rested there?  Had the
man let no chance light in on his character in
the rector's presence?  Very little; and that little did not set him forth in a morally alluring
aspect.   His way in the world had lain evidently
in doubtful places; familiarity with the small
villainies of vagabonds peeped out of him now
and then; and, more significant still, he habitually slept the light, suspicious sleep of a man
who has been accustomed to close his eyes in
doubt of the company under the same roof with
him.   Down to the very latest moment of the
rector's experience of him—down to that present
Friday night—his conduct had been persistently
secret and unaccountable to the very last.   After
bringing Mr. Brock's letter to the hotel, he had
mysterious disappeared from the house without
leaving any message for his companions, and

without letting anybody see whether he had or had not received a letter himself. At nightfall he had come back stealthily in the darkness, had been caught on the stairs by Allan, eager to tell him of the change in the rector's plans, had listened to the news without a word of remark, and had ended by sulkily locking himself into his own room. What was there in his favor to set against such revelations of his character as these —against his wandering eyes, his obstinate reserve with the rector, his ominous silence on the subject of family and friends? Little or nothing: the sum of all his merits began and ended with his gratitude to Allan.

Mr. Brock left his seat on the side of the bed, trimmed his candle, and, still lost in his own thoughts, looked out absently at the night. The change of place brought no new ideas with it. His retrospect over his own past life had amply satisfied him that his present sense of responsibility rested on no merely fanciful grounds, and, having brought him to that point, had left him there, standing at the window, and seeing nothing but the total darkness in his own mind faithfully reflected by the total darkness of the night.

"If I only had a friend to apply to!" thought the rector. "If I could only find some one to help me in this miserable place!"

At the moment when the aspiration crossed his mind, it was suddenly answered by a low knock at the door, and a voice said softly in the passage outside, "Let me come in."

After an instant's pause to steady his nerves, Mr. Brock opened the door, and found himself, at one o'clock in the morning, standing face to face on the threshold of his own bedroom with Ozias Midwinter.

"Are you ill?" asked the rector, as soon as his astonishment would allow him to speak.

"I have come here to make a clean breast of it!" was the strange answer. "Will you let me in?"

With those words he walked into the room, his eyes on the ground, his lips ashy pale, and his hand holding something hidden behind him.

"I saw the light under your door," he went on, without looking up, and without moving his hand, "and I know the trouble on your mind which is keeping you from your rest. You are going away to-morrow morning, and you don't like leaving Mr. Armadale alone with a stranger like me."

Startled as he was, Mr. Brock saw the serious necessity of being plain with a man who had come at that time, and had said those words to him.

"You have guessed right," he answered. "I stand in the place of a father to Allan Armadale, and I am naturally unwilling to leave him, at his age, with a man whom I don't know."

Ozias Midwinter took a step forward to the table. His wandering eyes rested on the rector's New Testament, which was one of the objects lying on it.

"You have read that Book, in the years of

a long life, to many congregations," he said. "Has it taught you mercy to your miserable fellow-creatures?"

Without waiting to be answered, he looked Mr. Brock in the face for the first time, and brought his hidden hand slowly into view.

"Read that," he said; "and, for Christ's sake, pity me when you know who I am."

He laid a letter of many pages on the table. It was the letter that Mr. Neal had posted at Wildbad nineteen years since.

---

## CHAPTER II.

### THE MAN REVEALED.

THE first cool breathings of the coming dawn fluttered through the open window as Mr. Brock read the closing lines of the Confession. He put it from him in silence, without looking up. The first shock of discovery had struck his mind, and had passed away again. At his age, and with his habits of thought, his grasp was not strong enough to hold the whole revelation that had fallen on him. All his heart, when he closed the manuscript, was with the memory of the woman who had been the beloved friend of his later and happier life; all his thoughts were busy with the miserable secret of her treason to her own father which the letter had disclosed.

He was startled out of the narrow limits of his own little grief by the vibration of the table at which he sat, under a hand that was laid on it heavily. The instinct of reluctance was strong in him; but he conquered it, and looked up. There, silently confronting him in the mixed light of the yellow candle flame and the faint gray dawn, stood the castaway of the village inn—the inheritor of the fatal Armadale name·

Mr. Brock shuddered as the terror of the present time and the darker terror yet of the future that might be coming rushed back on him at the sight of the man's face. The man saw it, and spoke first.

"Is my father's crime looking at you out of *my* eyes?" he asked. "Has the ghost of the drowned man followed me into the room?"

The suffering and the passion that he was forcing back shook the hand that he still kept on the table, and stifled the voice in which he spoke until it sank to a whisper.

"I have no wish to treat you otherwise than justly and kindly," answered Mr. Brock. "Do me justice on my side, and believe that I am incapable of cruelly holding you responsible for your father's crime."

The reply seemed to compose him. He bowed his head in silence, and took up the confession from the table.

"Have you read this through?" he asked, quietly.

"Every word of it, from first to last."

"Have I dealt openly with you so far. Has Ozias Midwinter—"

"Do you still call yourself by that name," interrupted Mr. Brock, "now your true name is known to me?"

"Since I have read my father's confession," was the answer, "I like my ugly alias better than ever. Allow me to repeat the question which I was about to put to you a minute since: Has Ozias Midwinter done his best thus far to enlighten Mr. Brock?"

The rector evaded a direct reply. "Few men in your position," he said, "would have had the courage to show me that letter."

"Don't be too sure, sir, of the vagabond you picked up at the inn till you know a little more of him than you know now. You have got the secret of my birth, but you are not in possession yet of the story of my life. You ought to know it, and you shall know it, before you leave me alone with Mr. Armadale. Will you wait, and rest a little while, or shall I tell it you now?"

"Now," said Mr. Brock, still as far away as ever from knowing the real character of the man before him.

Everything Ozias Midwinter said, everything Ozias Midwinter did, was against him. He had spoken with a sardonic indifference, almost with an insolence of tone, which would have repelled the sympathies of any man who heard him. And now, instead of placing himself at the table, and addressing his story directly to the rector, he withdrew silently and ungraciously to the window-seat. There he sat, his face averted, his hands mechanically turning the leaves of his father's letter till he came to the last. With his eyes fixed on the closing lines of the manuscript, and with a strange mixture of recklessness and sadness in his voice, he began his promised narrative in these words:

"The first thing you know of me," he said, "is what my father's confession has told you already. He mentions here that I was a child, asleep on his breast, when he spoke his last words in this world, and when a stranger's hand wrote them down for him at his deathbed. That stranger's name, as you may have noticed, is signed on the cover—'Alexander Neal, Writer to the Signet, Edinburgh.' The first recollection I have is of Alexander Neal beating me with a horsewhip (I dare say I deserved it), in the character of my stepfather."

"Have you no recollection of your mother at the same time?" asked Mr. Brock.

"Yes; I remember her having shabby old clothes made up to fit me, and having fine new frocks bought for her two children by her second husband. I remember the servants laughing at me in my old things, and the horsewhip finding its way to my shoulders again for losing my temper and tearing my shabby clothes. My next recollection gets on to a year or two later. I remember myself locked up in a lumber-room, with a bit of bread and a mug of water, wondering what it was that made my mother and my stepfather seem to hate the very sight of me. I never settled that question till yesterday, and then I solved the mystery, when my father's letter was put into my hands. My mother knew what had really happened on board the French timber ship, and my stepfather knew what had really happened, and they were both well aware that the shameful secret which they would fain have kept from every living creature was a secret which would be one day revealed to *me*. There was no help for it—the confession was in the executor's hands, and there was I, an ill-conditioned brat, with my mother's negro blood in my face, and my murdering father's passions in my heart, inheritor of their secret in spite of them! I don't wonder at the horsewhip now, or the shabby old clothes, or the bread and water in the lumber-room. Natural penalties all of them, sir, which the child was beginning to pay already for the father's sin."

Mr. Brock looked at the swarthy, secret face, still obstinately turned away from him. "Is this the stark insensibility of a vagabond," he asked himself, "or the despair, in disguise, of a miserable man?"

"School is my next recollection," the other went on—"a cheap place in a lost corner of Scotland. I was left there, with a bad character to help me at starting. I spare you the story of the master's cane in the schoolroom, and the boys' kicks in the playground. I dare say there was ingrained ingratitude in my nature; at any rate, I ran away. The first person who met me asked my name. I was too young and too foolish to know the importance of concealing it, and, as a matter of course, I was taken back to school the same evening. The result taught me a lesson which I have not forgotten since. In a day or two more, like the vagabond I was, I ran away for the second time. The school watch-dog had had his instructions, I suppose: he stopped me before I got outside the gate. Here is his mark, among the rest, on the back of my hand. His master's marks I can't show you; they are all on my back. Can you believe in my perversity? There was a devil in me that no dog could worry out. I ran away again as soon as I left my bed, and this time I got off. At nightfall I found myself (with a pocketful of the school oatmeal) lost on a moor. I lay down on the fine soft heather, under the lee of a great gray rock. Do you think I felt lonely? Not I! I was away from the master's cane, away from my schoolfellows' kicks, away from my mother, away from my stepfather; and I lay down that night under my good friend the rock, the happiest boy in all Scotland!"

Through the wretched childhood which that one significant circumstance disclosed, Mr. Brock began to see dimly how little was really strange, how little really unaccountable, in the character of the man who was now speaking to him.

"I slept soundly," Midwinter continued, "under my friend the rock. When I woke in the morning, I found a sturdy old man with a fiddle sitting on one side of me, and two performing dogs on the other. Experience had made me too sharp to tell the truth when the man put his first

I SLEPT SOUNDLY UNDER MY FRIEND THE ROCK.

—Armadale, Vol. Eight, page 146.

questions. He didn't press them; he gave me a
good breakfast out of his knapsack, and he let
me romp with the dogs. 'I'll tell you what,'
he said, when he had got my confidence in this
manner, 'you want three things, my man: you
want a new father, a new family, and a new
name. I'll be your father; I'll let you have the
dogs for your brothers; and, if you'll promise
to be very careful of it, I'll give you my own
name into the bargain. Ozias Midwinter, Junior, you have had a good breakfast; if you want
a good dinner, come along with me!' He got
up, the dogs trotted after him, and I trotted after
the dogs. Who was my new father? you will
ask. A half-breed gypsy, sir; a drunkard, a
ruffian, and a thief—and the best friend I ever
had! Isn't a man your friend who gives you
your food, your shelter, and your education?
Ozias Midwinter taught me to dance the High-
land fling, to throw somersaults, to walk on
stilts, and to sing songs to his fiddle. Sometimes we roamed the country, and performed
at fairs. Sometimes we tried the large towns,
and enlivened bad company over its cups. I
was a nice, lively little boy of eleven years old,
and bad company, the women especially, took
a fancy to me and my nimble feet. I was vagabond enough to like the life. The dogs and
I lived together, ate, and drank, and slept together. I can't think of those poor little four-
footed brothers of mine, even now, without a
choking in the throat. Many is the beating we
three took together; many is the hard day's

dancing we did together; many is the night
we have slept together, and whimpered together,
on the cold hill-side. I'm not trying to distress
you, sir; I'm only telling you the truth. The
life with all its hardships was a life that fitted
me, and the half-breed gypsy who gave me his
name, ruffian as he was, was a ruffian I liked."

"A man who beat you!" exclaimed Mr. Brock,
in astonishment.

"Didn't I tell you just now, sir, that I lived
with the dogs? and did you ever hear of a dog
who liked his master the worse for beating him?
Hundreds of thousands of miserable men, women,
and children would have liked that man (as I
liked him) if he had always given them what he
always gave me—plenty to eat. It was stolen
food mostly, and my new gypsy father was generous with it. He seldom laid the stick on us
when he was sober; but it diverted him to hear
us yelp when he was drunk. He died drunk, and
enjoyed his favorite amusement with his last
breath. One day (when I had been two years in
his service), after giving us a good dinner out on
the moor, he sat down with his back against a
stone, and called us up to divert himself with his
stick. He made the dogs yelp first, and then he
called to me. I didn't go very willingly; he had
been drinking harder than usual, and the more he
drank the better he liked his after-dinner amusement. He was in high good-humor that day,
and he hit me so hard that he toppled over, in
his drunken state, with the force of his own
blow. He fell with his face in a puddle, and

lay there without moving. I and the dogs stood at a distance, and looked at him: we thought he was feigning, to get us near and have another stroke at us. He feigned so long that we ventured up to him at last. It took me some time to pull him over; he was a heavy man. When I did get him on his back, he was dead. We made all the outcry we could; but the dogs were little, and I was little, and the place was lonely; and no help came to us. I took his fiddle and his stick; I said to my two brothers, 'Come along, we must get our own living now;' and we went away heavy-hearted, and left him on the moor. Unnatural as it may seem to you, I was sorry for him. I kept his ugly name through all my after-wanderings, and I have enough of the old leaven left in me to like the sound of it still. Midwinter or Armadale, never mind my name now, we will talk of that afterward; you must know the worst of me first."

"Why not the best of you?" said Mr. Brock, gently.

"Thank you, sir; but I am here to tell the truth. We will get on, if you please, to the next chapter in my story. The dogs and I did badly, after our master's death; our luck was against us. I lost one of my little brothers—the best performer of the two; he was stolen, and I never recovered him. My fiddle and my stilts were taken from me next, by main force, by a tramp who was stronger than I. These misfortunes drew Tommy and me—I beg your pardon, sir, I mean the dog—closer together than ever.

I think we had some kind of dim foreboding on both sides that we had not done with our misfortunes yet; anyhow, it was not very long before we were parted forever. We were neither of us thieves (our master had been satisfied with teaching us to dance); but we both committed an invasion of the rights of property, for all that. Young creatures, even when they are half starved, cannot resist taking a run sometimes on a fine morning. Tommy and I could not resist taking a run into a gentleman's plantation; the gentleman preserved his game; and the gentleman's keeper knew his business. I heard a gun go off; you can guess the rest. God preserve me from ever feeling such misery again as I felt when I lay down by Tommy, and took him, dead and bloody, in my arms! The keeper attempted to part us; I bit him, like the wild animal I was. He tried the stick on me next; he might as well have tried it on one of the trees. The noise reached the ears of two young ladies riding near the place—daughters of the gentleman on whose property I was a trespasser. They were too well brought up to lift their voices against the sacred right of preserving game, but they were kind-hearted girls, and they pitied me, and took me home with them. I remember the gentlemen of the house (keen sportsmen all of them) roaring with laughter as I went by the windows, crying, with my little dead dog in my arms. Don't suppose I complain of their laughter; it did me good service; it roused the indignation of the two ladies. One of them took me into her own garden, and showed me a place where I might bury my dog under the flowers, and be sure that no other hands should ever disturb him again. The other went to her father, and persuaded him to give the forlorn little vagabond a chance in the house, under one of the upper servants. Yes! you have been cruising in company with a man who was once a footboy. I saw you look at me, when I amused Mr. Armadale by laying the cloth on board the yacht. Now you know why I laid it so neatly, and forgot nothing. It has been my good fortune to see something of society; I have helped to fill its stomach and black its boots. My experience of the servants' hall was not a long one. Before I had worn out my first suit of livery, there was a scandal in the house. It was the old story; there is no need to tell it over again for the thousandth time. Loose money left on a table, and not found there again; all the servants with characters to appeal to except the foot-boy, who had been rashly taken on trial. Well! well! I was lucky in that house to the last; I was not prosecuted for taking what I had not only never touched, but never even seen: I was only turned out. One morning I went in my old clothes to the grave where I had buried Tommy. I gave the place a kiss; I said good-by to my little dead dog; and there I was, out in the world again, at the ripe age of thirteen years!"

"In that friendless state, and at that tender age," said Mr. Brock, "did no thought cross your mind of going home again?"

"I went home again, sir, that very night—I slept on the hill-side. What other home had I? In a day or two's time I drifted back to the large towns and the bad company, the great open country was so lonely to me, now I had lost the dogs! Two sailors picked me up next. I was a handy lad, and I got a cabin-boy's berth on board a coasting-vessel. A cabin-boy's berth means dirt to live in, offal to eat, a man's work on a boy's shoulders, and the rope's-end at regular intervals. The vessel touched at a port in the Hebrides. I was as ungrateful as usual to my best benefactors; I ran away again. Some women found me, half dead of starvation, in the northern wilds of the Isle of Skye. It was near the coast, and I took a turn with the fishermen next. There was less of the rope's-end among my new masters; but plenty of exposure to wind and weather, and hard work enough to have killed a boy who was not a seasoned tramp like me. I fought through it till the winter came, and then the fishermen turned me adrift again. I don't blame them; food was scarce, and mouths were many. With famine staring the whole community in the face, why should they keep a boy who didn't belong to them? A great city was my only chance in the winter-time; so I went to Glasgow, and all but stepped into the lion's mouth as soon as I got there. I was minding an empty cart on the Broomielaw, when I heard my stepfather's voice on the pavement side of the horse by which I was standing. He had met some person whom he knew, and, to my terror and surprise, they were talking about me. Hidden behind the horse, I heard enough of their conversation to know that I had narrowly escaped discovery before I went on board the coasting-vessel. I had met at that time with another vagabond boy of my own age; we had quarreled and parted. The day after, my stepfather's inquiries were made in that very district, and it became a question with him (a good personal description being unattainable in either case) which of the two boys he should follow. One of them, he was informed, was known as "Brown," and the other as "Midwinter." Brown was just the common name which a cunning runaway boy would be most likely to assume; Midwinter, just the remarkable name which he would be most likely to avoid. The pursuit had accordingly followed Brown, and had allowed me to escape. I leave you to imagine whether I was not doubly and trebly determined to keep my gypsy master's name after that. But my resolution did not stop here. I made up my mind to leave the country altogether. After a day or two's lurking about the outward-bound vessels in port, I found out which sailed first, and hid myself on board. Hunger tried hard to force me out before the pilot had left; but hunger was not new to me, and I kept my place. The pilot was out of the vessel when I made my appearance on deck, and there was nothing for it but to keep me or throw me overboard. The captain said (I have no doubt quite truly) that he would have preferred throwing me overboard; but the

majesty of the law does sometimes stand the
friend even of a vagabond like me. In that
way I came back to a sea-life. In that way I
learned enough to make me handy and useful
(as I saw you noticed) on board Mr. Armadale's
yacht. I sailed more than one voyage, in more
than one vessel, to more than one part of the
world; and I might have followed the sea for
life, if I could only have kept my temper under
every provocation that could be laid on it. I had
learned a great deal; but, not having learned
that, I made the last part of my last voyage
home to the port of Bristol in irons; and I saw
the inside of a prison for the first time in my life,
on a charge of mutinous conduct to one of my
officers. You have heard me with extraordinary
patience, sir, and I am glad to tell you, in return,
that we are not far now from the end of my story.
You found some books, if I remember right, when
you searched my luggage at the Somersetshire
inn?"

Mr. Brock answered in the affirmative.

"Those books mark the next change in my life
—and the last, before I took the usher's place at
the school. My term of imprisonment was not a
long one. Perhaps my youth pleaded for me;
perhaps the Bristol magistrates took into consideration the time I had passed in irons on
board ship. Anyhow, I was just turned seventeen when I found myself out on the world again.
I had no friends to receive me; I had no place to
go to. A sailor's life, after what had happened,
was a life I recoiled from in disgust. I stood in

the crowd on the bridge at Bristol, wondering
what I should do with my freedom now I had
got it back. Whether I had altered in the prison,
or whether I was feeling the change in character
that comes with coming manhood, I don't know;
but the old reckless enjoyment of the old vagabond life seemed quite worn out of my nature.
An awful sense of loneliness kept me wandering
about Bristol, in horror of the quiet country, till
after nightfall. I looked at the lights kindling
in the parlor windows, with a miserable envy
of the happy people inside. A word of advice
would have been worth something to me at that
time. Well! I got it: a policeman advised me
to move on. He was quite right; what else could
I do? I looked up at the sky, and there was my
old friend of many a night's watch at sea, the
north star. 'All points of the compass are alike
to me,' I thought to myself; 'I'll go *your* way.'
Not even the star would keep me company that
night. It got behind a cloud, and left me alone
in the rain and darkness. I groped my way to a
cart-shed, fell asleep, and dreamed of old times,
when I served my gypsy master and lived with
the dogs. God! what I would have given when
I woke to have felt Tommy's little cold muzzle in
my hand! Why am I dwelling on these things?
Why don't I get on to the end? You shouldn't
encourage me, sir, by listening so patiently.
After a week more of wandering, without hope
to help me, or prospects to look to, I found myself in the streets of Shrewsbury, staring in at
the windows of a book-seller's shop. An old

man came to the shop door, looked about him, and saw me. 'Do you want a job?' he asked. 'And are you not above doing it cheap?' The prospect of having something to do, and some human creature to speak a word to, tempted me, and I did a day's dirty work in the book-seller's warehouse for a shilling. More work followed at the same rate. In a week I was promoted to sweep out the shop and put up the shutters. In no very long time after, I was trusted to carry the books out; and when quarter-day came, and the shop-man left, I took his place. Wonderful luck! you will say; here I had found my way to a friend at last. I had found my way to one of the most merciless misers in England; and I had risen in the little world of Shrewsbury by the purely commercial process of underselling all my competitors. The job in the warehouse had been declined at the price by every idle man in the town, and I did it. The regular porter received his weekly pittance under weekly protest. I took two shillings less, and made no complaint. The shop-man gave warning on the ground that he was underfed as well as underpaid. I received half his salary, and lived contentedly on his reversionary scraps. Never were two men so well suited to each other as that book-seller and I. *His* one object in life was to find somebody who would work for him at starvation wages. *My* one object in life was to find somebody who would give me an asylum over my head. Without a single sympathy in common—without a vestige of feeling of any sort, hostile or friendly, growing up between us on either side—without wishing each other good-night when we parted on the house stairs, or good-morning when we met at the shop counter, we lived alone in that house, strangers from first to last, for two whole years. A dismal existence for a lad of my age, was it not? You are a clergyman and a scholar —surely you can guess what made the life endurable to me?"

Mr. Brock remembered the well-worn volumes which had been found in the usher's bag. "The books made it endurable to you," he said.

The eyes of the castaway kindled with a new light.

"Yes!" he said, "the books—the generous friends who met me without suspicion — the merciful masters who never used me ill! The only years of my life that I can look back on with something like pride are the years I passed in the miser's house. The only unalloyed pleasure I have ever tasted is the pleasure that I found for myself on the miser's shelves. Early and late, through the long winter nights and the quiet summer days, I drank at the fountain of knowledge, and never wearied of the draught. There were few customers to serve, for the books were mostly of the solid and scholarly kind. No responsibilities rested on me, for the accounts were kept by my master, and only the small sums of money were suffered to pass through my hands. He soon found out enough of me to know that my honesty was to be trusted, and that my patience might be counted on, treat me

as he might.   The one insight into *his* character
which I obtained, on my side, widened the distance between us to its last limits.   He was a
confirmed opium-eater in secret—a prodigal in
laudanum, though a miser in all besides.   He
never confessed his frailty, and I never told him
I had found it out.   He had his pleasure apart
from *me*, and I had my pleasure apart from *him*.
Week after week, month after .month, there we
sat, without a friendly word ever passing between us—I, alone with my book at the counter;
he, alone with his ledger in the parlor, dimly
visible to me through the dirty window-pane of
the glass door, sometimes poring over his figures,
sometimes lost and motionless for hours in the
ecstasy of his opium trance.   Time passed, and
made no impression on us; the seasons of two
years came and went, and found us still unchanged.   One morning, at the opening of the
third year, my master did not appear, as usual,
to give me my allowance for breakfast.   I went
upstairs, and found him helpless in his bed.   He
refused to trust me with the keys of the cupboard,
or to let me send for a doctor.   I bought a morsel
of bread, and went back to my books, with no
more feeling for *him* (I honestly confess it) than
he would have had for *me* under the same circumstances.   An hour or two later I was roused
from my reading by an occasional customer of
ours, a retired medical man.   He went upstairs.
I was glad to get rid of him and return to my
books.   He came down again, and disturbed me
once more.   'I don't much like you, my lad,' he

said; 'but I think it my duty to say that you
will soon have to shift for yourself. You are no
great favorite in the town, and you may have
some difficulty in finding a new place. Provide
yourself with a written character from your master before it is too late.' He spoke to me coldly.
I thanked him coldly on my side, and got my
character the same day. Do you think my master let me have it for nothing? Not he! He
bargained with me on his deathbed. I was his
creditor for a month's salary, and he wouldn't
write a line of my testimonial until I had first
promised to forgive him the debt. Three days
afterward he died, enjoying to the last the happiness of having overreached his shop-man. 'Aha!'
he whispered, when the doctor formally summoned me to take leave of him, 'I got you
cheap!' Was Ozias Midwinter's stick as cruel
as that? I think not. Well! there I was, out
on the world again, but surely with better prospects this time. I had taught myself to read
Latin, Greek, and German; and I had got my
written character to speak for me. All useless!
The doctor was quite right; I was not liked in
the town. The lower order of the people despised
me for selling my services to the miser at the
miser's price. As for the better classes, I did
with them (God knows how!) what I have always done with everybody, except Mr. Armadale—I produced a disagreeable impression at
first sight; I couldn't mend it afterward; and
there was an end of me in respectable quarters.
It is quite likely I might have spent all my sav-

ings, my puny little golden offspring of two
years' miserable growth, but for a school advertisement which I saw in a local paper.   The
heartlessly mean terms that were offered encouraged me to apply; and I got the place.   How
I prospered in it, and what became of me next,
there is no need to tell you.   The thread of my
story is all wound off; my vagabond life stands
stripped of its mystery; and you know the worst
of me at last.''

A moment of silence followed those closing
words.   Midwinter rose from the window-seat,
and came back to the table with the letter from
Wildbad in his hand.

"My father's confession has told you who I
am; and my own confession has told you what
my life has been," he said, addressing Mr. Brock,
without taking the chair to which the rector
pointed.   "I promised to make a clean breast
of it when I first asked leave to enter this room.
Have I kept my word?"

"It is impossible to doubt it," replied Mr.
Brock.   "You have established your claim on
my confidence and my sympathy.   I should be
insensible, indeed, if I could know what I now
know of your childhood and your youth, and not
feel something of Allan's kindness for Allan's
friend."

"Thank you, sir," said Midwinter, simply
and gravely.

He sat down opposite Mr. Brock at the table
for the first time.

"In a few hours you will have left this place," he proceeded. "If I can help you to leave it with your mind at ease, I will. There is more to be said between us than we have said up to this time. My future relations with Mr. Armadale are still left undecided; and the serious question raised by my father's letter is a question which we have neither of us faced yet."

He paused, and looked with a momentary impatience at the candle still burning on the table, in the morning light. The struggle to speak with composure, and to keep his own feelings stoically out of view, was evidently growing harder and harder to him.

"It may possibly help your decision," he went on, "if I tell you how I determined to act toward Mr. Armadale—in the matter of the similarity of our names—when I first read this letter, and when I had composed myself sufficiently to be able to think at all." He stopped, and cast a second impatient look at the lighted candle. "Will you excuse the odd fancy of an odd man?" he asked, with a faint smile. "I want to put out the candle: I want to speak of the new subject, in the new light."

He extinguished the candle as he spoke, and let the first tenderness of the daylight flow uninterruptedly into the room.

"I must once more ask your patience," he resumed, "if I return for a moment to myself and my circumstances. I have already told you that my stepfather made an attempt to discover me some years after I had turned my back on the

Scotch school. He took that step out of no anxiety of his own, but simply as the agent of my
father's trustees. In the exercise of their discretion, they had sold the estates in Barbadoes (at
the time of the emancipation of the slaves, and
the ruin of West Indian property) for what the
estates would fetch. Having invested the proceeds, they were bound to set aside a sum for my
yearly education. This responsibility obliged
them to make the attempt to trace me—a fruitless attempt, as you already know. A little
later (as I have been since informed) I was
publicly addressed by an advertisement in the
newspapers, which I never saw. Later still,
when I was twenty-one, a second advertisement
appeared (which I did see) offering a reward for
evidence of my death. If I was alive, I had a
right to my half share of the proceeds of the
estates on coming of age; if dead, the money
reverted to my mother. I went to the lawyers,
and heard from them what I have just told you.
After some difficulty in proving my identity—
and after an interview with my stepfather, and
a message from my mother, which has hopelessly
widened the old breach between us—my claim
was allowed; and my money is now invested for
me in the funds, under the name that is really
my own."

Mr. Brock drew eagerly nearer to the table.
He saw the end now to which the speaker was
tending.

"Twice a year," Midwinter pursued, "I must
sign my own name to get my own income. At

all other times, and under all other circumstances, I may hide my identity under any name I please. As Ozias Midwinter, Mr. Armadale first knew me; as Ozias Midwinter he shall know me to the end of my days. Whatever may be the result of this interview—whether I win your confidence or whether I lose it—of one thing you may feel sure: your pupil shall never know the horrible secret which I have trusted to your keeping. This is no extraordinary resolution; for, as you know already, it costs me no sacrifice of feeling to keep my assumed name. There is nothing in my conduct to praise; it comes naturally out of the gratitude of a thankful man. Review the circumstances for yourself, sir, and set my own horror of revealing them to Mr. Armadale out of the question. If the story of the names is ever told, there can be no limiting it to the disclosure of my father's crime; it must go back to the story of Mrs. Armadale's marriage. I have heard her son talk of her; I know how he loves her memory. As God is my witness, he shall never love it less dearly through *me!*"

Simply as the words were spoken, they touched the deepest sympathies in the rector's nature: they took his thoughts back to Mrs. Armadale's death-bed. There sat the man against whom she had ignorantly warned him in her son's interests; and that man, of his own free-will, had laid on himself the obligation of respecting her secret for her son's sake! The memory of his own past efforts to destroy the very friendship out of which this resolution had sprung rose and reproached Mr. Brock. He held out his hand to Midwinter for the first time. "In her name, and in her son's name," he said, warmly, "I thank you."

Without replying, Midwinter spread the confession open before him on the table.

"I think I have said all that it was my duty to say," he began, "before we could approach the consideration of this letter. Whatever may have appeared strange in my conduct toward you and toward Mr. Armadale may be now trusted to explain itself. You can easily imagine the natural curiosity and surprise that I must have felt (ignorant as I then was of the truth) when the sound of Mr. Armadale's name first startled me as the echo of my own. You will readily understand that I only hesitated to tell him I was his namesake, because I hesitated to damage my position—in your estimation, if not in his— by confessing that I had come among you under an assumed name. And, after all that you have just heard of my vagabond life and my low associates, you will hardly wonder at the obstinate silence I maintained about myself, at a time when I did not feel the sense of responsibility which my father's confession has laid on me. We can return to these small personal explanations, if you wish it, at another time; they cannot be suffered to keep us from the greater interests which we must settle before you leave this place. We may come now—" His voice faltered, and he suddenly turned his face toward the window, so as to hide it from the rector's view. "We may come now," he repeated, his hand trembling visibly as it held the page, "to the murder on board the timber ship, and to the warning that has followed me from my father's grave."

Softly—as if he feared they might reach Allan, sleeping in the neighboring room—he read the last terrible words which the Scotchman's pen had written at Wildbad, as they fell from his father's lips:

"Avoid the widow of the man I killed—if the widow still lives. Avoid the maid whose wicked hand smoothed the way to the marriage—if the maid is still in her service. And, more than all, avoid the man who bears the same name as your own. Offend your best benefactor, if that benefactor's influence has connected you one with the other. Desert the woman who loves you, if that woman is a link between you and him. Hide yourself from him under an assumed name. Put the mountains and the seas between you; be ungrateful; be unforgiving; be all that is most repellent to your own gentler nature, rather than live under the same roof and breathe the same air with that man. Never let the two Allan Armadales meet in this world; never, never, never!"

After reading those sentences, he pushed the manuscript from him, without looking up. The fatal reserve which he had been in a fair way of conquering but a few minutes since, possessed itself of him once more. Again his eyes wandered; again his voice sank in tone. A stranger who had heard his story, and who saw him now, would have said, "His look is lurking, his manner is bad; he is, every inch of him, his father's son."

"I have a question to ask you," said Mr. Brock, breaking the silence between them, on his side. "Why have you just read that passage in your father's letter?"

"To force me into telling you the truth," was the answer. "You must know how much there is of my father in me before you trust me to be Mr. Armadale's friend. I got my letter yesterday, in the morning. Some inner warning troubled me, and I went down on the sea-shore by myself before I broke the seal. Do you believe the dead can come back to the world they once lived in? I believe my father came back in that bright morning light, through the glare of that broad sunshine and the roar of that joyful sea, and watched me while I read. When I got to the words that you have just heard, and when I knew that the very end which he had died dreading was the end that had really come, I felt the horror that had crept over him in his last moments creeping over me. I struggled against myself, as *he* would have had me struggle. I tried to be all that was most repellent to my own gentler nature; I tried to think pitilessly of putting the mountains and the seas between me and the man who bore my name. Hours passed before I could prevail on myself to go back and run the risk of meeting Allan Armadale in this house. When I did get back, and when he met me at night on the stairs, I thought

I was looking him in the face as *my* father looked *his* father in the face when the cabin door closed between them. Draw your own conclusions, sir. Say, if you like, that the inheritance of my father's heathen belief in fate is one of the inheritances he has left to me. I won't dispute it; I won't deny that all through yesterday *his* superstition was *my* superstition. The night came before I could find my way to calmer and brighter thoughts. But I did find my way. You may set it down in my favor that I lifted myself at last above the influence of this horrible letter. Do you know what helped me?"

"Did you reason with yourself?"

"I can't reason about what I feel."

"Did you quiet your mind by prayer?"

"I was not fit to pray."

"And yet something guided you to the better feeling and the truer view?"

"Something did."

"What was it?"

"My love for Allan Armadale."

He cast a doubting, almost a timid look at Mr. Brock as he gave that answer, and, suddenly leaving the table, went back to the window-seat.

"Have I no right to speak of him in that way?" he asked, keeping his face hidden from the rector. "Have I not known him long enough; have I not done enough for him yet? Remember what my experience of other men had been when I first saw his hand held out to me—when I first heard his voice speaking to me in my sick-room. What had I known of strangers' hands all through my childhood? I had only known them as hands raised to threaten and to strike me. *His* hand put my pillow straight, and patted me on the shoulder, and gave me my food and drink. What had I known of other men's voices, when I was growing up to be a man myself? I had only known them as voices that jeered, voices that cursed, voices that whispered in corners with a vile distrust. *His* voice said to me, 'Cheer up, Midwinter! we'll soon bring you round again. You'll be strong enough in a week to go out for a drive with me in our Somersetshire lanes.' Think of the gypsy's stick; think of the devils laughing at me when I went by their windows with my little dead dog in my arms; think of the master who cheated me of my month's salary on his deathbed—and ask your own heart if the miserable wretch whom Allan Armadale has treated as his equal and his friend has said too much in saying that he loves him? I do love him! It *will* come out of me; I can't keep it back. I love the very ground he treads on! I would give my life—yes, the life that is precious to me now, because his kindness has made it a happy one—I tell you I would give my life—"

The next words died away on his lips; the hysterical passion rose, and conquered him. He stretched out one of his hands with a wild gesture of entreaty to Mr. Brock; his head sank on the window-sill and he burst into tears.

Even then the hard discipline of the man's life asserted itself. He expected no sympathy, he counted on no merciful human respect for human weakness. The cruel necessity of self-suppression was present to his mind, while the tears were pouring over his cheeks. "Give me a minute," he said, faintly. "I'll fight it down in a minute; I won't distress you in this way again."

True to his resolution, in a minute he had fought it down. In a minute more he was able to speak calmly.

"We will get back, sir, to those better thoughts which have brought me from my room to yours," he resumed. "I can only repeat that I should never have torn myself from the hold which this letter fastened on me, if I had not loved Allan Armadale with all that I have in me of a brother's love. I said to myself, 'If the thought of leaving him breaks my heart, the thought of leaving him is wrong!' That was some hours since, and I am in the same mind still. I can't believe—I won't believe—that a friendship which has grown out of nothing but kindness on one side, and nothing but gratitude on the other, is destined to lead to an evil end. Judge, you who are a clergyman, between the dead father, whose word is in these pages, and the living son, whose word is now on his lips! What is it appointed me to do, now that I am breathing the same air, and living under the same roof with the son of the man whom my father killed—to perpetuate my father's crime by mortally injuring him, or to atone for my father's crime by giving him the devotion of my whole life? The last of those two faiths is my faith, and shall be my faith, happen what may. In the strength of that better conviction, I have come here to trust you with my father's secret, and to confess the wretched story of my own life. In the strength of that better conviction, I can face you resolutely with the one plain question, which marks the one plain end of all that I have come here to say. Your pupil stands at the starting-point of his new career, in a position singularly friendless; his one great need is a companion of his own age on whom he can rely. The time has come, sir, to decide whether I am to be that companion or not. After all you have heard of Ozias Midwinter, tell me plainly, will you trust him to be Allan Armadale's friend?''

Mr. Brock met that fearlessly frank question by a fearless frankness on his side.

''I believe you love Allan,'' he said, ''and I believe you have spoken the truth. A man who has produced that impression on me is a man whom I am bound to trust. I trust you.''

Midwinter started to his feet, his dark face flushing deep; his eyes fixed brightly and steadily, at last, on the rector's face. ''A light!'' he exclaimed, tearing the pages of his father's letter, one by one, from the fastening that held them. ''Let us destroy the last link that holds us to the horrible past! Let us see this confession a heap of ashes before we part!''

''Wait!'' said Mr. Brock. ''Before you burn it, there is a reason for looking at it once more.''

The parted leaves of the manuscript dropped from Midwinter's hands. Mr. Brock took them up, and sorted them carefully until he found the last page.

"I view your father's superstition as you view it," said the rector. "But there is a warning given you here, which you will do well (for Allan's sake and for your own sake) not to neglect. The last link with the past will not be destroyed when you have burned these pages. One of the actors in this story of treachery and murder is not dead yet. Read those words."

He pushed the page across the table, with his finger on one sentence. Midwinter's agitation misled him. He mistook the indication, and read, "Avoid the widow of the man I killed, if the widow still lives."

"Not that sentence," said the rector. "The next."

Midwinter read it: "Avoid the maid whose wicked hand smoothed the way to the marriage, if the maid is still in her service."

"The maid and the mistress parted," said Mr. Brock, "at the time of the mistress's marriage. The maid and the mistress met again at Mrs. Armadale's residence in Somersetshire last year. I myself met the woman in the village, and I myself know that her visit hastened Mrs. Armadale's death. Wait a little, and compose yourself; I see I have startled you."

He waited as he was bid, his color fading away to a gray paleness, and the light in his clear brown eyes dying out slowly. What the rector had said had produced no transient impression on him; there was more than doubt, there was

alarm in his face, as he sat lost in his own
thoughts. Was the struggle of the past night
renewing itself already? Did he feel the horror
of his hereditary superstition creeping over him
again?

"Can you put me on my guard against her?"
he asked, after a long interval of silence. "Can
you tell me her name?"

"I can only tell you what Mrs. Armadale told
me," answered Mr. Brock. "The woman acknowledged having been married in the long
interval since she and her mistress had last met.
But not a word more escaped her about her past
life. She came to Mrs. Armadale to ask for
money, under a plea of distress. She got the
money, and she left the house, positively refusing, when the question was put to her, to mention
her married name."

"You saw her yourself in the village. What
was she like?"

"She kept her veil down. I can't tell you."

"You can tell me what you *did* see?"

"Certainly. I saw, as she approached me,
that she moved very gracefully, that she had
a beautiful figure, and that she was a little over
the middle height. I noticed, when she asked
me the way to Mrs. Armadale's house, that her
manner was the manner of a lady, and that the
tone of her voice was remarkably soft and winning. Lastly, I remembered afterward that she
wore a thick black veil, a black bonnet, a black
silk dress, and a red Paisley shawl. I feel all
the importance of your possessing some better

means of identifying her than I can give you. But unhappily—"

He stopped. Midwinter was leaning eagerly across the table, and Midwinter's hand was laid suddenly on his arm.

"Is it possible that you know the woman?" asked Mr. Brock, surprised at the sudden change in his manner.

"No."

"What have I said, then, that has startled you so?"

"Do you remember the woman who threw herself from the river steamer?" asked the other —"the woman who caused that succession of deaths which opened Allan Armadale's way to the Thorpe Ambrose estate?"

"I remember the description of her in the police report," answered the rector.

"*That* woman," pursued Midwinter, "moved gracefully, and had a beautiful figure. *That* woman wore a black veil, a black bonnet, a black silk gown, and a red Paisley shawl—" He stopped, released his hold of Mr. Brock's arm, and abruptly resumed his chair. "Can it be the same?" he said to himself in a whisper. "*Is* there a fatality that follows men in the dark? And is it following *us* in that woman's footsteps?"

If the conjecture was right, the one event in the past which had appeared to be entirely disconnected with the events that had preceded it was, on the contrary, the one missing link which made the chain complete. Mr. Brock's comfort-

able common sense instinctively denied that
startling conclusion. He looked at Midwinter
with a compassionate smile.

"My young friend," he said, kindly, "have
you cleared your mind of all superstition as
completely as you think? Is what you have
just said worthy of the better resolution at which
you arrived last night?"

Midwinter's head drooped on his breast; the
color rushed back over his face; he sighed bitterly.

"You are beginning to doubt my sincerity,"
he said. "I can't blame you."

"I believe in your sincerity as firmly as ever,"
answered Mr. Brock. "I only doubt whether
you have fortified the weak places in your nature as strongly as you yourself suppose. Many
a man has lost the battle against himself far
oftener than you have lost it yet, and has nevertheless won his victory in the end. I don't
blame you, I don't distrust you. I only notice
what has happened, to put you on your guard
against yourself. Come! come! Let your own
better sense help you; and you will agree with
me that there is really no evidence to justify the
suspicion that the woman whom I met in Somersetshire, and the woman who attempted suicide
in London, are one and the same. Need an old
man like me remind a young man like you that
there are thousands of women in England with
beautiful figures—thousands of women who are
quietly dressed in black silk gowns and red
Paisley shawls?"

Midwinter caught eagerly at the suggestion; too eagerly, as it might have occurred to a harder critic on humanity than Mr. Brock.

"You are quite right, sir," he said, "and I am quite wrong. Tens of thousands of women answer the description, as you say. I have been wasting time on my own idle fancies, when I ought to have been carefully gathering up facts. If this woman ever attempts to find her way to Allan, I must be prepared to stop her." He began searching restlessly among the manuscript leaves scattered about the table, paused over one of the pages, and examined it attentively. "This helps me to something positive," he went on; "this helps me to a knowledge of her age. She was twelve at the time of Mrs. Armadale's marriage; add a year, and bring her to thirteen; add Allan's age (twenty-two), and we make her a woman of five-and-thirty at the present time. I know her age; and I know that she has her own reasons for being silent about her married life. This is something gained at the outset, and it may lead, in time, to something more." He looked up brightly again at Mr. Brock. "Am I in the right way now, sir? Am I doing my best to profit by the caution which you have kindly given me?"

"You are vindicating your own better sense," answered the rector, encouraging him to trample down his own imagination, with an Englishman's ready distrust of the noblest of the human faculties. "You are paving the way for your own happier life."

"Am I?" said the other, thoughtfully.

He searched among the papers once more, and stopped at another of the scattered pages.

"The ship!" he exclaimed, suddenly, his color changing again, and his manner altering on the instant.

"What ship?" asked the rector.

"The ship in which the deed was done," Midwinter answered, with the first signs of impatience that he had shown yet. "The ship in which my father's murderous hand turned the lock of the cabin door."

"What of it?" said Mr. Brock.

He appeared not to hear the question; his eyes remained fixed intently on the page that he was reading.

"A French vessel, employed in the timber trade," he said, still speaking to himself—"a French vessel, named *La Grâce de Dieu.* If my father's belief had been the right belief—if the fatality had been following me, step by step, from my father's grave, in one or other of my voyages, I should have fallen in with that ship." He looked up again at Mr. Brock. "I am quite sure about it now," he said. "Those women are two, and not one."

Mr. Brock shook his head.

"I am glad you have come to that conclusion," he said. "But I wish you had reached it in some other way."

Midwinter started passionately to his feet, and, seizing on the pages of the manuscript with both hands, flung them into the empty fire-place.

"For God's sake let me burn it!" he exclaimed. "As long as there is a page left, I shall read it. And, as long as I read it, my father gets the better of me, in spite of myself!"

Mr. Brock pointed to the match-box. In another moment the confession was in flames. When the fire had consumed the last morsel of paper, Midwinter drew a deep breath of relief.

"I may say, like Macbeth: 'Why, so, being gone, I am a man again!'" he broke out with a feverish gayety. "You look fatigued, sir; and no wonder," he added, in a lower tone. "I have kept you too long from your rest—I will keep you no longer. Depend on my remembering what you have told me; depend on my standing between Allan and any enemy, man or woman, who comes near him. Thank you, Mr. Brock; a thousand thousand times, thank you! I came into this room the most wretched of living men; I can leave it now as happy as the birds that are singing outside!"

As he turned to the door, the rays of the rising sun streamed through the window, and touched the heap of ashes lying black in the black fireplace. The sensitive imagination of Midwinter kindled instantly at the sight.

"Look!" he said, joyously. "The promise of the Future shining over the ashes of the Past!"

An inexplicable pity for the man, at the moment of his life when he needed pity least, stole over the rector's heart when the door had closed, and he was left by himself again.

"Poor fellow!" he said, with an uneasy surprise at his own compassionate impulse. "Poor
fellow!"

---

## CHAPTER III.

### DAY AND NIGHT.

THE morning hours had passed; the noon had
come and gone; and Mr. Brock had started
on the first stage of his journey home.

After parting from the rector in Douglas
Harbor, the two young men had returned to
Castletown, and had there separated at the
hotel door, Allan walking down to the water-
side to look after his yacht, and Midwinter
entering the house to get the rest that he
needed after a sleepless night.

He darkened his room; he closed his eyes,
but no sleep came to him. On this first day
of the rector's absence, his sensitive nature extravagantly exaggerated the responsibility which
he now held in trust for Mr. Brock. A nervous
dread of leaving Allan by himself, even for a
few hours only, kept him waking and doubting,
until it became a relief rather than a hardship
to rise from the bed again, and, following in
Allan's footsteps, to take the way to the water-
side which led to the yacht.

The repairs of the little vessel were nearly
completed. It was a breezy, cheerful day; the
land was bright, the water was blue, the quick
waves leaped crisply in the sunshine, the men

were singing at their work. Descending to the
cabin, Midwinter discovered his friend busily
occupied in attempting to set the place to rights.
Habitually the least systematic of mortals, Allan
now and then awoke to an overwhelming sense
of the advantages of order, and on such occasions a perfect frenzy of tidiness possessed him.
He was down on his knees, hotly and wildly at
work, when Midwinter looked in on him; and
was fast reducing the neat little world of the
cabin to its original elements of chaos, with a
misdirected energy wonderful to see.

"Here's a mess!" said Allan, rising composedly on the horizon of his own accumulated litter. "Do you know, my dear fellow,
I begin to wish I had let well alone!"

Midwinter smiled, and came to his friend's
assistance with the natural neat-handedness of
a sailor.

The first object that he encountered was Allan's
dressing-case, turned upside down, with half the
contents scattered on the floor, and with a duster
and a hearth-broom lying among them. Replac-
ing the various objects which formed the furniture of the dressing-case one by one, Midwinter
lighted unexpectedly on a miniature portrait, of
the old-fashioned oval form, primly framed in
a setting of small diamonds.

"You don't seem to set much value on this,"
he said. "What is it?"

Allan bent over him, and looked at the miniature.

"It belonged to my mother," he answered;

"and I set the greatest value on it. It is a portrait of my father."

Midwinter put the miniature abruptly into Allan's hands, and withdrew to the opposite side of the cabin.

"You know best where the things ought to be put in your own dressing-case," he said, keeping his back turned on Allan. "I'll make the place tidy on this side of the cabin, and you shall make the place tidy on the other."

He began setting in order the litter scattered about him on the cabin table and on the floor. But it seemed as if fate had decided that his friend's personal possessions should fall into his hands that morning, employ them where he might. One among the first objects which he took up was Allan's tobacco jar, with the stopper missing, and with a letter (which appeared by the bulk of it to contain inclosures) crumpled into the mouth of the jar in the stopper's place.

"Did you know that you had put this here?" he asked. "Is the letter of any importance?"

Allan recognized it instantly. It was the first of the little series of letters which had followed the cruising party to the Isle of Man—the letter which young Armadale had briefly referred to as bringing him "more worries from those everlasting lawyers," and had then dismissed from further notice as recklessly as usual.

"This is what comes of being particularly careful," said Allan; "here is an instance of my extreme thoughtfulness. You may not think it, but I put the letter there on purpose. Every time I went to the jar, you know, I was sure to see the letter; and every time I saw the letter, I was sure to say to myself, 'This must be answered.' There's nothing to laugh at; it was a perfectly sensible arrangement, if I could only have remembered where I put the jar. Suppose I tie a knot in my pocket-handkerchief this time? You have a wonderful memory, my dear fellow. Perhaps you'll remind me in the course of the day, in case I forget the knot next."

Midwinter saw his first chance, since Mr. Brock's departure, of usefully filling Mr. Brock's place.

"Here is your writing-case," he said; "why not answer the letter at once? If you put it away again, you may forget it again."

"Very true," returned Allan. "But the worst of it is, I can't quite make up my mind what answer to write. I want a word of advice. Come and sit down here, and I'll tell you all about it."

With his loud boyish laugh—echoed by Midwinter, who caught the infection of his gayety—he swept a heap of miscellaneous incumbrances off the cabin sofa, and made room for his friend and himself to take their places. In the high flow of youthful spirits, the two sat down to their trifling consultation over a letter lost in a tobacco jar. It was a memorable moment to both of them, lightly as they thought of it at the time. Before they had risen again from their places, they had taken the first irrevocable step together on the dark and tortuous road of their future lives.

Vol. 8

Reduced to plain facts, the question on which
Allan now required his friend's advice may be
stated as follows:

While the various arrangements connected
with the succession to Thorpe Ambrose were
in progress of settlement, and while the new
possessor of the estate was still in London, a
question had necessarily arisen relating to the
person who should be appointed to manage the
property. The steward employed by the Blanchard family had written, without loss of time, to
offer his services. Although a perfectly competent and trustworthy man, he failed to find
favor in the eyes of the new proprietor. Acting,
as usual, on his first impulses, and resolved, at
all hazards, to install Midwinter as a permanent
inmate at Thorpe Ambrose, Allan had determined
that the steward's place was the place exactly
fitted for his friend, for the simple reason that it
would necessarily oblige his friend to live with
him on the estate. He had accordingly written
to decline the proposal made to him without consulting Mr. Brock, whose disapproval he had
good reason to fear; and without telling Midwinter, who would probably (if a chance were
allowed him of choosing) have declined taking
a situation which his previous training had by
no means fitted him to fill.

Further correspondence had followed this decision, and had raised two new difficulties which
looked a little embarrassing on the face of them,
but which Allan, with the assistance of his lawyers, easily contrived to solve. The first diffi-

culty, of examining the outgoing steward's books, was settled by sending a professional accountant to Thorpe Ambrose; and the second difficulty, of putting the steward's empty cottage to some profitable use (Allan's plans for his friend comprehending Midwinter's residence under his own roof), was met by placing the cottage on the list of an active house agent in the neighboring county town. In this state the arrangements had been left when Allan quitted London. He had heard and thought nothing more of the matter, until a letter from his lawyers had followed him to the Isle of Man, inclosing two proposals to occupy the cottage, both received on the same day, and requesting to hear, at his earliest convenience, which of the two he was prepared to accept.

Finding himself, after having conveniently forgotten the subject for some days past, placed face to face once more with the necessity for decision, Allan now put the two proposals into his friend's hands, and, after a rambling explanation of the circumstances of the case, requested to be favored with a word of advice. Instead of examining the proposals, Midwinter unceremoniously put them aside, and asked the two very natural and very awkward questions of who the new steward was to be, and why he was to live in Allan's house?

"I'll tell you who, and I'll tell you why, when we get to Thorpe Ambrose," said Allan. "In the meantime we'll call the steward X. Y. Z., and we'll say he lives with me, because I'm devilish sharp, and I mean to keep him under

my own eye. You needn't look surprised. I
know the man thoroughly well; he requires a
good deal of management. If I offered him the
steward's place beforehand, his modesty would
get in his way, and he would say 'No.' If I
pitch him into it neck and crop, without a word
of warning and with nobody at hand to relieve
him of the situation, he'll have nothing for it
but to consult my interests, and say 'Yes.' X.
Y. Z. is not at all a bad fellow, I can tell you.
You'll see him when we go to Thorpe Ambrose;
and I rather think you and he will get on uncommonly well together."

The humorous twinkle in Allan's eye, the sly
significance in Allan's voice, would have betrayed
his secret to a prosperous man. Midwinter was
as far from suspecting it as the carpenters who
were at work above them on the deck of the
yacht.

"Is there no steward now on the estate?" he
asked, his face showing plainly that he was far
from feeling satisfied with Allan's answer. "Is
the business neglected all this time?"

"Nothing of the sort!" returned Allan. "The
business is going with 'a wet sheet and a flowing
sea, and a wind that follows free.' I'm not joking;
I'm only metaphorical. A regular accountant
has poked his nose into the books, and a steady-
going lawyer's clerk attends at the office once a
week. That doesn't look like neglect, does it?
Leave the new steward alone for the present,
and just tell me which of those two tenants you
would take, if you were in my place.'

Midwinter opened the proposals, and read them attentively.

The first proposal was from no less a person than the solicitor at Thorpe Ambrose, who had first informed Allan at Paris of the large fortune that had fallen into his hands. This gentleman wrote personally to say that he had long admired the cottage, which was charmingly situated within the limits of the Thorpe Ambrose grounds. He was a bachelor, of studious habits, desirous of retiring to a country seclusion after the wear and tear of his business hours; and he ventured to say that Mr. Armadale, in accepting him as a tenant, might count on securing an unobtrusive neighbor, and on putting the cottage into responsible and careful hands.

The second proposal came through the house agent, and proceeded from a total stranger. The tenant who offered for the cottage, in this case, was a retired officer in the army—one Major Milroy. His family merely consisted of an invalid wife and an only child — a young lady. His references were unexceptionable; and he, too, was especially anxious to secure the cottage, as the perfect quiet of the situation was exactly what was required by Mrs. Milroy in her feeble state of health.

"Well, which profession shall I favor?" asked Allan. "The army or the law?"

"There seems to me to be no doubt about it," said Midwinter. "The lawyer has been already in correspondence with you; and the lawyer's claim is, therefore, the claim to be preferred."

"I knew you would say that. In all the thousands of times I have asked other people for advice, I never yet got the advice I wanted. Here's this business of letting the cottage as an instance. I'm all on the other side myself. I want to have the major."

"Why?"

Young Armadale laid his forefinger on that part of the agent's letter which enumerated Major Milroy's family, and which contained the three words—"a young lady."

"A bachelor of studious habits walking about my grounds," said Allan, "is not an interesting object; a young lady is. I have not the least doubt Miss Milroy is a charming girl. Ozias Midwinter of the serious countenance! think of her pretty muslin dress flitting about among your trees and committing trespasses on your property; think of her adorable feet trotting into your fruit-garden, and her delicious fresh lips kissing your ripe peaches; think of her dimpled hands among your early violets, and her little cream-colored nose buried in your blush-roses. What does the studious bachelor offer me in exchange for the loss of all this? He offers me a rheumatic brown object in gaiters and a wig. No! no! Justice is good, my dear friend; but, believe me, Miss Milroy is better."

"Can you be serious about any mortal thing, Allan?"

"I'll try to be, if you like. I know I ought to take the lawyer; but what can I do if the major's daughter keeps running in my head?"

Midwinter returned resolutely to the just and sensible view of the matter, and pressed it on his friend's attention with all the persuasion of which he was master. After listening with exemplary patience until he had done, Allan swept a supplementary accumulation of litter off the cabin table, and produced from his waistcoat pocket a half-crown coin.

"I've got an entirely new idea," he said. "Let's leave it to chance."

The absurdity of the proposal—as coming from a landlord—was irresistible. Midwinter's gravity deserted him.

"I'll spin," continued Allan, "and you shall call. We must give precedence to the army, of course; so we'll say Heads, the major; Tails, the lawyer. One spin to decide. Now, then, look out!"

He spun the half-crown on the cabin table.

"Tails!" cried Midwinter, humoring what he believed to be one of Allan's boyish jokes.

The coin fell on the table with the Head uppermost.

"You don't mean to say you are really in earnest!" said Midwinter, as the other opened his writing-case and dipped his pen in the ink.

"Oh, but I am, though!" replied Allan. "Chance is on my side, and Miss Milroy's; and you're outvoted, two to one. It's no use arguing. The major has fallen uppermost, and the major shall have the cottage. I won't leave it to the lawyers; they'll only be worrying me with more letters. I'll write myself."

He wrote his answers to the two proposals, literally in two minutes. One to the house agent: "Dear sir, I accept Major Milroy's offer; let him come in when he pleases. Yours truly, Allan Armadale." And one to the lawyer: "Dear sir, I regret that circumstances prevent me from accepting your proposal. Yours truly," etc. "People make a fuss about letter-writing," Allan remarked, when he had done. "*I* find it easy enough."

He wrote the addresses on his two notes, and stamped them for the post, whistling gayly. While he had been writing, he had not noticed how his friend was occupied. When he had done, it struck him that a sudden silence had fallen on the cabin; and, looking up, he observed that Midwinter's whole attention was strangely concentrated on the half-crown as it lay head uppermost on the table. Allan suspended his whistling in astonishment.

"What on earth are you doing?" he asked.

"I was only wondering," replied Midwinter.

"What about?" persisted Allan.

"I was wondering," said the other, handing him back the half-crown, "whether there is such a thing as chance."

Half an hour later the two notes were posted; and Allan, whose close superintendence of the repairs of the yacht had hitherto allowed him but little leisure time on shore, had proposed to while away the idle hours by taking a walk in Castletown. Even Midwinter's nervous anxiety to deserve Mr. Brock's confidence in him could

detect nothing objectionable in this harmless
proposal, and the young men set forth together
to see what they could make of the metropolis
of the Isle of Man.

It is doubtful if there is a place on the habitable
globe which, regarded as a sight-seeing invest-
ment offering itself to the spare attention of strangers, yields so small a percentage of interest in
return as Castletown. Beginning with the water-
side, there was an inner harbor to see, with a
drawbridge to let vessels through; an outer
harbor, ending in a dwarf lighthouse; a view
of a flat coast to the right, and a view of a flat
coast to the left. In the central solitudes of the
city, there was a squat gray building called "the
castle"; also a memorial pillar dedicated to one
Governor Smelt, with a flat top for a statue, and
no statue standing on it; also a barrack, holding
the half-company of soldiers allotted to the isl-
and, and exhibiting one spirit-broken sentry at
its lonely door. The prevalent color of the town
was faint gray. The few shops open were parted
at frequent intervals by other shops closed and
deserted in despair. The weary lounging of boatmen on shore was trebly weary here; the youth
of the district smoked together in speechless de-
pression under the lee of a dead wall; the ragged
children said mechanically: "Give us a penny,"
and before the charitable hand could search the
merciful pocket, lapsed away again in misan-
thropic doubt of the human nature they addressed.
The silence of the grave overflowed the church-
yard, and filled this miserable town. But one edi-

fice, prosperous to look at, rose consolatory in the
desolation of these dreadful streets. Frequented
by the students of the neighboring "College of
King William," this building was naturally
dedicated to the uses of a pastry-cook's shop.
Here, at least (viewed through the friendly
medium of the window), there was something
going on for a stranger to see; for here, on high
stools, the pupils of the college sat, with swinging legs and slowly moving jaws, and, hushed
in the horrid stillness of Castletown, gorged their
pastry gravely, in an atmosphere of awful silence.

"Hang me if I can look any longer at the
boys and the tarts!" said Allan, dragging his
friend away from the pastry-cook's shop. "Let's
try if we can't find something else to amuse us
in the next street."

The first amusing object which the next street
presented was a carver-and-gilder's shop, expiring feebly in the last stage of commercial decay.
The counter inside displayed nothing to view
but the recumbent head of a boy, peacefully
asleep in the unbroken solitude of the place.
In the window were exhibited to the passing
stranger three forlorn little fly-spotted frames;
a small posting-bill, dusty with long-continued
neglect, announcing that the premises were to
let; and one colored print, the last of a series
illustrating the horrors of drunkenness, on the
fiercest temperance principles. The composition
—representing an empty bottle of gin, an im-
mensely spacious garret, a perpendicular Script-

ure reader, and a horizontal expiring family—
appealed to public favor, under the entirely un-
objectionable title of "The Hand of Death."
Allan's resolution to extract amusement from
Castletown by main force had resisted a great
deal, but it failed him at this stage of the in-
vestigations. He suggested trying an excursion to some other place. Midwinter, readily
agreeing, they went back to the hotel to make
inquiries.

Thanks to the mixed influence of Allan's ready
gift of familiarity, and total want of method in
putting his questions, a perfect deluge of information flowed in on the two strangers, relating
to every subject but the subject which had actually brought them to the hotel. They made
various interesting discoveries in connection with
the laws and constitution of the Isle of Man, and
the manners and customs of the natives. To
Allan's delight, the Manxmen spoke of England
as of a well-known adjacent island, situated at
a certain distance from the central empire of
the Isle of Man. It was further revealed to the
two Englishmen that this happy little nation
rejoiced in laws of its own, publicly proclaimed
once a year by the governor and the two head
judges, grouped together on the top of an ancient
mound, in fancy costumes appropriate to the occasion. Possessing this enviable institution, the
island added to it the inestimable blessing of a
local parliament, called the House of Keys, an
assembly far in advance of the other parliament
belonging to the neighboring island, in this re-

spect—that the members dispensed with the people, and solemnly elected each other. With these and many more local particulars, extracted from all sorts and conditions of men in and about the hotel, Allan whiled away the weary time in his own essentially desultory manner, until the gossip died out of itself, and Midwinter (who had been speaking apart with the landlord) quietly recalled him to the matter in hand. The finest coast scenery in the island was said to be to the westward and the southward, and there was a fishing town in those regions called Port St. Mary, with a hotel at which travelers could sleep. If Allan's impressions of Castletown still inclined him to try an excursion to some other place, he had only to say so, and a carriage would be produced immediately. Allan jumped at the proposal, and in ten minutes more he and Midwinter were on their way to the western wilds of the island.

With trifling incidents, the day of Mr. Brock's departure had worn on thus far. With trifling incidents, in which not even Midwinter's nervous watchfulness could see anything to distrust, it was still to proceed, until the night came—a night which one at least of the two companions was destined to remember to the end of his life.

Before the travelers had advanced two miles on their road, an accident happened. The horse fell, and the driver reported that the animal had seriously injured himself. There was no alternative but to send for another carriage to Castletown, or to get on to Port St. Mary on foot.

Deciding to walk, Midwinter and Allan had not gone far before they were overtaken by a gentleman driving alone in an open chaise. He civilly introduced himself as a medical man, living close to Port St. Mary, and offered seats in his carriage. Always ready to make new acquaintances, Allan at once accepted the proposal. He and the doctor (whose name was ascertained to be Hawbury) became friendly and familiar before they had been five minutes in the chaise together; Midwinter, sitting behind them, reserved and silent, on the back seat. They separated just outside Port St. Mary, before Mr. Hawbury's house, Allan boisterously admiring the doctor's neat French windows and pretty flower-garden and lawn, and wringing his hand at parting as if they had known each other from boyhood upward. Arrived in Port St. Mary, the two friends found themselves in a second Castletown on a smaller scale. But the country round, wild, open, and hilly, deserved its reputation. A walk brought them well enough on with the day—still the harmless, idle day that it had been from the first—to see the evening near at hand. After waiting a little to admire the sun, setting grandly over hill, and heath, and crag, and talking, while they waited, of Mr. Brock and his long journey home, they returned to the hotel to order their early supper. Nearer and nearer the night, and the adventure which the night was to bring with it, came to the two friends; and still the only incidents that happened were incidents to be laughed at, if they were noticed at all. The supper was badly cooked; the waiting-maid was impenetrably stupid; the old-fashioned bell-rope in the coffee-room had come down in Allan's hands, and, striking in its descent a painted china shep-herdess on the chimney-piece, had laid the figure in fragments on the floor. Events as trifling as these were still the only events that had hap-pened, when the twilight faded, and the lighted candles were brought into the room.

Finding Midwinter, after the double fatigue of a sleepless night and a restless day, but little inclined for conversation, Allan left him rest-ing on the sofa, and lounged into the passage of the hotel, on the chance of discovering some-body to talk to. Here another of the trivial incidents of the day brought Allan and Mr. Hawbury together again, and helped—whether happily or not, yet remained to be seen—to strengthen. the acquaintance between them on either side.

The "bar" of the hotel was situated at one end of the passage, and the landlady was in attend-ance there, mixing a glass of liquor for the doc-tor, who had just looked in for a little gossip. On Allan's asking permission to make a third in the drinking and the gossiping, Mr. Hawbury civilly handed him the glass which the landlady had just filled. It contained cold brandy-and-water. A marked change in Allan's face, as he suddenly drew back and asked for whisky instead, caught the doctor's medical eye. "A case of nervous antipathy," said Mr. Hawbury,

quietly taking the glass away again. The remark obliged Allan to acknowledge that he had
an insurmountable loathing (which he was foolish enough to be a little ashamed of mentioning)
to the smell and taste of brandy. No matter
with what diluting liquid the spirit was mixed,
the presence of it, instantly detected by his
organs of taste and smell, turned him sick and
faint if the drink touched his lips. Starting
from this personal confession, the talk turned
on antipathies in general; and the doctor acknowledged, on his side, that he took a professional interest in the subject, and that he possessed a collection of curious cases at home, which
his new acquaintance was welcome to look at,
if Allan had nothing else to do that evening, and
if he would call, when the medical work of the
day was over, in an hour's time.

Cordially accepting the invitation (which was
extended to Midwinter also, if he cared to profit
by it), Allan returned to the coffee-room to look
after his friend. Half asleep and half awake,
Midwinter was still stretched on the sofa, with
the local newspaper just dropping out of his
languid hand.

"I heard your voice in the passage," he said,
drowsily. "Whom were you talking to?"

"The doctor," replied Allan. "I am going to
smoke a cigar with him, in an hour's time. Will
you come too?"

Midwinter assented with a weary sigh. Always shyly unwilling to make new acquaintances, fatigue increased the reluctance he now

felt to become Mr. Hawbury's guest. As matters stood, however, there was no alternative but to go; for, with Allan's constitutional imprudence, there was no safely trusting him alone anywhere, and more especially in a stranger's house. Mr. Brock would certainly not have left his pupil to visit the doctor alone; and Midwinter was still nervously conscious that he occupied Mr. Brock's place.

"What shall we do till it's time to go?" asked Allan, looking about him. "Anything in this?" he added, observing the fallen newspaper, and picking it up from the floor.

"I'm too tired to look. If you find anything interesting, read it out," said Midwinter, thinking that the reading might help to keep him awake.

Part of the newspaper, and no small part of it, was devoted to extracts from books recently published in London. One of the works most largely laid under contribution in this manner was of the sort to interest Allan: it was a highly spiced narrative of Traveling Adventures in the wilds of Australia. Pouncing on an extract which described the sufferings of the traveling-party, lost in a trackless wilderness, and in danger of dying by thirst, Allan announced that he had found something to make his friend's flesh creep, and began eagerly to read the passage aloud.

Resolute not to sleep, Midwinter followed the progress of the adventure, sentence by sentence, without missing a word. The consultation of the lost travelers, with death by thirst staring them in the face; the resolution to press on while their strength lasted; the fall of a heavy shower, the vain efforts made to catch the rain-water, the transient relief experienced by sucking their wet clothes; the sufferings renewed a few hours after; the night advance of the strongest of the party, leaving the weakest behind; the following a flight of birds when morning dawned; the discovery by the lost men of the broad pool of water that saved their lives—all this Midwinter's fast-failing attention mastered painfully, Allan's voice growing fainter and fainter on his ear with every sentence that was read. Soon the next words seemed to drop away gently, and nothing but the slowly sinking sound of the voice was left. Then the light in the room darkened gradually, the sound dwindled into delicious silence, and the last waking impressions of the weary Midwinter came peacefully to an end.

The next event of which he was conscious was a sharp ringing at the closed door of the hotel. He started to his feet, with the ready alacrity of a man whose life has accustomed him to wake at the shortest notice. An instant's look round showed him that the room was empty, and a glance at his watch told him that it was close on midnight. The noise made by the sleepy servant in opening the door, and the tread the next moment of quick footsteps in the passage, filled him with a sudden foreboding of something wrong. As he hurriedly stepped forward to go out and make inquiry, the door of the coffee-room opened, and the doctor stood before him.

"I am sorry to disturb you," said Mr. Hawbury. "Don't be alarmed; there's nothing wrong."

"Where is my friend?" asked Midwinter.

"At the pier head," answered the doctor. "I am, to a certain extent, responsible for what he is doing now; and I think some careful person, like yourself, ought to be with him."

The hint was enough for Midwinter. He and the doctor set out for the pier immediately, Mr. Hawbury mentioning, on the way, the circumstances under which he had come to the hotel.

Punctual to the appointed hour Allan had made his appearance at the doctor's house, explaining that he had left his weary friend so fast asleep on the sofa that he had not had the heart to wake him. The evening had passed pleasantly, and the conversation had turned on many subjects, until, in an evil hour, Mr. Hawbury had dropped a hint which showed that he was fond of sailing, and that he possessed a pleasure-boat of his own in the harbor. Excited on the instant by his favorite topic, Allan had left his host no hospitable alternative but to take him to the pier head and show him the boat. The beauty of the night and the softness of the breeze had done the rest of the mischief; they had filled Allan with irresistible longings for a sail by moonlight. Prevented from accompanying his guest by professional hindrances which obliged him to remain on shore, the doctor, not knowing what else to do, had ventured on disturbing Midwinter, rather than take the responsibility of allowing Mr. Armadale (no matter how well he might be accustomed to the sea) to set off on a sailing trip at midnight entirely by himself.

The time taken to make this explanation brought Midwinter and the doctor to the pier head. There, sure enough, was young Armadale in the boat, hoisting the sail, and singing the sailor's "Yo-heave-ho!" at the top of his voice.

"Come along, old boy!" cried Allan. "You're just in time for a frolic by moonlight!"

Midwinter suggested a frolic by daylight, and an adjournment to bed in the meantime.

"Bed!" cried Allan, on whose harum-scarum high spirits Mr. Hawbury's hospitality had certainly not produced a sedative effect. "Hear him, doctor! one would think he was ninety! Bed, you drowsy old dormouse! Look at that, and think of bed if you can!"

He pointed to the sea. The moon was shining in the cloudless heaven; the night-breeze blew soft and steady from the land; the peaceful waters rippled joyfully in the silence and the glory of the night. Midwinter turned to the doctor with a wise resignation to circumstances: he had seen enough to satisfy him that all words of remonstrance would be words simply thrown away.

"How is the tide?" he asked.

Mr. Hawbury told him.

"Are there oars in the boat?"

"Yes."

"I am well used to the sea," said Midwinter, descending the pier steps. "You may trust me to take care of my friend, and to take care of the boat."

"Good-night, doctor!" shouted Allan. "Your whisky-and-water is delicious — your boat's a little beauty—and you're the best fellow I ever met in my life!"

The doctor laughed and waved his hand, and the boat glided out from the harbor, with Midwinter at the helm.

As the breeze then blew, they were soon abreast of the westward headland, bounding the Bay of Poolvash, and the question was started whether they should run out to sea or keep along the shore. The wisest proceeding, in the event of the wind failing them, was to keep by the land. Midwinter altered the course of the boat, and they sailed on smoothly in a south - westerly direction, abreast of the coast.

Little by little the cliffs rose in height, and the rocks, massed wild and jagged, showed rifted black chasms yawning deep in their sea-ward sides. Off the bold promontory called Spanish Head, Midwinter looked ominously at his watch. But Allan pleaded hard for half an hour more, and for a glance at the famous channel of the Sound, which they were now fast nearing, and of which he had heard some startling stories from the workmen employed on his yacht. The new change which Midwinter's compliance with this request rendered it necessary to make in the course of the boat brought her close to the wind; and revealed, on one side, the grand view of the southernmost shores of the Isle of Man, and, on the other, the black precipices of the islet called the Calf, separated from the mainland by the dark and dangerous channel of the Sound.

Once more Midwinter looked at his watch. "We have gone far enough," he said. "Stand by the sheet!"

"Stop!" cried Allan, from the bows of the boat. "Good God! here's a wrecked ship right ahead of us!"

Midwinter let the boat fall off a little, and looked where the other pointed.

There, stranded midway between the rocky boundaries on either side of the Sound—there, never again to rise on the living waters from her grave on the sunken rock; lost and lonely in the quiet night; high, and dark, and ghostly in the yellow moonshine, lay the Wrecked Ship.

"I know the vessel," said Allan, in great excitement. "I heard my workmen talking of her yesterday. She drifted in here, on a pitch-dark night, when they couldn't see the lights; a poor old worn-out merchantman, Midwinter, that the ship-brokers have bought to break up. Let's run in and have a look at her."

Midwinter hesitated. All the old sympathies of his sea-life strongly inclined him to follow Allan's suggestion; but the wind was falling light, and he distrusted the broken water and the swirling currents of the channel ahead.

"This is an ugly place to take a boat into when you know nothing about it," he said.

"Nonsense!" returned Allan. "It's as light as day, and we float in two feet of water."

Before Midwinter could answer, the current caught the boat, and swept them onward through the channel straight toward the wreck.

"Lower the sail," said Midwinter, quietly, "and ship the oars. We are running down on her fast enough now, whether we like it or not."

Both well accustomed to the use of the oar, they brought the course of the boat under sufficient control to keep her on the smoothest side of the channel—the side which was nearest to the Islet of the Calf. As they came swiftly up with the wreck, Midwinter resigned his oar to Allan; and, watching his opportunity, caught a hold with the boat-hook on the fore-chains of the vessel. The next moment they had the boat safely in hand, under the lee of the wreck.

The ship's ladder used by the workmen hung over the fore-chains. Mounting it, with the boat's rope in his teeth, Midwinter secured one end, and lowered the other to Allan in the boat. "Make that fast," he said, "and wait till I see if it's all safe on board." With those words, he disappeared behind the bulwark.

"Wait?" repeated Allan, in the blankest astonishment at his friend's excessive caution. "What on earth does he mean? I'll be hanged if I wait. Where one of us goes, the other goes too!"

He hitched the loose end of the rope round the forward thwart of the boat, and, swinging himself up the ladder, stood the next moment on the deck. "Anything very dreadful on board?" he inquired sarcastically, as he and his friend met.

Midwinter smiled. "Nothing whatever," he replied. "But I couldn't be sure that we were to have the whole ship to ourselves till I got over the bulwark and looked about me."

Allan took a turn on the deck, and surveyed the wreck critically from stem to stern.

"Not much of a vessel," he said; "the Frenchmen generally build better ships than this."

Midwinter crossed the deck, and eyed Allan in a momentary silence.

"Frenchmen?" he repeated, after an interval. "Is this vessel French?"

"Yes."

"How do you know?"

"The men I have got at work on the yacht told me. They know all about her."

Midwinter came a little nearer. His swarthy face began to look, to Allan's eyes, unaccountably pale in the moonlight.

"Did they mention what trade she was engaged in?"

"Yes; the timber trade."

As Allan gave that answer, Midwinter's lean brown hand clutched him fast by the shoulder, and Midwinter's teeth chattered in his head like the teeth of a man struck by a sudden chill.

"Did they tell you her name?" he asked, in a voice that dropped suddenly to a whisper.

"They did, I think. But it has slipped my

memory.—Gently, old fellow; these long claws of yours are rather tight on my shoulder."

"Was the name—? ' He stopped, removed his hand, and dashed away the great drops that were gathering on his forehead. "Was the name *La Grâce de Dieu?*"

"How the deuce did you come to know it? That's the name, sure enough. *La Grâce de Dieu.*"

At one bound, Midwinter leaped on the bulwark of the wreck.

"The boat!" he cried, with a scream of horror that rang far and wide through the stillness of the night, and brought Allan instantly to his side.

The lower end of the carelessly hitched rope was loose on the water, and ahead, in the track of the moonlight, a small black object was floating out of view. The boat was adrift.

## CHAPTER IV.

### THE SHADOW OF THE PAST.

ONE stepping back under the dark shelter of the bulwark, and one standing out boldly in the yellow light of the moon, the two friends turned face to face on the deck of the timber ship, and looked at each other in silence. The next moment Allan's inveterate recklessness seized on the grotesque side of the situation by main force. He seated himself astride on the bulwark, and burst out boisterously into his loudest and heartiest laugh.

"All my fault," he said; "but there's no help for it now. Here we are, hard and fast in a trap of our own setting; and there goes the last of the doctor's boat! Come out of the dark, Midwinter; I can't half see you there, and I want to know what's to be done next."

Midwinter neither answered nor moved. Allan left the bulwark, and, mounting the forecastle, looked down attentively at the waters of the Sound.

"One thing is pretty certain," he said. "With the current on that side, and the sunken rocks on this, we can't find our way out of the scrape by swimming, at any rate. So much for the prospect at this end of the wreck. Let's try how things look at the other. Rouse up, messmate!" he called out, cheerfully, as he passed Midwinter. "Come and see what the old tub of a timber ship has got to show us astern." He sauntered on, with his hands in his pockets, humming the chorus of a comic song.

His voice had produced no apparent effect on his friend; but, at the light touch of his hand in passing, Midwinter started, and moved out slowly from the shadow of the bulwark. "Come along!" cried Allan, suspending his singing for a moment, and glancing back. Still, without a word of answer, the other followed. Thrice he stopped before he reached the stern end of the wreck: the first time, to throw aside his hat, and push back his hair from his forehead and temples; the second time, reeling giddy, to hold for a moment by a ring-bolt close at hand; the last time (though Allan was plainly visible a few yards ahead), to look stealthily behind him, with the furtive scrutiny of a man who believes that other footsteps are following him in the dark. "Not yet!" he whispered to himself, with eyes that searched the empty air. "I shall see him astern, with his hand on the lock of the cabin door"

The stern end of the wreck was clear of the ship-breakers' lumber, accumulated in the other parts of the vessel. Here, the one object that rose visible on the smooth surface of the deck was the low wooden structure which held the cabin door and roofed in the cabin stairs. The wheel-house had been removed, the binnacle had been removed, but the cabin entrance, and all that had belonged to it, had been left untouched. The scuttle was on, and the door was closed.

On gaining the after-part of the vessel, Allan walked straight to the stern, and looked out to sea over the taffrail. No such thing as a boat was in view anywhere on the quiet, moon-brightened waters. Knowing Midwinter's sight to be better than his own, he called out, " Come up here, and see if there's a fisherman within hail of us." Hearing no reply, he looked back. Midwinter had followed him as far as the cabin, and had stopped there. He called again in a louder voice, and beckoned impatiently. Midwinter had heard the call, for he looked up,

but still he never stirred from his place. There he stood, as if he had reached the utmost limits of the ship and could go no further.

Allan went back and joined him. It was not easy to discover what he was looking at, for he kept his face turned away from the moonlight; but it seemed as if his eyes were fixed, with a strange expression of inquiry, on the cabin door. "What is there to look at there?" Allan asked. "Let's see if it's locked." As he took a step forward to open the door, Midwinter's hand seized him suddenly by the coat collar and forced him back. The moment after, the hand relaxed without losing its grasp, and trembled violently, like the hand of a man completely unnerved.

"Am I to consider myself in custody?" asked Allan, half astonished and half amused. "Why in the name of wonder do you keep staring at the cabin door? Any suspicious noises below? It's no use disturbing the rats—if that's what you mean—we haven't got a dog with us. Men? Living men they can't be; for they would have heard us and come on deck. Dead men? Quite impossible! No ship's crew could be drowned in a land-locked place like this, unless the vessel broke up under them—and here's the vessel as steady as a church to speak for herself. Man alive, how your hand trembles! What is there to scare you in that rotten old cabin? What are you shaking and shivering about? Any company of the supernatural sort on board? Mercy preserve us! (as the old women say) do you see a ghost?"

"*I see two!*" answered the other, driven headlong into speech and action by a maddening temptation to reveal the truth. "Two!" he repeated, his breath bursting from him in deep, heavy gasps, as he tried vainly to force back the horrible words. "The ghost of a man like you, drowning in the cabin! And the ghost of a man like me, turning the lock of the door on him!"

Once more young Armadale's hearty laughter rang out loud and long through the stillness of the night.

"Turning the lock of the door, is he?" said Allan, as soon as his merriment left him breath enough to speak. "That's a devilish unhandsome action, Master Midwinter, on the part of your ghost. The least I can do, after that, is to let mine out of the cabin, and give him the run of the ship."

With no more than a momentary exertion of his superior strength, he freed himself easily from Midwinter's hold. "Below there!" he called out, gayly, as he laid his strong hand on the crazy lock, and tore open the cabin door. "Ghost of Allan Armadale, come on deck!" In his terrible ignorance of the truth, he put his head into the doorway and looked down, laughing, at the place where his murdered father had died. "Pah!" he exclaimed, stepping back suddenly, with a shudder of disgust. "The air is foul already; and the cabin is full of water."

It was true. The sunken rocks on which the vessel lay wrecked had burst their way through

her lower timbers astern, and the water had
welled up through the rifted wood. Here,
where the deed had been done, the fatal parallel
between past and present was complete. What
the cabin had been in the time of the fathers,
that the cabin was now in the time of the sons.

Allan pushed the door to again with his foot,
a little surprised at the sudden silence which appeared to have fallen on his friend from the moment when he had laid his hand on the cabin
lock. When he turned to look, the reason of the
silence was instantly revealed. Midwinter had
dropped on the deck. He lay senseless before the
cabin door; his face turned up, white and still,
to the moonlight, like the face of a dead man.

In a moment Allan was at his side. He looked
uselessly round the lonely limits of the wreck,
as he lifted Midwinter's head on his knee, for a
chance of help, where all chance was ruthlessly
cut off. "What am I to do?" he said to himself, in the first impulse of alarm. "Not a drop
of water near, but the foul water in the cabin."
A sudden recollection crossed his memory, tho
florid color rushed back over his face, and he
drew from his pocket a wicker-covered flask.
"God bless the doctor for giving me this before
we sailed!" he broke out, fervently, as he poured
down Midwinter's throat some drops of the raw
whisky which the flask contained. The stimulant acted instantly on the sensitive system of
the swooning man. He sighed faintly, and
slowly opened his eyes. "Have I been dreaming?" he asked, looking up vacantly in Allan's

face. His eyes wandered higher, and encountered the dismantled masts of the wreck rising weird and black against the night sky. He shuddered at the sight of them, and hid his face on Allan's knee. "No dream!" he murmured to himself, mournfully. "Oh me, no dream!"

"You have been overtired all day," said Allan, "and this infernal adventure of ours has upset you. Take some more whisky, it's sure to do you good. Can you sit by yourself, if I put you against the bulwark, so?"

"Why by myself? Why do you leave me?" asked Midwinter.

Allan pointed to the mizzen shrouds of the wreck, which were still left standing. "You are not well enough to rough it here till the workmen come off in the morning," he said. "We must find our way on shore at once, if we can. I am going up to get a good view all round, and see if there's a house within hail of us."

Even in the moment that passed while those few words were spoken, Midwinter's eyes wandered back distrustfully to the fatal cabin door. "Don't go near it!" he whispered. "Don't try to open it, for God's sake!"

"No, no," returned Allan, humoring him. "When I come down from the rigging, I'll come back here." He said the words a little constrainedly, noticing, for the first time while he now spoke, an underlying distress in Midwinter's face, which grieved and perplexed him. "You're not angry with me?" he said, in his simple, sweet-tempered way. "All this is my fault, I know; and I was a brute and a fool to laugh at you, when I ought to have seen you were ill. I am so sorry, Midwinter. Don't be angry with me!"

Midwinter slowly raised his head. His eyes rested with a mournful interest, long and tenderly, on Allan's anxious face.

"Angry?" he repeated, in his lowest, gentlest tones. "Angry with *you?*—Oh, my poor boy, were you to blame for being kind to me when I was ill in the old west-country inn? And was I to blame for feeling your kindness thankfully? Was it our fault that we never doubted each other, and never knew that we were traveling together blindfold on the way that was to lead us here? The cruel time is coming, Allan, when we shall rue the day we ever met. Shake hands, brother, on the edge of the precipice—shake hands while we are brothers still!"

Allan turned away quickly, convinced that his mind had not yet recovered the shock of the fainting fit. "Don't forget the whisky!" he said, cheerfully, as he sprang into the rigging, and mounted to the mizzen-top.

It was past two, the moon was waning, and the darkness that comes before dawn was beginning to gather round the wreck. Behind Allan, as he now stood looking out from the elevation of the mizzen-top, spread the broad and lonely sea. Before him were the low, black, lurking rocks, and the broken waters of the channel, pouring white and angry into the vast calm

Vol. 8                                        —H

of the westward ocean beyond. On the right
hand, heaved back grandly from the water-side,
were the rocks and precipices, with their little
table-lands of grass between; the sloping downs,
and upward-rolling heath solitudes of the Isle of
Man. On the left hand rose the craggy sides
of the Islet of the Calf, here rent wildly into
deep black chasms, there lying low under long
sweeping acclivities of grass and heath. No
sound rose, no light was visible, on either shore.
The black lines of the topmost masts of the wreck
looked shadowy and faint in the darkening mystery of the sky; the land breeze had dropped;
the small shoreward waves fell noiseless: far
or near, no sound was audible but the cheerless
bubbling of the broken water ahead, pouring
through the awful hush of silence in which earth
and ocean waited for the coming day.

Even Allan's careless nature felt the solemn
influence of the time. The sound of his own
voice startled him when he looked down and
hailed his friend on deck.

"I think I see one house," he said. "Here-
away, on the mainland to the right." He looked
again, to make sure, at a dim little patch of
white, with faint white lines behind it, nestling
low in a grassy hollow, on the main island. "It
looks like a stone house and inclosure," he resumed. "I'll hail it, on the chance." He passed
his arm round a rope to steady himself, made a
speaking - trumpet of his hands, and suddenly
dropped them again without uttering a sound.
"It's so awfully quiet," he whispered to himself.

"I'm half afraid to call out." He looked down
again on deck. "I shan't startle you, Midwinter, shall I?" he said, with an uneasy laugh.
He looked once more at the faint white object,
in the grassy hollow. "It won't do to have
come up here for nothing," he thought, and
made a speaking-trumpet of his hands again.
This time he gave the hail with the whole power
of his lungs. "On shore there!" he shouted,
turning his face to the main island. "Ahoy-
hoy-hoy!"

The last echoes of his voice died away and
were lost. No sound answered him but the
cheerless bubbling of the broken water ahead.

He looked down again at his friend, and saw
the dark figure of Midwinter rise erect, and pace
the deck backward and forward, never disappearing out of sight of the cabin when it retired
toward the bows of the wreck, and never passing beyond the cabin when it returned toward
the stern. "He is impatient to get away,"
thought Allan; "I'll try again." He hailed
the land once more, and, taught by previous
experience, pitched his voice in its highest key.

This time another sound than the sound of the
bubbling water answered him. The lowing of
frightened cattle rose from the building in the
grassy hollow, and traveled far and drearily
through the stillness of the morning air. Allan
waited and listened. If the building was a
farmhouse the disturbance among the beasts
would rouse the men. If it was only a cattle-
stable, nothing more would happen. The low-

ing of the frightened brutes rose and fell drearily, the minutes passed, and nothing happened.

"Once more!" said Allan, looking down at the restless figure pacing beneath him. For the third time he hailed the land. For the third time he waited and listened.

In a pause of silence among the cattle, he heard behind him, on the opposite shore of the channel, faint and far among the solitudes of the Islet of the Calf, a sharp, sudden sound, like the distant clash of a heavy door - bolt drawn back. Turning at once in the new direction, he strained his eyes to look for a house. The last faint rays of the waning moonlight trembled here and there on the higher rocks, and on the steeper pinnacles of ground, but great strips of darkness lay dense and black over all the land between; and in that darkness the house, if house there were, was lost to view.

"I have roused somebody at last," Allan called out, encouragingly, to Midwinter, still walking to and fro on the deck, strangely indifferent to all that was passing above and beyond him. "Look out for the answering hail!" And with his face set toward the islet, Allan shouted for help.

The shout was not answered, but mimicked with a shrill, shrieking derision, with wilder and wilder cries, rising out of the deep distant darkness, and mingling horribly the expression of a human voice with the sound of a brute's. A sudden suspicion crossed Allan's mind, which made his head swim and turned his hand cold

as it held the rigging. In breathless silence
he looked toward the quarter from which the
first mimicry of his cry for help had come.
After a moment's pause the shrieks were renewed, and the sound of them came nearer. Suddenly a figure, which seemed the figure of a
man, leaped up black on a pinnacle of rock,
and capered and shrieked in the waning gleam
of the moonlight. The screams of a terrified
woman mingled with the cries of the capering
creature on the rock. A red spark flashed out
in the darkness from a light kindled in an invisible window. The hoarse shouting of a man's
voice in anger was heard through the noise. A
second black figure leaped up on the rock, struggled with the first figure, and disappeared with
it in the darkness. The cries grew fainter and
fainter, the screams of the woman were stilled,
the hoarse voice of the man was heard again for
a moment, hailing the wreck in words made un-
intelligible by the distance, but in tones plainly
expressive of rage and fear combined. Another
moment, and the clang of the door-bolt was
heard again, the red spark of light was quenched
in darkness, and all the islet lay quiet in the
shadows once more. The lowing of the cattle
on the main-land ceased, rose again, stopped.
Then, cold and cheerless as ever, the eternal
bubbling of the broken water welled up through
the great gap of silence—the one sound left, as
the mysterious stillness of the hour fell like a
mantle from the heavens, and closed over the
wreck.

Allan descended from his place in the mizzen-top, and joined his friend again on deck.

"We must wait till the ship-breakers come off to their work," he said, meeting Midwinter half-way in the course of his restless walk. "After what has happened, I don't mind confessing that I've had enough of hailing the land. Only think of there being a madman in that house ashore, and of my waking him! Horrible, wasn't it?"

Midwinter stood still for a moment, and looked at Allan, with the perplexed air of a man who hears circumstances familiarly mentioned to which he is himself a total stranger. He appeared, if such a thing had been possible, to have passed over entirely without notice all that had just happened on the Islet of the Calf.

"Nothing is horrible *out* of this ship," he said. "Everything is horrible *in* it."

Answering in those strange words, he turned away again, and went on with his walk.

Allan picked up the flask of whisky lying on the deck near him, and revived his spirits with a dram. "Here's one thing on board that isn't horrible," he retorted briskly, as he screwed on the stopper of the flask; "and here's another," he added, as he took a cigar from his case and lit it. "Three o'clock!" he went on, looking at his watch, and settling himself comfortably on deck, with his back against the bulwark. "Day-break isn't far off; we shall have the piping of the birds to cheer us up before long. I say, Mid-winter, you seem to have quite got over that un-lucky fainting fit. How you do keep walking!

Come here and have a cigar, and make yourself comfortable. What's the good of tramping backward and forward in that restless way?"

"I am waiting," said Midwinter.

"Waiting! What for?"

"For what is to happen to you or to me—or to both of us—before we are out of this ship."

"With submission to your superior judgment, my dear fellow, I think quite enough has happened already. The adventure will do very well as it stands now; more of it is more than I want." He took another dram of whisky, and rambled on, between the puffs of his cigar, in his usual easy way. "I've not got your fine imagination, old boy; and I hope the next thing that happens will be the appearance of the workmen's boat. I suspect that queer fancy of yours has been running away with you while you were down here all by yourself. Come, now, what were you thinking of while I was up in the mizzen-top frightening the cows?"

Midwinter suddenly stopped. "Suppose I tell you?" he said.

"Suppose you do?"

The torturing temptation to reveal the truth, roused once already by his companion's merciless gayety of spirit, possessed itself of Midwinter for the second time. He leaned back in the dark against the high side of the ship, and looked down in silence at Allan's figure, stretched comfortably on the deck. "Rouse him," the fiend whispered, subtly, "from that ignorant self-possession and that pitiless repose. Show him the place where the deed was done; let him know it with your knowledge, and fear it with your dread. Tell him of the letter you burned, and of the words no fire can destroy which are living in your memory now. Let him see your mind as it was yesterday, when it roused your sinking faith in your own convictions, to look back on your life at sea, and to cherish the comforting remembrance that, in all your voyages, you had never fallen in with this ship. Let him see your mind as it is now, when the ship has got you at the turning-point of your new life, at the outset of your friendship with the one man of all men whom your father warned you to avoid. Think of those death-bed words, and whisper them in his ear, that he may think of them, too: 'Hide yourself from him under an assumed name. Put the mountains and the seas between you; be ungrateful, be unforgiving; be all that is most repellent to your own gentler nature, rather than live under the same roof and breathe the same air with that man.' " So the tempter counseled. So, like a nòisome exhalation from the father's grave, the father's influence rose and poisoned the mind of the son.

The sudden silence surprised Allan; he looked back drowsily over his shoulder. "Thinking again!" he exclaimed, with a weary yawn.

Midwinter stepped out from the shadow, and came nearer to Allan than he had come yet. "Yes," he said, "thinking of the past and the future."

"The past and the future?" repeated Allan,

shifting himself comfortably into a new position. "For my part, I'm dumb about the past. It's a sore subject with me: the past means the loss of the doctor's boat. Let's talk about the future. Have you been taking a practical view? as dear old Brock calls it. Have you been considering the next serious question that concerns us both when we get back to the hotel—the question of breakfast?"

After an instant's hesitation, Midwinter took a step nearer. "I have been thinking of your future and mine," he said; "I have been thinking of the time when your way in life and my way in life will be two ways instead of one."

"Here's the daybreak!" cried Allan. "Look up at the masts; they're beginning to get clear again already. I beg your pardon. What were you saying?"

Midwinter made no reply. The struggle between the hereditary superstition that was driving him on, and the unconquerable affection for Allan that was holding him back, suspended the next words on his lips. He turned aside his face in speechless suffering. "Oh, my father!" he thought, "better have killed me on that day when I lay on your bosom, than have let me live for this."

"What's that about the future?" persisted Allan. "I was looking for the daylight; I didn't hear."

Midwinter controlled himself, and answered: "You have treated me with your usual kindness," he said, "in planning to take me with

you to Thorpe Ambrose. I think, on reflection,
I had better not intrude myself where I am not
known and not expected." His voice faltered,
and he stopped again. The more he shrank from
it, the clearer the picture of the happy life that
he was resigning rose on his mind.

Allan's thoughts instantly reverted to the
mystification about the new steward which he
had practiced on his friend when they were consulting together in the cabin of the yacht. "Has
he been turning it over in his mind?" wondered
Allan; "and is he beginning at last to suspect
the truth? I'll try him.—Talk as much nonsense, my dear fellow, as you like," he rejoined,
"but don't forget that you are engaged to see
me established at Thorpe Ambrose, and to give
me your opinion of the new steward."

Midwinter suddenly stepped forward again,
close to Allan.

"I am not talking about your steward or your
estate," he burst out passionately; "I am talking about myself. Do you hear? Myself! I
am not a fit companion for you. You don't
know who I am." He drew back into the
shadowy shelter of the bulwark as suddenly
as he had come out from it. "O God! I can't
tell him," he said to himself, in a whisper.

For a moment, and for a moment only, Allan
was surprised. "Not know who you are?" Even
as he repeated the words, his easy goodhumor got
the upper-hand again. He took up the whisky
flask, and shook it significantly. "I say," he
resumed, "how much of the doctor's medicine

did you take while I was up in the mizzen-top?"

The light tone which he persisted in adopting stung Midwinter to the last pitch of exasperation. He came out again into the light, and stamped his foot angrily on the deck. "Listen to me!" he said. "You don't know half the low things I have done in my lifetime. I have been a tradesman's drudge; I have swept out the shop and put up the shutters; I have carried parcels through the street, and waited for my master's money at his customers' doors."

"I have never done anything half as useful," returned Allan, composedly. "Dear old boy, what an industrious fellow you have been in your time!"

"I've been a vagabond and a blackguard in my time," returned the other, fiercely; "I've been a street tumbler, a tramp, a gypsy's boy! I've sung for half-pence with dancing dogs on the high-road! I've worn a foot-boy's livery, and waited at table! I've been a common sailors' cook, and a starving fisherman's Jack-of-all-trades! What has a gentleman in your position in common with a man in mine? Can you take *me* into the society at Thorpe Ambrose? Why, my very name would be a reproach to you. Fancy the faces of your new neighbors when their foot-men announce Ozias Midwinter and Allan Armadale in the same breath!" He burst into a harsh laugh, and repeated the two names again, with a scornful bitterness of emphasis which insisted pitilessly on the marked contrast between them.

Something in the sound of his laughter jarred painfully even on Allan's easy nature. He raised himself on the deck and spoke seriously for the first time. "A joke's a joke, Midwinter," he said, "as long as you don't carry it too far. I remember your saying something of the same sort to me once before when I was nursing you in Somersetshire. You forced me to ask you if I deserved to be kept at arms-length by *you* of all the people in the world. Don't force me to say so again. Make as much fun of me as you please, old fellow, in any other way. *That* way hurts me."

Simple as the words were, and simply as they had been spoken, they appeared to work an instant revolution in Midwinter's mind. His impressible nature recoiled as from some sudden shock. Without a word of reply, he walked away by himself to the forward part of the ship. He sat down on some piled planks between the masts, and passed his hand over his head in a vacant, bewildered way. Though his father's belief in fatality was his own belief once more—though there was no longer the shadow of a doubt in his mind that the woman whom Mr. Brock had met in Somersetshire, and the woman who had tried to destroy herself in London, were one and the same—though all the horror that mastered him when he first read the letter from Wildbad had now mastered him again, Allan's appeal to their past experience of each other had come home to his heart, with a force more irresistible than the force of his superstition itself.

In the strength of that very superstition, he now sought the pretext which might encourage him to sacrifice every less generous feeling to the one predominant dread of wounding the sympathies of his friend. "Why distress him?" he whispered to himself. "We are not at the end here: there is the Woman behind us in the dark. Why resist him when the mischief's done, and the caution comes too late? What *is* to be *will* be. What have I to do with the future? and what has he?"

He went back to Allan, sat down by his side, and took his hand. "Forgive me," he said, gently; "I have hurt you for the last time." Before it was possible to reply, he snatched up the whisky flask from the deck. "Come!" he exclaimed, with a sudden effort to match his friend's cheerfulness, "you have been trying the doctor's medicine, why shouldn't I?"

Allan was delighted. "This is something like a change for the better," he said; "Midwinter is himself again. Hark! there are the birds. Hail, smiling morn! smiling morn!" He sang the words of the glee in his old, cheerful voice, and clapped Midwinter on the shoulder in his old, hearty may. "How did you manage to clear your head of those confounded megrims? Do you know you were quite alarming about something happening to one or other of us before we were out of this ship?"

"Sheer nonsense!" returned Midwinter, contemptuously. "I don't think my head has ever been quite right since that fever; I've got a bee in my bonnet, as they say in the North. Let's talk of something else. About those people you have let the cottage to? I wonder whether the agent's account of Major Milroy's family is to be depended on? There might be another lady in the household besides his wife and his daughter."

"Oho!" cried Allan, "*you're* beginning to think of nymphs among the trees, and flirtations in the fruit-garden, are you? Another lady, eh? Suppose the major's family circle won't supply another? We shall have to spin that half-crown again, and toss up for which is to have the first chance with Miss Milroy."

For once Midwinter spoke as lightly and carelessly as Allan himself. "No, no," he said, "the major's landlord has the first claim to the notice of the major's daughter. I'll retire into the background, and wait for the next lady who makes her appearance at Thorpe Ambrose."

"Very good. I'll have an address to the women of Norfolk posted in the park to that effect," said Allan. "Are you particular to a shade about size or complexion? What's your favorite age?"

Midwinter trifled with his own superstition, as a man trifles with the loaded gun that may kill him, or with the savage animal that may maim him for life. He mentioned the age (as he had reckoned it himself) of the woman in the black gown and the red Paisley shawl.

"Five-and-thirty," he said.

As the words passed his lips, his factitious

spirits deserted him. He left his seat, impenetrably deaf to all Allan's efforts at rallying him on his extraordinary answer, and resumed his restless pacing of the deck in dead silence. Once more the haunting thought which had gone to and fro with him in the hour of darkness went to and fro with him now in the hour of daylight.

Once more the conviction possessed itself of his mind that something was to happen to Allan or to himself before they left the wreck.

Minute by minute the light strengthened in the eastern sky; and the shadowy places on the deck of the timber ship revealed their barren emptiness under the eye of day. As the breeze rose again, the sea began to murmur wakefully in the morning light. Even the cold bubbling of the broken water changed its cheerless note, and softened on the ear as the mellowing flood of daylight poured warm over it from the rising sun. Midwinter paused near the forward part of the ship, and recalled his wandering attention to the passing time. The cheering influences of the hour were round him, look where he might. The happy morning smile of the summer sky, so brightly merciful to the old and weary earth, lavished its all-embracing beauty even on the wreck. The dew that lay glittering on the inland fields lay glittering on the deck, and the worn and rusted rigging was gemmed as brightly as the fresh green leaves on shore. Insensibly, as he looked round, Midwinter's thoughts reverted to the comrade who had

shared with him the adventure of the night.
He returned to the after-part of the ship, and
spoke to Allan as he advanced.  Receiving no
answer, he approached the recumbent figure and
looked closer at it.  Left to his own resources,
Allan had let the fatigues of the night take their
own way with him.  His head had sunk back;
his hat had fallen off; he lay stretched at full
length on the deck of the timber ship, deeply and
peacefully asleep.

Midwinter resumed his walk; his mind lost in
doubt; his own past thoughts seeming suddenly
to have grown strange to him.  How darkly his
forebodings had distrusted the coming time, and
how harmlessly that time had come!  The sun
was mounting in the heavens, the hour of release
was drawing nearer and nearer, and of the two
Armadales imprisoned in the fatal ship, one was
sleeping away the weary time, and the other
was quietly watching the growth of the new
day.

The sun climbed higher; the hour wore on.
With the latent distrust of the wreck which
still clung to him, Midwinter looked inquiringly on either shore for signs of awakening
human life.  The land was still lonely.  The
smoke wreaths that were soon to rise from cottage chimneys had not risen yet.

After a moment's thought he went back again
to the after-part of the vessel, to see if there
might be a fisherman's boat within hail astern
of them.  Absorbed for the moment by the new
idea, he passed Allan hastily, after barely notic-

ing that he still lay asleep. One step more would
have brought him to the taffrail, when that step
was suspended by a sound behind him, a sound
like a faint groan. He turned, and looked at
the sleeper on the deck. He knelt softly, and
looked closer.

"It has come!" he whispered to himself. "Not
to *me*—but to *him*."

It had come, in the bright freshness of the
morning; it had come, in the mystery and terror
of a Dream. The face which Midwinter had
last seen in perfect repose was now the distorted
face of a suffering man. The perspiration stood
thick on Allan's forehead, and matted his curl-
ing hair. His partially opened eyes showed nothing but the white of the eyeball gleaming blindly.
His outstretched hands scratched and struggled
on the deck. From moment to moment he moaned
and muttered helplessly; but the words that
escaped him were lost in the grinding and gnash-
ing of his teeth. There he lay—so near in the
body to the friend who bent over him; so far
away in the spirit, that the two might have
been in different worlds—there he lay, with the
morning sunshine on his face, in the torture of
his dream.

One question, and one only, rose in the mind
of the man who was looking at him. What had
the fatality which had imprisoned him in the
wreck decreed that he should see?

Had the treachery of Sleep opened the gates
of the grave to that one of the two Armadales
whom the other had kept in ignorance of the

truth? Was the murder of the father revealing itself to the son—there, on the very spot where the crime had been committed—in the vision of a dream?

With that question overshadowing all else in his mind, the son of the homicide knelt on the deck, and looked at the son of the man whom his father's hand had slain.

The conflict between the sleeping body and the waking mind was strengthening every moment. The dreamer's helpless groaning for deliverance grew louder; his hands raised themselves, and clutched at the empty air. Struggling with the all-mastering dread that still held him, Midwinter laid his hand gently on Allan's forehead. Light as the touch was, there were mysterious sympathies in the dreaming man that answered it. His groaning ceased, and his hands dropped slowly. There was an instant of suspense, and Midwinter looked closer. His breath just fluttered over the sleeper's face. Before the next breath had risen to his lips, Allan suddenly sprang up on his knees—sprang up, as if the call of a trumpet had rung on his ear, awake in an instant.

"You have been dreaming," said Midwinter, as the other looked at him wildly, in the first bewilderment of waking.

Allan's eyes began to wander about the wreck, at first vacantly, then with a look of angry surprise. "Are we here still?" he said, as Midwinter helped him to his feet. "Whatever else I do on board this infernal ship," he added, after a moment, "I won't go to sleep again!"

As he said those words, his friend's eyes searched his face in silent inquiry. They took a turn together on the deck.

"Tell me your dream," said Midwinter, with a strange tone of suspicion in his voice, and a strange appearance of abruptness in his manner.

"I can't tell it yet," returned Allan. "Wait a little till I'm my own man again."

They took another turn on the deck. Midwinter stopped, and spoke once more.

"Look at me for a moment, Allan," he said.

There was something of the trouble left by the dream, and something of natural surprise at the strange request just addressed to him, in Allan's face, as he turned it full on the speaker; but no shadow of ill-will, no lurking lines of distrust anywhere. Midwinter turned aside quickly, and hid, as he best might, an irrepressible outburst of relief.

"Do I look a little upset?" asked Allan, taking his arm, and leading him on again. "Don't make yourself nervous about me if I do. My head feels wild and giddy, but I shall soon get over it."

For the next few minutes they walked backward and forward in silence, the one bent on dismissing the terror of the dream from his thoughts, the other bent on discovering what the terror of the dream might be. Relieved of the dread that had oppressed it, the superstitious nature of Midwinter had leaped to its next conclusion at a bound. What if the sleeper had been visited by another revelation than the revelation of the

Past? What if the dream had opened those un-
turned pages in the book of the Future which
told the story of his life to come? The bare
doubt that it might be so strengthened tenfold
Midwinter's longing to penetrate the mystery
which Allan's silence still kept a secret from
him.

"Is your head more composed?" he asked.
"Can you tell me your dream now?"

While he put the question, a last memorable
moment in the Adventure of the Wreck was at
hand.

They had reached the stern, and were just
turning again when Midwinter spoke. As Allan
opened his lips to answer, he looked out mechanically to sea. Instead of replying, he suddenly
ran to the taffrail, and waved his hat over his
head, with a shout of exultation.

Midwinter joined him, and saw a large six-
oared boat pulling straight for the channel of
the Sound. A figure, which they both thought
they recognized, rose eagerly in the stern-sheets
and returned the waving of Allan's hat. The
boat came nearer, the steersman called to them
cheerfully, and they recognized the doctor's voice.

"Thank God you're both above water!" said
Mr. Hawbury, as they met him on the deck of
the timber ship. "Of all the winds of heaven,
which wind blew you here?"

He looked at Midwinter as he made the inquiry, but it was Allan who told him the story
of the night, and Allan who asked the doctor
for information in return. The one absorbing

interest in Midwinter's mind — the interest of penetrating the mystery of the dream—kept him silent throughout. Heedless of all that was said or done about him, he watched Allan, and followed Allan, like a dog, until the time came for getting down into the boat. Mr. Hawbury's professional eye rested on him curiously, noting his varying color, and the incessant restlessness of his hands. "I wouldn't change nervous systems with that man for the largest fortune that could be offered me," thought the doctor as he took the boat's tiller, and gave the oarsmen their order to push off from the wreck.

Having reserved all explanations on his side until they were on their way back to Port St. Mary, Mr. Hawbury next addressed himself to the gratification of Allan's curiosity. The circumstances which had brought him to the rescue of his two guests of the previous evening were simple enough. The lost boat had been met with at sea by some fishermen of Port Erin, on the western side of the island, who at once recognized it as the doctor's property, and at once sent a messenger to make inquiry at the doctor's house. The man's statement of what had happened had naturally alarmed Mr. Hawbury for the safety of Allan and his friend. He had immediately secured assistance, and, guided by the boatman's advice, had made first for the most dangerous place on the coast — the only place, in that calm weather, in which an accident could have happened to a boat sailed by experienced men — the channel of the Sound.

After thus accounting for his welcome appearance on the scene, the doctor hospitably insisted that his guests of the evening should be his guests of the morning as well. It would still be too early when they got back for the people at the hotel to receive them, and they would find bed and breakfast at Mr. Hawbury's house.

At the first pause in the conversation between Allan and the doctor, Midwinter, who had neither joined in the talk nor listened to the talk, touched his friend on the arm. "Are you better?" he asked, in a whisper. "Shall you soon be composed enough to tell me what I want to know?"

Allan's eyebrows contracted impatiently; the subject of the dream, and Midwinter's obstinacy in returning to it, seemed to be alike distasteful to him. He hardly answered with his usual good humor. "I suppose I shall have no peace till I tell you," he said, "so I may as well get it over at once."

"No!" returned Midwinter, with a look at the doctor and his oarsmen. "Not where other people can hear it—not till you and I are alone."

"If you wish to see the last, gentlemen, of your quarters for the night," interposed the doctor, "now is your time! The coast will shut the vessel out in a minute more."

In silence on the one side and on the other, the two Armadales looked their last at the fatal ship. Lonely and lost they had found the wreck in the mystery of the summer night; lonely and lost they left the wreck in the radiant beauty of the summer morning.

An hour later the doctor had seen his guests established in their bedrooms, and had left them to take their rest until the breakfast hour arrived.

Almost as soon as his back was turned, the doors of both rooms opened softly, and Allan and Midwinter met in the passage.

"Can you sleep after what has happened?" asked Allan.

Midwinter shook his head. "You were coming to my room, were you not?" he said. "What for?"

"To ask you to keep me company. What were *you* coming to *my* room for?"

"To ask you to tell me your dream."

"Damn the dream! I want to forget all about it."

"And *I* want to know all about it."

Both paused; both refrained instinctively from saying more. For the first time since the beginning of their friendship they were on the verge of a disagreement, and that on the subject of the dream. Allan's good temper just stopped them on the brink.

"You are the most obstinate fellow alive," he said; "but if you will know all about it, you must know all about it, I suppose. Come into my room, and I'll tell you."

He led the way, and Midwinter followed. The door closed and shut them in together.

# CHAPTER V.

### THE SHADOW OF THE FUTURE.

WHEN Mr. Hawbury joined his guests in the breakfast-room, the strange contrast of character between them which he had noticed already was impressed on his mind more strongly than ever. One of them sat at the well-spread table, hungry and happy, ranging from dish to dish, and declaring that he had never made such a breakfast in his life. The other sat apart at the window; his cup thanklessly deserted before it was empty, his meat left ungraciously half-eaten on his plate. The doctor's morning greeting to the two accurately expressed the differing impressions which they had produced on his mind.

He clapped Allan on the shoulder, and saluted him with a joke. He bowed constrainedly to Midwinter, and said, "I am afraid you have not recovered the fatigues of the night."

"It's not the night, doctor, that has damped his spirits," said Allan. "It's something I have been telling him. It is not my fault, mind. If I had only known beforehand that he believed in dreams, I wouldn't have opened my lips."

"Dreams?" repeated the doctor, looking at Midwinter directly, and addressing him under a mistaken impression of the meaning of Allan's words. "With your constitution, you ought to be well used to dreaming by this time."

"This way, doctor; you have taken the wrong

turning!" cried Allan. "I'm the dreamer, not he. Don't look astonished; it wasn't in this comfortable house; it was on board that confounded timber ship. The fact is, I fell asleep just before you took us off the wreck; and it's not to be denied that I had a very ugly dream. Well, when we got back here—"

"Why do you trouble Mr. Hawbury about a matter that cannot possibly interest him?" asked Midwinter, speaking for the first time, and speaking very impatiently.

"I beg your pardon," returned the doctor, rather sharply; "so far as I have heard, the matter does interest me."

"That's right, doctor!" said Allan. "Be interested, I beg and pray; I want you to clear his head of the nonsense he has got in it now. What do you think? He will have it that my dream is a warning to me to avoid certain people; and he actually persists in saying that one of those people is—himself! Did you ever hear the like of it? I took great pains; I explained the whole thing to him. I said, warning be hanged; it's all indigestion! You don't know what I ate and drank at the doctor's supper-table; I do. Do you think he would listen to me? Not he. You try him next; you're a professional man, and he must listen to you. Be a good fellow, doctor, and give me a certificate of indigestion; I'll show you my tongue with pleasure."

"The sight of your face is quite enough," said Mr. Hawbury. "I certify, on the spot, that you never had such a thing as an indigestion in your

life. Let's hear about the dream, and see what
we can make of it, if you have no objection,
that is to say."

Allan pointed at Midwinter with his fork.

"Apply to my friend, there," he said; "he has
got a much better account of it than I can give
you. If you'll believe me, he took it all down
in writing from my own lips; and he made me
sign it at the end, as if it was my 'last dying
speech and confession' before I went to the gal-
lows. Out with it, old boy—I saw you put it in
your pocket-book—out with it!"

"Are you really in earnest?" asked Midwinter, producing his pocket-book with a reluctance
which was almost offensive under the circumstances, for it implied distrust of the doctor in
the doctor's own house.

Mr. Hawbury's color rose. "Pray don't show
it to me, if you feel the least unwillingness," he
said, with the elaborate politeness of an offended
man.

"Stuff and nonsense!" cried Allan. "Throw
it over here!"

Instead of complying with that characteristic
request, Midwinter took the paper from the
pocket-book, and, leaving his place, approached
Mr. Hawbury. "I beg your pardon," he said,
as he offered the doctor the manuscript with his
own hand. His eyes dropped to the ground, and
his face darkened, while he made the apology.
"A secret, sullen fellow," thought the doctor,
thanking him with formal civility; "his friend
is worth ten thousand of him." Midwinter went

back to the window, and sat down again in silence, with the old impenetrable resignation which had once puzzled Mr. Brock.

"Read that, doctor," said Allan, as Mr. Hawbury opened the written paper. "It's not told in my roundabout way; but there's nothing added to it, and nothing taken away. It's exactly what I dreamed, and exactly what I should have written myself, if I had thought the thing worth putting down on paper, and if I had had the knack of writing—which," concluded Allan, composedly stirring his coffee, "I haven't, except it's letters; and I rattle *them* off in no time."

Mr. Hawbury spread the manuscript before him on the breakfast-table, and read these lines:

## "Allan Armadale's Dream.

"Early on the morning of June the first, eighteen hundred and fifty-one, I found myself (through circumstances which it is not important to mention in this place) left alone with a friend of mine—a young man about my own age—on board the French timber ship named *La Grâce de Dieu*, which ship then lay wrecked in the channel of the Sound between the main-land of the Isle of Man and the islet called the Calf. Having not been in bed the previous night, and feeling overcome by fatigue, I fell asleep on the deck of the vessel. I was in my usual good health at the time, and the morning was far enough advanced for the sun to have risen. Under these circumstances, and at that period of the day, I passed from sleeping to dreaming. As clearly as

I can recollect it, after the lapse of a few hours, this was the succession of events presented to me by the dream:

"1. The first event of which I was conscious was the appearance of my father. He took me silently by the hand; and we found ourselves in the cabin of a ship.

"2. Water rose slowly over us in the cabin; and I and my father sank through the water together.

"3. An interval of oblivion followed; and then the sense came to me of being left alone in the darkness.

"4. I waited.

"5. The darkness opened, and showed me the vision—as in a picture—of a broad, lonely pool, surrounded by open ground. Above the further margin of the pool I saw the cloudless western sky, red wtih the light of sunset.

"6. On the near margin of the pool there stood the Shadow of a Woman.

"7. It was the shadow only. No indication was visible to me by which I could identify it, or compare it with any living creature. The long robe showed me that it was the shadow of a woman, and showed me nothing more.

"8. The darkness closed again — remained with me for an interval — and opened for the second time.

"9. I found myself in a room, standing before a long window. The only object of furniture or of ornament that I saw (or that I can now remember having seen) was a little statue placed near me. The window opened on a lawn and flower-garden; and the rain was pattering heavily against the glass.

"10. I was not alone in the room. Standing opposite to me at the window was the Shadow of a Man.

"11. I saw no more of it; I knew no more of it than I saw and knew of the shadow of the woman. But the shadow of the man moved. It stretched out its arm toward the statue; and the statue fell in fragments on the floor.

"12. With a confused sensation in me, which was partly anger and partly distress, I stooped to look at the fragments. When I rose again, the Shadow had vanished, and I saw no more.

"13. The darkness opened for the third time, and showed me the Shadow of the Woman and the Shadow of the Man together.

"14. No surrounding scene (or none that I can now call to mind) was visible to me.

"15. The Man-Shadow was the nearest; the Woman-Shadow stood back. From where she stood, there came a sound as of the pouring of a liquid softly. I saw her touch the shadow of the man with one hand, and with the other give him a glass. He took the glass, and gave it to me. In the moment when I put it to my lips, a deadly faintness mastered me from head to foot. When I came to my senses again, the Shadows had vanished, and the third vision was at an end.

"16. The darkness closed over me again; and the interval of oblivion followed.

"17. I was conscious of nothing more, till I felt the morning sun shine on my face, and heard my friend tell me that I had awakened from a dream." . . . .

After reading the narrative attentively to the last line (under which appeared Allan's signature), the doctor looked across the breakfast-table at Midwinter, and tapped his fingers on the manuscript with a satirical smile.

"Many men, many opinions," he said. "I don't agree with either of you about this dream. Your theory," he added, looking at Allan, with a smile, "we have disposed of already: the supper that _you_ can't digest is a supper which has yet to be discovered. My theory we will come to presently; your friend's theory claims attention first." He turned again to Midwinter, with his anticipated triumph over a man whom he disliked a little too plainly visible in his face and manner. "If I understand rightly," he went on, "you believe that this dream is a warning, supernaturally addressed to Mr. Armadale, of dangerous events that are threatening him, and of dangerous people connected with those events, whom he would do wisely to avoid. May I inquire whether you have arrived at this conclusion as an habitual believer in dreams, or as having reasons of your own for attaching especial importance to this one dream in particular?"

"You have stated what my conviction is quite accurately," returned Midwinter, chafing under the doctor's looks and tones. "Excuse me if I

ask you to be satisfied with that admission, and
to let me keep my reasons to myself."

"That's exactly what he said to me," interposed Allan. "I don't believe he has got any
reasons at all."

"Gently! gently!" said Mr. Hawbury. "We
can discuss the subject without intruding ourselves into anybody's secrets. Let us come to
my own method of dealing with the dream next.
Mr. Midwinter will probably not be surprised to
hear that I look at this matter from an essentially
practical point of view."

"I shall not be at all surprised," retorted Midwinter. "The view of a medical man, when
he has a problem in humanity to solve, seldom
ranges beyond the point of his dissecting-knife."

The doctor was a little nettled on his side.
"Our limits are not quite so narrow as that," he
said; "but I willingly grant you that there are
some articles of your faith in which we doctors
don't believe. For example, we don't believe
that a reasonable man is justified in attaching
a supernatural interpretation to any phenomenon
which comes within the range of his senses, until he has certainly ascertained that there is no
such thing as a natural explanation of it to be
found in the first instance."

"Come; that's fair enough, I'm sure," exclaimed Allan. "He hit you hard with the
'dissecting - knife,' doctor; and now you have
hit him back again with your 'natural explanation.' Let's have it."

"By all means," said Mr. Hawbury. "Here

it is. There is nothing at all extraordinary in my theory of dreams: it is the theory accepted by the great mass of my profession. A dream is the reproduction, in the sleeping state of the brain, of images and impressions produced on it in the waking state; and this reproduction is more or less involved, imperfect, or contradictory, as the action of certain faculties in the dreamer is controlled more or less completely by the influence of sleep. Without inquiring further into this latter part of the subject—a very curious and interesting part of it—let us take the theory, roughly and generally, as I have just stated it, and apply it at once to the dream now under consideration." He took up the written paper from the table, and dropped the formal tone (as of a lecturer addressing an audience) into which he had insensibly fallen. "I see one event already in this dream," he resumed, "which I know to be the reproduction of a waking impression produced on Mr. Armadale in my own presence. If he will only help me by exerting his memory, I don't despair of tracing back the whole succession of events set down here to something that he has said or thought, or seen or done, in the four-and-twenty hours, or less, which preceded his falling asleep on the deck of the timber ship."

"I'll exert my memory with the greatest pleasure," said Allan. "Where shall we start from?"

"Start by telling me what you did yesterday, before I met you and your friend on the road to this place," replied Mr. Hawbury. "We will say, you got up and had your breakfast. What next?"

"We took a carriage next," said Allan, "and drove from Castletown to Douglas to see my old friend, Mr. Brock, off by the steamer to Liverpool. We came back to Castletown, and separated at the hotel door. Midwinter went into the house, and I went on to my yacht in the harbor.—By-the-bye, doctor, remember you have promised to go cruising with us before we leave the Isle of Man."

"Many thanks; but suppose we keep to the matter in hand. What next?"

Allan hesitated. In both senses of the word his mind was at sea already.

"What did you do on board the yacht?"

"Oh, I know! I put the cabin to rights—thoroughly to rights. I give you my word of honor, I turned every blessed thing topsy-turvy. And my friend there came off in a shore-boat and helped me.—Talking of boats, I have never asked you yet whether your boat came to any harm last night. If there's any damage done, I insist on being allowed to repair it."

The doctor abandoned all further attempts at the cultivation of Allan's memory in despair.

"I doubt if we shall be able to reach our object conveniently in this way," he said. "It will be better to take the events of the dream in their regular order, and to ask the questions that naturally suggest themselves as we go on. Here are the first two events to begin with. You dream that your father appears to you—that you and he find yourselves in the cabin of a ship— that the water rises over you, and that you sink

in it together. Were you down in the cabin of
the wreck, may I ask?"

"I couldn't be down there," replied Allan,
"as the cabin was full of water. I looked in
and saw it, and shut the door again."

"Very good," said Mr. Hawbury. "Here are
the waking impressions clear enough, so far.
You have had the cabin in your mind; and you
have had the water in your mind; and the sound
of the channel current (as I well know without
asking) was the last sound in your ears when
you went to sleep. The idea of drowning comes
too naturally out of such impressions as these to
need dwelling on. Is there anything else before
we go on? Yes; there is one more circumstance
left to account for."

"The most important circumstance of all,"
remarked Midwinter, joining in the conversation, without stirring from his place at the window.

"You mean the appearance of Mr. Armadale's
father? I was just coming to that," answered
Mr. Hawbury. "Is your father alive?" he
added, addressing himself to Allan once more.

"My father died before I was born."

The doctor started. "This complicates it a
little," he said. "How did you know that the
figure appearing to you in the dream was the
figure of your father?"

Allan hesitated again. Midwinter drew his
chair a little away from the window, and looked
at the doctor attentively for the first time.

"Was your father in your thoughts before you

went to sleep?" pursued Mr. Hawbury. "Was there any description of him—any portrait of him at home—in your mind?"

"Of course there was!" cried Allan, suddenly seizing the lost recollection. "Midwinter! you remember the miniature you found on the floor of the cabin when we were putting the yacht to rights? You said I didn't seem to value it; and I told you I did, because it was a portrait of my father—"

"And was the face in the dream like the face in the miniature?" asked Mr. Hawbury.

"Exactly like! I say, doctor, this is beginning to get interesting!"

"What do you say now?" asked Mr. Hawbury, turning toward the window again.

Midwinter hurriedly left his chair, and placed himself at the table with Allan. Just as he had once already taken refuge from the tyranny of his own superstition in the comfortable common sense of Mr. Brock, so, with the same headlong eagerness, with the same straightforward sincerity of purpose, he now took refuge in the doctor's theory of dreams. "I say what my friend says," he answered, flushing with a sudden enthusiasm; "this is beginning to get interesting. Go on; pray go on."

The doctor looked at his strange guest more indulgently than he had looked yet. "You are the only mystic I have met with," he said, "who is willing to give fair evidence fair play. I don't despair of converting you before our inquiry comes to an end. Let us get on to the next set of events," he resumed, after referring for a moment to the manuscript. "The interval of oblivion which is described as succeeding the first of the appearances in the dream may be easily disposed of. It means, in plain English, the momentary cessation of the brain's intellectual action, while a deeper wave of sleep flows over it, just as the sense of being alone in the darkness, which follows, indicates the renewal of that action, previous to the reproduction of another set of impressions. Let us see what they are. A lonely pool, surrounded by an open country; a sunset sky on the further side of the pool; and the shadow of a woman on the near side. Very good; now for it, Mr. Armadale! How did that pool get into your head? The open country you saw on your way from Castletown to this place. But we have no pools or lakes hereabouts; and you can have seen none recently elsewhere, for you came here after a cruise at sea. Must we fall back on a picture, or a book, or a conversation with your friend?"

Allan looked at Midwinter. "I don't remember talking about pools or lakes," he said. "Do you?"

Instead of answering the question, Midwinter suddenly appealed to the doctor.

"Have you got the last number of the Manx newspaper?" he asked.

The doctor produced it from the sideboard. Midwinter turned to the page containing those extracts from the recently published "Travels in Australia," which had roused Allan's interest on

the previous evening, and the reading of which
had ended by sending his friend to sleep. There
—in the passage describing the sufferings of the
travelers from thirst, and the subsequent discovery which saved their lives—there, appearing at the climax of the narrative, was the broad
pool of water which had figured in Allan's
dream!

"Don't put away the paper," said the doctor,
when Midwinter had shown it to him, with the
necessary explanation. "Before we are at the
end of the inquiry, it is quite possible we may
want that extract again. We have got at the
pool. How about the sunset? Nothing of that
sort is referred to in the newspaper extract.
Search your memory again, Mr. Armadale; we
want your waking impression of a sunset, if
you please."

Once more, Allan was at a loss for an answer;
and, once more, Midwinter's ready memory
helped him through the difficulty.

"I think I can trace our way back to this impression, as I traced our way back to the other,"
he said, addressing the doctor. "After we got
here yesterday afternoon, my friend and I took a
long walk over the hills—"

"That's it!" interposed Allan. "I remember.
The sun was setting as we came back to the hotel
for supper, and it was such a splendid red sky,
we both stopped to look at it. And then we
talked about Mr. Brock, and wondered how far
he had got on his journey home. My memory
may be a slow one at starting, doctor; but when

it's once set going, stop it if you can! I haven't half done yet.''

"Wait one minute, in mercy to Mr. Midwinter's memory and mine," said the doctor. "We have traced back to your waking impressions the vision of the open country, the pool, and the sunset. But the Shadow of the Woman has not been accounted for yet. Can you find us the original of this mysterious figure in the dream landscape?''

Allan relapsed into his former perplexity, and Midwinter waited for what was to come, with his eyes fixed in breathless interest on the doctor's face. For the first time there was unbroken silence in the room. Mr. Hawbury looked interrogatively from Allan to Allan's friend. Neither of them answered him. Between the shadow and the shadow's substance there was a great gulf of mystery, impenetrable alike to all three of them.

"Patience," said the doctor, composedly. "Let us leave the figure by the pool for the present, and try if we can't pick her up again as we go on. Allow me to observe, Mr. Midwinter, that it is not very easy to identify a shadow; but we won't despair. This impalpable lady of the lake may take some consistency when we next meet with her.''

Midwinter made no reply. From that moment his interest in the inquiry began to flag.

"What is the next scene in the dream?" pursued Mr. Hawbury, referring to the manuscript. "Mr. Armadale finds himself in a room. He is standing before a long window opening on a lawn and flower - garden, and the rain is pattering against the glass. The only thing he sees in the room is a little statue; and the only company he has is the Shadow of a Man standing opposite to him. The Shadow stretches out its arm, and the statue falls in fragments on the floor; and the dreamer, in anger and distress at the catastrophe (observe, gentlemen, that here the sleeper's reasoning faculty wakes up a little, and the dream passes rationally, for a moment, from cause to effect), stoops to look at the broken pieces. When he looks up again, the scene has vanished. That is to say, in the ebb and flow of sleep, it is the turn of the flow now, and the brain rests a little. What's the matter, Mr. Armadale? Has that restive memory of yours run away with you again?"

"Yes," said Allan. "I'm off at full gallop. I've run the broken statue to earth; it's nothing more nor less than a china shepherdess I knocked off the mantel-piece in the hotel coffee-room, when I rang the bell for supper last night. I say, how well we get on; don't we? It's like guessing a riddle. Now, then, Midwinter! your turn next."

"No!" said the doctor. "My turn, if you please. I claim the long window, the garden, and the lawn, as my property. You will find the long window, Mr. Armadale, in the next room. If you look out, you'll see the garden and lawn in front of it; and, if you'll exert that wonderful memory of yours, you will recollect that you were good enough to take special and complimentary notice of my smart French window and my neat garden, when I drove you and your friend to Port St. Mary yesterday.''

"Quite right," rejoined Allan; "so I did. But what about the rain that fell in the dream? I haven't seen a drop of rain for the last week.''

Mr. Hawbury hesitated. The Manx newspaper which had been left on the table caught his eye. "If we can think of nothing else," he said, "let us try if we can't find the idea of the rain where we found the idea of the pool." He looked through the extract carefully. "I have got it!" he exclaimed. "Here is rain described as having fallen on these thirsty Australian travelers, before they discovered the pool. Behold the shower, Mr. Armadale, which got into your mind when you read the extract to your friend last night! And behold the dream, Mr. Midwinter, mixing up separate waking impressions just as usual!''

"Can you find the waking impression which accounts for the human figure at the window?'' asked Midwinter; "or are we to pass over the Shadow of the Man as we have passed over the Shadow of the Woman already?''

He put the question with scrupulous courtesy of manner, but with a tone of sarcasm in his voice which caught the doctor's ear, and set up the doctor's controversial bristles on the instant.

"When you are picking up shells on the beach, Mr. Midwinter, you usually begin with the shells that lie nearest at hand," he rejoined. "We are picking up facts now; and those that are easiest to get at are the facts we will take first. Let the Shadow of the Man and the Shadow of the Woman pair off together for the present; we won't lose sight of them, I promise you. All in good time, my dear sir; all in good time!"

He, too, was polite, and he, too, was sarcastic. The short truce between the opponents was at an end already. Midwinter returned significantly to his former place by the window. The doctor instantly turned his back on the window more significantly still. Allan, who never quarreled with anybody's opinion, and never looked below the surface of anybody's conduct, drummed cheerfully on the table with the handle of his knife. "Go on, doctor!" he called out; "my wonderful memory is as fresh as ever."

"Is it?" said Mr. Hawbury, referring again to the narrative of the dream. "Do you remember what happened when you and I were gossiping with the landlady at the bar of the hotel last night?"

"Of course I do! You were kind enough to hand me a glass of brandy-and-water, which the landlady had just mixed for your own drinking. And I was obliged to refuse it because, as I told you, the taste of brandy always turns me sick and faint, mix it how you please."

"Exactly so," returned the doctor. "And here is the incident reproduced in the dream. You see the man's shadow and the woman's shadow together this time. You hear the pouring out of liquid (brandy from the hotel bottle, and water from the hotel jug); the glass is handed by the woman-shadow (the landlady) to the man-shadow (myself); the man-shadow hands it to you (exactly what I did); and the faintness (which you had previously described to me) follows in due course. I am shocked to identify these mysterious appearances, Mr. Midwinter, with such miserably unromantic originals as a woman who keeps a hotel, and a man who physics a country district. But your friend himself will tell you that the glass of brandy-and-water was prepared by the landlady, and that it reached him by passing from her hand to mine. We have picked up the shadows, exactly as I anticipated; and we have only to account now—which may be done in two words—for the manner of their appearance in the dream. After having tried to introduce the waking impression of the doctor and the landlady separately, in connection with the wrong set of circumstances, the dreaming mind comes right at the third trial, and introduces the doctor and the landlady together, in connection with the right set of circumstances. There it is in a nutshell!—Permit me to hand you back the manuscript, with my best thanks for your very complete and striking confirmation of the rational theory of dreams." Saying those words, Mr. Hawbury returned the written paper to Midwinter, with the pitiless politeness of a conquering man.

"Wonderful! not a point missed anywhere from beginning to end! By Jupiter!" cried Allan, with the ready reverence of intense ignorance. "What a thing science is!"

"Not a point missed, as you say," remarked the doctor, complacently. "And yet I doubt if we have succeeded in convincing your friend."

"You have *not* convinced me," said Midwinter. "But I don't presume on that account to say that you are wrong."

He spoke quietly, almost sadly. The terrible conviction of the supernatural origin of the dream, from which he had tried to escape, had possessed itself of him again. All his interest in the argument was at an end; all his sensitiveness to its irritating influences was gone. In the case of any other man, Mr. Hawbury would have been mollified by such a concession as his adversary had now made to him; but he disliked Midwinter too cordially to leave him in the peaceable enjoyment of an opinion of his own.

"Do you admit," asked the doctor, more pugnaciously than ever, "that I have traced back every event of the dream to a waking impression which preceded it in Mr. Armadale's mind?"

"I have no wish to deny that you have done so," said Midwinter, resignedly.

"Have I identified the shadows with their living originals?"

"You have identified them to your own satisfaction, and to my friend's satisfaction. Not to mine."

"Not to yours? Can *you* identify them?"

"No. I can only wait till the living originals stand revealed in the future."

"Spoken like an oracle, Mr. Midwinter! Have

you any idea at present of who those living originals may be?"

"I have. I believe that coming events will
identify the Shadow of the Woman with a person
whom my friend has not met with yet; and the
Shadow of the Man with myself."

Allan attempted to speak. The doctor stopped
him. "Let us clearly understand this," he said
to Midwinter. "Leaving your own case out of
the question for the moment, may I ask how a
shadow, which has no distinguishing mark about
it, is to be identified with a living woman whom
your friend doesn't know?"

Midwinter's color rose a little. He began to
feel the lash of the doctor's logic.

"The landscape picture of the dream has its
distinguishing marks," he replied; "and in that
landscape the living woman will appear when
the living woman is first seen."

"The same thing will happen, I suppose,"
pursued the doctor, "with the man-shadow which
you persist in identifying with yourself. You will
be associated in the future with a statue broken
in your friend's presence, with a long window
looking out on a garden, and with a shower of
rain pattering against the glass? Do you say that?"

"I say that."

"And so again, I presume, with the next
vision? You and the mysterious woman will be
brought together in some place now unknown,
and will present to Mr. Armadale some liquid
yet unnamed, which will turn him faint?—Do
you seriously tell me you believe this?"

"I seriously tell you I believe it."

"And, according to your view, these fulfill-ments of the dream will mark the progress of certain coming events, in which Mr. Armadale's happiness, or Mr. Armadale's safety, will be dangerously involved?"

"That is my firm conviction."

The doctor rose, laid aside his moral dissect-ing-knife, considered for a moment, and took it up again.

"One last question," he said. "Have you any reason to give for going out of your way to adopt such a mystical view as this, when an unan-swerably rational explanation of the dream lies straight before you?'

"No reason," replied Midwinter, "that I can give, either to you or to my friend."

The doctor looked at his watch with the air of a man who is suddenly reminded that he has been wasting his time.

"We have no common ground to start from," he said; "and if we talk till doomsday, we should not agree. Excuse my leaving you rather abruptly. It is later than I thought; and my morning's batch of sick people are waiting for me in the surgery. I have convinced *your* mind, Mr. Armadale, at any rate; so the time we have given to this discussion has not been altogether lost. Pray stop here, and smoke your cigar. I shall be at your service again in less than an hour." He nodded cordially to Allan, bowed formally to Midwinter, and quitted the room.

As soon as the doctor's back was turned, Allan

left his place at the table, and appealed to his friend, with that irresistible heartiness of manner which had always found its way to Midwinter's sympathies, from the first day when they met at the Somersetshire inn.

"Now the sparring-match between you and the doctor is over," said Allan, "I have got two words to say on my side. Will you do something for my sake which you won't do for your own?"

Midwinter's face brightened instantly. "I will do anything you ask me," he said.

"Very well. Will you let the subject of the dream drop out of our talk altogether from this time forth?"

"Yes, if you wish it."

"Will you go a step further? Will you leave off thinking about the dream?"

"It's hard to leave off thinking about it, Allan. But I will try."

"That's a good fellow! Now give me that trumpery bit of paper, and let's tear it up, and have done with it."

He tried to snatch the manuscript out of his friend's hand; but Midwinter was too quick for him, and kept it beyond his reach.

"Come! come!" pleaded Allan. "I've set my heart on lighting my cigar with it."

Midwinter hesitated painfully. It was hard to resist Allan; but he did resist him. "I'll wait a little," he said, "before you light your cigar with it."

"How long? Till to-morrow?"

"Longer."

"Till we leave the Isle of Man?"

"Longer."

"Hang it—give me a plain answer to a plain question! How long *will* you wait?"

Midwinter carefully restored the paper to its place in his pocket-book.

"I'll wait," he said, "till we get to Thorpe Ambrose."

### THE END OF THE FIRST BOOK.

---

## BOOK THE SECOND

---

## CHAPTER I.

### LURKING MISCHIEF.

1. *From Ozias Midwinter to Mr. Brock.*

"Thorpe Ambrose, June 15, 1851.

"DEAR MR. BROCK—Only an hour since we reached this house, just as the servants were locking up for the night. Allan has gone to bed, worn out by our long day's journey, and has left me in the room they call the library, to tell you the story of our journey to Norfolk. Being better seasoned than he is to fatigues of all kinds, my eyes are quite wakeful enough for writing a letter, though the clock on the chimney-piece points to midnight, and we have been traveling since ten in the morning.

"The last news you had of us was news sent by Allan from the Isle of Man. If I am not mistaken, he wrote to tell you of the night we passed on board the wrecked ship. Forgive me, dear Mr. Brock, if I say nothing on that subject until time has helped me to think of it with a quieter mind. The hard fight against myself must all be fought over again; but I will win it yet, please God; I will, indeed.

"There is no need to trouble you with any account of our journeyings about the northern and western districts of the island, or of the short cruises we took when the repairs of the yacht were at last complete. It will be better if I get on at once to the morning of yesterday, the fourteenth. We had come in with the night-tide to Douglas Harbor, and, as soon as the post-office was open, Allan, by my advice, sent on shore for letters. The messenger returned with one letter only, and the writer of it proved to be the former mistress of Thorpe Ambrose—Mrs. Blanchard.

"You ought to be informed, I think, of the contents of this letter, for it has seriously influenced Allan's plans. He loses everything, sooner or later, as you know, and he has lost the letter already. So I must give you the substance of what Mrs. Blanchard wrote to him, as plainly as I can.

"The first page announced the departure of the ladies from Thorpe Ambrose. They left on the day before yesterday, the thirteenth, having, after much hesitation, finally decided on going abroad, to visit some old friends settled in Italy, in the neighborhood of Florence. It appears to be quite possible that Mrs. Blanchard and her niece may settle there, too, if they can find a suitable house and grounds to let. They both like the Italian country and the Italian people, and they are well enough off to please themselves. The elder lady has her jointure, and the younger is in possession of all her father's fortune.

"The next page of the letter was, in Allan's opinion, far from a pleasant page to read.

"After referring, in the most grateful terms, to the kindness which had left her niece and herself free to leave their old home at their own time, Mrs. Blanchard added that Allan's considerate conduct had produced such a strongly favorable impression among the friends and dependents of the family that they were desirous of giving him a public reception on his arrival among them. A preliminary meeting of the tenants on the estate and the principal persons in the neighboring town had already been held to discuss the arrangements, and a letter might be expected shortly from the clergyman inquiring when it would suit Mr. Armadale's convenience to take possession personally and publicly of his estates in Norfolk.

"You will now be able to guess the cause of our sudden departure from the Isle of Man. The first and foremost idea in your old pupil's mind, as soon as he had read Mrs. Blanchard's account of the proceedings at the meeting, was the idea of escaping the public reception, and the one certain way he could see of avoiding it was to start for Thorpe Ambrose before the clergyman's letter could reach him.

"I tried hard to make him think a little before he acted on his first impulse in this matter; but he only went on packing his portmanteau in his own impenetrably good-humored way. In ten minutes his luggage was ready, and in five minutes more he had given the crew their directions for taking the yacht back to Somersetshire. The steamer to Liverpool was alongside of us in the harbor, and I had really no choice but to go on board with him or to let him go by himself. I spare you the account of our stormy voyage, of our detention at Liverpool, and of the trains we missed on our journey across the country. You know that we have got here safely, and that is enough. What the servants think of the new squire's sudden appearance among them, without a word of warning, is of no great consequence. What the committee for arranging the public reception may think of it when the news flies abroad to-morrow is, I am afraid, a more serious matter.

"Having already mentioned the servants, I may proceed to tell you that the latter part of Mrs. Blanchard's letter was entirely devoted to instructing Allan on the subject of the domestic establishment which she has left behind her. It seems that all the servants, indoors and out (with three exceptions), are waiting here, on the chance that Allan will continue them in their places. Two of these exceptions are readily accounted for: Mrs. Blanchard's maid and Miss Blanchard's maid go abroad with their mistresses. The third exceptional case is the case of the upper house-maid; and here there is a little hitch. In plain words, the house-maid has been sent away at a moment's notice, for what Mrs. Blanchard rather mysteriously describes as 'levity of conduct with a stranger.'

"I am afraid you will laugh at me, but I must confess the truth. I have been made so distrustful (after what happened to us in the Isle of Man) of even the most trifling misadventures which connect themselves in any way with Allan's introduction to his new life and prospects, that I have already questioned one of the men-servants here about this apparently unimportant matter of the house-maid's going away in disgrace.

"All I can learn is that a strange man had been noticed hanging suspiciously about the grounds; that the house-maid was so ugly a woman as to render it next to a certainty that he had some underhand purpose to serve in making himself agreeable to her; and that he has not as yet been seen again in the neighborhood since the day of her dismissal. So much for the one servant who has been turned out at Thorpe Ambrose. I can only hope there is no trouble for Allan brewing in that quarter. As for the other servants who remain, Mrs. Blanchard describes them, both men and women, as perfectly trustworthy, and they will all, no doubt, continue to occupy their present places.

"Having now done with Mrs. Blanchard's letter, my next duty is to beg you, in Allan's name and with Allan's love, to come here and stay with him at the earliest moment when you can leave Somersetshire. Although I cannot presume to think that my own wishes will have any special influence in determining you to accept this invitation, I must nevertheless acknowledge that I have a reason of my own for earnestly desiring to see you here. Allan has innocently caused me a new anxiety about my future relations with him, and I sorely need your advice to show me the right way of setting that anxiety at rest.

"The difficulty which now perplexes me relates to the steward's place at Thorpe Ambrose. Before to-day I only knew that Allan had hit on some plan of his own for dealing with this matter, rather strangely involving, among other results, the letting of the cottage which was the old steward's place of abode, in consequence of the new steward's contemplated residence in the great house. A chance word in our conversation on the journey here led Allan into speaking out more plainly than he had spoken yet, and I heard to my unutterable astonishment that the person who was at the bottom of the whole arrangement about the steward was no other than myself!

"It is needless to tell you how I felt this new instance of Allan's kindness. The first pleasure of hearing from his own lips that I had deserved the strongest proof he could give of his confidence in me was soon dashed by the pain which mixes itself with all pleasure—at least, with all that I have ever known. Never has my past life seemed so dreary to look back on as it seems now, when I feel how entirely it has unfitted me to take the place of all others that I should have liked to occupy in my friend's service. I mustered courage to tell him that I had none of the business knowledge and business experience which his steward ought to possess. He generously met the objection by telling me that I could learn; and he has promised to send to London for the person who has already been employed for the time being in the steward's office, and who will, therefore, be perfectly competent to teach me.

"Do you, too, think I can learn? If you do, I will work day and night to instruct myself. But if (as I am afraid) the steward's duties are of far too serious a kind to be learned off-hand by a man so young and so inexperienced as I am, then pray hasten your journey to Thorpe Ambrose, and exert your influence over Allan personally. Nothing less will induce him to pass me over, and to employ a steward who is really fit to take the place. Pray, pray act in this matter as you think best for Allan's interests. Whatever disappointment I may feel, *he* shall not see it.

"Believe me, dear Mr. Brock,
"Gratefuly yours,
"OZIAS MIDWINTER.

"P.S.—I open the envelope again to add one word more. If you have heard or seen anything since your return to Somersetshire of the woman in the black dress and the red shawl, I hope you will not forget, when you write, to let me know it.                                    O. M."

## 2. *From Mrs. Oldershaw to Miss Gwilt.*

"Ladies' Toilet Repository, Diana Street, Pimlico,
Wednesday.

"MY DEAR LYDIA—To save the post, I write to you, after a long day's worry at my place of business, on the business letter-paper, having news since we last met which it seems advisable to send you at the earliest opportunity.

"To begin at the beginning. After carefully considering the thing, I am quite sure you will do wisely with young Armadale if you hold your tongue about Madeira and all that happened there. Your position was, no doubt, a very strong one with his mother. You had privately helped her in playing a trick on her own father; you had been ungratefully dismissed, at a pitiably tender age, as soon as you had served her purpose; and, when you came upon her suddenly, after a separation of more than twenty years, you found her in failing health, with a grown-up son, whom she had kept in total ignorance of the true story of her marriage.

"Have you any such advantages as these with the young gentleman who has survived her? If he is not a born idiot he will decline to believe your shocking aspersions on the memory of his mother; and—seeing that you have no proofs at this distance of time to meet him with—there is an end of your money-grubbing in the golden Armadale diggings. Mind, I don't dispute that the old lady's heavy debt of obligation, after what you did for her in Madeira, is not paid yet; and that the son is the next person to settle with you, now the mother has slipped through your fingers. Only squeeze him the right way, my dear, that's what I venture to suggest — squeeze him the right way.

"And which is the right way? That question brings me to my news.

"Have you thought again of that other notion of yours of trying your hand on this lucky young gentleman, with nothing but your own good looks and your own quick wits to help you? The idea hung on my mind so strangely after you were gone that it ended in my sending a little note to my lawyer, to have the will under which young Armadale has got his fortune examined at Doctor's Commons. The result turns out to be something infinitely more encouraging than either you or I could possibly have hoped for. After the lawyer's report to me, there cannot be a moment's doubt of what you ought to do. In two words, Lydia, take the bull by the horns—and marry him!

"I am quite serious. He is much better worth the venture than you suppose. Only persuade him to make you Mrs. Armadale, and you may set all after-discoveries at flat defiance. As long

as he lives, you can make your own terms with
him; and, if he dies, the will entitles you, in
spite of anything he can say or do—with children or without them—to an income chargeable
on his estate of *twelve hundred a year for life*.
There is no doubt about this; the lawyer himself has looked at the will. Of course, Mr.
Blanchard had his son and his son's widow in
his eye when he made the provision. But, as
it is not limited to any one heir by name, and
not revoked anywhere, it now holds as good with
young Armadale as it would have held under
other circumstances with Mr. Blanchard's son.
What a chance for you, after all the miseries and
the dangers you have gone through, to be mistress of Thorpe Ambrose, if he lives; to have
an income for life, if he dies! Hook him, my
poor dear; hook him at any sacrifice.

"I dare say you will make the same objection
when you read this which you made when we
were talking about it the other day; I mean the
objection of your age.

"Now, my good creature, just listen to me.
The question is—not whether you were five-and-
thirty last birthday; we will own the dreadful
truth, and say you were—but whether you do
look, or don't look, your real age. My opinion
on this matter ought to be, and is, one of the
best opinions in London. I have had twenty
years' experience among our charming sex in
making up battered old faces and worn-out old
figures to look like new, and I say positively you
don't look a day over thirty, if as much. If you

will follow my advice about dressing, and use one or two of my applications privately, I guarantee to put you back three years more. I will forfeit all the money I shall have to advance for you in this matter, if, when I have ground you young again in my wonderful mill, you look more than seven-and-twenty in any man's eyes living—except, of course, when you wake anxious in the small hours of the morning; and then, my dear, you will be old and ugly in the retirement of your own room, and it won't matter.

" 'But,' you may say, 'supposing all this, here I am, even with your art to help me, looking a good six years older than he is; and that is against me at starting.' Is it? Just think again. Surely, your own experience must have shown you that the commonest of all common weaknesses, in young fellows of this Armadale's age, is to fall in love with women older than themselves. Who are the men who really appreciate us in the bloom of our youth (I'm sure I have cause to speak well of the bloom of youth; I made fifty guineas to-day by putting it on the spotted shoulders of a woman old enough to be your mother)—who are the men, I say, who are ready to worship us when we are mere babies of seventeen? The gay young gentlemen in the bloom of their own youth? No! The cunning old wretches who are on the wrong side of forty.

"And what is the moral of this, as the story-books say?

"The moral is that the chances, with such a head as you have got on your shoulders, are all in your favor. If you feel your present forlorn position, as I believe you do; if you know what a charming woman (in the men's eyes) you can still be when you please; and if all your old resolution has really come back, after that shocking outbreak of desperation on board the steamer (natural enough, I own, under the dreadful provocation laid on you), you will want no further persuasion from me to try this experiment. Only to think of how things turn out! If the other young booby had not jumped into the river after you, *this* young booby would never have had the estate. It really looks as if fate had determined that you were to be Mrs. Armadale, of Thorpe Ambrose; and who can control his fate, as the poet says?

"Send me one line to say Yes or No; and believe me your attached old friend,

"MARIA OLDERSHAW."

### 3. *From Miss Gwilt to Mrs. Oldershaw.*

"Richmond, Thursday.

'YOU OLD WRETCH—I won't say Yes or No till I have had a long, long look at my glass first. If you had any real regard for anybody but your wicked old self, you would know that the bare idea of marrying again (after what I have gone through) is an idea that makes my flesh creep.

"But there can be no harm in your sending me

a little more information while I am making up my mind. You have got twenty pounds of mine still left out of those things you sold for me; send ten pounds here for my expenses, in a post-office order, and use the other ten for making private inquiries at Thorpe Ambrose. I want to know when the two Blanchard women go away, and when young Armadale stirs up the dead ashes in the family fire-place. Are you quite sure he will turn out as easy to manage as you think? If he takes after his hypocrite of a mother, I can tell you this—Judas Iscariot has come to life again.

"I am very comfortable in this lodging. There are lovely flowers in the garden, and the birds wake me in the morning delightfully. I have hired a reasonably good piano. The only man I care two straws about—don't be alarmed; he was laid in his grave many a long year ago, under the name of BEETHOVEN—keeps me company, in my lonely hours. The landlady would keep me company, too, if I would only let her. I hate women. The new curate paid a visit to the other lodger yesterday, and passed me on the lawn as he came out. My eyes have lost nothing yet, at any rate, though I *am* five-and-thirty; the poor man actually blushed when I looked at him! What sort of color do you think he would have turned, if one of the little birds in the garden had whispered in his ear, and told him the true story of the charming Miss Gwilt?

"Good-by, Mother Oldershaw. I rather doubt

whether I am yours, or anybody's, affectionately; but we all tell lies at the bottoms of our letters, don't we? If you are my attached old friend, I must, of course, be yours affectionately.

"LYDIA GWILT.

"P.S.—Keep your odious powders and paints and washes for the spotted shoulders of your customers; not one of them shall touch my skin, I promise you. If you really want to be useful, try and find out some quieting draught to keep me from grinding my teeth in my sleep. I shall break them one of these nights; and then what will become of my beauty, I wonder?"

### 4. *From Mrs. Oldershaw to Miss Gwilt.*

"Ladies' Toilet Repository, Tuesday.

"MY DEAR LYDIA—It is a thousand pities your letter was not addressed to Mr. Armadale; your graceful audacity would have charmed him. It doesn't affect me; I am so well used to audacity in my way of life, you know. Why waste your sparkling wit, my love, on your own impenetrable Oldershaw? It only splutters and goes out. Will you try and be serious this next time? I have news for you from Thorpe Ambrose, which is beyond a joke, and which must not be trifled with.

"An hour after I got your letter I set the inquiries on foot. Not knowing what consequences they might lead to, I thought it safest to begin in the dark. Instead of employing any of the people whom I have at my own disposal (who know

you and know me), I went to the **Private Inquiry** Office in Shadyside Place, and put the
matter in the inspector's hands, in the character
of a perfect stranger, and without mentioning
you at all. This was not the ¦cheapest way of
going to work, I own; but it was the safest
way, which is of much greater consequence.

"The inspector and I understood each other in
ten minutes; and the right person for the purpose—the most harmless looking young man you
ever saw in your life—was produced immediately.
He left for Thorpe Ambrose an hour after I saw
him. I arranged to call at the office on the after-
noons of Saturday, Monday, and to-day for news.
There was no news till to-day; and there I found
our confidential agent just returned to town, and
waiting to favor me with a full account of his
trip to Norfolk.

"First of all, let me quiet your mind about
those two questions of yours; I have got answers to both the one and the other. The Blanchard women go away to foreign parts on the thirteenth, and young Armadale is at this moment
cruising somewhere at sea in his yacht. There
is talk at Thorpe Ambrose of giving him a public
reception, and of calling a meeting of the local
grandees to settle it all. The speechifying and
fuss on these occasions generally wastes plenty
of time, and the public reception is not thought
likely to meet the new squire much before the
end of the month.

"If our messenger had done no more for us
than this, I think he would have earned his

money. But the harmless young man is a regular Jesuit at a private inquiry, with this great advantage over all the Popish priests I have ever seen, that he has not got his slyness written in his face.

"Having to get his information through the female servants in the usual way, he addressed himself, with admirable discretion, to the ugliest woman in the house. 'When they are nice-looking, and can pick and choose,' as he neatly expressed it to me, 'they waste a great deal of valuable time in deciding on a sweetheart. When they are ugly, and haven't got the ghost of a chance of choosing, they snap at a sweetheart, if he comes their way, li $\pm$ e a starved dog at a bone.' Acting on these excellent principles, our confidential agent succeeded, after certain unavoidable delays, in addressing himself to the upper housemaid at Thorpe Ambrose, and took full possession of her confidence at the first interview. Bearing his instructions carefully in mind, he encouraged the woman to chatter, and was favored, of course, with all the gossip of the servants' hall. The greater part of it (as repeated to me) was of no earthly importance. But I listened patiently, and was rewarded by a valuable discovery at last. Here it is.

"It seems there is an ornamental cottage in the grounds at Thorpe Ambrose. For some reason unknown, young Armadale has chosen to let it, and a tenant has come in already. He is a poor half-pay major in the army, named Milroy, a meek sort of man, by all accounts, with a turn for occupying himself in mechanical pursuits, and with a domestic incumbrance in the shape of a bedridden wife, who has not been seen by anybody. Well, and what of all this? you will ask, with that sparkling impatience which becomes you so well. My dear Lydia, don't sparkle! The man's family affairs seriously concern us both, for, as ill luck will have it, the man has got a daughter!

"You may imagine how I questioned our agent, and how our agent ransacked his memory, when I stumbled, in due course, on such a discovery as this. If Heaven is responsible for women's chattering tongues, Heaven be praised! From Miss Blanchard to Miss Blanchard's maid; from Miss Blanchard's maid to Miss Blanchard's aunt's maid; from Miss Blanchard's aunt's maid, to the ugly housemaid; from the ugly housemaid to the harmless-looking young man—so the stream of gossip trickled into the right reservoir at last, and thirsty Mother Oldershaw has drunk it all up.

"In plain English, my dear, this is how it stands. The major's daughter is a minx just turned sixteen; lively and nice-looking (hateful little wretch!), dowdy in her dress (thank Heaven!) and deficient in her manners (thank Heaven again!). She has been brought up at home. The governess who last had charge of her left before her father moved to Thorpe Ambrose. Her education stands wofully in want of a finishing touch, and the major doesn't quite know what to do next. None of his friends can recommend him a new governess, and he doesn't like the notion of sending the girl to school. So matters rest at present, on the major's own showing; for so the major expressed himself at a morning call which the father and daughter paid to the ladies at the great house.

"You have now got my promised news, and you will have little difficulty, I think, in agreeing with me that the Armadale business must be settled at once, one way or the other. If, with your hopeless prospects, and with what I may call your family claim on this young fellow, you decide on giving him up, I shall have the pleasure of sending you the balance of your account with me (seven-and-twenty shillings), and shall then be free to devote myself entirely to my own proper business. If, on the contrary, you decide to try your luck at Thorpe Ambrose, then (there being no kind of doubt that the major's minx will set her cap at the young squire) I should be glad to hear how you mean to meet the double difficulty of inflaming Mr. Armadale and extinguishing Miss Milroy.

"Affectionately yours,
"MARIA OLDERSHAW."

5. *From Miss Gwilt to Mrs. Oldershaw.*
(*First Answer.*)

"Richmond, Wednesday Morning.

"MRS. OLDERSHAW—Send me my seven-and-twenty shillings, and devote yourself to your own proper business. Yours, L. G."

### 6. *From Miss Gwilt to Mrs. Oldershaw.*
### (*Second Answer.*)

"Richmond, Wednesday Night.

"DEAR OLD LOVE — Keep the seven-and-twenty shillings, and burn my other letter. I have changed my mind.

"I wrote the first time after a horrible night. I write this time after a ride on horseback, a tumbler of claret, and the breast of a chicken. Is that explanation enough? Please say Yes, for I want to go back to my piano.

"No; I can't go back yet; I must answer your question first. But are you really so very simple as to suppose that I don't see straight through you and your letter? You know that the major's difficulty is our opportunity as well as I do; but you want me to take the responsibility of making the first proposal, don't you? Suppose I take it in your own roundabout way? Suppose I say, 'Pray don't ask me how I propose inflaming Mr. Armadale and extinguishing Miss Milroy; the question is so shockingly abrupt I really can't answer it. Ask me, instead, if it is the modest ambition of my life to become Miss Milroy's governess?' Yes, if you please, Mrs. Oldershaw, and if you will assist me by becoming my reference.

"There it is for you! If some serious disaster happens (which is quite possible), what a comfort it will be to remember that it was all my fault!

"Now I have done this for you, will you do

something for me. I want to dream away the little time I am likely to have left here in my own way. Be a merciful Mother Oldershaw, and spare me the worry of looking at the Ins and Outs, and adding up the chances For and Against, in this new venture of mine. Think for me, in short, until I am obliged to think for myself.

"I had better not write any more, or I shall say something savage that you won't like. I am in one of my tempers to-night. I want a husband to vex, or a child to beat, or something of that sort. Do you ever like to see the summer insects kill themselves in the candle? I do, sometimes. Good-night, Mrs. Jezebel. The longer you can leave me here the better. The air agrees with me, and I am looking charmingly.

"L. G."

### 7. *From Mrs. Oldershaw to Miss Gwilt.*

"Thursday.

"MY DEAR LYDIA— Some persons in my situation might be a little offended at the tone of your last letter. But I am so fondly attached to you! And when I love a person, it is so very hard, my dear, for that person to offend me! Don't ride quite so far, and only drink half a tumblerful of claret next time. I say no more.

"Shall we leave off our fencing - match and come to serious matters now? How curiously hard it always seems to be for women to understand each other, especially when they have got their pens in their hands! But suppose we try.

"Well, then, to begin with: I gather from your letter that you have wisely decided to try the Thorpe Ambrose experiment, and to secure, if you can, an excellent position at starting by becoming a member of Major Milroy's household. If the circumstances turn against you, and some other woman gets the governess's place (about which I shall have something more to say presently), you will then have no choice but to make Mr. Armadale's acquaintance in some other character. In any case, you will want my assistance; and the first question, therefore, to set at rest between us is the question of what I am willing to do, and what I can do, to help you.

"A woman, my dear Lydia, with your appearance, your manners, your abilities, and your education, can make almost any excursions into society that she pleases if she only has money in her pocket and a respectable reference to appeal to in cases of emergency. As to the money, in the first place. I will engage to find it, on condition of your remembering my assistance with adequate pecuniary gratitude if you win the Armadale prize. Your promise so to remember me, embodying the terms in plain figures, shall be drawn out on paper by my own lawyer, so that we can sign and settle at once when I see you in London.

"Next, as to the reference.

"Here, again, my services are at your disposal, on another condition. It is this: that you present yourself at Thorpe Ambrose, under the name to which you have returned ever since that dreadful business of your marriage; I mean your own maiden name of Gwilt. I have only one motive in insisting on this; I wish to run no needless risks. My experience, as confidential adviser of my customers, in various romantic cases of private embarrassment, has shown me that an assumed name is, nine times out of ten, a very unnecessary and a very dangerous form of deception. Nothing could justify your assuming a name but the fear of young Armadale's detecting you—a fear from which we are fortunately relieved by his mother's own conduct in keeping your early connection with her a profound secret from her son and from everybody.

"The next, and last, perplexity to settle relates, my dear, to the chances for and against your finding your way, in the capacity of governess, into Major Milroy's house. Once inside the door, with your knowledge of music and languages, if you can keep your temper, you may be sure of keeping the place. The only doubt, as things are now, is whether you can get it.

"In the major's present difficulty about his daughter's education, the chances are, I think, in favor of his advertising for a governess. Say he does advertise, what address will he give for applicants to write to?

"If he gives an address in London, good-by to all chances in your favor at once; for this plain reason, that we shall not be able to pick out his advertisement from the advertisements of other people who want governesses, and who will give them addresses in London as well. If, on the other hand, our luck helps us, and he refers his correspondents to a shop, post-office, or what not *at Thorpe Ambrose*, there we have our advertiser as plainly picked out for us as we can wish. In this last case, I have little or no doubt—with me for your reference—of your finding your way into the major's family circle. We have one great advantage over the other women who will answer the advertisement. Thanks to my inquiries on the spot, I know Major Milroy to be a poor man; and we will fix the salary you ask at a figure that is sure to tempt him. As for the style of the letter, if you and I together can't write a modest and interesting application for the vacant place, I should like to know who can?

"All this, however, is still in the future. For the present my advice is, stay where you are, and dream to your heart's content, till you hear from me again. I take in *The Times* regularly, and you may trust my wary eye not to miss the right advertisement. We can luckily give the major time, without doing any injury to our own interests; for there is no fear just yet of the girl's getting the start of you. The public reception, as we know, won't be ready till near the end of the month; and we may safely trust young Armadale's vanity to keep him out of his new house until his flatterers are all assembled to welcome him.

"It's odd, isn't it, to think how much depends on this half-pay officer's decision? For my part, I shall wake every morning now with the same question in my mind: If the major's advertise-

ment appears, which will the major say—Thorpe
Ambrose, or London?

"Ever, my dear Lydia, affectionately yours,
                          "MARIA OLDERSHAW."

## CHAPTER II.

### ALLAN AS A LANDED GENTLEMAN.

EARLY on the morning after his first night's
rest at Thorpe Ambrose, Allan rose and surveyed
the prospect from his bedroom window, lost in
the dense mental bewilderment of feeling himself
to be a stranger in his own house.

The bedroom looked out over the great front
door, with its portico, its terrace and flight of
steps beyond, and, further still, the broad sweep
of the well-timbered park to close the view. The
morning mist nestled lightly about the distant
trees; and the cows were feeding sociably, close
to the iron fence which railed off the park from
the drive in front of the house. "All mine!"
thought Allan, staring in blank amazement at
the prospect of his own possessions. "Hang me
if I can beat it into my head yet. All mine!"

He dressed, left his room, and walked along
the corridor which led to the staircase and hall,
opening the doors in succession as he passed them.

The rooms in this part of the house were bedrooms and dressing-rooms, light, spacious, perfectly furnished; and all empty, except the one
bed-chamber next to Allan's, which had been ap-

propriated to Midwinter. He was still sleeping when his friend looked in on him, having sat late into the night writing his letter to Mr. Brock. Allan went on to the end of the first corridor, turned at right angles into a second, and, that passed, gained the head of the great staircase. "No romance here," he said to himself, looking down the handsomely carpeted stone stairs into the bright modern hall. "Nothing to startle Midwinter's fidgety nerves in this house." There was nothing, indeed; Allan's essentially superficial observation had not misled him for once. The mansion of Thorpe Ambrose (built after the pulling down of the dilapidated old manor-house) was barely fifty years old. Nothing picturesque, nothing in the slightest degree suggestive of mystery and romance, appeared in any part of it. It was a purely conventional country house—the product of the classical idea filtered judiciously through the commercial English mind. Viewed on the outer side, it presented the spectacle of a modern manufactory trying to look like an ancient temple. Viewed on the inner side, it was a marvel of luxurious comfort in every part of it, from basement to roof. "And quite right, too," thought Allan, sauntering contentedly down the broad, gently graduated stairs. "Deuce take all mystery and romance! Let's be clean and comfortable, that's what I say."

Arrived in the hall, the new master of Thorpe Ambrose hesitated, and looked about him, uncertain which way to turn next.

The four reception-rooms on the ground-floor opened into the hall, two on either side. Allan tried the nearest door on his right hand at a venture, and found himself in the drawing-room. Here the first sign of life appeared, under life's most attractive form. A young girl was in solitary possession of the drawing-room. The duster in her hand appeared to associate her with the domestic duties of the house; but at that particular moment she was occupied in asserting the rights of nature over the obligations of service. In other words, she was attentively contemplating her own face in the glass over the mantelpiece.

"There! there! don't let me frighten you," said Allan, as the girl started away from the glass, and stared at him in unutterable confusion. "I quite agree with you, my dear; your face is well worth looking at. Who are you? Oh, the house-maid. And what's your name? Susan, eh? Come! I like your name, to begin with. Do you know who I am, Susan? I'm your master, though you may not think it. Your character? Oh, yes! Mrs. Blanchard gave you a capital character. You shall stop here; don't be afraid. And you'll be a good girl, Susan, and wear smart little caps and aprons and bright ribbons, and you'll look nice and pretty, and dust the furniture, won't you?"

With this summary of a house-maid's duties, Allan sauntered back into the hall, and found more signs of life in that quarter. A man-servant appeared on this occasion, and bowed, as be-

came a vassal in a linen jacket, before his liege
lord in a wide-awake hat.

"And who may you be?" asked Allan. "Not
the man who let us in last night? Ah, I thought
not. The second footman, eh? Character? Oh,
yes; capital character. Stop here, of course. You
can valet me, can you? Bother valeting me! I
like to put on my own clothes, and brush them,
too, when they *are* on; and, if I only knew how
to black my own boots, by George, I should like
to do it! What room's this? Morning-room,
eh? And here's the dining - room, of course.
Good heavens, what a table! it's as long as
my yacht, and longer. I say, by-the-by, what's
your name? Richard, is it? Well, Richard, the
vessel I sail in is a vessel of my own building?
What do you think of that? You look to me
just the right sort of man to be my steward on
board. If you're not sick at sea—oh, you *are*
sick at sea? Well, then, we'll say nothing more
about it. And what room is this? Ah, yes;
the library, of course—more in Mr. Midwinter's
way than mine. Mr. Midwinter is the gentleman who came here with me last night; and
mind this, Richard, you're all to show him as
much attention as you show me. Where are we
now? What's this door at the back? Billiard-
room and smoking-room, eh? Jolly. Another
door! and more stairs! Where do they go to?
and who's this coming up? Take your time,
ma'am; you're not quite so young as you were
once—take your time."

The object of Allan's humane caution was a

corpulent elderly woman of the type called "motherly." Fourteen stairs were all that separated her from the master of the house; she ascended them with fourteen stoppages and fourteen sighs. Nature, various in all things, is infinitely various in the female sex. There are some women whose personal qualities reveal the Loves and the Graces; and there are other women whose personal qualities suggest the Perquisites and the Grease Pot. This was one of the other women.

"Glad to see you looking so well, ma'am," said Allan, when the cook, in the majesty of her office, stood proclaimed before him. "Your name is Gripper, is it? I consider you, Mrs. Gripper, the most valuable person in the house. For this reason, that nobody in the house eats a heartier dinner every day than I do. Directions? Oh, no; I've no directions to give. I leave all that to you. Lots of strong soup, and joints done with the gravy in them—there's my notion of good feeding, in two words. Steady! Here's somebody else. Oh, to be sure — the butler! Another valuable person. We'll go right through all the wine in the cellar, Mr. Butler; and if I can't give you a sound opinion after that, we'll persevere boldly, and go right through it again. Talking of wine — halloo! here are more of them coming up stairs. There! there! don't trouble yourselves. You've all got capital characters, and you shall all stop here along with me. What was I saying just now? Something about wine; so it was. I'll tell you

what, Mr. Butler, it isn't every day that a new
master comes to Thorpe Ambrose; and it's my
wish that we should all start together on the
best possible terms.   Let the servants have a
grand jollification downstairs to celebrate my
arrival, and give them what they like to drink
my health in.   It's a poor heart, Mrs. Gripper,
that never rejoices, isn't it?   No; I won't look
at the cellar now: I want to go out, and get a
breath of fresh air before breakfast.   Where's
Richard?   I say, have I got a garden here?
Which side of the house is it!   That side, eh?
You needn't show me round.   I'll go alone,
Richard, and lose myself, if I can, in my own
property.''

With those words Allan descended the terrace
steps in front of the house, whistling cheerfully.
He had met the serious responsibility of settling
his domestic establishment to his own entire
satisfaction.   ''People talk of the difficulty of
managing their servants,'' thought Allan.
''What on earth do they mean?   I don't see
any difficulty at all.''   He opened an ornamental gate leading out of the drive at the side of the
house, and, following the footman's directions,
entered the shrubbery that sheltered the Thorpe
Ambrose gardens.   ''Nice shady sort of place
for a cigar,'' said Allan, as he sauntered along,
with his hands in his pockets.   ''I wish I could
beat it into my head that it really belongs to *me*.''

The shrubbery opened on the broad expanse of
a flower garden, flooded bright in its summer
glory by the light of the morning sun.

On one side, an archway, broken through a wall, led into the fruit garden. On the other, a terrace of turf led to ground on a lower level, laid out as an Italian garden. Wandering past the fountains and statues, Allan reached another shrubbery, winding its way apparently to some remote part of the grounds. Thus far, not a human creature had been visible or audible anywhere; but, as he approached the end of the second shrubbery, it struck him that he heard something on the other side of the foliage. He stopped and listened. There were two voices speaking distinctly—an old voice that sounded very obstinate, and a young voice that sounded very angry.

"It's no use, miss," said the old voice. "I mustn't allow it, and I won't allow it. What would Mr. Armadale say?"

"If Mr. Armadale is the gentleman I take him for, you old brute!" replied the young voice, "he would say, 'Come into my garden, Miss Milroy, as often as you like, and take as many nosegays as you please.'"

Allan's bright blue eyes twinkled mischievously. Inspired by a sudden idea, he stole softly to the end of the shrubbery, darted round the corner of it, and, vaulting over a low ring fence, found himself in a trim little paddock, crossed by a gravel walk. At a short distance down the walk stood a young lady, with her back toward him, trying to force her way past an impenetrable old man, with a rake in his hand, who stood obstinately in front of her, shaking his head.

"COME INTO MY GARDEN, MISS MILROY, AS OFTEN AS YOU LIKE."
—Armadale, Vol. Eight, page 287.

"Come into my garden, Miss Milroy, as often as you like, and take as many nosegays as you please," cried Allan, remorselessly repeating her own words.

The young lady turned round, with a scream; her muslin dress, which she was holding up in front, dropped from her hand, and a prodigious lapful of flowers rolled out on the gravel walk.

Before another word could be said, the impenetrable old man stepped forward, with the utmost composure, and entered on the question of his own personal interests, as if nothing whatever had happened, and nobody was present but his new master and himself.

"I bid you humbly welcome to Thorpe Ambrose, sir," said this ancient of the gardens. "My name is Abraham Sage. I've been employed in the grounds for more than forty years; and I hope you'll be pleased to continue me in my place."

So, with vision inexorably limited to the horizon of his own prospects, spoke the gardener, and spoke in vain. Allan was down on his knees on the gravel walk, collecting the fallen flowers, and forming his first impressions of Miss Milroy from the feet upward.

She was pretty; she was not pretty; she charmed, she disappointed, she charmed again. Tried by recognized line and rule, she was too short and too well developed for her age. And yet few men's eyes would have wished her figure other than it was. Her hands were so prettily plump and dimpled that it was hard to see how

red they were with the blessed exuberance of
youth and health. Her feet apologized gracefully for her old and ill fitting shoes; and her
shoulders made ample amends for the misde-
meanor in muslin which covered them in the
shape of a dress. Her dark-gray eyes were lovely
in their clear softness of color, in their spirit,
tenderness, and sweet good humor of expression;
and her hair (where a shabby old garden hat allowed it to be seen) was of just that lighter shade
of brown which gave value by contrast to the
darker beauty of her eyes. But these attractions
passed, the little attendant blemishes and imper-
fections of this self-contradictory girl began
again. Her nose was too short, her mouth was
too large, her face was too round and too rosy.
The dreadful justice of photography would have
had no mercy on her; and the sculptors of classical Greece would have bowed her regretfully out
of their studios. Admitting all this, and more,
the girdle round Miss Milroy's waist was the
girdle of Venus nevertheless; and the passkey
that opens the general heart was the key she carried, if ever a girl possessed it yet. Before Allan
had picked up his second handful of flowers,
Allan was in love with her.

"Don't! pray don't, Mr. Armadale!" she
said, receiving the flowers under protest, as
Allan vigorously showered them back into the
lap of her dress. "I am so ashamed! I didn't
mean to invite myself in that bold way into your
garden; my tongue ran away with me—it did,
indeed! What can I say to excuse myself?

Oh, Mr. Armadale, what must you think of me!''

Allan suddenly saw his way to a compliment, and tossed it up to her forthwith, with the third handful of flowers.

"I'll tell you what I think, Miss Milroy," he said, in his blunt, boyish way. "I think the luckiest walk I ever took in my life was the walk this morning that brought me here."

He looked eager and handsome. He was not addressing a woman worn out with admiration, but a girl just beginning a woman's life; and it did him no harm, at any rate, to speak in the character of master of Thorpe Ambrose. The penitential expression on Miss Milroy's face gently melted away; she looked down, demure and smiling, at the flowers in her lap.

"I deserve a good scolding," she said. "I don't deserve compliments, Mr. Armadale—least of all from *you*."

"Oh, yes, you do!" cried the headlong Allan, getting briskly on his legs. "Besides, it isn't a compliment; it's true. You are the prettiest— I beg your pardon, Miss Milroy! *my* tongue ran away with me that time."

Among the heavy burdens that are laid on female human nature, perhaps the heaviest, at the age of sixteen, is the burden of gravity. Miss Milroy struggled, tittered, struggled again, and composed herself for the time being.

The gardener, who still stood where he had stood from the first, immovably waiting for his next opportunity, saw it now, and gently pushed

his personal interests into the first gap of silence
that had opened within his reach since Allan's
appearance on the scene.

"I humbly bid you welcome to Thorpe Ambrose, sir," said Abraham Sage, beginning obstinately with his little introductory speech for
the second time. "My name—"

Before he could deliver himself of his name,
Miss Milroy looked accidentally in the horticul-
turist's pertinacious face, and instantly lost her
hold on her gravity beyond recall. Allan, never
backward in following a boisterous example of
any sort, joined in her laughter with right good-
will. The wise man of the gardens showed no
surprise, and took no offense. He waited for
another gap of silence, and walked in again
gently with his personal interests the moment
the two young people stopped to take breath.

"I have been employed in the grounds," proceeded Abraham Sage, irrepressibly, "for more
than forty years—"

"You shall be employed in the grounds for
forty more, if you'll only hold your tongue and
take yourself off!" cried Allan, as soon as he
could speak.

"Thank you kindly, sir," said the gardener,
with the utmost politeness, but with no present
signs either of holding his tongue or of taking
himself off.

"Well?" said Allan.

Abraham Sage carefully cleared his throat,
and shifted his rake from one hand to the other.
He looked down the length of his own invaluable

implement, with a grave interest and attention, seeing, apparently, not the long handle of a rake, but the long perspective of a vista, with a supplementary personal interest established at the end of it. "When more convenient, sir," resumed this immovable man, "I should wish respectfully to speak to you about my son. Perhaps it may be more convenient in the course of the day? My humble duty, sir, and my best thanks. My son is strictly sober. He is accustomed to the stables, and he belongs to the Church of England—without incumbrances." Having thus planted his offspring provisionally in his master's estimation, Abraham Sage shouldered his invaluable rake, and hobbled slowly out of view.

"If that's a specimen of a trustworthy old servant," said Allan, "I think I'd rather take my chance of being cheated by a new one. You shall not be troubled with him again, Miss Milroy, at any rate. All the flower-beds in the garden are at your disposal, and all the fruit in the fruit season, if you'll only come here and eat it."

"Oh, Mr. Armadale, how very, very kind you are. How can I thank you?"

Allan saw his way to another compliment—an elaborate compliment, in the shape of a trap, this time.

"You can do me the greatest possible favor," he said. "You can assist me in forming an agreeable impression of my own grounds."

"Dear me! how?" asked Miss Milroy, innocently.

Allan judiciously closed the trap on the spot
in these words: "By taking me with you, Miss
Milroy, on your morning walk." He spoke,
smiled, and offered his arm.

She saw the way, on her side, to a little flirtation. She rested her hand on his arm, blushed,
hesitated, and suddenly took it away again.

"I don't think it's quite right, Mr. Armadale," she said, devoting herself with the
deepest attention to her collection of flowers.
"Oughtn't we to have some old lady here?
Isn't it improper to take your arm until I
know you a little better than I do now? I
am obliged to ask; I have had so little instruction; I have seen so little of society, and one of
papa's friends once said my manners were too
bold for my age. What do *you* think?"

"I think it's a very good thing your papa's
friend is not here now," answered the outspoken
Allan; "I should quarrel with him to a dead
certainty. As for society, Miss Milroy, nobody
knows less about it than I do; but if we *had*
an old lady here, I must say myself I think she
would be uncommonly in the way. Won't you?"
concluded Allan, imploringly offering his arm
for the second time. "Do!"

Miss Milroy looked up at him sidelong from her
flowers. "You are as bad as the gardener, Mr.
Armadale!" She looked down again in a flutter
of indecision. "I'm sure it's wrong," she said,
and took his arm the instant afterward without
the slightest hesitation.

They moved away together over the daisied

turf of the paddock, young and bright and happy, with the sunlight of the summer morning shining cloudless over their flowery path.

"And where are we going to, now?" asked Allan. "Into another garden?"

She laughed gayly. "How very odd of you, Mr. Armadale, not to know, when it all belongs to you! Are you really seeing Thorpe Ambrose this morning for the first time? How indescribably strange it must feel! No, no; don't say any more complimentary things to me just yet. You may turn my head if you do. We haven't got the old lady with us; and I really must take care of myself. Let me be useful; let me tell you all about your own grounds. We are going out at that little gate, across one of the drives in the park, and then over the rustic bridge, and then round the corner of the plantation—where do you think? To where I live, Mr. Armadale; to the lovely little cottage that you have let to papa. Oh, if you only knew how lucky we thought ourselves to get it!"

She paused, looked up at her companion, and stopped another compliment on the incorrigible Allan's lips.

"I'll drop your arm," she said, coquettishly, "if you do! We *were* lucky to get the cottage, Mr. Armadale. Papa said he felt under an obligation to you for letting it, the day we got in. And *I* said I felt under an obligation, no longer ago than last week."

"You, Miss Milroy!" exclaimed Allan.

"Yes. It may surprise you to hear it; but

if you hadn't let the cottage to papa, I believe
I should have suffered the indignity and misery
of being sent to school."

Allan's memory reverted to the half-crown
that he had spun on the cabin-table of the
yacht, at Castletown. "If she only knew that
I had tossed up for it!" he thought, guiltily.

"I dare say you don't understand why I should
feel such a horror of going to school," pursued
Miss Milroy, misinterpreting the momentary
silence on her companion's side. "If I had
gone to school in early life—I mean at the age
when other girls go—I shouldn't have minded it
now. But I had no such chance at the time. It
was the time of mamma's illness and of papa's
unfortunate speculation; and as papa had nobody
to comfort him but me, of course I stayed at
home. You needn't laugh; I was of some use,
I can tell you. I helped papa over his trouble,
by sitting on his knee after dinner, and asking
him to tell me stories of all the remarkable people
he had known when he was about in the great
world, at home and abroad. Without me to
amuse him in the evening, and his clock to
occupy him in the daytime—"

"His clock?" repeated Allan.

"Oh, yes! I ought to have told you. Papa is
an extraordinary mechanical genius. You will
say so, too, when you see his clock. It's nothing like so large, of course, but it's on the model
of the famous clock at Strasbourg. Only think,
he began it when I was eight years old; and
(though I was sixteen last birthday) it isn't

finished yet! Some of our friends were quite
surprised he should take to such a thing when
his troubles began. But papa himself set that
right in no time; he reminded them that Louis
the Sixteenth took to lock‑making when *his*
troubles began, and then everybody was per‑
fectly satisfied.'' She stopped, and changed
color confusedly. "Oh, Mr. Armadale,'' she
said, in genuine embarrassment this time, "here
is my unlucky tongue running away with me
again! I am talking to you already as if I had
known you for years! This is what papa's friend
meant when he said my manners were too bold.
It's quite true; I have a dreadful way of getting
familiar with people, if—'' She checked her‑
self suddenly, on the brink of ending the sen‑
tence by saying, "if I like them.''

"No, no; do go on!'' pleaded Allan. "It's a
fault of mine to be familiar, too. Besides, we
*must* be familiar; we are such near neighbors.
I'm rather an uncultivated sort of fellow, and I
don't know quite how to say it; but I want your
cottage to be jolly and friendly with my house,
and my house to be jolly and friendly with your
cottage. There's my meaning, all in the wrong
words. Do go on, Miss Milroy; pray go on!''

She smiled and hesitated. "I don't exactly
remember where I was,'' she replied, "I only re‑
member I had something I wanted to tell you.
This comes, Mr. Armadale, of my taking your
arm. I should get on so much better, if you
would only consent to walk separately. You
won't? Well, then, will you tell me what it

was I wanted to say? Where was I before I went wandering off to papa's troubles and papa's clock?''

"At school!" replied Allan, with a prodigious effort of memory.

"*Not* at school, you mean," said Miss Milroy; "and all through *you*. Now I can go on again, which is a great comfort. I am quite serious, Mr. Armadale, in saying that I should have been sent to school, if you had said No when papa proposed for the cottage. This is how it happened. When we began moving in, Mrs. Blanchard sent us a most kind message from the great house to say that her servants were at our disposal, if we wanted any assistance. The least papa and I could do, after that, was to call and thank her. We saw Mrs. Blanchard and Miss Blanchard. Mistress was charming, and miss looked perfectly lovely in her mourning. I'm sure you admire her? She's tall and pale and graceful—quite your idea of beauty, I should think?''

"Nothing like it," began Allan. "My idea of beauty at the present moment—''

Miss Milroy felt it coming, and instantly took her hand off his arm.

"I mean I have never seen either Mrs. Blanchard or her niece," added Allan, precipitately, correcting himself.

Miss Milroy tempered justice with mercy, and put her hand back again.

"How extraordinary that you should never have seen them!" she went on. "Why, you

are a perfect stranger to everything and everybody at Thorpe Ambrose! Well, after Miss
Blanchard and I had sat and talked a little
while, I heard my name on Mrs. Blanchard's
lips, and instantly held my breath. She was
asking papa if I had finished my education.
Out came papa's great grievance directly. My
old governess, you must know, left us to be married just before we came here, and none of our
friends could produce a new one whose terms
were reasonable. 'I'm told, Mrs. Blanchard, by
people who understand it better than I do,' says
papa, 'that advertising is a risk. It all falls on
me, in Mrs. Milroy's state of health, and I suppose I must end in sending my little girl to
school. Do you happen to know of a school
within the means of a poor man?' Mrs. Blanchard shook her head; I could have kissed her on
the spot for doing it. 'All my experience, Major
Milroy,' says this perfect angel of a woman, 'is
in favor of advertising. My niece's governess
was originally obtained by an advertisement,
and you may imagine her value to us when I
tell you she lived in our family for more than
ten years.' I could have gone down on both
my knees and worshiped Mrs. Blanchard then
and there; and I only wonder I didn't! Papa
was struck at the time—I could see that—and he
referred to it again on the way home. 'Though
I have been long out of the world, my dear,' says
papa, 'I know a highly-bred woman and a sensible woman when I see her. Mrs. Blanchard's
experience puts advertising in a new light; I

must think about it.' He *has* thought about it, and (though he hasn't openly confessed it to me) I know that he decided to advertise, no later than last night. So, if papa thanks you for letting the cottage, Mr. Armadale, I thank you, too. But for you, we should never have known darling Mrs. Blanchard; and but for darling Mrs. Blanchard, I should have been sent to school."

Before Allan could reply, they turned the corner of the plantation, and came in sight of the cottage. Description of it is needless; the civilized universe knows it already. It was the typical cottage of the drawing-master's early lessons in neat shading and the broad pencil touch— with the trim thatch, the luxuriant creepers, the modest lattice - windows, the rustic porch, and the wicker bird-cage, all complete.

"Isn't it lovely?" said Miss Milroy. "Do come in!"

"May I?" asked Allan. "Won't the major think it too early?"

"Early or late, I am sure papa will be only too glad to see you."

She led the way briskly up the garden path, and opened the parlor door. As Allan followed her into the little room, he saw, at the further end of it, a gentleman sitting alone at an old-fashioned writing-table, with his back turned to his visitor.

"Papa! a surprise for you!" said Miss Milroy, rousing him from his occupation. "Mr. Armadale has come to Thorpe Ambrose; and I have brought him here to see you."

The major started; rose, bewildered for the moment; recovered himself immediately, and advanced to welcome his young landlord, with hospitable, outstretched hand.

A man with a larger experience of the world and a finer observation of humanity than Allan possessed would have seen the story of Major Milroy's life written in Major Milroy's face. The home troubles that had struck him were plainly betrayed in his stooping figure and his wan, deeply wrinkled cheeks, when he first showed himself on rising from his chair. The changeless influence of one monotonous pursuit and one monotonous habit of thought was next expressed in the dull, dreamy self-absorption of his manner and his look while his daughter was speaking to him. The moment after, when he had roused himself to welcome his guest, was the moment which made the self-revelation complete. Then there flickered in the major's weary eyes a faint reflection of the spirit of his happier youth. Then there passed over the major's dull and dreamy manner a change which told unmistakably of social graces and accomplishments, learned at some past time in no ignoble social school; a man who had long since taken his patient refuge from trouble in his own mechanical pursuit; a man only roused at intervals to know himself again for what he once had been. So revealed to all eyes that could read him aright, Major Milroy now stood before Allan, on the first morning of an acquaintance which **was** destined to be an event in Allan's life.

"I am heartily glad to see you, Mr. Armadale," he said, speaking in the changeless quiet,
subdued tone peculiar to most men whose occu-
pations are of the solitary and monotonous kind.
"You have done me one favor already by taking
me as your tenant, and you now do me another
by paying this friendly visit. If you have not
breakfasted already, let me waive all ceremony
on my side, and ask you to take your place at
our little table."

"With the greatest pleasure, Major Milroy, if
I am not in the way," replied Allan, delighted
at his reception. "I was sorry to hear from Miss
Milroy that Mrs. Milroy is an invalid. Perhaps
my being here unexpectedly; perhaps the sight
of a strange face—"

"I understand your hesitation, Mr. Armadale," said the major; "but it is quite unnecessary. Mrs. Milroy's illness keeps her entirely
confined to her own room.—Have we got everything we want on the table, my love?" he went
on, changing the subject so abruptly that a closer
observer than Allan might have suspected it was
distasteful to him. "Will you come and make
tea?"

Miss Milroy's attention appeared to be already
pre-engaged; she made no reply. While her
father and Allan had been exchanging civilities,
she had been putting the writing-table in order,
and examining the various objects scattered on
it with the unrestrained curiosity of a spoiled
child. The moment after the major had spoken
to her, she discovered a morsel of paper hidden

between the leaves of the blotting-book, snatched it up, looked at it, and turned round instantly, with an exclamation of surprise.

"Do my eyes deceive me, papa?" she asked. "Or were you really and truly writing *the* advertisement when I came in?"

"I had just finished it," replied her father. "But, my dear, Mr. Armadale is here—we are waiting for breakfast."

"Mr. Armadale knows all about it," rejoined Miss Milroy. "I told him in the garden."

"Oh, yes!" said Allan. "Pray, don't make a stranger of me, major! If it's about the governess, I've got something (in an indirect sort of way) to do with it too."

Major Milroy smiled. Before he could answer, his daughter, who had been reading the advertisement, appealed to him eagerly, for the second time.

"Oh, papa," she said, "there's one thing here I don't like at all! Why do you put grandmamma's initials at the end? Why do you tell them to write to grandmamma's house in London?"

"My dear! your mother can do nothing in this matter, as you know. And as for me (even if I went to London), questioning strange ladies about their characters and accomplishments is the last thing in the world that I am fit to do. Your grandmamma is on the spot; and your grandmamma is the proper person to receive the letters, and to make all the necessary inquiries."

"But I want to see the letters myself," per-

sisted the spoiled child. "Some of them are sure
to be amusing—"

"I don't apologize for this very unceremonious
reception of you, Mr. Armadale," said the major,
turning to Allan, with a quaint and quiet humor.
"It may be useful as a warning, if you ever
chance to marry and have a daughter, not to
begin, as I have done, by letting her have her
own way."

Allan laughed, and Miss Milroy persisted.

"Besides," she went on, "I should like to help
in choosing which letters we answer, and which
we don't. I think I ought to have some voice
in the selection of my own governess. Why not
tell them, papa, to send their letters down here
—to the post-office or the stationer's, or anywhere you like? When you and I have read
them, we can send up the letters we prefer to
grandmamma; and she can ask all the questions, and pick out the best governess, just as
you have arranged already, without leaving ME
entirely in the dark, which I consider (don't
you, Mr. Armadale?) to be quite inhuman. Let
me alter the address, papa; do, there's a
darling!"

"We shall get no breakfast, Mr. Armadale, if
I don't say Yes," said the major good-humoredly.
"Do as you like, my dear," he added, turning to
his daughter. "As long as it ends in your grandmamma's managing the matter for us, the rest
is of very little consequence."

Miss Milroy took up her father's pen, drew it
through the last line of the advertisement, and

wrote the altered address with her own hand as follows:

"*Apply, by letter, to M., Post-office, Thorpe Ambrose, Norfolk.*"

"There!" she said, bustling to her place at the breakfast-table. "The advertisement may go to London now; and, if a governess *does* come of it, oh, papa, who in the name of wonder will she be?—Tea or coffee, Mr. Armadale? I'm really ashamed of having kept you waiting. But it is such a comfort," she added, saucily, "to get all one's business off one's mind before breakfast!"

Father, daughter, and guest sat down together sociably at the little round table, the best of good neighbors and good friends already.

Three days later, one of the London newsboys got *his* business off his mind before breakfast. His district was Diana Street, Pimlico; and the last of the morning's newspapers which he disposed of was the newspaper he left at Mrs. Oldershaw's door.

---

## CHAPTER III.

### THE CLAIMS OF SOCIETY.

MORE than an hour after Allan had set forth on his exploring expedition through his own grounds, Midwinter rose, and enjoyed, in his turn, a full view by daylight of the magnificence of the new house.

Refreshed by his long night's rest, he descended the great staircase as cheerfully as Allan himself. One after another, he, too, looked into the spacious rooms on the ground floor in breathless astonishment at the beauty and the luxury which surrounded him. "The house where I lived in service when I was a boy, was a fine one," he thought, gayly; "but it was nothing to this! I wonder if Allan is as surprised and delighted as I am?" The beauty of the summer morning drew him out through the open hall door, as it had drawn his friend out before him. He ran briskly down the steps, humming the burden of one of the old vagabond tunes which he had danced to long since in the old vagabond time. Even the memories of his wretched childhood took their color, on that happy morning, from the bright medium through which he looked back at them. "If I was not out of practice," he thought to himself, as he leaned on the fence and looked over at the park, "I could try some of my old tumbling tricks on that delicious grass." He turned, noticed two of the servants talking together near the shrubbery, and asked for news of the master of the house.

The men pointed with a smile in the direction of the gardens; Mr. Armadale had gone that way more than an hour since, and had met (as had been reported) with Miss Milroy in the grounds. Midwinter followed the path through

the shrubbery, but, on reaching the flower garden, stopped, considered a little, and retraced his
steps. "If Allan has met with the young lady,"
he said to himself, "Allan doesn't want me."
He laughed as he drew that inevitable inference,
and turned considerately to explore the beauties
of Thorpe Ambrose on the other side of the
house.

Passing the angle of the front wall of the
building, he descended some steps, advanced
along a paved walk, turned another angle, and
found himself in a strip of garden ground at the
back of the house.

Behind him was a row of small rooms situated
on the level of the servants' offices. In front of
him, on the further side of the little garden, rose
a wall, screened by a laurel hedge, and having
a door at one end of it, leading past the stables
to a gate that opened on the high-road. Perceiv-
ing that he had only discovered thus far the
shorter way to the house, used by the servants
and trades-people, Midwinter turned back again,
and looked in at the window of one of the rooms
on the basement story as he passed it. Were
these the servants' offices? No; the offices were
apparently in some other part of the ground-floor;
the window he had looked in at was the window
of a lumber-room. The next two rooms in the
row were both empty. The fourth window,
when he approached it, presented a little variety.
It served also as a door; and it stood open to the
garden at that moment.

Attracted by the book-shelves which he no-

ticed on one of the walls, Midwinter stepped into
the room.

The books, few in number, did not detain him
long; a glance at their backs was enough without taking them down. The Waverley Novels,
Tales by Miss Edgeworth, and by Miss Edgeworth's many followers, the Poems of Mrs.
Hemans, with a few odd volumes of the illustrated gift-books of the period, composed the
bulk of the little library. Midwinter turned to
leave the room, when an object on one side of
the window, which he had not previously noticed, caught his attention and stopped him. It
was a statuette standing on a bracket—a reduced
copy of the famous Niobe of the Florence Mu-
seum. He glanced from the statuette to the
window, with a sudden doubt which set his
heart throbbing fast. It was a French window.
He looked out with a suspicion which he had
not felt yet. The view before him was the view
of a lawn and garden. For a moment his mind
struggled blindly to escape the conclusion which
had seized it, and struggled in vain. Here, close
round him and close before him—here, forcing
him mercilessly back from the happy present to
the horrible past, was the room that Allan had
seen in the Second Vision of the Dream.

He waited, thinking and looking round him
while he thought. There was wonderfully little
disturbance in his face and manner; he looked
steadily from one to the other of the few objects
in the room, as if the discovery of it had saddened rather than surprised him. Matting of

some foreign sort covered the floor. Two cane chairs and a plain table comprised the whole of the furniture. The walls were plainly papered, and bare—broken to the eye in one place by a door leading into the interior of the house; in another, by a small stove; in a third, by the book-shelves which Midwinter had already noticed. He returned to the books, and this time he took some of them down from the shelves.

The first that he opened contained lines in a woman's handwriting, traced in ink that had faded with time. He read the inscription— "Jane Armadale, from her beloved father. Thorpe Ambrose, October, 1828." In the second, third, and fourth volumes that he opened, the same inscription re-appeared. His previous knowledge of dates and persons helped him to draw the true inference from what he saw. The books must have belonged to Allan's mother; and she must have inscribed them with her name, in the interval of time between her return to Thorpe Ambrose from Madeira and the birth of her son. Midwinter passed on to a volume on another shelf—one of a series containing the writings of Mrs. Hemans. In this case, the blank leaf at the beginning of the book was filled on both sides with a copy of verses, the writing being still in Mrs. Armadale's hand. The verses were headed "Farewell to Thorpe Ambrose," and were dated "March, 1829"—two months only after Allan had been born.

Entirely without merit in itself, the only in-

terest of the little poem was in the domestic
story that it told.

The very room in which Midwinter then stood
was described—with the view on the garden, the
window made to open on it, the book-shelves, the
Niobe, and other more perishable ornaments which
Time had destroyed. Here, at variance with her
brothers, shrinking from her friends, the widow
of the murdered man had, on her own acknowledgment, secluded herself, without other comfort
than the love and forgiveness of her father, until
her child was born. The father's mercy and the
father's recent death filled many verses, happily
too vague in their commonplace expression of pen-
itence and despair to give any hint of the marriage story in Madeira to any reader who looked
at them ignorant of the truth. A passing reference to the writer's estrangement from her surviving relatives, and to her approaching departure from Thorpe Ambrose, followed. Last came
the assertion of the mother's resolution to separate
herself from all her old associations; to leave behind her every possession, even to the most trifling
thing she had, that could remind her of the miserable past; and to date her new life in the future
from the birthday of the child who had been
spared to console her—who was now the one
earthly object that could still speak to her of
love and hope. So the old story of passionate
feeling that finds comfort in phrases rather than
not find comfort at all was told once again. So
the poem in the faded ink faded away to its
end.

Midwinter put the book back with a heavy sigh, and opened no other volume on the shelves. "Here in the country house, or there on board the wreck," he said, bitterly, "the traces of my father's crime follow me, go where I may." He advanced toward the window, stopped, and looked back into the lonely, neglected little room. "Is *this* chance?" he asked himself. "The place where his mother suffered is the place he sees in the Dream; and the first morning in the new house is the morning that reveals it, not to *him*, but to *me*. Oh, Allan! Allan! how will it end?"

The thought had barely passed through his mind before he heard Allan's voice, from the paved walk at the side of the house, calling to him by his name. He hastily stepped out into the garden. At the same moment Allan came running round the corner, full of voluble apologies for having forgotten, in the society of his new neighbors, what was due to the laws of hospitality and the claims of his friend.

"I really haven't missed you," said Midwinter; "and I am very, very glad to hear that the new neighbors have produced such a pleasant impression on you already."

He tried, as he spoke, to lead the way back by the outside of the house; but Allan's flighty attention had been caught by the open window and the lonely little room. He stepped in immediately. Midwinter followed, and watched him in breathless anxiety as he looked round. Not the slightest recollection of the Dream troubled

Allan's easy mind. Not the slightest reference
to it fell from the silent lips of his friend.

"Exactly the sort of place I should have expected you to hit on!" exclaimed Allan, gayly.
"Small and snug and unpretending. I know
you, Master Midwinter! You'll be slipping off
here when the county families come visiting,
and I rather think on those dreadful occasions
you won't find me far behind you. What's the
matter? You look ill and out of spirits. Hungry?
Of course you are! unpardonable of me to have
kept you waiting. This door leads somewhere,
I suppose; let's try a short cut into the house.
Don't be afraid of my not keeping you company
at breakfast. I didn't eat much at the cottage;
I feasted my eyes on Miss Milroy, as the poets
say. Oh, the darling! the darling! she turns
you topsy-turvy the moment you look at her.
As for her father, wait till you see his wonderful clock! It's twice the size of the famous clock
at Strasbourg, and the most tremendous striker
ever heard yet in the memory of man!"

Singing the praises of his new friends in this
strain at the top of his voice, Allan hurried Midwinter along the stone passages on the basement
floor, which led, as he had rightly guessed, to a
staircase communicating with the hall. They
passed the servants' offices on the way. At the
sight of the cook and the roaring fire, disclosed
through the open kitchen door, Allan's mind
went off at a tangent, and Allan's dignity scattered itself to the four winds of heaven, as usual.

"Aha, Mrs. Gripper, there you are with your

pots and pans, and your burning fiery furnace! One had need be Shadrach, Meshach, and the other fellow to stand over that. Breakfast as soon as ever you like. Eggs, sausages, bacon, kidneys, marmalade, water - cresses, coffee, and so forth. My friend and I belong to the select few whom it's a perfect privilege to cook for. Voluptuaries, Mrs. Gripper, voluptuaries, both of us. You'll see," continued Allan, as they went on toward the stairs, "I shall make that worthy creature young again; I'm better than a doctor for Mrs. Gripper. When she laughs, she shakes her fat sides; and when she shakes her fat sides, she exerts her muscular system; and when she exerts her muscular system— Ha! here's Susan again. Don't squeeze yourself flat against the banisters, my dear; if you don't mind hustling *me* on the stairs, I rather like hustling *you*. She looks like a full-blown rose when she blushes, doesn't she? Stop, Susan! I've some orders to give. Be very particular with Mr. Midwinter's room: shake up his bed like mad, and dust his furniture till those nice round arms of yours ache again. Nonsense, my dear fellow! I'm not too familiar with them; I'm only keeping them up to their work. Now, then, Richard! where do we breakfast? Oh, here. Between ourselves, Midwinter, these splendid rooms of mine are a size too large for me; I don't feel as if I should ever be on intimate terms with my own furniture. My views in life are of the snug and slovenly sort—a kitchen chair, you know, and a low ceiling. Man wants but little here below, and wants that little long. That's not exactly the right quotation; but it expresses my meaning, and we'll let alone correcting it till the next opportunity."

"I beg your pardon," interposed Midwinter, "here is something waiting for you which you have not noticed yet."

As he spoke, he pointed a little impatiently to a letter lying on the breakfast-table. He could conceal the ominous discovery which he had made that morning, from Allan's knowledge; but he could not conquer the latent distrust of circumstances which was now raised again in his superstitious nature—the instinctive suspicion of everything that happened, no matter how common or how trifling the event, on the first memorable day when the new life began in the new house.

Allan ran his eye over the letter, and tossed it across the table to his friend. "I can't make head or tail of it," he said; "can you?"

Midwinter read the letter, slowly, aloud. "Sir —I trust you will pardon the liberty I take in sending these few lines to wait your arrival at Thorpe Ambrose. In the event of circumstances not disposing you to place your law business in the hands of Mr. Darch—" He suddenly stopped at that point, and considered a little.

"Darch is our friend the lawyer," said Allan, supposing Midwinter had forgotten the name. "Don't you remember our spinning the half-crown on the cabin table, when I got the two offers for the cottage? Heads, the major; tails, the lawyer. This is the lawyer."

Without making any reply, Midwinter resumed reading the letter. "In the event of circumstances not disposing you to place your law business in the hands of Mr. Darch, I beg to say that I shall be happy to take charge of your interests, if you feel willing to honor me with your confidence. Inclosing a reference (should you desire it) to my agents in London, and again apologizing for this intrusion, I beg to remain, sir, respectfully yours, A. PEDGIFT, Sen."

"Circumstances?" repeated Midwinter, as he laid the letter down. "What circumstances can possibly indispose you to give your law business to Mr. Darch?"

"Nothing can indispose me," said Allan. "Besides being the family lawyer here, Darch was the first to write me word at Paris of my coming in for my fortune; and, if I have got any business to give, of course he ought to have it."

Midwinter still looked distrustfully at the open letter on the table. "I am sadly afraid, Allan, there is something wrong already," he said. "This man would never have ventured on the application he has made to you, unless he had some good reason for believing he would succeed. If you wish to put yourself right at starting, you will send to Mr. Darch this morning to tell him you are here, and you will take no notice for the present of Mr. Pedgift's letter."

Before more could be said on either side, the footman made his appearance with the breakfast tray. He was followed, after an interval, by the butler, a man of the essentially confidential kind, with a modulated voice, a courtly manner, and a bulbous nose. Anybody but Allan would have seen in his face that he had come into the room having a special communication to make to his master. Allan, who saw nothing under the surface, and whose head was running on the lawyer's letter, stopped him bluntly with the point-blank question: "Who's Mr. Pedgift?"

The butler's sources of local knowledge opened confidentially on the instant. Mr. Pedgift was the second of the two lawyers in the town. Not so long established, not so wealthy, not so universally looked up to as old Mr. Darch. Not doing the business of the highest people in the county, and not mixing freely with the best society, like old Mr. Darch. A very sufficient man, in his way, nevertheless. Known as a perfectly competent and respectable practitioner all round the neighborhood. In short, professionally next best to Mr. Darch; and personally superior to him (if the expression might be permitted) in this respect—that Darch was a Crusty One, and Pedgift wasn't.

Having imparted this information, the butler, taking a wise advantage of his position, glided, without a moment's stoppage, from Mr. Pedgift's character to the business that had brought him into the breakfast-room. The Midsummer Audit was near at hand; and the tenants were accustomed to have a week's notice of the rent-day dinner. With this necessity pressing, and with no orders given as yet, and no steward in office at Thorpe Ambrose, it appeared desirable that some confidential person should bring the matter forward. The butler was that confidential person; and he now ventured accordingly to trouble his master on the subject.

At this point Allan opened his lips to interrupt, and was himself interrupted before he could utter a word.

"Wait!" interposed Midwinter, seeing in Allan's face that he was in danger of being publicly announced in the capacity of steward. "Wait!" he repeated, eagerly, "till I can speak to you first."

The butler's courtly manner remained alike unruffled by Midwinter's sudden interference and by his own dismissal from the scene. Nothing but the mounting color in his bulbous nose betrayed the sense of injury that animated him as he withdrew. Mr. Armadale's chance of regaling his friend and himself that day with the best wine in the cellar trembled in the balance, as the butler took his way back to the basement story.

"This is beyond a joke, Allan," said Midwinter, when they were alone. "Somebody must meet your tenants on the rent-day who is really fit to take the steward's place. With the best will in the world to learn, it is impossible for *me* to master the business at a week's notice. Don't, pray don't let your anxiety for my welfare put you in a false position with other people! I should never forgive myself if I was the unlucky cause—"

"Gently, gently!" cried Allan, amazed at his

friend's extraordinary earnestness. "If I write to London by to-night's post for the man who came down here before, will that satisfy you?"

Midwinter shook his head. "Our time is short," he said; "and the man may not be at liberty. Why not try in the neighborhood first? You were going to write to Mr. Darch. Send at once, and see if he can't help us between this and post-time."

Allan withdrew to a side-table on which writing materials were placed. "You shall breakfast in peace, you old fidget," he replied, and addressed himself forthwith to Mr. Darch, with his usual Spartan brevity of epistolary expression. "Dear Sir—Here I am, bag and baggage. Will you kindly oblige me by being my lawyer? I ask this, because I want to consult you at once. Please look in in the course of the day, and stop to dinner if you possibly can. Yours truly, ALLAN ARMADALE." Having read this composition aloud with unconcealed admiration of his own rapidity of literary execution, Allan addressed the letter to Mr. Darch, and rang the bell. "Here, Richard, take this at once, and wait for an answer. And, I say, if there's any news stirring in the town, pick it up and bring it back with you. See how I manage my servants!" continued Allan, joining his friend at the breakfast-table. "See how I adapt myself to my new duties! I haven't been down here one clear day yet, and I'm taking an interest in the neighborhood already."

Breakfast over, the two friends went out to

idle away the morning under the shade of a tree in the park. Noon came, and Richard never appeared. One o'clock struck, and still there were no signs of an answer from Mr. Darch. Midwinter's patience was not proof against the delay. He left Allan dozing on the grass, and went to the house to make inquiries. The town was described as little more than two miles distant; but the day of the week happened to be market day, and Richard was being detained no doubt by some of the many acquaintances whom he would be sure to meet with on that occasion.

Half an hour later the truant messenger returned, and was sent out to report himself to his master under the tree in the park.

"Any answer from Mr. Darch?" asked Midwinter, seeing that Allan was too lazy to put the question for himself.

"Mr. Darch was engaged, sir. I was desired to say that he would send an answer."

"Any news in the town?" inquired Allan, drowsily, without troubling himself to open his eyes.

"No, sir; nothing in particular."

Observing the man suspiciously as he made that reply, Midwinter detected in his face that he was not speaking the truth. He was plainly embarrassed, and plainly relieved when his master's silence allowed him to withdraw. After a little consideration, Midwinter followed, and overtook the retreating servant on the drive before the house.

"Richard," he said, quietly, "if I was to

guess that there *is* some news in the town, and that you don't like telling it to your master, should I be guessing the truth?"

The man started and changed color. "I don't know how you have found it out," he said; "but I can't deny you have guessed right."

"If you let me hear what the news is, I will take the responsibility on myself of telling Mr. Armadale."

After some little hesitation, and some distrustful consideration, on his side, of Midwinter's face, Richard at last prevailed on himself to repeat what he had heard that day in the town.

The news of Allan's sudden appearance at Thorpe Ambrose had preceded the servant's arrival at his destination by some hours. Whereever he went, he found his master the subject of public discussion. The opinion of Allan's conduct among the leading townspeople, the resident gentry of the neighborhood, and the principal tenants on the estate was unanimously unfavorable. Only the day before, the committee for managing the public reception of the new squire had sketched the progress of the procession; had settled the serious question of the triumphal arches; and had appointed a competent person to solicit subscriptions for the flags, the flowers, the feasting, the fireworks, and the band. In less than a week more the money could have been collected, and the rector would have written to Mr. Armadale to fix the day. And now, by Allan's own act, the public welcome waiting to honor him had been cast back contemptuously in the public teeth! Everybody took for granted (what was unfortunately true) that he had received private information of the contemplated proceedings. Everybody declared that he had purposely stolen into his own house like a thief in the night (so the phrase ran) to escape accepting the offered civilities of his neighbors. In brief, the sensitive self-importance of the little town was wounded to the quick, and of Allan's once enviable position in the estimation of the neighborhood not a vestige remained.

For a moment, Midwinter faced the messenger of evil tidings in silent distress. That moment past, the sense of Allan's critical position roused him, now the evil was known, to seek the remedy.

"Has the little you have seen of your master, Richard, inclined you to like him?" he asked.

This time the man answered without hesitation, "A pleasanter and kinder gentleman than Mr. Armadale no one could wish to serve."

"If you think that," pursued Midwinter, "you won't object to give me some information which will help your master to set himself right with his neighbors. Come into the house."

He led the way into the library, and, after asking the necessary questions, took down in writing a list of the names and addresses of the most influential persons living in the town and its neighborhood. This done, he rang the bell for the head footman, having previously sent Richard with a message to the stables, directing an open carriage to be ready in an hour's time.

"When the late Mr. Blanchard went out to

make calls in the neighborhood, it was your place to go with him, was it not?" he asked, when the upper servant appeared. "Very well. Be ready in an hour's time, if you please, to go out with Mr. Armadale." Having given that order, he left the house again on his way back to Allan, with the visiting list in his hand. He smiled a little sadly as he descended the steps. "Who would have imagined," he thought, "that my foot-boy's experience of the ways of gentle-folks would be worth looking back at one day for Allan's sake?"

The object of the popular odium lay inno-cently slumbering on the grass, with his garden hat over his nose, his waistcoat unbuttoned, and his trousers wrinkled half way up his out-stretched legs. Midwinter roused him without hesitation, and remorselessly repeated the serv-ant's news.

Allan accepted the disclosure thus forced on him without the slightest disturbance of temper. "Oh, hang 'em!" was all he said. "Let's have another cigar." Midwinter took the cigar out of his hand, and, insisting on his treating the matter seriously, told him in plain words that he must set himself right with his offended neighbors by calling on them personally to make his apologies. Allan sat up on the grass in as-tonishment; his eyes opened wide in incredulous dismay. Did Midwinter positively meditate forcing him into a "chimney-pot hat," a nicely brushed frock-coat, and a clean pair of gloves? Was it actually in contemplation to shut him up in a carriage, with his footman on the box and his card-case in his hand, and send him round from house to house, to tell a pack of fools that he begged their pardon for not letting them make a public show of him? If anything so outrageously absurd as this was really to be done, it could not be done that day, at any rate. He had promised to go back to the charming Milroy at the cottage, and to take Midwinter with him. What earthly need had he of the good opinion of the resident gentry? The only friends he wanted were the friends he had got already. Let the whole neighborhood turn its back on him if it liked; back or face, the Squire of Thorpe Ambrose didn't care two straws about it.

After allowing him to run on in this way until his whole stock of objections was exhausted, Midwinter wisely tried his personal influence next. He took Allan affectionately by the hand. "I am going to ask a great favor," he said. "If you won't call on these people for your own sake, will you call on them to please *me?*"

Allan delivered himself of a groan of despair, stared in mute surprise at the anxious face of his friend, and good-humoredly gave way. As Midwinter took his arm, and led him back to the house, he looked round with rueful eyes at the cattle hard by, placidly whisking their tails in the pleasant shade. "Don't mention it in the neighborhood," he said; "I should like to change places with one of my own cows."

Midwinter left him to dress, engaging to return when the carriage was at the door. Allan's

toilet did not promise to be a speedy one. He
began it by reading his own visiting cards; and
he advanced it a second stage by looking into his
wardrobe, and devoting the resident gentry to
the infernal regions. Before he could discover
any third means of delaying his own proceedings, the necessary pretext was unexpectedly
supplied by Richard's appearance with a note
in his hand. The messenger had just called
with Mr. Darch's answer. Allan briskly shut
up the wardrobe, and gave his whole attention
to the lawyer's letter. The lawyer's letter rewarded him by the following lines:

"SIR—I beg to acknowledge the receipt of
your favor of to-day's date, honoring me with
two proposals; namely, ONE inviting me to act
as your legal adviser, and ONE inviting me to
pay you a visit at your house. In reference
to the first proposal, I beg permission to decline
it with thanks. With regard to the second proposal, I have to inform you that circumstances
have come to my knowledge relating to the letting of the cottage at Thorpe Ambrose which
render it impossible for me (in justice to myself) to accept your invitation. I have ascertained, sir, that my offer reached you at the
same time as Major Milroy's; and that, with
both proposals thus before you, you gave the
preference to a total stranger, who addressed
you through a house agent, over a man who
had faithfully served your relatives for two
generations, and who had been the first person

to inform you of the most important event in
your life. After this specimen of your estimate
of what is due to the claims of common courtesy
and common justice, I cannot flatter myself that
I possess any of the qualities which would fit me
to take my place on the list of your friends.

"I remain, sir, your obedient servant,

"JAMES DARCH."

"Stop the messenger!" cried Allan, leaping
to his feet, his ruddy face aflame with indignation. "Give me pen, ink, and paper! By the
Lord Harry, they're a nice set of people in these
parts; the whole neighborhood is in a conspiracy
to bully me!" He snatched up the pen in a fine
frenzy of epistolary inspiration. "Sir—I despise
you and your letter.—" At that point the pen
made a blot, and the writer was seized with
a momentary hesitation. "Too strong," he
thought; "I'll give it to the lawyer in his
own cool and cutting style." He began again
on a clean sheet of paper. "Sir—You remind
me of an Irish bull. I mean that story in 'Joe
Miller' where Pat remarked, in the hearing of
a wag hard by, that 'the reciprocity was all on
one side.' *Your* reciprocity is all on one side.
You take the privilege of refusing to be my lawyer, and then you complain of my taking the
privilege of refusing to be your landlord." He
paused fondly over those last words. "Neat!"
he thought. "Argument and hard hitting both
in one. I wonder where my knack of writing
comes from?" He went on, and finished the

letter in two more sentences. "As for your casting my invitation back in my teeth, I beg to inform you my teeth are none the worse for it. I am equally glad to have nothing to say to you, either in the capacity of a friend or a tenant.—ALLAN ARMADALE." He nodded exultantly at his own composition, as he addressed it and sent it down to the messenger. "Darch's hide must be a thick one," he said, "if he doesn't feel *that!*"

The sound of the wheels outside suddenly recalled him to the business of the day. There was the carriage waiting to take him on his round of visits; and there was Midwinter at his post, pacing to and fro on the drive.

"Read that," cried Allan, throwing out the lawyer's letter; "I've written him back a smasher."

He bustled away to the wardrobe to get his coat. There was a wonderful change in him; he felt little or no reluctance to pay the visits now. The pleasurable excitement of answering Mr. Darch had put him in a fine aggressive frame of mind for asserting himself in the neighborhood. "Whatever else they may say of me, they shan't say I was afraid to face them." Heated red-hot with that idea, he seized his hat and gloves, and hurrying out of the room, met Midwinter in the corridor with the lawyer's letter in his hand.

"Keep up your spirits!" cried Allan, seeing the anxiety in his friend's face, and misinterpreting the motive of it immediately. "If Darch can't be counted on to send us a helping hand into the steward's office, Pedgift can."

"My dear Allan, I was not thinking of that; I was thinking of Mr. Darch's letter. I don't defend this sour-tempered man; but I am afraid we must admit he has some cause for complaint. Pray don't give him another chance of putting you in the wrong. Where is your answer to his letter?"

"Gone!" replied Allan. "I always strike while the iron's hot—a word and a blow, and the blow first, that's my way. Don't, there's a good fellow, don't fidget about the steward's books and the rent-day. Here! here's a bunch of keys they gave me last night: one of them opens the room where the steward's books are; go in and read them till I come back. I give you my sacred word of honor I'll settle it all with Pedgift before you see me again."

"One moment," interposed Midwinter, stopping him resolutely on his way out to the carriage. "I say nothing against Mr. Pedgift's fitness to possess your confidence, for I know nothing to justify me in distrusting him. But he has not introduced himself to your notice in a very delicate way; and he has not acknowledged (what is quite clear to my mind) that he knew of Mr. Darch's unfriendly feeling toward you when he wrote. Wait a little before you go to this stranger; wait till we can talk it over together to-night."

"Wait!" replied Allan. "Haven't I told you that I always strike while the iron's hot?

Trust my eye for character, old boy; I'll look Pedgift through and through, and act accordingly. Don't keep me any longer, for Heaven's sake. I'm in a fine humor for tackling the resident gentry; and if I don't go at once, I'm afraid it may wear off."

With that excellent reason for being in a hurry, Allan boisterously broke away. Before it was possible to stop him again, he had jumped into the carriage and had left the house.

---

## CHAPTER IV.

### THE MARCH OF EVENTS.

MIDWINTER'S face darkened when the last trace of the carriage had disappeared from view. "I have done my best," he said, as he turned back gloomily into the house. "If Mr. Brock himself were here, Mr. Brock could do no more!"

He looked at the bunch of keys which Allan had thrust into his hand, and a sudden longing to put himself to the test over the steward's books took possession of his sensitive self-tormenting nature. Inquiring his way to the room in which the various movables of the steward's office had been provisionally placed after the letting of the cottage, he sat down at the desk, and tried how his own unaided capacity would guide him through the business records of the Thorpe Ambrose estate. The result exposed his own ignorance unanswerably before his own eyes. The ledgers bewildered him; the leases, the plans, and even the correspondence itself, might have been written, for all he could understand of them, in an unknown tongue. His memory reverted bitterly as he left the room again to his two years' solitary self-instruction in the Shrewsbury book-seller's shop. "If I could only have worked at a business!" he thought. "If I could only have known that the company of poets and philosophers was company too high for a vagabond like me!"

He sat down alone in the great hall; the silence of it fell heavier and heavier on his sinking spirits; the beauty of it exasperated him, like an insult from a purse-proud man. "Curse the place!" he said, snatching up his hat and stick. "I like the bleakest hillside I ever slept on better than I like this house!"

He impatiently descended the door-steps, and stopped on the drive, considering by which direction he should leave the park for the country beyond. If he followed the road taken by the carriage, he might risk unsettling Allan by accidentally meeting him in the town. If he went out by the back gate, he knew his own nature well enough to doubt his ability to pass the room of the dream without entering it again. But one other way remained: the way which he had taken, and then abandoned again, in the morning. There was no fear of disturbing Allan and the major's daughter now. Without further hesitation, Midwinter set forth through the gardens to explore the open country on that side of the estate.

Thrown off its balance by the events of the day, his mind was full of that sourly savage resistance to the inevitable self-assertion of wealth, so amiably deplored by the prosperous and the rich; so bitterly familiar to the unfortunate and the poor. "The heather-bell costs nothing!" he thought, looking contemptuously at the masses of rare and beautiful flowers that surrounded him; "and the buttercups and daisies are as bright as the best of you!" He followed the artfully contrived ovals and squares of the Italian garden with a vagabond indifference to the symmetry of their construction and the ingenuity of their design. "How many pounds a foot did *you* cost?" he said, looking back with scornful eyes at the last path as he left it. "Wind away over high and low like the sheep-walk on the mountain-side, if you can!"

He entered the shrubbery which Allan had entered before him; crossed the paddock and the rustic bridge beyond; and reached the major's cottage. His ready mind seized the right conclusion at the first sight of it; and he stopped before the garden gate, to look at the trim little residence which would never have been empty, and would never have been let, but for Allan's ill-advised resolution to force the steward's situation on his friend.

The summer afternoon was warm; the summer air was faint and still. On the upper and the lower floor of the cottage the windows were all open. From one of them, on the upper story, the sound of voices was startlingly audible in the quiet of the park as Midwinter paused on the outer side of the garden inclosure. The voice of a woman, harsh, high, and angrily complaining—a voice with all the freshness and the melody gone, and with nothing but the hard power of it left—was the discordantly predominant sound. With it, from moment to moment, there mingled the deeper and quieter tones, soothing and compassionate, of the voice of a man. Although the distance was too great to allow Midwinter to distinguish the words that were spoken, he felt the impropriety of remaining within hearing of the voices, and at once stepped forward to continue his walk.

At the same moment, the face of a young girl (easily recognizable as the face of Miss Milroy, from Allan's description of her) appeared at the open window of the room. In spite of himself, Midwinter paused to look at her. The expression of the bright young face, which had smiled so prettily on Allan, was weary and disheartened. After looking out absently over the park, she suddenly turned her head back into the room, her attention having been apparently struck by something that had just been said in it. "Oh, mamma, mamma," she exclaimed, indignantly, "how *can* you say such things!" The words were spoken close to the window; they reached Midwinter's ears, and hurried him away before he heard more. But the self-disclosure of Major Milroy's domestic position had not reached its end yet. As Midwinter turned the corner of the garden fence, a tradesman's boy was handing a parcel in at the wicket gate to the woman servant. "Well," said the boy, with the irrepressible impudence of his class, "how is the missus?" The woman lifted her hand to box his ears. "How is the missus?" she repeated, with an angry toss of her head, as the boy ran off. "If it would only please God to take the missus, it would be a blessing to everybody in the house."

No such ill-omened shadow as this had passed over the bright domestic picture of the inhabitants of the cottage, which Allan's enthusiasm had painted for the contemplation of his friend. It was plain that the secret of the tenants had been kept from the landlord so far. Five minutes more of walking brought Midwinter to the park gates. "Am I fated to see nothing and hear nothing to-day, which can give me heart and hope for the future?" he thought, as he angrily swung back the lodge gate. "Even the people Allan has let the cottage to are people whose lives are imbittered by a household misery which it is *my* misfortune to have found out!"

He took the first road that lay before him, and walked on, noticing little, immersed in his own thoughts.

More than an hour passed before the necessity of turning back entered his mind. As soon as the idea occurred to him, he consulted his watch, and determined to retrace his steps, so as to be at the house in good time to meet Allan on his return. Ten minutes of walking brought him back to a point at which three roads met, and one moment's observation of the place satisfied him that he had entirely failed to notice at the time by which of the three roads he had advanced. No sign-post was to be seen; the country on either side was lonely and flat, intersected by broad drains and ditches. Cattle were grazing here and there, and a windmill rose in the distance above the pollard willows that fringed the low horizon. But not a house was to be seen, and not a human creature appeared on the visible perspective of any one of the three roads. Midwinter glanced back in the only direction left to look at—the direction of the road along which he had just been walking. There, to his relief, was the figure of a man, rapidly advancing toward him, of whom he could ask his way.

The figure came on, clad from head to foot in dreary black—a moving blot on the brilliant white surface of the sun-brightened road. He was a lean, elderly, miserably respectable man. He wore a poor old black dress-coat, and a cheap brown wig, which made no pretense of being his own natural hair. Short black trousers clung like attached old servants round his wizen legs; and rusty black gaiters hid all they could of his knobbed, ungainly feet  Black crape added its mite to the decayed and dingy wretchedness of his old beaver hat; black mohair in the obsolete form of a stock drearily encircled his neck and rose as high as his haggard jaws. The one morsel of color he carried about him was a lawyer's bag of blue serge, as lean and limp as himself.

The one attractive feature in his clean-shaven, weary old face was a neat set of teeth—teeth (as honest as his wig) which said plainly to all inquiring eyes, "We pass our nights on his looking-glass, and our days in his mouth."

All the little blood in the man's body faintly reddened his fleshless cheeks as Midwinter advanced to meet him, and asked the way to Thorpe Ambrose. His weak, watery eyes looked hither and thither in a bewilderment painful to see. If he had met with a lion instead of a man, and if the few words addressed to him had been words expressing a threat instead of a question, he could hardly have looked more confused and alarmed than he looked now. For the first time in his life, Midwinter saw his own shy uneasiness in the presence of strangers reflected, with tenfold intensity of nervous suffering, in the face of another man—and that man old enough to be his father.

"Which do you please to mean, sir—the town or the house? I beg your pardon for asking, but they both go by the same name in these parts."

He spoke with a timid gentleness of tone, an ingratiatory smile, and an anxious courtesy of manner, all distressingly suggestive of his being accustomed to receive rough answers in exchange for his own politeness from the persons whom he habitually addressed.

"I was not aware that both the house and the town went by the same name," said Midwinter; "I meant the house." He instinctively conquered his own shyness as he answered in those words, speaking with a cordiality of manner which was very rare with him in his intercourse with strangers.

The man of miserable respectability seemed to feel the warm return of his own politeness gratefully; he brightened and took a little courage. His lean forefinger pointed eagerly to the right road. "That way, sir," he said, "and when you come to two roads next, please take the left one of the two. I am sorry I have business the other way, I mean in the town. I should have been happy to go with you and show you. Fine summer weather, sir, for walking? You can't miss your way if you keep to the left. Oh, don't mention it! I'm afraid I have detained you, sir. I wish you a pleasant walk back, and —good-morning."

By the time he had made an end of speaking (under an impression apparently that the more he talked the more polite he would be) he had lost his courage again. He darted away down his own road, as if Midwinter's attempt to thank him involved a series of trials too terrible to confront. In two minutes more, his black retreating figure had lessened in the distance till it looked again, what it had once looked already, a moving blot on the brilliant white surface of the sun-brightened road.

The man ran strangely in Midwinter's thoughts while he took his way back to the house. He was at a loss to account for it. It never occurred to him that he might have been insensibly reminded of himself, when he saw the plain traces of past misfortune and present nervous suffering in the poor wretch's face. He blindly resented his own perverse interest in this chance foot passenger on the high-road, as he had resented all else that had happened to him since the beginning of the day. "Have I made another unlucky discovery?" he asked himself, impatiently. "Shall I see this man again, I wonder? Who can he be?"

Time was to answer both those questions before many days more had passed over the inquirer's head.

Allan had not returned when Midwinter reached the house. Nothing had happened but the arrival of a message of apology from the cottage. "Major Milroy's compliments, and he was sorry that Mrs. Milroy's illness would prevent his receiving Mr. Armadale that day." It was plain that Mrs. Milroy's occasional fits of suffering (or of ill temper) created no mere transitory disturbance of the tranquillity of the household. Drawing this natural inference, after what he had himself heard at the cottage nearly three hours since, Midwinter withdrew into the library to wait patiently among the books until his friend came back.

It was past six o'clock when the well-known hearty voice was heard again in the hall. Allan burst into the library, in a state of irrepressible excitement, and pushed Midwinter back unceremoniously into the chair from which he was just rising, before he could utter a word.

"Here's a riddle for you, old boy!" cried Allan. "Why am I like the resident manager of the Augean stable, before Hercules was called in to sweep the litter out? Because I have had my place to keep up, and I've gone and made an infernal mess of it! Why don't you laugh? By George, he doesn't see the point! Let's try again. Why am I like the resident manager—"

"For God's sake, Allan, be serious for a moment!" interposed Midwinter. "You don't know how anxious I am to hear if you have recovered the good opinion of your neighbors."

"That's just what the riddle was intended to tell you!" rejoined Allan. "But if you will have it in so many words, my own impression is that you would have done better not to disturb me under that tree in the park. I've been calculating it to a nicety, and I beg to inform you that I have sunk exactly three degrees lower in the estimation of the resident gentry since I had the pleasure of seeing you last."

"You *will* have your joke out," said Midwinter, bitterly. "Well, if I can't laugh, I can wait."

"My dear fellow, I'm not joking; I really mean what I say. You shall hear what happened; you shall have a report in full of my first visit. It will do, I can promise you, as a sample for all the rest. Mind this, in the first place, I've gone wrong with the best possible intentions. When I started for these visits, I own I was angry with that old brute of a lawyer, and I

certainly had a notion of carrying things with a
high hand. But it wore off somehow on the
road; and the first family I called on, I went
in, as I tell you, with the best possible intentions. Oh, dear, dear! there was the same
spick-and-span reception-room for me to wait
in, with the neat conservatory beyond, which
I saw again and again and again at every other
house I went to afterward. There was the same
choice selection of books for me to look at—a religious book, a book about the Duke of Welling-
ton, a book about sporting, and a book about
nothing in particular, beautifully illustrated with
pictures. Down came papa with his nice white
hair, and mamma with her nice lace cap; down
came young mister with the pink face and straw-
colored whiskers, and young miss with the plump
cheeks and the large petticoats. Don't suppose
there was the least unfriendliness on my side; I
always began with them in the same way—I insisted on shaking hands all round. That staggered them to begin with. When I came to the
sore subject next—the subject of the public reception—I give you my word of honor I took
the greatest possible pains with my apologies.
It hadn't the slightest effect; they let my apologies in at one ear and out at the other, and then
waited to hear more  Some men would have
been disheartened: I tried another way with
them; I addressed myself to the master of the
house, and put it pleasantly next. 'The fact is,'
I said, 'I wanted to escape the speechifying—my
getting up, you know, and telling you to your

I ADDRESSED MYSELF TO THE MASTER OF THE HOUSE.

face you're the best of men, and I beg to propose your health; and your getting up and telling me to my face I'm the best of men, and you beg to thank me; and so on, man after man, praising each other and pestering each other all round the table.' That's how I put it, in an easy, light-handed, convincing sort of way. Do you think any of them took it in the same friendly spirit? Not one! It's my belief they had got their speeches ready for the reception, with the flags and the flowers, and that they're secretly angry with me for stopping their open mouths just as they were ready to begin. Anyway, whenever we came to the matter of the speech-ifying (whether they touched it first or I), down I fell in their estimation the first of those three steps I told you of just now. Don't suppose I made no efforts to get up again! I made desperate efforts. I found they were all anxious to know what sort of life I had led before I came in for the Thorpe Ambrose property, and I did my best to satisfy them. And what came of that, do you think? Hang me, if I didn't disappoint them for the second time! When they found out that I had actually never been to Eton or Harrow, or Oxford or Cambridge, they were quite dumb with astonishment. I fancy they thought me a sort of outlaw. At any rate, they all froze up again; and down I fell the second step in their estimation. Never mind! I wasn't to be beaten; I had promised you to do my best, and I did it. I tried cheerful small-talk about the neighborhood next   The women said nothing in particular; the men, to my unutterable astonishment, all began to condole with me. I shouldn't be able to find a pack of hounds, they said, within twenty miles of my house; and they thought it only right to prepare me for the disgracefully careless manner in which the Thorpe Ambrose covers had been preserved. I let them go on condoling with me, and then what do you think I did? I put my foot in it again. 'Oh, don't take that to heart!' I said; 'I don't care two straws about hunting or shooting, either. When I meet with a bird in my walk, I can't for the life of me feel eager to kill it; I rather like to see the bird flying about and enjoying itself.' You should have seen their faces! They had thought me a sort of outlaw before; now they evidently thought me mad. Dead silence fell upon them all; and down I tumbled the third step in the general estimation. It was just the same at the next house, and the next and the next. The devil possessed us all, I think. It *would* come out, now in one way, and now in another, that I couldn't make speeches—that I had been brought up without a university education—and that I could enjoy a ride on horseback without galloping after a wretched stinking fox or a poor distracted little hare. These three unlucky defects of mine are not excused, it seems, in a country gentleman (especially when he has dodged a public reception to begin with). I think I got on best, upon the whole, with the wives and daughters. The women and I always fell, sooner or later, on the subject of

Mrs. Blanchard and her niece. We invariably agreed that they had done wisely in going to Florence; and the only reason we had to give for our opinion was that we thought their minds would be benefited after their sad bereavement, by the contemplation of the masterpieces of Italian art. Every one of the ladies—I solemnly declare it—at every house I went to, came sooner or later to Mrs. and Miss Blanchard's bereavement and the masterpieces of Italian art. What we should have done without that bright idea to help us, I really don't know. The one pleasant thing at any of the visits was when we all shook our heads together, and declared that the masterpieces would console them. As for the rest of it, there's only one thing more to be said. What I might be in other places I don't know: I'm the wrong man in the wrong place here. Let me muddle on for the future in my own way, with my own few friends; and ask me anything else in the world, as long as you don't ask me to make any more calls on my neighbors."

With that characteristic request, Allan's report of his exploring expedition among the resident gentry came to a close. For a moment Midwinter remained silent. He had allowed Allan to run on from first to last without uttering a word on his side. The disastrous result of the visits—coming after what had happened earlier in the day; and threatening Allan, as it did, with exclusion from all local sympathies at the very outset of his local career—had broken down Midwinter's power of resisting the stealthily depressing influence of his own superstition. It was with an effort that he now looked up at Allan; it was with an effort that he roused himself to answer.

"It shall be as you wish," he said, quietly. "I am sorry for what has happened; but I am not the less obliged to you, Allan, for having done what I asked you."

His head sank on his breast, and the fatalist resignation which had once already quieted him on board the wreck now quieted him again. "What *must* be, *will* be," he thought once more. "What have I to do with the future, and what has he?"

"Cheer up!" said Allan. "*Your* affairs are in a thriving condition, at any rate. I paid one pleasant visit in the town, which I haven't told you of yet. I've seen Pedgift, and Pedgift's son, who helps him in the office. They're the two jolliest lawyers I ever met with in my life; and, what's more, they can produce the very man you want to teach you the steward's business."

Midwinter looked up quickly. Distrust of Allan's discovery was plainly written in his face already; but he said nothing.

"I thought of you," Allan proceeded, "as soon as the two Pedgifts and I had had a glass of wine all round to drink to our friendly connection. The finest sherry I ever tasted in my life; I've ordered some of the same—but that's not the question just now. In two words I told these worthy fellows your difficulty, and in two seconds old Pedgift understood all about it. 'I have got

the man in my office,' he said, 'and before the
audit-day comes, I'll place him with the greatest
pleasure at your friend's disposal.' "

At this last announcement, Midwinter's distrust found its expression in words. He questioned Allan unsparingly.

The man's name, it appeared, was Bashwood.
He had been some time (how long Allan could
not remember) in Mr. Pedgift's service. He
had been previously steward to a Norfolk gentleman (name forgotten) in the westward district
of the county. He had lost the steward's place,
through some domestic trouble, in connection
with his son, the precise nature of which Allan
was not able to specify. Pedgift vouched for
him, and Pedgift would send him to Thorpe Ambrose two or three days before the rent-day dinner. He could not be spared, for office reasons,
before that time. There was no need to fidget
about it; Pedgift laughed at the idea of there
being any difficulty with the tenants. Two or
three days' work over the steward's books with
a man to help Midwinter who practically understood that sort of thing would put him all right
for the audit; and the other business would keep
till afterward.

"Have you seen this Mr. Bashwood yourself,
Allan?" asked Midwinter, still obstinately on his
guard.

"No," replied Allan: "he was out—out with
the bag, as young Pedgift called it. They tell
me he's a decent elderly man. A little broken
by his troubles, and a little apt to be nervous

and confused in his manner with strangers; but
thoroughly competent and thoroughly to be depended on—those are Pedgift's own words.''

Midwinter paused and considered a little, with
a new interest in the subject. The strange man
whom he had just heard described, and the
strange man of whom he had asked his way
where the three roads met, were remarkably
like each other. Was this another link in the
fast-lengthening chain of events? Midwinter
grew doubly determined to be careful, as the
bare doubt that it might be so passed through
his mind.

"When Mr. Bashwood comes," he said, "will
you let me see him, and speak to him, before
anything definite is done?''

"Of course I will!" rejoined Allan. He
stopped and looked at his watch. "And I'll
tell you what I'll do for you, old boy, in the
meantime," he added; "I'll introduce you to
the prettiest girl in Norfolk! There's just time
to run over to the cottage before dinner. Come
along, and be introduced to Miss Milroy.''

"You can't introduce me to Miss Milroy to-
day," replied Midwinter; and he repeated the
message of apology which had been brought
from the major that afternoon. Allan was surprised and disappointed; but he was not to be
foiled in his resolution to advance himself in
the good graces of the inhabitants of the cottage.
After a little consideration he hit on a means of
turning the present adverse circumstances to
good account. "I'll show a proper anxiety for

Mrs. Milroy's recovery," he said, gravely. "I'll send her a basket of strawberries, with my best respects, to-morrow morning."

Nothing more happened to mark the end of that first day in the new house.

The one noticeable event of the next day was another disclosure of Mrs. Milroy's infirmity of temper. Half an hour after Allan's basket of strawberries had been delivered at the cottage, it was returned to him intact (by the hands of the invalid lady's nurse), with a short and sharp message, shortly and sharply delivered. "Mrs. Milroy's compliments and thanks. Strawberries invariably disagreed with her." If this curiously petulant acknowledgment of an act of politeness was intended to irritate Allan, it failed entirely in accomplishing its object. Instead of being offended with the mother, he sympathized with the daughter. "Poor little thing," was all he said, "she must have a hard life of it with such a mother as that!"

He called at the cottage himself later in the day, but Miss Milroy was not to be seen; she was engaged upstairs. The major received his visitor in his working apron—far more deeply immersed in his wonderful clock, and far less readily accessible to outer influences, than Allan had seen him at their first interview. His manner was as kind as before; but not a word more could be extracted from him on the subject of his wife than that Mrs. Milroy "had not improved since yesterday."

The two next days passed quietly and uneventfully. Allan persisted in making his inquiries at the cottage; but all he saw of the major's daughter was a glimpse of her on one occasion at a window on the bedroom floor. Nothing more was heard from Mr. Pedgift; and Mr. Bashwood's appearance was still delayed. Midwinter declined to move in the matter until time enough had passed to allow of his first hearing from Mr. Brock, in answer to the letter which he had addressed to the rector on the night of his arrival at Thorpe Ambrose. He was unusually silent and quiet, and passed most of his hours in the library among the books. The time wore on wearily. The resident gentry acknowledged Allan's visit by formally leaving their cards. Nobody came near the house afterward; the weather was monotonously fine. Allan grew a little restless and dissatisfied. He began to resent Mrs. Milroy's illness; he began to think regretfully of his deserted yacht.

The next day—the twentieth—brought some news with it from the outer world. A message was delivered from Mr. Pedgift, announcing that his clerk, Mr. Bashwood, would personally present himself at Thorpe Ambrose on the following day; and a letter in answer to Midwinter was received from Mr. Brock.

The letter was dated the 18th, and the news which it contained raised not Allan's spirits only, but Midwinter's as well.

On the day on which he wrote, Mr. Brock announced that he was about to journey to London;

having been summoned thither on business connected with the interests of a sick relative, to whom he stood in the position of trustee. The business completed, he had good hope of finding one or other of his clerical friends in the metropolis who would be able and willing to do duty for him at the rectory; and, in that case, he trusted to travel on from London to Thorpe Ambrose in a week's time or less. Under these circumstances, he would leave the majority of the subjects on which Midwinter had written to him to be discussed when they met. But as time might be of importance, in relation to the stewardship of the Thorpe Ambrose estate, he would say at once that he saw no reason why Midwinter should not apply his mind to learning the steward's duties, and should not succeed in rendering himself invaluably serviceable in that way to the interests of his friend.

Leaving Midwinter reading and re-reading the rector's cheering letter, as if he was bent on getting every sentence in it by heart, Allan went out rather earlier than usual, to make his daily inquiry at the cottage—or, in plainer words, to make a fourth attempt at improving his acquaintance with Miss Milroy. The day had begun encouragingly, and encouragingly it seemed destined to go on. When Allan turned the corner of the second shrubbery, and entered the little paddock where he and the major's daughter had first met, there was Miss Milroy herself loitering to and fro on the grass, to all appearance on the watch for somebody.

She gave a little start when Allan appeared, and came forward without hesitation to meet him. She was not in her best looks. Her rosy complexion had suffered under confinement to the house, and a marked expression of embarrassment clouded her pretty face.

"I hardly know how to confess it, Mr. Armadale," she said, speaking eagerly, before Allan could utter a word, "but I certainly ventured here this morning in the hope of meeting with you. I have been very much distressed; I have only just heard, by accident, of the manner in which mamma received the present of fruit you so kindly sent to her. Will you try to excuse her? She has been miserably ill for years, and she is not always quite herself. After your being so very, very kind to me (and to papa), I really could not help stealing out here in the hope of seeing you, and telling you how sorry I was. Pray forgive and forget, Mr. Armadale— pray do!" her voice faltered over the last words, and, in her eagerness to make her mother's peace with him, she laid her hand on his arm.

Allan was himself a little confused. Her earnestness took him by surprise, and her evident conviction that he had been offended honestly distressed him. Not knowing what else to do, he followed his instincts, and possessed himself of her hand to begin with.

"My dear Miss Milroy, if you say a word more you will distress *me* next," he rejoined, unconsciously pressing her hand closer and closer, in the embarrassment of the moment. "I never

was in the least offended; I made allowances—
upon my honor I did—for poor Mrs Milroy's
illness. Offended!" cried Allan, reverting
energetically to the old complimentary strain.
"I should like to have my basket of fruit sent
back every day—if I could only be sure of its
bringing you out into the paddock the first thing
in the morning."

Some of Miss Milroy's missing color began to
appear again in her cheeks. "Oh, Mr. Armadale, there is really no end to your kindness,"
she said; "you don't know how you relieve me!"
She paused; her spirits rallied with as happy a
readiness of recovery as if they had been the
spirits of a child; and her native brightness of
temper sparkled again in her eyes, as she looked
up, shyly smiling in Allan's face. "Don't you
think," she asked, demurely, "that it is almost
time now to let go of my hand?"

Their eyes met. Allan followed his instincts
for the second time. Instead of releasing her
hand, he lifted it to his lips and kissed it. All
the missing tints of the rosier sort returned to
Miss Milroy's complexion on the instant. She
snatched away her hand as if Allan had burned
it.

"I'm sure *that's* wrong, Mr. Armadale," she
said, and turned her head aside quickly, for she
was smiling in spite of herself.

"I meant it as an apology for—for holding
your hand too long," stammered Allan. "An
apology can't be wrong—can it?"

There are occasions, though not many, when

the female mind accurately appreciates an appeal to the force of pure reason. This was one of the occasions. An abstract proposition had been presented to Miss Milroy, and Miss Milroy was convinced. If it was meant as an apology, that, she admitted, made all the difference. "I only hope," said the little coquet, looking at him slyly, "you're not misleading me. Not that it matters much now," she added, with a serious shake of her head. "If we *have* committed any improprieties, Mr. Armadale, we are not likely to have the opportunity of committing many more."

"You're not going away?" exclaimed Allan, in great alarm.

"Worse than that, Mr. Armadale. My new governess is coming."

"Coming?" repeated Allan. "Coming already?"

"As good as coming, I ought to have said— only I didn't know you wished me to be so very particular. We got the answers to the advertisements this morning. Papa and I opened them and read them together half an hour ago; and we both picked out the same letter from all the rest. I picked it out, because it was so prettily expressed; and papa picked it out because the terms were so reasonable. He is going to send the letter up to grandmamma in London by to-day's post, and, if she finds everything satisfactory on inquiry, the governess is to be engaged. You don't know how dreadfully nervous I am getting about it already; a strange governess is such an awful prospect. But it is not quite so

bad as going to school; and I have great hopes
of this new lady, because she writes such a nice
letter! As I said to papa, it almost reconciles
me to her horrid, unromantic name."

"What is her name?" asked Allan. "Brown?
Grubb? Scraggs? Anything of that sort?"

"Hush! hush! Nothing quite so horrible as
that. Her name is Gwilt. Dreadfully unpoeti-
cal, isn't it? Her reference must be a respectable person, though; for she lives in the same
part of London as grandmamma. Stop, Mr. Armadale! we are going the wrong way. No; I can't
wait to look at those lovely flowers of yours this
morning, and, many thanks, I can't accept your
arm. I have stayed here too long already. Papa
is waiting for his breakfast; and I must run back
every step of the way. Thank you for making
those kind allowances for mamma; thank you
again and again, and good-by!"

"Won't you shake hands?" asked Allan.

She gave him her hand. "No more apologies,
if you please, Mr. Armadale," she said, saucily.
Once more their eyes met, and once more the
plump dimpled little hand found its way to
Allan's lips. "It isn't an apology this time!"
cried Allan, precipitately defending himself.
"It's—it's a mark of respect."

She started back a few steps, and burst out
laughing. "You won't find me in your grounds
again, Mr. Armadale," she said, merrily, "till I
have got Miss Gwilt to take care of me!" With
that farewell, she gathered up her skirts, and ran
back across the paddock at the top of her speed.

Allan stood watching her in speechless admiration till she was out of sight. His second interview with Miss Milroy had produced an extraordinary effect on him. For the first time since he had become the master of Thorpe Ambrose, he was absorbed in serious consideration of what he owed to his new position in life. "The question is," pondered Allan, "whether I hadn't better set myself right with my neighbors by becoming a married man? I'll take the day to consider; and if I keep in the same mind about it, I'll consult Midwinter to-morrow morning."

When the morning came, and when Allan descended to the breakfast-room, resolute to consult his friend on the obligations that he owed to his neighbors in general, and to Miss Milroy in particular, no Midwinter was to be seen. On making inquiry, it appeared that he had been observed in the hall; that he had taken from the table a letter which the morning's post had brought to him; and that he had gone back immediately to his own room. Allan at once ascended the stairs again, and knocked at his friend's door.

"May I come in?" he asked.

"Not just now," was the answer.

"You have got a letter, haven't you?" persisted Allan. "Any bad news? Anything wrong?"

"Nothing. I'm not very well this morning. Don't wait breakfast for me; I'll come down as soon as I can."

No more was said on either side. Allan returned to the breakfast-room a little disappointed. He had set his heart on rushing headlong into his consultation with Midwinter, and here was the consultation indefinitely delayed. "What an odd fellow he is!" thought Allan. "What on earth can he be doing, locked in there by himself?"

He was doing nothing. He was sitting by the window, with the letter which had reached him that morning open in his hand. The handwriting was Mr. Brock's, and the words written were these:

"MY DEAR MIDWINTER—I have literally only two minutes before post time to tell you that I have just met (in Kensington Gardens) with the woman whom we both only know, thus far, as the woman with the red Paisley shawl. I have traced her and her companion (a respectable-looking elderly lady) to their residence—after having distinctly heard Allan's name mentioned between them. Depend on my not losing sight of the woman until I am satisfied that she means no mischief at Thorpe Ambrose; and expect to hear from me again as soon as I know how this strange discovery is to end.

"Very truly yours,     DECIMUS BROCK."

After reading the letter for the second time, Midwinter folded it up thoughtfully, and placed it in his pocket-book, side by side with the manuscript narrative of Allan's dream.

"Your discovery will not end with *you*, Mr. Brock," he said. "Do what you will with the woman, when the time comes the woman will be here."

## CHAPTER V.

### MOTHER OLDERSHAW ON HER GUARD.

1. *From Mrs. Oldershaw (Diana Street, Pimlico) to Miss Gwilt (West Place, Old Brompton).*

"Ladies' Toilet Repository, June 20th,
Eight in the Evening.

"MY DEAR LYDIA—About three hours have passed, as well as I can remember, since I pushed you unceremoniously inside my house in West Place, and, merely telling you to wait till you saw me again, banged the door to between us, and left you alone in the hall. I know your sensitive nature, my dear, and I am afraid you have made up your mind by this time that never yet was a guest treated so abominably by her hostess as I have treated you.

"The delay that has prevented me from explaining my strange conduct is, believe me, a delay for which I am not to blame. One of the many delicate little difficulties which beset so essentially confidential a business as mine occurred here (as I have since discovered) while we were taking the air this afternoon in Kensington Gardens. I see no chance of being able to get back to you for some hours to come, and I have a word of very urgent caution for your private ear, which has been too long delayed already. So I must use the spare minutes as they come, and write.

"Here is caution the first. On no account venture outside the door again this evening, and be very careful, while the daylight lasts, not to show yourself at any of the front windows. I have reason to fear that a certain charming person now staying with me may possibly be watched. Don't be alarmed, and don't be impatient; you shall know why.

"I can only explain myself by going back to our unlucky meeting in the Gardens with that reverend gentleman who was so obliging as to follow us both back to my house.

"It crossed my mind, just as we were close to the door, that there might be a motive for the parson's anxiety to trace us home, far less creditable to his taste, and far more dangerous to both of us, than the motive you supposed him to have. In plainer words, Lydia, I rather doubted whether you had met with another admirer; and I strongly suspected that you had encountered another enemy instead. There was no time to tell you this. There was only time to see you safe into the house, and to make sure of the parson (in case my suspicions were right) by treating him as he had treated us; I mean, by following him in his turn.

"I kept some little distance behind him at first, to turn the thing over in my mind, and to be

satisfied that my doubts were not misleading me.
We have no concealments from each other; and
you shall know what my doubts were.

"I was not surprised at *your* recognizing *him;*
he is not at all a common-looking old man; and
you had seen him twice in Somersetshire—once
when you asked your way of him to Mrs. Armadale's house, and once when you saw him again
on your way back to the railroad. But I was a
little puzzled (considering that you had your
veil down on both those occasions, and your veil
down also when we were in the Gardens) at *his*
recognizing *you.* I doubted his remembering
your figure in a summer dress after he had only
seen it in a winter dress; and though we were
talking when he met us, and your voice is one
among your many charms, I doubted his remembering your voice, either. And yet I felt persuaded that he knew you. 'How?' you will
ask. My dear, as ill-luck would have it, we
were speaking at the time of young Armadale.
I firmly believe that the name was the first thing
that struck him; and when he heard *that*, your
voice certainly and your figure perhaps, came
back to his memory. 'And what if it did?' you
may say. Think again, Lydia, and tell me
whether the parson of the place where Mrs.
Armadale lived was not likely to be Mrs. Armadale's friend? If he *was* her friend, the
very first person to whom she would apply for
advice after the manner in which you frightened
her, and after what you most injudiciously said
on the subject of appealing to her son, would be

the clergyman of the parish—and the magistrate, too, as the landlord at the inn himself told you.

"You will now understand why I left you in that extremely uncivil manner, and I may go on to what happened next.

"I followed the old gentleman till he turned into a quiet street, and then accosted him, with respect for the Church written (I flatter myself) in every line of my face.

" 'Will you excuse me,' I said, 'if I venture to inquire, sir, whether you recognized the lady who was walking with me when you happened to pass us in the Gardens?'

" 'Will you excuse my asking, ma'am, why you put that question?' was all the answer I got.

" 'I will endeavor to tell you, sir,' I said. 'If my friend is not an absolute stranger to you, I should wish to request your attention to a very delicate subject, connected with a lady deceased, and with her son who survives her.'

"He was staggered; I could see that. But he was sly enough at the same time to hold his tongue and wait till I said something more.

" 'If I am wrong, sir, in thinking that you recognized my friend,' I went on, 'I beg to apologize. But I could hardly suppose it possible that a gentleman in your profession would follow a lady home who was a total stranger to him.'

"There I had him. He colored up (fancy that, at his age!), and owned the truth, in defense of his own precious character.

" 'I have met with the lady once before, and

I acknowledge that I recognized her in the Gardens,' he said. 'You will excuse me if I decline entering into the question of whether I did or did not purposely follow her home. If you wish to be assured that your friend is not an absolute stranger to me, you now have that assurance; and if you have anything particular to say to me, I leave you to decide whether the time has come to say it.'

"He waited, and looked about. I waited, and looked about. He said the street was hardly a fit place to speak of a delicate subject in. I said the street was hardly a fit place to speak of a . delicate subject in. He didn't offer to take me to where he lived. I didn't offer to take him to where I lived. Have you ever seen two strange cats, my dear, nose to nose on the tiles? If you have, you have seen the parson and me done to the life.

" 'Well, ma'am,' he said, at last, 'shall we go on with our conversation in spite of circumstances?'

" 'Yes, sir,' I said; 'we are both of us, fort-unately, of an age to set circumstances at defiance' (I had seen the old wretch looking at my gray hair, and satisfying himself that his character was safe if he *was* seen with me).

"After all this snapping and snarling, we came to the point at last. I began by telling him that I feared his interest in you was not of the friendly sort. He admitted that much—of course, in defense of his own character once more. I next repeated to him everything you

had told me about your proceedings in Somersetshire, when we first found that he was following us home. Don't be alarmed, my dear—
I was acting on principle. If you want to make
a dish of lies digestible, always give it a garnish
of truth. Well, having appealed to the reverend
gentleman's confidence in this manner, I next
declared that you had become an altered woman
since he had seen you last. I revived that dead
wretch, your husband (without mentioning
names, of course), established him (the first
place I thought of) in business at the Brazils,
and described a letter which he had written,
offering to forgive his erring wife, if she would
repent and go back to him. I assured the parson that your husband's noble conduct had softened your obdurate nature; and then, thinking
I had produced the right impression, I came
boldly to close quarters with him. I said, 'At
the very time when you met us, sir, my unhappy friend was speaking in terms of touching
self-reproach of her conduct to the late Mrs. Armadale. She confided to me her anxiety to
make some atonement, if possible, to Mrs. Armadale's son; and it is at her entreaty (for she
cannot prevail on herself to face you) that I now
beg to inquire whether Mr. Armadale is still in
Somersetshire, and whether he would consent to
take back in small installments the sum of money
which my friend acknowledges that she received
by practicing on Mrs. Armadale's fears.' Those
were my very words. A neater story (accounting
so nicely for everything) was never told; it was

a story to melt a stone. But this Somersetshire parson is harder than stone itself. I blush for *him*, my dear, when I assure you that he was evidently insensible enough to disbelieve every word I said about your reformed character, your husband in the Brazils, and your penitent anxiety to pay the money back. It is really a disgrace that such a man should be in the Church; such cunning as his is in the last degree unbecoming in a member of a sacred profession.

" 'Does your friend propose to join her husband by the next steamer?' was all he condescended to say, when I had done.

"I acknowledge I was angry. I snapped at him. I said, 'Yes, she does.'

" 'How am I to communicate with her?' he asked.

"I snapped at him again. 'By letter—through me.'

" ' At what address, ma'am?'

"There I had him once more. 'You have found my address out for yourself, sir,' I said. 'The directory will tell you my name, if you wish to find that out for yourself also; otherwise, you are welcome to my card.'

" 'Many thanks, ma'am. If your friend wishes to communicate with Mr. Armadale, I will give you *my* card in return.'

" 'Thank you, sir.'

" 'Thank you, ma'am.'

" 'Good-afternoon, sir.'

" 'Good-afternoon, ma'am.'

"So we parted. I went my way to an appointment at my place of business, and he went his in a hurry; which is of itself suspicious. What I can't get over is his heartlessness. Heaven help the people who send for *him* to comfort them on their death-beds!

"The next consideration is, What are we to do? If we don't find out the right way to keep this old wretch in the dark, he may be the ruin of us at Thorpe Ambrose just as we are within easy reach of our end in view. Wait up till I come to you, with my mind free, I hope, from the other difficulty which is worrying me here. Was there ever such ill luck as ours? Only think of that man deserting his congregation, and coming to London just at the very time when we have answered Major Milroy's advertisement, and may expect the inquiries to be made next week! I have no patience with him; his bishop ought to interfere.

"Affectionately yours,
"MARIA OLDERSHAW."

2. *From Miss Gwilt to Mrs. Oldershaw.*

"West Place, June 20th.

"MY POOR OLD DEAR—How very little you know of my sensitive nature, as you call it! Instead of feeling offended when you left me, I went to your piano, and forgot all about you till your messenger came. Your letter is irresistible; I have been laughing over it till I am quite out of breath. Of all the absurd stories I ever read, the story you addressed to the Somersetshire clergyman is the most ridiculous. And as for your interview with him in the street, it is a perfect sin to keep it to ourselves. The public ought really to enjoy it in the form of a farce at one of the theaters.

"Luckily for both of us (to come to serious matters), your messenger is a prudent person. He sent upstairs to know if there was an answer. In the midst of my merriment I had presence of mind enough to send downstairs and say 'Yes.'

"Some brute of a man says, in some book which I once read, that no woman can keep two separate trains of ideas in her mind at the same time. I declare you have almost satisfied me that the man is right. What! when you have escaped unnoticed to your place of business, and when you suspect this house to be watched, you propose to come back here, and to put it in the parson's power to recover the lost trace of you! What madness! Stop where you are; and when you have got over your difficulty at Pimlico (it is some woman's business, of course; what worries women are!), be so good as to read what I have got to say about our difficulty at Brompton.

"In the first place, the house (as you supposed) is watched.

"Half an hour after you left me, loud voices in the street interrupted me at the piano, and I went to the window. There was a cab at the house opposite, where they let lodgings; and an old man, who looked like a respectable servant, was wrangling with the driver about his fare. An elderly gentleman came out of the house, and stopped them. An elderly gentleman returned into the house, and appeared cautiously at the front drawing-room window. You know him, you worthy creature; he had the bad taste, some few hours since, to doubt whether you were telling him the truth. Don't be afraid, he didn't see me. When he looked up, after settling with the cab driver, I was behind the curtain. I have been behind the curtain once or twice since; and I have seen enough to satisfy me that he and his servant will relieve each other at the window, so as never to lose sight of your house here, night or day. That the parson suspects the real truth is of course impossible. But that he firmly believes I mean some mischief to young Armadale, and that you have entirely confirmed him in that conviction, is as plain as that two and two make four. And this has happened (as you helplessly remind me) just when we have answered the advertisement, and when we may expect the major's inquiries to be made in a few days' time.

"Surely, here is a terrible situation for two women to find themselves in? A fiddlestick's end for the situation! We have got an easy way out of it—thanks, Mother Oldershaw, to what I myself forced you to do, not three hours before the Somersetshire clergyman met with us.

"Has that venomous little quarrel of ours this morning—after we had pounced on the major's advertisement in the newspaper—quite slipped out of your memory? Have you forgotten how I persisted in my opinion that you were a great

deal too well known in London to appear safely
as my reference in your own name, or to receive
an inquiring lady or gentleman (as you were rash
enough to propose) in your own house? Don't
you remember what a passion you were in when
I brought our dispute to an end by declining to
stir a step in the matter, unless I could conclude
my application to Major Milroy by referring him
to an address at which you were totally unknown, and to a name which might be anything
you pleased, as long as it was not yours? What
a look you gave me when you found there was
nothing for it but to drop the whole speculation
or to let me have my own way! How you fumed
over the lodging hunting on the other side of the
Park! and how you groaned when you came
back, possessed of furnished apartments in respectable Bayswater, over the useless expense
I had put you to!

"What do you think of those furnished apartments *now*, you obstinate old woman? Here
we are, with discovery threatening us at our
very door, and with no hope of escape unless
we can contrive to disappear from the parson in
the dark. And there are the lodgings in Bayswater, to which no inquisitive strangers have
traced either you or me, ready and waiting to
swallow us up—the lodgings in which we can
escape all further molestation, and answer the
major's inquiries at our ease. Can you see, at
last, a little further than your poor old nose? Is
there anything in the world to prevent your safe
disappearance from Pimlico to-night, and your

safe establishment at the new lodgings, in the
character of my respectable reference, half an
hour afterward? Oh, fie, fie, Mother Oldershaw! Go down on your wicked old knees,
and thank your stars that you had a she-devil
like me to deal with this morning!

"Suppose we come now to the only difficulty
worth mentioning—*my* difficulty. Watched as
I am in this house, how am I to join you without bringing the parson or the parson's servant
with me at my heels?

"Being to all intents and purposes a prisoner
here, it seems to me that I have no choice but to
try the old prison plan of escape—a change of
clothes. I have been looking at your house-
maid. Except that we are both light, her face
and hair and my face and hair are as unlike each
other as possible. But she is as nearly as can be
my height and size; and (if she only knew how
to dress herself, and had smaller feet) her figure
is a very much better one than it ought to be for
a person in her station in life.

"My idea is, to dress her in the clothes I wore
in the Gardens to-day; to send her out, with our
reverend enemy in full pursuit of her; and, as
soon as the coast is clear, to slip away myself
and join you. The thing would be quite impossible, of course, if I had been seen with my
veil up; but, as events have turned out, it is one
advantage of the horrible exposure which followed my marriage that I seldom show myself
in public, and never, of course, in such a popu-
lous place as London, without wearing a thick

veil and keeping that veil down. If the house-maid wears my dress, I don't really see why the house-maid may not be counted on to represent me to the life.

"The one question is, Can the woman be trusted? If she can, send me a line, telling her, on your authority, that she is to place herself at my disposal. I won't say a word till I have heard from you first.

"Let me have my answer to-night. As long as we were only talking about my getting the governess's place, I was careless enough how it ended. But now that we have actually answered Major Milroy's advertisement, I am in earnest at last. I mean to be Mrs. Armadale of Thorpe Ambrose; and woe to the man or woman who tries to stop me! Yours,

"LYDIA GWILT.

"P.S.—I open my letter again to say that you need have no fear of your messenger being followed on his return to Pimlico. He will drive to a public-house where he is known, will dismiss the cab at the door, and will go out again by a back way which is only used by the landlord and his friends.—L. G."

3. *From Mrs. Oldershaw to Miss Gwilt.*

"Diana Street, 10 o'clock.

"MY DEAR LYDIA—You have written me a heartless letter. If you had been in my trying position, harassed as I was when I wrote to you, I should have made allowances for my friend when I found my friend not so sharp as usual.

But the vice of the present age is a want of consideration for persons in the decline of life. Morally speaking, you are in a sad state, my dear; and you stand much in need of a good example. You shall have a good example—I forgive you.

"Having now relieved my mind by the performance of a good action, suppose I show you next (though I protest against the vulgarity of the expression) that I *can* see a little further than my poor old nose?

"I will answer your question about the housemaid first. You may trust her implicitly. She has had her troubles, and has learned discretion. She also looks your age; though it is only her due to say that, in this particular, she has some years the advantage of you. I inclose the necessary directions which will place her entirely at your disposal.

"And what comes next?

"Your plan for joining me at Bayswater comes next. It is very well as far as it goes; but it stands sadly in need of a little judicious improvement. There is a serious necessity (you shall know why presently) for deceiving the parson far more completely than you propose to deceive him. I want him to see the house-maid's face under circumstances which will persuade him that it is *your* face. And then, going a step further, I want him to see the house-maid leave London, under the impression that he has seen *you* start on the first stage of your journey to the Brazils. He didn't believe in that journey when

I announced it to him this afternoon in the street. He may believe in it yet, if you follow the directions I am now going to give you.

"To-morrow is Saturday. Send the house-maid out in your walking dress of to-day, just as you propose; but don't stir out yourself, and don't go near the window. Desire the woman to keep her veil down, to take half an hour's walk (quite unconscious, of course, of the parson or his servant at her heels), and then to come back to you. As soon as she appears, send her instantly to the open window, instructing her to lift her veil carelessly and look out. Let her go away again after a minute or two, take off her bonnet and shawl, and then appear once more at the window, or, better still, in the balcony outside. She may show herself again occasionally (not too often) later in the day. And to-morrow—as we have a professional gentleman to deal with—by all means send her to church. If these proceedings don't persuade the parson that the house-maid's face is your face, and if they don't make him readier to believe in your reformed character than he was when I spoke to him, I have lived sixty years, my love, in this vale of tears to mighty little purpose.

"The next day is Monday. I have looked at the shipping advertisements, and I find that a steamer leaves Liverpool for the Brazils on Tuesday. Nothing could be more convenient; we will start you on your voyage under the parson's own eyes. You may manage it in this way:

"At one o'clock send out the man who cleans the knives and forks to get a cab; and when he has brought it up to the door, let him go back and get a second cab, which he is to wait in himself, round the corner, in the square. Let the house-maid (still in your dress) drive off, with the necessary boxes, in the first cab to the North-western Railway. When she is gone, slip out yourself to the cab waiting round the corner, and come to me at Bayswater. They may be prepared to follow the house-maid's cab, because they have seen it at the door; but they won't be prepared to follow your cab, because it has been hidden round the corner. When the house-maid has got to the station, and has done her best to disappear in the crowd (I have chosen the mixed train at 2 : 10, so as to give her every chance), you will be safe with me; and whether they do or do not find out that she does not really start for Liverpool won't matter by that time. They will have lost all trace of *you;* and they may follow the house-maid half over London, if they like. She has my instructions (inclosed) to leave the empty boxes to find their way to the lost luggage office, and to go to her friends in the City, and stay there till I write word that I want her again.

"And what is the object of all this?

"My dear Lydia, the object is your future security (and mine). We may succeed, or we may fail, in persuading the parson that you have actually gone to the Brazils. If we succeed, we are relieved of all fear of him. If we fail, he

-M

will warn young Armadale to be careful *of a woman like my house-maid, and not of a woman like you.* This last gain is a very important one; for we don't know that Mrs. Armadale may not have told him your maiden name. In that event, the 'Miss Gwilt' whom he will describe as having slipped through his fingers here will be so entirely unlike the 'Miss Gwilt' established at Thorpe Ambrose, as to satisfy everybody that it is not a case of similarity of persons, but only a case of similarity of names.

"What do you say now to my improvement on your idea? Are my brains not quite so addled as you thought them when you wrote? Don't suppose I'm at all overboastful about my own ingenuity. Cleverer tricks than this trick of mine are played off on the public by swindlers, and are recorded in the newspapers every week. I only want to show you that my assistance is not less necessary to the success of the Armadale speculation now than it was when I made our first important discoveries, by means of the harmless-looking young man and the private inquiry office in Shadyside Place.

"There is nothing more to say that I know of, except that I am just going to start for the new lodging, with a box directed in my new name. The last expiring moments of Mother Oldershaw, of the Toilet Repository, are close at hand, and the birth of Miss Gwilt's respectable reference, Mrs. Mandeville, will take place in a cab in five minutes' time. I fancy I must be still young at heart, for I am quite in love already with my romantic name; it sounds almost as pretty as Mrs. Armadale of Thorpe Ambrose, doesn't it?

"Good-night, my dear, and pleasant dreams. If any accident happens between this and Monday, write to me instantly by post. If no accident happens you will be with me in excellent time for the earliest inquiries that the major can possibly make. My last words are, don't go out, and don't venture near the front windows till Monday comes.

"Affectionately yours,            M. O."

## CHAPTER VI.

### MIDWINTER IN DISGUISE.

TOWARD noon on the day of the twenty-first, Miss Milroy was loitering in the cottage garden —released from duty in the sick-room by an improvement in her mother's health—when her attention was attracted by the sound of voices in the park. One of the voices she instantly recognized as Allan's; the other was strange to her. She put aside the branches of a shrub near the garden palings, and, peeping through, saw Allan approaching the cottage gate, in company with a slim, dark, undersized man, who was talking and laughing excitably at the top of his voice. Miss Milroy ran indoors to warn her father of Mr. Armadale's arrival, and to add that he was bringing with him a noisy stranger, who was, in all probability, the friend generally repoited to be staying with the squire at the great house.

Had the major's daughter guessed right? Was the squire's loud-talking, loud-laughing companion the shy, sensitive Midwinter of other times? It was even so. In Allan's presence, that morning, an extraordinary change had passed over the ordinarily quiet demeanor of Allan's friend.

When Midwinter had first appeared in the breakfast-room, after putting aside Mr. Brock's startling letter, Allan had been too much occupied to pay any special attention to him. The undecided difficulty of choosing the day for the audit dinner had pressed for a settlement once more, and had been fixed at last (under the butler's advice) for Saturday, the twenty-eighth of the month. It was only on turning round to remind Midwinter of the ample space of time which the new arrangement allowed for mastering the steward's books, that even Allan's flighty attention had been arrested by a marked change in the face that confronted him. He had openly noticed the change in his usual blunt manner, and had been instantly silenced by a fretful, almost an angry, reply. The two had sat down together to breakfast without the usual cordiality, and the meal had proceeded gloomily, till Midwinter himself broke the silence by bursting into the strange outbreak of gayety which had revealed in Allan's eyes a new side to the character of his friend.

As usual with most of Allan's judgments, here

again the conclusion was wrong. It was no new
side to Midwinter's character that now presented
itself · it was only a new aspect of the one ever-
recurring struggle of Midwinter's life.

Irritated by Allan's discovery of the change
in him, and dreading the next questions that
Allan's curiosity might put, Midwinter had
roused himself to efface, by main force, the
impression which his own altered appearance
had produced. It was one of those efforts which
no men compass so resolutely as the men of his
quick temper and his sensitive feminine organization. With his whole mind still possessed by
the firm belief that the Fatality had taken one
great step nearer to Allan and himself since the
rector's adventure in Kensington Gardens—with
his face still betraying what he had suffered,
under the renewed conviction that his father's
death-bed warning was now, in event after
event, asserting its terrible claim to part him,
at any sacrifice, from the one human creature
whom he loved—with the fear still busy at his
heart that the first mysterious vision of Allan's
Dream might be a vision realized, before the
new day that now saw the two Armadales together was a day that had passed over their
heads—with these triple bonds, wrought by his
own superstition, fettering him at that moment
as they had never fettered him yet, he mercilessly
spurred his resolution to the desperate effort of
rivaling, in Allan's presence, the gayety and
good spirits of Allan himself.

He talked and laughed, and heaped his plate

indiscriminately from every dish on the breakfast-table. He made noisily merry with jests
that had no humor, and stories that had no
point. He first astonished Allan, then amused
him, then won his easily encouraged confidence
on the subject of Miss Milroy. He shouted with
laughter over the sudden development of Allan's
views on marriage, until the servants downstairs
began to think that their master's strange friend
had gone mad. Lastly, he had accepted Allan's
proposal that he should be presented to the major's
daughter, and judge of her for himself, as readily, nay, more readily than it would have been accepted by the least diffident man living. There
the two now stood at the cottage gate—Midwinter's voice rising louder and louder over Allan's
—Midwinter's natural manner disguised (how
madly and miserably none but he knew!) in a
coarse masquerade of boldness—the outrageous,
the unendurable boldness of a shy man.

They were received in the parlor by the major's
daughter, pending the arrival of the major himself.

Allan attempted to present his friend in the
usual form. To his astonishment, Midwinter
took the words flippantly out of his lips, and
introduced himself to Miss Milroy with a confident look, a hard laugh, and a clumsy assump-
tion of ease which presented him at his worst.
His artificial spirits, lashed continuously into
higher and higher effervescence since the morning, were now mounting hysterically beyond his
own control. He looked and spoke with that

terrible freedom of license which is the necessary consequence, when a diffident man has
thrown off his reserve, of the very effort by
which he has broken loose from his own restraints. He involved himself in ·a confused
medley of apologies that were not wanted, and
of compliments that might have overflattered
the vanity of a savage. He looked backward
and forward from Miss Milroy to Allan, and
declared jocosely that he understood now why
his friend's morning walks were always taken
in the same direction. He asked her questions
about her mother, and cut short the answers she
gave him by remarks on the weather. In one
breath, he said she must feel the day insufferably
hot, and in another he protested that he quite
envied her in her cool muslin dress.

The major came in.

Before he could say two words, Midwinter
overwhelmed him with the same frenzy of familiarity, and the same feverish fluency of
speech. He expressed his interest in Mrs. Milroy's health in terms which would have been
exaggerated on the lips of a friend of the family.
He overflowed into a perfect flood of apologies
for disturbing the major at his mechanical pursuits. He quoted Allan's extravagant account
of the clock, and expressed his own anxiety to see
it in terms more extravagant still. He paraded
his superficial book knowledge of the great clock
at Strasbourg, with far-fetched jests on the extraordinary automaton figures which that clock
puts in·motion—on the procession of the Twelve

Apostles, which walks out under the dial at noon, and on the toy cock, which crows at St. Peter's appearance — and this before a man who had studied every wheel in that complex machinery, and who had passed whole years of his life in trying to imitate it. "I hear you have outnumbered the Strasbourg apostles, and outcrowed the Strasbourg cock," he exclaimed, with the tone and manner of a friend habitually privileged to waive all ceremony; "and I am dying, absolutely dying, major, to see your wonderful clock!"

Major Milroy had entered the room with his mind absorbed in his own mechanical contrivances as usual. But the sudden shock of Midwinter's familiarity was violent enough to recall him instantly to himself, and to make him master again, for the time, of his social resources as a man of the world.

"Excuse me for interrupting you," he said, stopping Midwinter for the moment, by a look of steady surprise. "I happen to have seen the clock at Strasbourg; and it sounds almost absurd in my ears (if you will pardon me for saying so) to put my little experiment in any light of comparison with that wonderful achievement. There is nothing else of the kind like it in the world!" He paused, to control his own mounting enthusiasm; the clock at Strasbourg was to Major Milroy what the name of Michael Angelo was to Sir Joshua Reynolds. "Mr. Armadale's kindness has led him to exaggerate a little," pursued the major, smiling at Allan, and passing over another attempt of Midwinter's to seize on the talk, as if no such attempt had been made. "But as there does happen to be this one point of resemblance between the great clock abroad and the little clock at home, that they both show what they can do on the stroke of noon, and as it is close on twelve now, if you still wish to visit my workshop, Mr. Midwinter, the sooner I show you the way to it the better." He opened the door, and apologized to Midwinter, with marked ceremony, for preceding him out of the room.

"What do you think of my friend?" whispered Allan, as he and Miss Milroy followed.

"Must I tell you the truth, Mr. Armadale?" she whispered back.

"Of course!"

"Then I don't like him at all!"

"He's the best and dearest fellow in the world," rejoined the outspoken Allan. "You'll like him better when you know him better—I'm sure you will!"

Miss Milroy made a little grimace, implying supreme indifference to Midwinter, and saucy surprise at Allan's earnest advocacy of the merits of his friend. "Has he got nothing more interesting to say to me than *that*," she wondered, privately, "after kissing my hand twice yesterday morning?"

They were all in the major's workroom before Allan had the chance of trying a more attractive subject. There, on the top of a rough wooden case, which evidently contained the machinery, was the wonderful clock. The dial was crowned by a glass pedestal placed on rock-work in carved ebony; and on the top of the pedestal sat the inevitable figure of Time, with his everlasting scythe in his hand. Below the dial was a little platform, and at either end of it rose two miniature sentry-boxes, with closed doors. Externally, this was all that appeared, until the magic moment came when the clock struck twelve at noon.

It wanted then about three minutes to twelve; and Major Milroy seized the opportunity of explaining what the exhibition was to be, before the exhibition began.

"At the first words, his mind fell back again into its old absorption over the one employment of his life. He turned to Midwinter (who had persisted in talking all the way from the parlor, and who was talking still) without a trace left in his manner of the cool and cutting composure with which he had spoken but a few minutes before. The noisy, familiar man, who had been an ill-bred intruder in the parlor, became a privileged guest in the workshop, for *there* he possessed the all-atoning social advantage of being new to the performances of the wonderful clock.

"At the first stroke of twelve, Mr. Midwinter," said the major, quite eagerly, "keep your eye on the figure of Time: he will move his scythe, and point it downward to the glass pedestal. You will next see a little printed card appear behind the glass, which will tell you the day of the month and the day of the week. At the last stroke of the clock, Time will lift his scythe again into its former position, and the chimes will ring a peal. The peal will be succeeded by the playing of a tune—the favorite march of my old regiment—and then the final performance of the clock will follow. The sentry-boxes, which you may observe at each side, will both open at the same moment. In one of them you will see the sentinel appear; and from the other a corporal and two privates will march across the platform to relieve the guard, and will then disappear, leaving the new sentinel at his post. I must ask your kind allowances for this last part of the performance. The machinery is a little complicated, and there are defects in it which I am ashamed to say I have not yet succeeded in remedying as I could wish. Sometimes the figures go all wrong, and sometimes they go all right. I hope they may do their best on the occasion of your seeing them for the first time."

As the major, posted near his clock, said the last words, his little audience of three, assembled at the opposite end of the room, saw the hour-hand and the minute-hand on the dial point together to twelve. The first stroke sounded, and Time, true to the signal, moved his scythe. The day of the month and the day of the week announced themselves in print through the glass pedestal next; Midwinter applauding their appearance with a noisy exaggeration of surprise, which Miss Milroy mistook for coarse sarcasm directed at her father's pursuits, and which Allan (seeing that she was offended) attempted to moderate by touching the elbow of his friend. Meanwhile, the performances of the clock went on. At the last stroke of twelve, Time lifted his scythe again, the chimes rang, the march tune of the major's old regiment followed; and the crowning exhibition of the relief of the guard announced itself in a preliminary trembling of the sentry-boxes, and a sudden disappearance of the major at the back of the clock.

The performance began with the opening of the sentry‐box on the right‐hand side of the platform, as punctually as could be desired; the door on the other side, however, was less tract-able—it remained obstinately closed.  Unaware of this hitch in the proceedings, the corporal and his two privates appeared in their places in a state of perfect discipline, tottered out across the platform, all three trembling in every limb, dashed themselves headlong against the closed door on the other side, and failed in producing the smallest impression on the immovable sentry presumed to be within.  An intermittent click-ing, as of the major's keys and tools at work, was heard in the machinery.  The corporal and his two privates suddenly returned, backward, across the platform, and shut themselves up with a bang inside their own door.  Exactly at the same moment, the other door opened for the first time, and the provoking sentry appeared with the utmost deliberation at his post, waiting to be relieved.  He was allowed to wait.  Nothing happened in the other box but an occasional knocking inside the door, as if the corporal and his privates were impatient to be let out.  The clicking of the major's tools was heard again among the machinery; the corporal and his party, suddenly restored to liberty, appeared in a violent hurry, and spun furiously across the platform. Quick as they were, however, the hitherto deliberate sentry on the other side now perversely showed himself to be quicker still. He disappeared like lightning into his own premises, the door closed smartly after him, the corporal and his privates dashed themselves headlong against it for the second time, and the major, appearing again round the corner of the clock, asked his audience innocently "if they would be good enough to tell him whether anything had gone wrong?"

The fantastic absurdity of the exhibition, heightened by Major Milroy's grave inquiry at the end of it, was so irresistibly ludicrous that the visitors shouted with laughter; and even Miss Milroy, with all her consideration for her father's sensitive pride in his clock, could not restrain herself from joining in the merriment which the catastrophe of the puppets had provoked. But there are limits even to the license of laughter; and these limits were ere long so outrageously overstepped by one of the little party as to have the effect of almost instantly silencing the other two. The fever of Midwinter's false spirits flamed out into sheer delirium as the performance of the puppets came to an end. His paroxysms of laughter followed each other with such convulsive violence that Miss Milroy started back from him in alarm, and even the patient major turned on him with a look which said plainly, Leave the room! Allan, wisely impulsive for once in his life, seized Midwinter by the arm, and dragged him out by main force into the garden, and thence into the park beyond.

"Good heavens! what has come to you!" he exclaimed, shrinking back from the tortured face before him, as he stopped and looked close at it for the first time.

For the moment, Midwinter was incapable of answering. The hysterical paroxysm was passing from one extreme to the other. He leaned against a tree, sobbing and gasping for breath, and stretched out his hand in mute entreaty to Allan to give him time.

"You had better not have nursed me through my fever," he said, faintly, as soon as he could speak. "I'm mad and miserable, Allan; I have never recovered it. Go back and ask them to forgive me; I am ashamed to go and ask them myself. I can't tell how it happened; I can only ask your pardon and theirs." He turned aside his head quickly so as to conceal his face. "Don't stop here," he said; "don't look at me; I shall soon get over it." Allan still hesitated, and begged hard to be allowed to take him back to the house. It was useless. "You break my heart with your kindness," he burst out, passionately. "For God's sake, leave me by myself!"

Allan went back to the cottage, and pleaded there for indulgence to Midwinter, with an earnestness and simplicity which raised him im-

mensely in the major's estimation, but which
totally failed to produce the same favorable impression on Miss Milroy. Little as she herself
suspected it, she was fond enough of Allan
already to be jealous of Allan's friend.

"How excessively absurd!" she thought, pet-
tishly. "As if either papa or I considered such
a person of the slightest consequence!"

"You will kindly suspend your opinion, won't
you, Major Milroy?" said Allan, in his hearty
way, at parting.

"With the greatest pleasure!" replied the
major, cordially shaking hands.

"And you, too, Miss Milroy?" added Allan.

Miss Milroy made a mercilessly formal bow.
"*My* opinion, Mr. Armadale, is not of the slightest consequence."

Allan left the cottage, sorely puzzled to account
for Miss Milroy's sudden coolness toward him.
His grand idea of conciliating the whole neighborhood by becoming a married man underwent
some modification as he closed the garden gate
behind him. The virtue called Prudence and
the Squire of Thorpe Ambrose became personally
acquainted with each other, on this occasion, for
the first time; and Allan, entering headlong as
usual on the high-road to moral improvement,
actually decided on doing nothing in a hurry!

A man who is entering on a course of reformation ought, if virtue is its own reward, to be a
man engaged in an essentially inspiriting pursuit. But virtue is not always its own reward;
and the way that leads to reformation is remark-

ably ill-lighted for so respectable a thoroughfare. Allan seemed to have caught the infection of his friend's despondency. As he walked home, he, too, began to doubt—in his widely different way, and for his widely different reasons — whether the life at Thorpe Ambrose was promising quite as fairly for the future as it had promised at first.

## CHAPTER VII.

### THE PLOT THICKENS.

Two messages were waiting for Allan when he returned to the house. One had been left by Midwinter. "He had gone out for a long walk, and Mr. Armadale was not to be alarmed if he did not get back till late in the day." The other message had been left by "a person from Mr. Pedgift's office," who had called, according to appointment, while the two gentlemen were away at the major's. "Mr. Bashwood's respects, and he would have the honor of waiting on Mr. Armadale again in the course of the evening."

Toward five o'clock, Midwinter returned, pale and silent. Allan hastened to assure him that his peace was made at the cottage; and then, to change the subject, mentioned Mr. Bashwood's message. Midwinter's mind was so preoccupied or so languid that he hardly seemed to remember the name. Allan was obliged to remind him that Bashwood was the elderly clerk, whom Mr. Pedgift had sent to be his instructor in the duties of the steward's office. He listened without making any remark, and withdrew to his room, to rest till dinner-time.

Left by himself, Allan went into the library, to try if he could while away the time over a book.

He took many volumes off the shelves, and put a few of them back again; and there he ended. Miss Milroy contrived in some mysterious manner to get, in this case, between the reader and the books. Her formal bow and her merciless parting speech dwelt, try how he might to forget them, on Allan's mind; he began to grow more and more anxious as the idle hour wore on, to recover his lost place in her favor. To call again that day at the cottage, and ask if he had been so unfortunate as to offend her, was impossible. To put the question in writing with the needful nicety of expression proved, on trying the experiment, to be a task beyond his literary reach. After a turn or two up and down the room, with his pen in his mouth, he decided on the more diplomatic course (which happened, in this case, to be the easiest course, too), of writing to Miss Milroy as cordially as if nothing had happened, and of testing his position in her good graces by the answer that she sent him back. An invitation of some kind (including her father, of course, but addressed directly to herself) was plainly the right thing to oblige her to send a written reply; but here the difficulty occurred of what the invitation was to be. A ball was not to be thought of, in his present position with the resident gentry. A dinner-party, with no indispensable elderly lady on the premises to receive Miss Milroy—except Mrs. Gripper, who could only receive her in the kitchen —was equally out of the question. What was the invitation to be? Never backward, when he wanted help, in asking for it right and left in every available direction, Allan, feeling himself at the end of his own resources, coolly rang the bell, and astonished the servant who answered it by inquiring how the late family at Thorpe Ambrose used to amuse themselves, and what sort of invitations they were in the habit of sending to their friends.

"The family did what the rest of the gentry did, sir," said the man, staring at his master in utter bewilderment. "They gave dinner-parties and balls. And in fine summer weather, sir, like this, they sometimes had lawn-parties and picnics—"

"That'll do!" shouted Allan. "A picnic's just the thing to please her. Richard, you're an invaluable man; you may go downstairs again."

Richard retired wondering, and Richard's master seized his ready pen.

"DEAR MISS MILROY—Since I left you it has suddenly struck me that we might have a picnic. A little change and amusement (what I should call a good shaking-up, if I wasn't writing to a young lady) is just the thing for you, after being so long indoors lately in Mrs. Milroy's room.

A picnic is a change, and (when the wine is good) amusement, too. Will you ask the major if he will consent to the picnic, and come? And if you have got any friends in the neighborhood who like a picnic, pray ask them too, for I have got none. It shall be your picnic, but I will provide everything and take everybody. You shall choose the day, and we will picnic where you like. I have set my heart on this picnic.

"Believe me, ever yours,

"ALLAN ARMADALE."

On reading over his composition before sealing it up, Allan frankly acknowledged to himself, this time, that it was not quite faultless. " 'Picnic' comes in a little too often," he said. "Never mind; if she likes the idea, she won't quarrel with that." He sent off the letter on the spot, with strict instructions to the messenger to wait for a reply.

In half an hour the answer came back on scented paper, without an erasure anywhere, fragrant to smell, and beautiful to see.

The presentation of the naked truth is one of those exhibitions from which the native delicacy of the female mind seems instinctively to revolt. Never were the tables turned more completely than they were now turned on Allan by his fair correspondent. Machiavelli himself would never have suspected, from Miss Milroy's letter, how heartily she had repented her petulance to the young squire as soon as his back was turned, and how extravagantly delighted she was when his invitation was placed in her hands. Her letter was the composition of a model young lady whose emotions are all kept under parental lock and key, and served out for her judiciously as occasion may require. "Papa," appeared quite as frequently in Miss Milroy's reply as "picnic" had appeared in Allan's invitation. "Papa" had been as considerately kind as Mr. Armadale in wishing to procure her a little change and amusement, and had offered to forego his usual quiet habits and join the picnic. With "papa's" sanction, therefore, she accepted, with much pleasure, Mr. Armadale's proposal; and, at "papa's" suggestion, she would presume on Mr. Armadale's kindness to add two friends of theirs, recently settled at Thorpe Ambrose, to the picnic party—a widow lady and her son; the latter in holy orders and in delicate health. If Tuesday next would suit Mr. Armadale, Tuesday next would suit "papa"—being the first day he could spare from repairs which were required by his clock. The rest, by "papa's" advice, she would beg to leave entirely in Mr. Armadale's hands; and, in the meantime, she would remain, with "papa's" compliments, Mr. Armadale's truly—ELEANOR MILROY."

Who would ever have supposed that the writer of that letter had jumped for joy when Allan's invitation arrived? Who would ever have suspected that there was an entry already in Miss Milroy's diary, under that day's date, to this effect: "The sweetest, dearest letter from *I-know-who;* I'll never behave unkindly to him

again as long as I live?" As for Allan, he was
charmed with the success of his maneuver. Miss
Milroy had accepted his invitation; consequently, Miss Milroy was not offended with him. It
was on the tip of his tongue to mention the correspondence to his friend when they met at dinner. But there was something in Midwinter's
face and manner (even plain enough for Allan
to see) which warned him to wait a little before
he said anything to revive the painful subject of
their visit to the cottage. By common consent
they both avoided all topics connected with
Thorpe Ambrose, not even the visit from Mr.
Bashwood, which was to come with the evening, being referred to by either of them. All
through the dinner they drifted further and
further back into the old endless talk of past
times about ships and sailing. When the butler
withdrew from his attendance at table, he came
downstairs with a nautical problem on his
mind, and asked his fellow-servants if they
any of them knew the relative merits "on a
wind" and "off a wind" of a schooner and a
brig.

The two young men had sat longer at table
than usual that day. When they went out into
the garden with their cigars, the summer twilight fell gray and dim on lawn and flower bed,
and narrowed round them by slow degrees the
softly fading circle of the distant view. The dew
was heavy, and, after a few minutes in the garden, they agreed to go back to the drier ground
on the drive in front of the house.

They were close to the turning which led into the shrubbery, when there suddenly glided out on them, from behind the foliage, a softly stepping black figure—a shadow, moving darkly through the dim evening light. Midwinter started back at the sight of it, and even the less finely strung nerves of his friend were shaken for the moment.

"Who the devil are you?" cried Allan.

The figure bared its head in the gray light, and came slowly a step nearer. Midwinter advanced a step on his side, and looked closer. It was the man of the timid manners and the mourning garments, of whom he had asked the way to Thorpe Ambrose where the three roads met.

"Who are you?" repeated Allan.

"I humbly beg your pardon, sir," faltered the stranger, stepping back again, confusedly. "The servants told me I should find Mr. Armadale—"

"What, are you Mr. Bashwood?"

"Yes, if you please, sir."

"I beg your pardon for speaking to you so roughly," said Allan; "but the fact is, you rather startled me. My name is Armadale (put on your hat, pray), and this is my friend, Mr. Midwinter, who wants your help in the steward's office."

"We hardly stand in need of an introduction," said Midwinter. "I met Mr. Bashwood out walking a few days since, and he was kind enough to direct me when I had lost my way."

"Put on your hat," reiterated Allan, as Mr.

Bashwood, still bareheaded, stood bowing speech-
lessly, now to one of the young men, and now to
the other. "My good sir, put on your hat, and
let me show you the way back to the house.
Excuse me for noticing it," added Allan, as the
man, in sheer nervous helplessness, let his hat
fall, instead of putting it back on his head; "but
you seem a little out of sorts; a glass of good
wine will do you no harm before you and my
friend come to business. Whereabouts did you
meet with Mr. Bashwood, Midwinter, when you
lost your way?"

"I am too ignorant of the neighborhood to
know. I must refer you to Mr. Bashwood."

"Come, tell us where it was," said Allan, trying, a little too abruptly, to set the man at his
ease, as they all three walked back to the
house.

The measure of Mr. Bashwood's constitutional
timidity seemed to be filled to the brim by the
loudness of Allan's voice and the bluntness of
Allan's request. He ran over in the same feeble
flow of words with which he had deluged Midwinter on the occasion when they first met.

"It was on the road, sir," he began, addressing himself alternately to Allan, whom
he called, "sir," and to Midwinter, whom he
called by his name, "I mean, if you please,
on the road to Little Gill Beck. A singular
name, Mr. Midwinter, and a singular place;
I don't mean the village; I mean the neighborhood—I mean the 'Broads' beyond the neighborhood. Perhaps you may have heard of the

Norfolk Broads, sir? What they call lakes in
other parts of England, they call Broads here.
The Broads are quite numerous; I think they
would repay a visit. You would have seen the
first of them, Mr. Midwinter, if you had walked
on a few miles from where I had the honor
of meeting you. Remarkably numerous, the
Broads, sir—situated between this and the sea.
About three miles from the sea, Mr. Midwinter
—about three miles. Mostly shallow, sir, with
rivers running between them. Beautiful; solitary. Quite a watery country, Mr. Midwinter;
quite separate, as it were, in itself. Parties
sometimes visit them, sir—pleasure parties in
boats. It's quite a little net-work of lakes, or,
perhaps—yes, perhaps, more correctly, pools.
There is good sport in the cold weather. The
wild fowl are quite numerous. Yes; the Broads
would repay a visit, Mr. Midwinter, the next
time you are walking that way. The distance
from here to Little Gill Beck, and then from
Little Gill Beck to Girdler Broad, which is the
first you come to, is altogether not more—" In
sheer nervous inability to leave off, he would apparently have gone on talking of the Norfolk
Broads for the rest of the evening, if one of his
two listeners had not unceremoniously cut him
short before he could find his way into a new
sentence.

"Are the Broads within an easy day's drive
there and back from this house?" asked Allan,
feeling, if they were, that the place for the picnic was discovered already.

"Oh, yes, sir; a nice drive—quite a nice easy drive from this beautiful place!"

They were by this time ascending the portico steps, Allan leading the way up, and calling to Midwinter and Mr. Bashwood to follow him into the library, where there was a lighted lamp.

In the interval which elapsed before the wine made its appearance, Midwinter looked at his chance acquaintance of the high-road with strangely mingled feelings of compassion and distrust — of compassion that strengthened in spite of him; of distrust that persisted in diminishing, try as he might to encourage it to grow. There, perched comfortless on the edge of his chair, sat the poor broken-down, nervous wretch, in his worn black garments, with his watery eyes, his honest old outspoken wig, his miserable mohair stock, and his false teeth that were incapable of deceiving anybody—there he sat, politely ill at ease; now shrinking in the glare of the lamp, now wincing under the shock of Allan's sturdy voice; a man with the wrinkles of sixty years in his face, and the manners of a child in the presence of strangers; an object of pity surely, if ever there was a pitiable object yet!

"Whatever else you're afraid of, Mr. Bashwood," cried Allan, pouring out a glass of wine, "don't be afraid of that! There isn't a headache in a hogshead of it! Make yourself comfortable; I'll leave you and Mr. Midwinter to talk your business over by yourselves. It's all in Mr. Mid-

winter's hands; he acts for me, and settles
everything at his own discretion."

He said those words with a cautious choice of
expression very uncharacteristic of him, and,
without further explanation, made abruptly for
the door. Midwinter, sitting near it, noticed
his face as he went out. Easy as the way was
into Allan's favor, Mr. Bashwood, beyond all
kind of doubt, had in some unaccountable manner failed to find it!

The two strangely assorted companions were
left together—parted widely, as it seemed on the
surface, from any possible interchange of sympathy; drawn invisibly one to the other, nevertheless, by those magnetic similarities of temperament which overleap all difference of age
or station, and defy all apparent incongruities
of mind and character. From the moment when
Allan left the room, the hidden Influence that
works in darkness began slowly to draw the two
men together, across the great social desert which
had lain between them up to this day.

Midwinter was the first to approach the subject
of the interview.

"May I ask," he began, "if you have been
made acquainted with my position here, and if
you know why it is that I require your assistance?"

Mr. Bashwood—still hesitating and still timid,
but manifestly relieved by Allan's departure—
sat further back in his chair, and ventured on
fortifying himself with a modest little sip of
wine.

"Yes, sir," he replied; "Mr. Pedgift informed me of all—at least I think I may say so—of all the circumstances. I am to instruct, or perhaps, I ought to say to advise—"

"No, Mr. Bashwood; the first word was the best word of the two. I am quite ignorant of the duties which Mr. Armadale's kindness has induced him to intrust to me. If I understand right, there can be no question of your capacity to instruct me, for you once filled a steward's situation yourself. May I inquire where it was?"

"At Sir John Mellowship's, sir, in West Norfolk. Perhaps you would like—I have got it with me — to see my testimonial? Sir John might have dealt more kindly with me; but I have no complaint to make; it's all done and over now!" His watery eyes looked more watery still, and the trembling in his hands spread to his lips as he produced an old dingy letter from his pocket-book and laid it open on the table.

The testimonial was very briefly and very coldly expressed, but it was conclusive as far as it went. Sir John considered it only right to say that he had no complaint to make of any want of capacity or integrity in his steward. If Mr. Bashwood's domestic position had been compatible with the continued performance of his duties on the estate, Sir John would have been glad to keep him. As it was, embarrassments caused by the state of Mr. Bashwood's personal affairs had rendered it undesirable that he should

continue in Sir John's service; and on that
ground, and that only, his employer and he
had parted. Such was Sir John's testimony
to Mr. Bashwood's character. As Midwinter
read the last lines, he thought of another testimonial, still in his own possession—of the written character which they had given him at the
school, when they turned their sick usher adrift
in the world. His superstition (distrusting all
new events and all new faces at Thorpe Ambrose) still doubted the man before him as obstinately as ever. But when he now tried to
put those doubts into words, his heart upbraided
him, and he laid the letter on the table in silence.

The sudden pause in the conversation appeared
to startle Mr. Bashwood. He comforted himself
with another little sip of wine, and, leaving the
letter untouched, burst irrepressibly into words,
as if the silence was quite unendurable to him.

"I am ready to answer any question, sir," he
began. "Mr. Pedgift told me that I must answer questions, because I was applying for a
place of trust. Mr. Pedgift said neither you nor
Mr. Armadale was likely to think the testimonial
sufficient of itself. Sir John doesn't say — he
might have put it more kindly, but I don't complain—Sir John doesn't say what the troubles
were that lost me my place. Perhaps you might
wish to know—" He stopped confusedly, looked
at the testimonial, and said no more.

"If no interests but mine were concerned in
the matter," rejoined Midwinter, "the testimonial would, I assure you, be quite enough

to satisfy me. But while I am learning my new duties, the person who teaches me will be really and truly the steward of my friend's estate. I am very unwilling to ask you to speak on what may be a painful subject, and I am sadly inexperienced in putting such questions as I ought to put; but, perhaps, in Mr. Armadale's interests, I ought to know something more, either from yourself, or from Mr. Pedgift, if you prefer it—'' He, too, stopped confusedly, looked at the testimonial, and said no more.

There was another moment of silence. The night was warm, and Mr. Bashwood, among his other misfortunes, had the deplorable infirmity of perspiring at the palms of the hands. He took out a miserable little cotton pocket-handkerchief, rolled it up into a ball, and softly dabbed it to and fro, from one hand to the other, with the regularity of a pendulum. Performed by other men, under other circumstances, the action might have been ridiculous. Performed by this man, at the crisis of the interview, the action was horrible.

"Mr. Pedgift's time is too valuable, sir, to be wasted on me," he said. "I will mention what ought to be mentioned myself—if you will please to allow me. I have been unfortunate in my family. It was very hard to bear, though it seems not much to tell. My wife — '' One of his hands closed fast on the pocket-handkerchief; he moistened his dry lips, struggled with himself, and went on.

"My wife, sir," he resumed, "stood a little in

my way; she did me (I am afraid I must confess)
some injury with Sir John.   Soon after I got the
steward's situation, she contracted—she took—
she fell into habits (I hardly know how to say it)
of drinking.   I couldn't break her of it, and I
couldn't always conceal it from Sir John's knowledge.  She broke out, and—and tried his patience
once or twice, when he came to my office on business.   Sir John excused it, not very kindly; but
still he excused it.   I don't complain of Sir John!
I don't complain now of my wife."   He pointed
a trembling finger at his miserable crape-covered
beaver hat on the floor.   "I'm in mourning for
her," he said, faintly.   "She died nearly a year
ago, in the county asylum here."

His mouth began to work convulsively.  He
took up the glass of wine at his side, and, instead of sipping it this time, drained it to the
bottom.   "I'm not much used to wine, sir," he
said, conscious, apparently, of the flush that flew
into his face as he drank, and still observant of
the obligations of politeness amid all the misery
of the recollections that he was calling up.

"I beg, Mr. Bashwood, you will not distress
yourself by telling me any more," said Midwinter, recoiling from any further sanction on his
part of a disclosure which had already bared the
sorrows of the unhappy man before him to the
quick.

"I'm much obliged to you, sir," replied Mr.
Bashwood.   "But if I don't detain you too long,
and if you will please to remember that Mr. Pedgift's directions to me were very particular—and,

besides, I only mentioned my late wife because
if she hadn't tried Sir John's patience to begin
with, things might have turned out differently—"
He paused, gave up the disjointed sentence in
which he had involved himself, and tried another.
"I had only two children, sir," he went on, advancing to a new point in his narrative, "a boy
and a girl. The girl died when she was a baby.
My son lived to grow up; and it was my son who
lost me my place. I did my best for him; I got
him into a respectable office in London. They
wouldn't take him without security. I'm afraid
it was imprudent; but I had no rich friends to
help me, and I became security. My boy turned
out badly, sir. He — perhaps you will kindly
understand what I mean, if I say he behaved
dishonestly. His employers consented, at my
entreaty, to let him off without prosecuting. I
begged very hard—I was fond of my son James
—and I took him home, and did my best to re-
form him. He wouldn't stay with me; he went
away again to London; he—I beg your pardon,
sir! I'm afraid I'm confusing things; I'm afraid
I'm wandering from the point."

"No, no," said Midwinter, kindly. "If you
think it right to tell me this sad story, tell it in
your own way. Have you seen your son since
he left you to go to London?"

"No, sir. He's in London still, for all I know.
When I last heard of him, he was getting his
bread—not very creditably. He was employed,
under the inspector, at the Private Inquiry Office
in Shadyside Place."

He spoke those words—apparently (as events then stood) the most irrelevant to the matter in hand that had yet escaped him; actually (as events were soon to be) the most vitally important that he had uttered yet—he spoke those words absently, looking about him in confusion, and trying vainly to recover the lost thread of his narrative.

Midwinter compassionately helped him. "You were telling me," he said, "that your son had been the cause of your losing your place. How did that happen?"

"In this way, sir," said Mr. Bashwood, getting back again excitedly into the right train of thought. "His employers consented to let him off; but they came down on his security; and I was the man. I suppose they were not to blame; the security covered their loss. I couldn't pay it all out of my savings; I had to borrow—on the word of a man, sir, I couldn't help it—I had to borrow. My creditor pressed me; it seemed cruel, but, if he wanted the money, I suppose it was only just. I was sold out of house and home. I dare say other gentlemen would have said what Sir John said; I dare say most people would have refused to keep a steward who had had the bailiffs after him, and his furniture sold in the neighborhood. That was how it ended, Mr. Midwinter. I needn't detain you any longer —here is Sir John's address, if you wish to apply to him." Midwinter generously refused to receive the address.

"Thank you kindly, sir," said Mr. Bashwood,

getting tremulously on his legs. "There is nothing more, I think, except—except that Mr. Pedgift will speak for me, if you wish to inquire into my conduct in his service. I'm very much indebted to Mr. Pedgift; he's a little rough with me sometimes, but, if he hadn't taken me into his office, I think I should have gone to the workhouse when I left Sir John, I was so broken down." He picked up his dingy old hat from the floor. "I won't intrude any longer, sir. I shall be happy to call again, if you wish to have time to consider before you decide."

"I want no time to consider after what you have told me," replied Midwinter, warmly, his memory busy, while he spoke, with the time when *he* had told *his* story to Mr. Brock, and was waiting for a generous word in return, as the man before him was waiting now. "To-day is Saturday," he went on. "Can you come and give me my first lesson on Monday morning? I beg your pardon," he added, interrupting Mr. Bashwood's profuse expressions of acknowledgment, and stopping him on his way out of the room; "there is one thing we ought to settle, ought we not? We haven't spoken yet about your own interest in this matter; I mean, about the terms." He referred, a little confusedly, to the pecuniary part of the subject. Mr. Bashwood (getting nearer and nearer to the door) answered him more confusedly still.

"Anything, sir—anything you think right. I won't intrude any longer; I'll leave it to you and Mr. Armadale."

"I will send for Mr. Armadale, if you like," said Midwinter, following him into the hall. "But I am afraid he has as little experience in matters of this kind as I have. Perhaps, if you see no objection, we might be guided by Mr. Pedgift?"

Mr. Bashwood caught eagerly at the last suggestion, pushing his retreat, while he spoke, as far as the front door. "Yes, sir—oh, yes, yes! nobody better than Mr. Pedgift. Don't—pray don't disturb Mr. Armadale!" His watery eyes looked quite wild with nervous alarm as he turned round for a moment in the light of the hall lamp to make that polite request. If sending for Allan had been equivalent to unchaining a ferocious watch-dog, Mr. Bashwood could hardly have been more anxious to stop the proceeding. "I wish you kindly good-evening, sir," he went on, getting out to the steps. "I'm much obliged to you. I will be scrupulously punctual on Monday morning—I hope—I think—I'm sure you will soon learn everything I can teach you. It's not difficult—oh dear, no—not difficult at all! I wish you kindly good-evening, sir. A beautiful night; yes, indeed, a beautiful night for a walk home."

With those words, all dropping out of his lips one on the top of the other, and without noticing, in his agony of embarrassment at effecting his departure, Midwinter's outstretched hand, he went noiselessly down the steps, and was lost in the darkness of the night.

As Midwinter turned to re-enter the house, the

dining-room door opened and his friend met him
in the hall.

"Has Mr. Bashwood gone?" asked Allan.

"He has gone," replied Midwinter, "after telling me a very sad story, and leaving me a little
ashamed of myself for having doubted him without any just cause. I have arranged that he is
to give me my first lesson in the steward's office
on Monday morning."

"All right," said Allan. "You needn't be
afraid, old boy, of my interrupting you over
your studies. I dare say I'm wrong—but I
don't like Mr. Bashwood."

"I dare say *I'm* wrong," retorted the other,
a little petulantly. "I do."

The Sunday morning found Midwinter in the
park, waiting to intercept the postman, on the
chance of his bringing more news from Mr.
Brock.

At the customary hour the man made his appearance, and placed the expected letter in Midwinter's hands. He opened it, far away from
all fear of observation this time, and read these
lines:

"MY DEAR MIDWINTER—I write more for the
purpose of quieting your anxiety than because I
have anything definite to say. In my last hurried letter I had no time to tell you that the elder
of the two women whom I met in the Gardens
had followed me, and spoken to me in the street.
I believe I may characterize what she said (with-

out doing her any injustice) as a tissue of false-
hoods from beginning to end. At any rate, she
confirmed me in the suspicion that some underhand proceeding is on foot, of which Allan is
destined to be the victim, and that the prime
mover in the conspiracy is the vile woman who
helped his mother's marriage and who hastened
his mother's death.

"Feeling this conviction, I have not hesitated
to do, for Allan's sake, what I would have done
for no other creature in the world. I have left
my hotel, and have installed myself (with my
old servant Robert) in a house opposite the
house to which I traced the two women. We
are alternately on the watch (quite unsuspected,
I am certain, by the people opposite) day and
night. All my feelings, as a gentleman and a
clergyman, revolt from such an occupation as
I am now engaged in; but there is no other
choice. I must either do this violence to my
own self-respect, or I must leave Allan, with his
easy nature, and in his assailable position, to defend himself against a wretch who is prepared,
I firmly believe, to take the most unscrupulous
advantage of his weakness and his youth. His
mother's dying entreaty has never left my memory; and, God help me, I am now degrading
myself in my own eyes in consequence.

"There has been some reward already for the
sacrifice. This day (Saturday) I have gained an
immense advantage—I have at last seen the woman's face. She went out with her veil down as
before; and Robert kept her in view, having my

instructions, if she returned to the house, not to follow her back to the door. She did return to the house; and the result of my precaution was, as I had expected, to throw her off her guard. I saw her face unveiled at the window, and afterward again in the balcony. If any occasion should arise for describing her particularly, you shall have the description. At present I need only say that she looks the full age (five-and-thirty) at which you estimated her, and that she is by no means so handsome a woman as I had (I hardly know why) expected to see.

"This is all I can now tell you. If nothing more happens by Monday or Tuesday next, I shall have no choice but to apply to my lawyers for assistance; though I am most unwilling to trust this delicate and dangerous matter in other hands than mine. Setting my own feelings, however, out of the question, the business which has been the cause of my journey to London is too important to be trifled with much longer as I am trifling with it now. In any and every case, depend on my keeping you informed of the progress of events; and believe me yours truly,

"DECIMUS BROCK."

Midwinter secured the letter as he had secured the letter that preceded it—side by side in his pocket-book with the narrative of Allan's Dream.

"How many days more?" he asked himself, as he went back to the house. "How many days more?"

Not many.   The time he was waiting for was a time close at hand.

Monday came, and brought Mr. Bashwood, punctual to the appointed hour.   Monday came, and found Allan immersed in his preparations for the picnic.   He held a series of interviews, at home and abroad, all through the day.   He transacted business with Mrs. Gripper, with the butler, and with the coachman, in their three several departments of eating, drinking, and driving.   He went to the town to consult his professional advisers on the subject of the Broads, and to invite both the lawyers, father and son (in the absence of anybody else in the neighborhood whom he could ask), to join the picnic.   Pedgift Senior (in his department) supplied general information, but begged to be excused from appearing at the picnic, on the score of business engagements.   Pedgift Junior (in his department) added all the details; and, casting business engagements to the winds, accepted the invitation with the greatest pleasure.   Returning from the lawyer's office, Allan's next proceeding was to go to the major's cottage and obtain Miss Milroy's approval of the proposed locality for the pleasure party.   This object accomplished, he returned to his own house, to meet the last difficulty now left to encounter— the difficulty of persuading Midwinter to join the expedition to the Broads.

On first broaching the subject, Allan found his friend impenetrably resolute to remain at

home. Midwinter's natural reluctance to meet
the major and his daughter after what had happened at the cottage, might probably have been
overcome. But Midwinter's determination not
to allow Mr. Bashwood's course of instruction to
be interrupted was proof against every effort that
could be made to shake it. After exerting his
influence to the utmost, Allan was obliged to
remain contented with a compromise. Midwinter promised, not very willingly, to join the party
toward evening, at the place appointed for a
gypsy tea-making, which was to close the proceedings of the day. To this extent he would
consent to take the opportunity of placing himself on a friendly footing with the Milroys. More
he could not concede, even to Allan's persuasion,
and for more it would be useless to ask.

The day of the picnic came. The lovely morning, and the cheerful bustle of preparation for
the expedition, failed entirely to tempt Midwinter into altering his resolution. At the regular
hour he left the breakfast-table to join Mr. Bashwood in the steward's office. The two were
quietly closeted over the books, at the back of the
house, while the packing for the picnic went on
in front. Young Pedgift (short in stature, smart
in costume, and self-reliant in manner) arrived
some little time before the hour for starting, to
revise all the arrangements, and to make any
final improvements which his local knowledge
might suggest. Allan and he were still busy in
consultation when the first hitch occurred in the
proceedings. The woman-servant from the cot-

tage was reported to be waiting below for an answer to a note from her young mistress, which was placed in Allan's hands.

On this occasion Miss Milroy's emotions had apparently got the better of her sense of propriety. The tone of the letter was feverish, and the handwriting wandered crookedly up and down in deplorable freedom from all proper restraint.

"Oh, Mr. Armadale" (wrote the major's daughter), "such a misfortune! What *are* we to do? Papa has got a letter from grandmamma this morning about the new governess. Her reference has answered all the questions, and she's ready to come at the shortest notice. Grandmamma thinks (how provoking!) the sooner the better; and she says we may expect her—I mean the governess—either to-day or to-morrow. Papa says (he *will* be so absurdly considerate to everybody!) that we can't allow Miss Gwilt to come here (if she comes to-day) and find nobody at home to receive her. What *is* to be done? I am ready to cry with vexation. I have got the worst possible impression (though grandmamma says she is a charming person) of Miss Gwilt. *Can* you suggest something, dear Mr. Armadale? I'm sure papa would give way if you could. Don't stop to write; send me a message back. I have got a new hat for the picnic; and oh, the agony of not knowing whether I am to keep it on or take it off. Yours truly, E. M."

"The devil take Miss Gwilt!" said Allan, staring at his legal adviser in a state of helpless consternation.

"With all my heart, sir—I don't wish to interfere," remarked Pedgift Junior. "May I ask what's the matter?"

Allan told him. Mr. Pedgift the younger might have his faults, but a want of quickness of resource was not among them.

"There's a way out of the difficulty, Mr. Armadale," he said. "If the governess comes to-day, let's have her at the picnic."

Allan's eyes opened wide in astonishment.

"All the horses and carriages in the Thorpe Ambrose stables are not wanted for this small party of ours," proceeded Pedgift Junior. "Of course not! Very good. If Miss Gwilt comes to-day, she can't possibly get here before five o'clock. Good again. You order an open carriage to be waiting at the major's door at that time, Mr. Armadale, and I'll give the man his directions where to drive to. When the governess comes to the cottage, let her find a nice little note of apology (along with the cold fowl, or whatever else they give her after her journey) begging her to join us at the picnic, and putting a carriage at her own sole disposal to take her there. Gad, sir!" said young Pedgift, gayly, "she *must* be a Touchy One if she thinks herself neglected after that!"

"Capital!" cried Allan. "She shall have every attention. I'll give her the pony-chaise and the white harness, and she shall drive herself, if she likes."

He scribbled a line to relieve Miss Milroy's apprehensions, and gave the necessary orders for the pony-chaise.    Ten minutes later, the carriages for the pleasure party were at the door.

"Now we've taken all this trouble about her," said Allan, reverting to the governess as they left the house, "I wonder, if she does come to-day, whether we shall see her at the picnic!"

"Depends entirely on her age, sir," remarked young Pedgift, pronouncing judgment with the happy confidence in himself which eminently distinguished him.    "If she's an old one, she'll be knocked up with the journey, and she'll stick to the cold fowl and the cottage.    If she's a young one, either I know nothing of women, or the pony in the white harness will bring her to the picnic."

They started for the major's cottage.

## CHAPTER VIII.

### THE NORFOLK BROADS.

THE little group gathered together in Major Milroy's parlor to wait for the carriages from Thorpe Ambrose would hardly have conveyed the idea, to any previously uninstructed person introduced among them, of a party assembled in expectation of a picnic.    They were almost dull enough, so far as outward appearances went, to have been a party assembled in expectation of a marriage.

Even Miss Milroy herself, though conscious of looking her best in her bright muslin dress and

her gayly feathered new hat, was at this in-
auspicious moment Miss Milroy under a cloud.
Although Allan's note had assured her, in Allan's
strongest language, that the one great object of
reconciling the governess's arrival with the celebration of the picnic was an object achieved, the
doubt still remained whether the plan proposed
—whatever it might be—would meet with her
father's approval. In a word, Miss Milroy declined to feel sure of her day's pleasure until the
carriage made its appearance and took her from
the door. The major, on his side, arrayed for
the festive occasion in a tight blue frock-coat
which he had not worn for years, and threatened
with a whole long day of separation from his old
friend and comrade the clock, was a man out of
his element, if ever such a man existed yet. As
for the friends who had been asked at Allan's
request—the widow lady (otherwise Mrs. Pentecost) and her son (the Reverend Samuel) in delicate health—two people less capable, apparently,
of adding to the hilarity of the day could hardly
have been discovered in the length and breadth
of all England. A young man who plays his
part in society by looking on in green spectacles,
and listening with a sickly smile, may be a
prodigy of intellect and a mine of virtue, but he
is hardly, perhaps, the right sort of man to have
at a picnic. An old lady afflicted with deafness,
whose one inexhaustible subject of interest is the
subject of her son, and who (on the happily rare
occasions when that son opens his lips) asks
everybody eagerly, "What does my boy say?"

is a person to be pitied in respect of her infirmities, and a person to be admired in respect of her maternal devotedness, but not a person, if the thing could possibly be avoided, to take to a picnic. Such a man, nevertheless, was the Reverend Samuel Pentecost, and such a woman was the Reverend Samuel's mother; and in the dearth of any other producible guests, there they were, engaged to eat, drink, and be merry for the day at Mr. Armadale's pleasure party to the Norfolk Broads.

The arrival of Allan, with his faithful follower, Pedgift Junior, at his heels, roused the flagging spirits of the party at the cottage. The plan for enabling the governess to join the picnic, if she arrived that day, satisfied even Major Milroy's anxiety to show all proper attention to the lady who was coming into his house. After writing the necessary note of apology and invitation, and addressing it in her very best handwriting to the new governess, Miss Milroy ran upstairs to say good-by to her mother, and returned with a smiling face and a side look of relief directed at her father, to announce that there was nothing now to keep any of them a moment longer indoors. The company at once directed their steps to the garden gate, and were there met face to face by the second great difficulty of the day. How were the six persons of the picnic to be divided between the two open carriages that were in waiting for them?

Here, again, Pedgift Junior exhibited his invaluable faculty of contrivance. This highly

cultivated young man possessed in an eminent
degree an accomplishment more or less peculiar
to all the young men of the age we live in: he
was perfectly capable of taking his pleasure without forgetting his business. Such a client as the
Master of Thorpe Ambrose fell but seldom in his
father's way, and to pay special but unobtrusive
attention to Allan all through the day was the
business of which young Pedgift, while proving
himself to be the life and soul of the picnic, never
once lost sight from the beginning of the merry-
making to the end. He had detected the state
of affairs between Miss Milroy and Allan at a
glance, and he at once provided for his client's
inclinations in that quarter by offering, in virtue of his local knowledge, to lead the way in
the first carriage, and by asking Major Milroy
and the curate if they would do him the honor
of accompanying him.

"We shall pass a very interesting place to a
military man, sir," said young Pedgift, addressing the major, with his happy and unblushing
confidence—"the remains of a Roman encampment. And my father, sir, who is a subscriber,"
proceeded this rising lawyer, turning to the curate, "wished me to ask your opinion of the new
Infant School buildings at Little Gill Beck.
Would you kindly give it me as we go along?"
He opened the carriage door, and helped in the
major and the curate before they could either of
them start any difficulties. The necessary result
followed. Allan and Miss Milroy rode together
in the same carriage, with the extra convenience

of a deaf old lady in attendance to keep the
squire's compliments within the necessary limits.

Never yet had Allan enjoyed such an interview
with Miss Milroy as the interview he now obtained on the road to the Broads.

The dear old lady, after a little anecdote or
two on the subject of her son, did the one thing
wanting to secure the perfect felicity of her two
youthful companions: she became considerately
blind for the occasion, as well as deaf. A quarter of an hour after the carriage left the major's
cottage, the poor old soul, reposing on snug cush-
ions, and fanned by a fine summer air, fell peace-
ably asleep. Allan made love, and Miss Milroy
sanctioned the manufacture of that occasionally
precious article of human commerce, sublimely
indifferent on both sides to a solemn bass accompaniment on two notes, played by the curate's
mother's unsuspecting nose. The only interruption to the love-making (the snoring, being a
thing more grave and permanent in its nature,
was not interrupted at all) came at intervals
from the carriage ahead. Not satisfied with having the major's Roman encampment and the
curate's Infant Schools on his mind, Pedgift
Junior rose erect from time to time in his place,
and, respectfully hailing the hindmost vehicle,
directed Allan's attention, in a shrill tenor voice,
and with an excellent choice of language, to objects of interest on the road. The only way to
quiet him was to answer, which Allan invariably
did by shouting back, "Yes, beautiful," upon
which young Pedgift disappeared again in the

recesses of the leading carriage, and took up the Romans and the Infants where he had left them last.

The scene through which the picnic party was now passing merited far more attention than it received either from Allan or Allan's friends.

An hour's steady driving from the major's cottage had taken young Armadale and his guests beyond the limits of Midwinter's solitary walk, and was now bringing them nearer and nearer to one of the strangest and loveliest aspects of nature which the inland landscape, not of Norfolk only, but of all England, can show. Little by little the face of the country began to change as the carriages approached the remote and lonely district of the Broads. The wheat fields and turnip fields became perceptibly fewer, and the fat green grazing grounds on either side grew wider and wider in their smooth and sweeping range. Heaps of dry rushes and reeds, laid up for the basket-maker and the thatcher, began to appear at the road-side. The old gabled cottages of the early part of the drive dwindled and disappeared, and huts with mud walls rose in their place. With the ancient church towers and the wind and water mills, which had hitherto been the only lofty objects seen over the low marshy flat, there now rose all round the horizon, gliding slow and distant behind fringes of pollard willows, the sails of invisible boats moving on invisible waters. All the strange and startling anomalies presented by an inland agricultural district, isolated from other districts by its intricate surrounding network of pools and streams —holding its communications and carrying its produce by water instead of by land—began to present themselves in closer and closer succession. Nets appeared on cottage pailings; little flat-bottomed boats lay strangely at rest among the flowers in cottage gardens; farmers' men passed to and fro clad in composite costume of the coast and the field, in sailors' hats, and fishermen's boots, and plowmen's smocks; and even yet the low-lying labyrinth of waters, embosomed in its mystery of solitude, was a hidden labyrinth still. A minute more, and the carriages took a sudden turn from the hard high-road into a little weedy lane. The wheels ran noiseless on the damp and spongy ground. A lonely outlying cottage appeared, with its litter of nets and boats. A few yards further on, and the last morsel of firm earth suddenly ended in a tiny creek and quay. One turn more to the end of the quay—and there, spreading its great sheet of water, far and bright and smooth, on the right hand and the left— there, as pure in its spotless blue, as still in its heavenly peacefulness, as the summer sky above it, was the first of the Norfolk Broads.

The carriages stopped, the love-making broke off, and the venerable Mrs. Pentecost, recovering the use of her senses at a moment's notice, fixed her eyes sternly on Allan the instant she woke.

"I see in your face, Mr. Armadale," said the old lady, sharply, "that you think I have been asleep."

The consciousness of guilt acts differently on the two sexes. In nine cases out of ten, it is a much more manageable consciousness with a woman than with a man. All the confusion, on this occasion, was on the man's side. While Allan reddened and looked embarrassed, the quickwitted Miss Milroy instantly embraced the old lady with a burst of innocent laughter. "He is quite incapable, dear Mrs. Pentecost," said the little hypocrite, "of anything so ridiculous as thinking you have been asleep!"

"All I wish Mr. Armadale to know," pursued the old lady, still suspicious of Allan, "is, that my head being giddy, I am obliged to close my eyes in a carriage. Closing the eyes, Mr. Armadale, is one thing, and going to sleep is another. Where is my son?"

The Reverend Samuel appeared silently at the carriage door, and assisted his mother to get out. ("Did you enjoy the drive, Sammy?" asked the old lady. "Beautiful scenery, my dear, wasn't it?") Young Pedgift, on whom all the arrangements for exploring the Broads devolved, bustled about, giving his orders to the boatman. Major Milroy, placid and patient, sat apart on an overturned punt, and privately looked at his watch. Was it past noon already? More than an hour past. For the first time, for many a long year, the famous clock at home had struck in an empty workshop. Time had lifted his wonderful scythe, and the corporal and his men had relieved guard, with no master's eye to watch their performances, with no master's hand to encourage them to do their best. The major sighed as he put his watch back in his pocket. "I'm afraid I'm too old for this sort of thing," thought the good man, looking about him dreamily. "I don't find I enjoy it as much as I thought I should. When are we going on the water, I wonder? Where's Neelie?"

Neelie—more properly Miss Milroy—was behind one of the carriages with the promoter of the picnic. They were immersed in the interesting subject of their own Christian names, and Allan was as near a pointblank proposal of marriage as it is well possible for a thoughtless young gentleman of two-and-twenty to be.

"Tell me the truth," said Miss Milroy, with her eyes modestly riveted on the ground. "When you first knew what my name was, you didn't like it, did you?"

"I like everything that belongs to you," rejoined Allan, vigorously. "I think Eleanor is a beautiful name; and yet, I don't know why, I think the major made an improvement when he changed it to Neelie."

"I can tell you why, Mr. Armadale," said the major's daughter, with great gravity. "There are some unfortunate people in this world whose names are—how can I express it?—whose names are misfits. Mine is a misfit. I don't blame my parents, for of course it was impossible to know when I was a baby how I should grow up. But as things are, I and my name don't fit each other. When you hear a young lady called Eleanor, you think of a tall, beautiful, interesting creature directly—the very opposite of *me!*

With my personal appearance, Eleanor sounds ridiculous; and Neelie, as you yourself remarked, is just the thing. No! no! don't say any more; I'm tired of the subject. I've got another name in my head, if we must speak of names, which is much better worth talking about than mine."

She stole a glance at her companion which said plainly enough, "The name is yours." Allan advanced a step nearer to her, and lowered his voice, without the slightest necessity, to a mysterious whisper. Miss Milroy instantly resumed her investigation of the ground. She looked at it with such extraordinary interest that a geologist might have suspected her of scientific flirtation with the superficial strata.

"What name are you thinking of?" asked Allan.

Miss Milroy addressed her answer, in the form of a remark, to the superficial strata—and let them do what they liked with it, in their capacity of conductors of sound. "If I had been a man," she said, "I should so like to have been called Allan!"

She felt his eyes on her as she spoke, and, turning her head aside, became absorbed in the graining of the panel at the back of the carriage. "How beautiful it is!" she exclaimed, with a sudden outburst of interest in the vast subject of varnish. "I wonder how they do it?"

Man persists, and woman yields. Allan declined to shift the ground from love-making to coach-making. Miss Milroy dropped the subject

"Call me by my name, if you really like it,"

he whispered, persuasively. "Call me 'Allan' for once; just to try."

She hesitated with a heightened color and a charming smile, and shook her head. "I couldn't just yet," she answered, softly.

"May I call you Neelie? Is it too soon?"

She looked at him again, with a sudden disturbance about the bosom of her dress, and a sudden flash of tenderness in her dark-gray eyes.

"You know best," she said, faintly, in a whisper.

The inevitable answer was on the tip of Allan's tongue. At the very instant, however, when he opened his lips, the abhorrent high tenor of Pedgift Junior, shouting for "Mr. Armadale," rang cheerfully through the quiet air. At the same moment, from the other side of the carriage, the lurid spectacles of the Reverend Samuel showed themselves officiously on the search; and the voice of the Reverend Samuel's mother (who had, with great dexterity, put the two ideas of the presence of water and a sudden movement among the company together) inquired distractedly if anybody was drowned? Sentiment flies and Love shudders at all demonstrations of the noisy kind. Allan said: "Damn it," and rejoined young Pedgift. Miss Milroy sighed, and took refuge with her father.

"I've done it, Mr. Armadale!" cried young Pedgift, greeting his patron gayly. "We can all go on the water together; I've got the biggest boat on the Broads. The little skiffs," he added, in a lower tone, as he led the way to the quay steps, "besides being ticklish and easily upset, won't hold more than two, with the boatman; and the major told me he should feel it his duty to go with his daughter, if we all separated in different boats. I thought *that* would hardly do, sir," pursued Pedgift Junior, with a respectfully sly emphasis on the words. "And, besides, if we had put the old lady into a skiff, with her weight (sixteen stone if she's a pound), we might have had her upside down in the water half her time, which would have occasioned delay, and thrown what you call a damp on the proceedings. Here's the boat, Mr. Armadale. What do you think of it?"

The boat added one more to the strangely anomalous objects which appeared at the Broads. It was nothing less than a stout old life-boat, passing its last declining years on the smooth fresh water, after the stormy days of its youth time on the wild salt sea. A comfortable little cabin for the use of fowlers in the winter season had been built amidships, and a mast and sail adapted for inland navigation had been fitted forward. There was room enough and to spare for the guests, the dinner, and the three men in charge. Allan clapped his faithful lieutenant approvingly on the shoulder; and even Mrs. Pentecost, when the whole party were comfortably established on board, took a comparatively cheerful view of the prospects of the picnic. "If anything happens," said the old lady, addressing the company generally, "there's one comfort for all of us. My son can swim."

The boat floated out from the creek into the placid waters of the Broad, and the full beauty of the scene opened on the view.

On the northward and westward, as the boat reached the middle of the lake, the shore lay clear and low in the sunshine, fringed darkly at certain points by rows of dwarf trees; and dotted here and there, in the opener spaces, with windmills and reed-thatched cottages, of puddled mud. Southward, the great sheet of water narrowed gradually to a little group of close-nestling islands which closed the prospect; while to the east a long, gently undulating line of reeds followed the windings of the Broad, and shut out all view of the watery wastes beyond. So clear and so light was the summer air that the one cloud in the eastern quarter of the heaven was the smoke-cloud left by a passing steamer three miles distant and more on the invisible sea. When the voices of the pleasure party were still, not a sound rose, far or near, but the faint ripple at the bows, as the men, with slow, deliberate strokes of their long poles, pressed the boat forward softly over the shallow water. The world and the world's turmoil seemed left behind forever on the land; the silence was the silence of enchantment—the delicious interflow of the soft purity of the sky and the bright tranquillity of the lake.

Established in perfect comfort in the boat—the major and his daughter on one side, the curate and his mother on the other, and Allan and young Pedgift between the two—the water party floated smoothly toward the little nest of islands at the end of the Broad. Miss Milroy was in raptures; Allan was delighted; and the major for once forgot his clock. Every one felt pleasurably, in their different ways, the quiet and beauty of the scene. Mrs. Pentecost, in her way, felt it like a clairvoyant—with closed eyes.

"Look behind you, Mr. Armadale," whispered young Pedgift. "I think the parson's beginning to enjoy himself."

An unwonted briskness—portentous apparently of coming speech—did certainly at that moment enliven the curate's manner. He jerked his head from side to side like a bird; he cleared his throat, and clasped his hands, and looked with a gentle interest at the company. Getting into spirits seemed, in the case of this excellent person, to be alarmingly like getting into the pulpit.

"Even in this scene of tranquillity," said the Reverend Samuel, coming out softly with his first contribution to the society in the shape of a remark, "the Christian mind—led, so to speak, from one extreme to another—is forcibly recalled to the unstable nature of all earthly enjoyments. How if this calm should not last? How if the winds rose and the waters became agitated?"

"You needn't alarm yourself about that, sir," said young Pedgift; "June's the fine season here —and you can swim."

Mrs. Pentecost (mesmerically affected, in all probability, by the near neighborhood of her son) opened her eyes suddenly and asked, with her customary eagerness: "What does my boy say?"

The Reverend Samuel repeated his words in the key that suited his mother's infirmity. The old lady nodded in high approval, and pursued her son's train of thought through the medium of a quotation.

"Ah!" sighed Mrs. Pentecost, with infinite relish, "He rides the whirlwind, Sammy, and directs the storm!"

"Noble words!" said the Reverend Samuel. "Noble and consoling words!"

"I say," whispered Allan, "if he goes on much longer in that way, what's to be done?"

"I told you, papa, it was a risk to ask them," added Miss Milroy, in another whisper.

"My dear!" remonstrated the major. "We knew nobody else in the neighborhood, and, as Mr. Armadale kindly suggested our bringing our friends, what could we do?"

"We can't upset the boat," remarked young Pedgift, with sardonic gravity. "It's a life-boat, unfortunately. May I venture to suggest putting something into the reverend gentleman's mouth, Mr. Armadale? It's close on three o'clock. What do you say to ringing the dinner-bell, sir?"

Never was the right man more entirely in the right place than Pedgift Junior at the picnic. In ten minutes more the boat was brought to a stand-still among the reeds; the Thorpe Ambrose hampers were unpacked on the roof of the cabin; and the current of the curate's eloquence was checked for the day.

How inestimably important in its moral results—and therefore how praiseworthy in itself—is the act of eating and drinking! The social virtues center in the stomach. A man who is not a better husband, father, and brother after dinner than before is, digestively speaking, an incurably vicious man. What hidden charms of character disclose themselves, what dormant amiabilities awaken, when our common humanity gathers together to pour out the gastric juice! At the opening of the hampers from Thorpe Ambrose, sweet Sociability (offspring of the happy union of Civilization and Mrs. Gripper) exhaled among the boating party, and melted in one friendly fusion the discordant elements of which that party had hitherto been composed. Now did the Reverend Samuel Pentecost, whose light had hitherto been hidden under a bushel, prove at last that he could do something by proving that he could eat. Now did Pedgift Junior shine brighter than ever he had shone yet in gems of caustic humor and exquisite fertilities of resource. Now did the squire, and the squire's charming guest, prove the triple connection between Champagne that sparkles, Love that grows bolder, and Eyes whose vocabulary is without the word No. Now did cheerful old times come back to the major's memory, and cheerful old stories not told for years find their way to the major's lips. And now did Mrs. Pentecost, coming out wakefully in the whole force of her estimable maternal character, seize on a supplementary fork, and ply that useful instrument incessantly between the choicest morsels in the whole round of dishes, and the few vacant places left available on the Reverend Samuel's plate. "Don't laugh at my son," cried the old lady, observing the merriment which her proceedings produced among the company. "It's my fault, poor dear—*I* make him eat!" And there are men in this world who, seeing virtues such as these developed at the table, as they are developed nowhere else, can, nevertheless, rank the glorious privilege of dining with the smallest of the diurnal personal worries which necessity imposes on mankind— with buttoning your waistcoat, for example, or lacing your stays! Trust no such monster as this with your tender secrets, your loves and hatreds, your hopes and fears. His heart is uncorrected by his stomach, and the social virtues are not in him.

The last mellow hours of the day and the first cool breezes of the long summer evening had met before the dishes were all laid waste, and the bottles as empty as bottles should be. This point in the proceedings attained, the picnic party looked lazily at Pedgift Junior to know what was to be done next. That inexhaustible functionary was equal as ever to all the calls on him. He had a new amusement ready before the quickest of the company could so much as ask him what that amusement was to be.

"Fond of music on the water, Miss Milroy?" he asked, in his airiest and pleasantest manner.

Miss Milroy adored music, both on the water

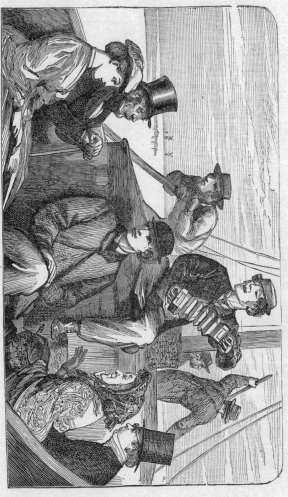

YOUNG PEDGIFT WAS TROUBLED WITH NO NERVOUS HESITATION.

—Armadale, Vol. Eight, page 445.

and the land—always excepting the one case when she was practicing the art herself on the piano at home.

"We'll get out of the reeds first," said young Pedgift. He gave his orders to the boatmen, dived briskly into the little cabin, and re-appeared with a concertina in his hand. "Neat, Miss Milroy, isn't it?" he observed, pointing to his initials, inlaid on the instrument in mother-of-pearl. "My name's Augustus, like my father's. Some of my friends knock off the 'A,' and call me 'Gustus Junior.' A small joke goes a long way among friends, doesn't it, Mr. Armadale? I sing a little to my own accompaniment, ladies and gentlemen; and, if quite agreeable, I shall be proud and happy to do my best."

"Stop!" cried Mrs. Pentecost; "I dote on music."

With this formidable announcement, the old lady opened a prodigious leather bag, from which she never parted night or day, and took out an ear-trumpet of the old-fashioned kind — something between a key-bugle and a French horn. "I don't care to use the thing generally," explained Mrs. Pentecost, "because I'm afraid of its making me deafer than ever. But I can't and won't miss the music. I dote on music. If you'll hold the other end, Sammy, I'll stick it in my ear. Neelie, my dear, tell him to begin."

Young Pedgift was troubled with no nervous hesitation. He began at once, not with songs of the light and modern kind, such as might have been expected from an amateur of his age and character, but with declamatory and patriotic bursts of poetry, set to the bold and blatant music which the people of England loved dearly at the earlier part of the present century, and which, whenever they can get it, they love dearly still. "The Death of Marmion," "The Battle of the Baltic," "The Bay of Biscay," "Nelson," under various vocal aspects, as exhibited by the late Braham—these were the songs in which the roaring concertina and strident tenor of Gustus Junior exulted together. "Tell me when you're tired, ladies and gentlemen," said the minstrel solicitor. "There's no conceit about *me*. Will you have a little sentiment by way of variety? Shall I wind up with 'The Mistletoe Bough' and 'Poor Mary Anne'? "

Having favored his audience with those two cheerful melodies, young Pedgift respectfully requested the rest of the company to follow his vocal example in turn, offering, in every case, to play "a running accompaniment" impromptu, if the singer would only be so obliging as to favor him with the key-note.

"Go on, somebody!" cried Mrs. Pentecost, eagerly. "I tell you again, I dote on music. We haven't had half enough yet, have we, Sammy?"

The Reverend Samuel made no reply. The unhappy man had reasons of his own—not exactly in his bosom, but a little lower—for remaining silent, in the midst of the general hilarity and the general applause. Alas for humanity! Even maternal love is alloyed with mortal fallibility. Owing much already to his excellent mother, the Reverend Samuel was now additionally indebted to her for a smart indigestion.

Nobody, however, noticed as yet the signs and tokens of internal revolution in the curate's face. Everybody was occupied in entreating everybody else to sing. Miss Milroy appealed to the founder of the feast. "Do sing something, Mr. Armadale," she said; "I should so like to hear you!"

"If you once begin, sir," added the cheerful Pedgift, "you'll find it get uncommonly easy as you go on. Music is a science which requires to be taken by the throat at starting."

"With all my heart," said Allan, in his good-humored way. "I know lots of tunes, but the worst of it is, the words escape me. I wonder if I can remember one of Moore's Melodies? My poor mother used to be fond of teaching me Moore's Melodies when I was a boy."

"Whose melodies?" asked Mrs. Pentecost. "Moore's? Aha! I know Tom Moore by heart."

"Perhaps in that case you will be good enough to help me, ma'am, if my memory breaks down," rejoined Allan. "I'll take the easiest melody in the whole collection, if you'll allow me. Everybody knows it—'Eveleen's Bower.'"

"I'm familiar, in a general sort of way, with the national melodies of England, Scotland, and Ireland," said Pedgift Junior. "I'll accompany you, sir, with the greatest pleasure. This is the sort of thing, I think." He seated himself cross-

legged on the roof of the cabin, and burst into a
complicated musical improvisation wonderful to
hear—a mixture of instrumental flourishes and
groans; a jig corrected by a dirge, and a dirge
enlivened by a jig. "That's the sort of thing,"
said young Pedgift, with his smile of supreme
confidence. "Fire away, sir!"

Mrs. Pentecost elevated her trumpet, and Allan
elevated his voice. "Oh, weep for the hour when
to Eveleen's Bower—" He stopped; the accompaniment stopped; the audience waited. "It's
a most extraordinary thing," said Allan; "I
thought I had the next line on the tip of my
tongue, and it seems to have escaped me. I'll
begin again, if you have no objection. 'Oh,
weep for the hour when to Eveleen's Bower—' "

" 'The lord of the valley with false vows
came,' " said Mrs. Pentecost.

"Thank you, ma'am," said Allan. "Now I
shall get on smoothly. 'Oh, weep for the hour
when to Eveleen's Bower, the lord of the valley
with false vows came. The moon was shining
bright—' "

"No!" said Mrs. Pentecost.

"I beg your pardon, ma'am," remonstrated
Allan. " 'The moon was shining bright—' "

"The moon wasn't doing anything of the
kind," said Mrs. Pentecost.

Pedgift Junior, foreseeing a dispute, perse-
vered *sotto voce* with the accompaniment, in
the interests of harmony.

"Moore's own words, ma'am," said **Allan**,
"in my mother's copy of the Melodies."

"Your mother's copy was wrong," retorted Mrs. Pentecost. "Didn't I tell you just now that I knew Tom Moore by heart?"

Pedgift Junior's peace-making concertina still flourished and groaned in the minor key.

"Well, what *did* the moon do?" asked Allan, in despair.

"What the moon *ought* to have done, sir, or Tom Moore wouldn't have written it so," rejoined Mrs. Pentecost. " 'The moon hid her light from the heaven that night, and wept behind her clouds o'er the maiden's shame!' I wish that young man would leave off playing," added Mrs. Pentecost, venting her rising irritation on Gustus Junior. "I've had enough of him—he tickles my ears."

"Proud, I'm sure, ma'am," said the unblushing Pedgift. "The whole science of music consists in tickling the ears."

"We seem to be drifting into a sort of argument," remarked Major Milroy, placidly. "Wouldn't it be better if Mr. Armadale went on with his song?"

"Do go on, Mr. Armadale!" added the major's daughter. "Do go on, Mr. Pedgift!"

"One of them doesn't know the words, and the other doesn't know the music," said Mrs. Pentecost. "Let them go on if they can!"

"Sorry to disappoint you, ma'am," said Pedgift Junior; "I'm ready to go on myself to any extent. Now, Mr. Armadale!"

Allan opened his lips to take up the unfinished melody where he had last left it. Before he could utter a note, the curate suddenly rose, with a ghastly face, and a hand pressed convulsively over the middle region of his waistcoat.

"What's the matter?" cried the whole boating party in chorus.

"I am exceedingly unwell," said the Reverend Samuel Pentecost. The boat was instantly in a state of confusion. "Eveleen's Bower" expired on Allan's lips, and even the irrepressible concertina of Pedgift was silenced at last. The alarm proved to be quite needless. Mrs. Pentecost's son possessed a mother, and that mother had a bag. In two seconds the art of medicine occupied the place left vacant in the attention of the company by the art of music.

"Rub it gently, Sammy," said Mrs. Pentecost. "I'll get out the bottles and give you a dose. It's his poor stomach, major. Hold my trumpet, somebody—and stop the boat. You take that bottle, Neelie, my dear; and you take this one, Mr. Armadale; and give them to me as I want them. Ah, poor dear, I know what's the matter with him! Want of power *here*, major—cold, acid, and flabby. Ginger to warm him; soda to correct him; sal volatile to hold him up. There, Sammy! drink it before it settles; and then go and lie down, my dear, in that dog-kennel of a place they call the cabin. No more music!" added Mrs. Pentecost, shaking her forefinger at the proprietor of the concertina—"unless it's a hymn, and that I don't object to."

Nobody appearing to be in a fit frame of mind for singing a hymn, the all-accomplished Pedgift drew upon his stores of local knowledge, and produced a new idea. The course of the boat was immediately changed under his direction. In a few minutes more, the company found themselves in a little island creek, with a lonely cottage at the far end of it, and a perfect forest of reeds closing the view all round them. "What do you say, ladies and gentlemen, to stepping on shore and seeing what a reed-cutter's cottage looks like?" suggested young Pedgift.

"We say yes, to be sure," answered Allan. "I think our spirits have been a little dashed by Mr. Pentecost's illness and Mrs. Pentecost's bag," he added, in a whisper to Miss Milroy. "A change of this sort is the very thing we want to set us all going again."

He and young Pedgift handed Miss Milroy out of the boat. The major followed. Mrs. Pentecost sat immovable as the Egyptian Sphinx, with her bag on her knees, mounting guard over "Sammy" in the cabin.

"We must keep the fun going, sir," said Allan, as he helped the major over the side of the boat. "We haven't half done yet with the enjoyment of the day."

His voice seconded his hearty belief in his own prediction to such good purpose that even Mrs. Pentecost heard him, and ominously shook her head.

"Ah!" sighed the curate's mother, "if you were as old as I am, young gentleman, you wouldn't feel quite so sure of the enjoyment of the day!"

So, in rebuke of the rashness of youth, spoke the caution of age. The negative view is notoriously the safe view, all the world over, and the Pentecost philosophy is, as a necessary consequence, generally in the right.

* * *

## CHAPTER IX.

### FATE OR CHANCE?

IT was close on six o'clock when Allan and his friends left the boat, and the evening influence was creeping already, in its mystery and its stillness, over the watery solitude of the Broads.

The shore in these wild regions was not like the shore elsewhere. Firm as it looked, the garden ground in front of the reed-cutter's cottage was floating ground, that rose and fell and oozed into puddles under the pressure of the foot. The boatmen who guided the visitors warned them to keep to the path, and pointed through gaps in the reeds and pollards to grassy places, on which strangers would have walked confidently, where the crust of earth was not strong enough to bear the weight of a child over the unfathomed depths of slime and water beneath. The solitary cottage, built of planks pitched black, stood on ground that had been steadied and strengthened by resting it on piles. A little wooden tower rose at one end of the roof, and served as a lookout post in the fowling season. From this elevation the eye ranged far and wide over a wilderness of winding water and lonesome marsh. If the reed-cutter had lost his boat, he would have been as completely isolated from all communication with town or village as if his place of abode had been a light - vessel instead of a cottage. Neither he nor his family complained of their solitude, or looked in any way the rougher or the worse for it. His wife received the visitors hospitably, in a snug little room, with a raftered ceiling, and windows which looked like windows in a cabin on board ship. His wife's father told stories of the famous days when the smugglers came up from the sea at night, rowing through the net-work of rivers with muffled oars till they gained the lonely Broads, and sank their spirit casks in the water, far from the coast-guard's reach. His wild little children played at hide-and - seek with the visitors; and the visitors ranged in and out of the cottage, and round and round the morsel of firm earth on which it stood, surprised and delighted by the novelty of all they saw. The one person who noticed the advance of the evening — the one person who thought of the flying time and the stationary Pentecosts in the boat — was young Pedgift. That experienced pilot of the Broads looked askance at his watch, and drew Allan aside at the first opportunity.

"I don't wish to hurry you, Mr. Armadale," said Pedgift Junior; "but the time is getting on, and there's a lady in the case."

"A lady?" repeated Allan.

"Yes, sir," rejoined young Pedgift. "A lady

from London; connected (if you'll allow me to jog your memory) with a pony-chaise and white harness.''

'Good heavens, the governess!'' cried Allan. "Why, we have forgotten all about her!''

"Don't be alarmed, sir; there's plenty of time, if we only get into the boat again. This is how it stands, Mr. Armadale. We settled, if you remember, to have the gypsy tea-making at the next 'Broad' to this—Hurle Mere?''

"Certainly,'' said Allan. "Hurle Mere is the place where my friend Midwinter has promised to come and meet us.''

"Hurle Mere is where the governess will be, sir, if your coachman follows my directions,'' pursued young Pedgift. "We have got nearly an hour's punting to do, along the twists and turns of the narrow waters (which they call The Sounds here) between this and Hurle Mere; and according to my calculations we must get on board again in five minutes, if we are to be in time to meet the governess and to meet your friend.''

"We mustn't miss my friend on any account,'' said Allan; "or the governess, either, of course. I'll tell the major.''

Major Milroy was at that moment preparing to mount the wooden watch-tower of the cottage to see the view. The ever useful Pedgift volunteered to go up with him, and rattle off all the necessary local explanations in half the time which the reed-cutter would occupy in describing his own neighborhood to a stranger.

Allan remained standing in front of the cottage, more quiet and more thoughtful than usual. His interview with young Pedgift had brought his absent friend to his memory for the first time since the picnic party had started. He was surprised that Midwinter, so much in his thoughts on all other occasions, should have been so long out of his thoughts now. Something troubled him, like a sense of self-reproach, as his mind reverted to the faithful friend at home, toiling hard over the steward's books, in his interests and for his sake. "Dear old fellow," thought Allan, "I shall be so glad to see him at the Mere; the day's pleasure won't be complete till he joins us!"

"Should I be right or wrong, Mr. Armadale, if I guessed that you were thinking of somebody?" asked a voice, softly, behind him.

Allan turned, and found the major's daughter at his side. Miss Milroy (not unmindful of a certain tender interview which had taken place behind a carriage) had noticed her admirer standing thoughtfully by himself, and had determined on giving him another opportunity, while her father and young Pedgift were at the top of the watch-tower.

"You know everything," said Allan, smiling. "I *was* thinking of somebody."

Miss Milroy stole a glance at him—a glance of gentle encouragement. There could be but one human creature in Mr. Armadale's mind after what had passed between them that morning! It would be only an act of mercy to take him back again at once to the interrupted conversation of a few hours since on the subject of names.

"I have been thinking of somebody, too," she said, half-inviting, half - repelling the coming avowal. "If I tell you the first letter of my Somebody's name, will you tell me the first letter of yours?"

"I will tell you anything you like," rejoined Allan, with the utmost enthusiasm.

She still shrank coquettishly from the very subject that she wanted to approach. "Tell me your letter first," she said, in low tones, looking away from him.

Allan laughed. "M," he said, "is my first letter."

She started a little. Strange that he should be thinking of her by her surname instead of her Christian name; but it mattered little as long as he *was* thinking of her.

"What is your letter?" asked Allan.

She blushed and smiled. "A — if you will have it!" she answered, in a reluctant little whisper. She stole another look at him, and luxuriously protracted her enjoyment of the coming avowal once more. "How many syllables is the name in?" she asked, drawing patterns shyly on the ground with the end of the parasol.

No man with the slightest knowledge of the sex would have been rash enough, in Allan's position, to tell her the truth. Allan, who knew nothing whatever of woman's natures, and who told the truth right and left in all morta. emergencies, answered as if he had been under examination in a court of justice.

"It's a name in three syllables," he said.

Miss Milroy's downcast eyes flashed up at him like lightning. "Three!" she repeated, in the blankest astonishment.

Allan was too inveterately straightforward to take the warning even now. "I'm not strong at my spelling, I know," he said, with his lighthearted laugh. "But I don't think I'm wrong in calling Midwinter a name in three syllables. I was thinking of my friend; but never mind my thoughts. Tell me who A is—tell me whom *you* were thinking of?"

"Of the first letter of the alphabet, Mr. Armadale, and I beg positively to inform you of nothing more!"

With that annihilating answer the major's daughter put up her parasol and walked back by herself to the boat.

Allan stood petrified with amazement. If Miss Milroy had actually boxed his ears (and there is no denying that she had privately longed to devote her hand to that purpose), he could hardly have felt more bewildered than he felt now. "What on earth have I done?" he asked himself, helplessly, as the major and young Pedgift joined him, and the three walked down together to the water-side. "I wonder what she'll say to me next?"

She said absolutely nothing; she never so much as looked at Allan when he took his place

in the boat. There she sat, with her eyes and
her complexion both much brighter than usual,
taking the deepest interest in the curate's progress toward recovery; in the state of Mrs. Pentecost's spirits; in Pedgift Junior (for whom she
ostentatiously made room enough to let him sit
beside her); in the scenery and the reed-cutter's
cottage; in everybody and everything but Allan
—whom she would have married with the greatest pleasure five minutes since. "I'll never forgive him," thought the major's daughter. "To
be thinking of that ill-bred wretch when I was
thinking of *him;* and to make me all but confess it before I found him out! Thank Heaven,
Mr. Pedgift is in the boat!"

In this frame of mind Miss Neelie applied herself forthwith to the fascination of Pedgift and
the discomfiture of Allan. "Oh, Mr. Pedgift,
how extremely clever and kind of you to think
of showing us that sweet cottage! Lonely, Mr.
Armadale? I don't think it's lonely at all; I
should like of all things to live there. What
would this picnic have been without you, Mr.
Pedgift; you can't think how I have enjoyed it
since we got into the boat. Cool, Mr. Armadale?
What can you possibly mean by saying it's cool;
it's the warmest evening we've had this summer. And the music, Mr. Pedgift; how nice
it was of you to bring your concertina! I wonder if I could accompany you on the piano? I
should so like to try. Oh, yes, Mr. Armadale,
no doubt you meant to do something musical,
too, and I dare say you sing very well when

you know the words; but, to tell you the truth,
I always did, and always shall, hate Moore's
Melodies!"

Thus, with merciless dexterity of manipula-
tion, did Miss Milroy work that sharpest female
weapon of offense, the tongue; and thus she
would have used it for some time longer, if
Allan had only shown the necessary jealousy,
or if Pedgift had only afforded the necessary encouragement. But adverse fortune had decreed
that she should select for her victims two men
essentially unassailable under existing circumstances. Allan was too innocent of all knowledge of female subtleties and susceptibilities to
understand anything, except that the charming
Neelie was unreasonably out of temper with him
without the slightest cause. The wary Pedgift,
as became one of the quick-witted youth of the
present generation, submitted to female influence, with his eye fixed immovably all the
time on his own interests. Many a young man
of the past generation, who was no fool, has
sacrificed everything for love. Not one young
man in ten thousand of the present generation,
*except* the fools, has sacrificed a half-penny.
The daughters of Eve still inherit their mother's
merits and commit their mother's faults. But
the sons of Adam, in these latter days, are men
who would have handed the famous apple back
with a bow, and a "Thanks, no; it might get me
into a scrape." When Allan—surprised and disappointed—moved away out of Miss Milroy's
reach to the forward part of the boat, Pedgift

Junior rose and followed him. "You're a very nice girl," thought this shrewdly sensible young man; "but a client's a client; and I am sorry to inform you, miss, it won't do." He set himself at once to rouse Allan's spirits by diverting his attention to a new subject. There was to be a regatta that autumn on one of the Broads, and his client's opinion as a yachtsman might be valuable to the committee. "Something new, I should think, to you, sir, in a sailing match on fresh water?" he said, in his most ingratiatory manner. And Allan, instantly interested, answered, "Quite new. Do tell me about it!"

As for the rest of the party at the other end of the boat, they were in a fair way to confirm Mrs. Pentecost's doubts whether the hilarity of the picnic would last the day out. Poor Neelie's natural feeling of irritation under the disappointment which Allan's awkwardness had inflicted on her was now exasperated into silent and settled resentment by her own keen sense of humiliation and defeat. The major had relapsed into his habitually dreamy, absent manner; his mind was turning monotonously with the wheels of his clock. The curate still secluded his indigestion from public view in the innermost recesses of the cabin; and the curate's mother, with a second dose ready at a moment's notice, sat on guard at the door. Women of Mrs. Pentecost's age and character generally enjoy their own bad spirits. "This," sighed the old lady, wagging her head with a smile of sour satisfaction, "is what you call a day's pleasure, is it?

Ah, what fools we all were to leave our comfortable homes!''

Meanwhile the boat floated smoothly along the windings of the watery labyrinth which lay between the two Broads. The view on either side was now limited to nothing but interminable rows of reeds. Not a sound was heard, far or near; not so much as a glimpse of cultivated or inhabited land appeared anywhere. "A trifle dreary hereabouts, Mr. Armadale," said the ever-cheerful Pedgift. "But we are just out of it now. Look ahead, sir! Here we are at Hurle Mere."

The reeds opened back on the right hand and the left, and the boat glided suddenly into the wide circle of a pool. Round the nearer half of the circle, the eternal reeds still fringed the margin of the water. Round the further half, the land appeared again, here rolling back from the pool in desolate sand-hills, there rising above it in a sweep of grassy shore. At one point the ground was occupied by a plantation, and at another by the out-buildings of a lonely old red brick house, with a strip of by-road near, that skirted the garden wall and ended at the pool. The sun was sinking in the clear heaven, and the water, where the sun's reflection failed to tinge it, was beginning to look black and cold. The solitude that had been soothing, the silence that had felt like an enchantment, on the other Broad, in the day's vigorous prime, was a solitude that saddened here—a silence that struck cold, in the stillness and melancholy of the day's decline.

The course of the boat was directed across the Mere to a creek in the grassy shore. One or two of the little flat-bottomed punts peculiar to the Broads lay in the creek; and the reed cutters to whom the punts belonged, surprised at the appearance of strangers, came out, staring silently, from behind an angle of the old garden wall. Not another sign of life was visible anywhere. No pony-chaise had been seen by the reed cutters; no stranger, either man or woman, had approached the shores of Hurle Mere that day.

Young Pedgift took another look at his watch, and addressed himself to Miss Milroy. "You may, or may not, see the governess when you get back to Thorpe Ambrose," he said; "but, as the time stands now, you won't see her here. You know best, Mr. Armadale," he added, turning to Allan, "whether your friend is to be depended on to keep his appointment?"

"I am certain he is to be depended on," replied Allan, looking about him in unconcealed disappointment at Midwinter's absence.

"Very good," pursued Pedgift Junior. "If we light the fire for our gypsy tea-making on the open ground there, your friend may find us out, sir, by the smoke. That's the Indian dodge for picking up a lost man on the prairie, Miss Milroy—and it's pretty nearly wild enough (isn't it?) to be a prairie here!"

There are some temptations—principally those of the smaller kind—which it is not in the defensive capacity of female human nature to resist. The temptation to direct the whole force of her influence, as the one young lady of the party, toward the instant overthrow of Allan's arrangement for meeting his friend, was too much for the major's daughter. She turned on the smiling Pedgift with a look which ought to have overwhelmed him. But who ever overwhelmed a solicitor?

"I think it's the most lonely, dreary, hideous place I ever saw in my life!" said Miss Neelie. "If you insist on making tea here, Mr. Pedgift, don't make any for me. No! I shall stop in the boat; and, though I am absolutely dying with thirst, I shall touch nothing till we get back again to the other Broad!"

The major opened his lips to remonstrate. To his daughter's infinite delight, Mrs. Pentecost rose from her seat before he could say a word, and, after surveying the whole landward prospect, and seeing nothing in the shape of a vehicle anywhere, asked indignantly whether they were going all the way back again to the place where they had left the carriages in the middle of the day. On ascertaining that this was, in fact, the arrangement proposed, and that, from the nature of the country, the carriages could not have been ordered round to Hurle Mere without, in the first instance, sending them the whole of the way back to Thorpe Ambrose, Mrs. Pentecost (speaking in her son's interests) instantly declared that no earthly power should induce her to be out on the water after dark. "Call me a boat!" cried the old lady, in great agitation. "Wherever there's water, there's a night mist, and wherever there's a night mist, my son Samuel catches cold. Don't talk to *me* about your moonlight and your tea-making — you're all mad! Hi! you two men there!" cried Mrs. Pentecost, hailing the silent reed cutters on shore. "Sixpence apiece for you, if you'll take me and my son back in your boat!"

Before young Pedgift could interfere, Allan himself settled the difficulty this time, with perfect patience and good temper.

"I can't think, Mrs. Pentecost, of your going back in any boat but the boat you have come out in," he said. "There is not the least need (as you and Miss Milroy don't like the place) for anybody to go on shore here but me. I *must* go on shore. My friend Midwinter never broke his promise to me yet; and I can't consent to leave Hurle Mere as long as there is a chance of his keeping his appointment. But there's not the least reason in the world why I should stand in the way on that account. You have the major and Mr. Pedgift to take care of you; and you can get back to the carriages before dark, if you go at once. I will wait here, and give my friend half an hour more, and then I can follow you in one of the reed-cutters' boats."

"That's the most sensible thing, Mr. Armadale, you've said to-day," remarked Mrs. Pentecost, seating herself again in a violent hurry.

"Tell them to be quick!" cried the old lady, shaking her fist at the boatmen. "Tell them to be quick!"

Allan gave the necessary directions, and stepped

on shore. The wary Pedgift (sticking fast to his client) tried to follow.

"We can't leave you here alone, sir," he said, protesting eagerly in a whisper. "Let the major take care of the ladies, and let me keep you company at the Mere."

"No, no!" said Allan, pressing him back. "They're all in low spirits on board. If you want to be of service to me, stop like a good fellow where you are, and do your best to keep the thing going." ·

He waved his hand, and the men pushed the boat off from the shore. The others all waved their hands in return except the major's daughter, who sat apart from the rest, with her face hidden under her parasol. The tears stood thick in Neelie's eyes. Her last angry feeling against Allan died out, and her heart went back to him penitently the moment he left the boat. "How good he is to us all!" she thought, "and what a wretch I am!" She got up with every generous impulse in her nature urging her to make atonement to him. She got up, reckless of appearances, and looked after him with eager eyes and flushed cheeks, as he stood alone on the shore. "Don't be long, Mr. Armadale!" she said, with a desperate disregard of what the rest of the company thought of her.

The boat was already far out in the water, and with all Neelie's resolution the words were spoken in a faint little voice, which failed to reach Allan's ears. The one sound he heard, as the boat gained the opposite extremity of the

Mere, and disappeared slowly among the reeds, was the sound of the concertina. The indefatigable Pedgift was keeping things going—evidently under the auspices of Mrs. Pentecost—by performing a sacred melody.

Left by himself, Allan lit a cigar, and took a turn backward and forward on the shore. "She might have said a word to me at parting!" he thought. "I've done everything for the best; I've as good as told her how fond of her I am, and this is the way she treats me!" He stopped, and stood looking absently at the sinking sun, and the fast-darkening waters of the Mere. Some inscrutable influence in the scene forced its way stealthily into his mind, and diverted his thoughts from Miss Milroy to his absent friend. He started, and looked about him.

The reed-cutters had gone back to their retreat behind the angle of the wall, not a living creature was visible, not a sound rose anywhere along the dreary shore. Even Allan's spirits began to get depressed  It was nearly an hour after the time when Midwinter had promised to be at Hurle Mere. He had himself arranged to walk to the pool (with a stable-boy from Thorpe Ambrose as his guide), by lanes and footpaths which shortened the distance by the road. The boy knew the country well, and Midwinter was habitually punctual at all his appointments. Had anything gone wrong at Thorpe Ambrose? Had some accident happened on the way? Determined to remain no longer doubting and idling by himself, Allan made up his mind to walk

inland from the Mere, on the chance of meeting
his friend. He went round at once to the angle
in the wall, and asked one of the reed-cutters to
show him the footpath to Thorpe Ambrose.

The man led him away from the road, and
pointed to a barely perceptible break in the outer
trees of the plantation. After pausing for one
more useless look around him, Allan turned his
back on the Mere and made for the trees.

For a few paces, the path ran straight through
the plantation. Thence it took a sudden turn;
and the water and the open country became both
lost to view. Allan steadily followed the grassy
track before him, seeing nothing and hearing
nothing, until he came to another winding of
the path. Turning in the new direction, he
saw dimly a human figure sitting alone at the
foot of one of the trees. Two steps nearer were
enough to make the figure familiar to him.
"Midwinter!" he exclaimed, in astonishment.
"This is not the place where I was to meet you!
What are you waiting for here?"

Midwinter rose, without answering. The evening dimness among the trees, which obscured his
face, made his silence doubly perplexing.

Allan went on eagerly questioning him. "Did
you come here by yourself?" he asked. "I thought
the boy was to guide you?"

This time Midwinter answered. "When we
got as far as these trees," he said, "I sent the
boy back. He told me I was close to the place,
and couldn't miss it."

"What made you stop here when he left

you?'' reiterated Allan. ''Why didn't you walk on?''

''Don't despise me,'' answered the other. ''I hadn't the courage!''

''Not the courage?'' repeated Allan. He paused a moment. ''Oh, I know!'' he resumed, putting his hand gayly on Midwinter's shoulder. ''You're still shy of the Milroys. What nonsense, when I told you myself that your peace was made at the cottage!''

''I wasn't thinking, Allan, of your friends at the cottage. The truth is, I'm hardly myself to-day. I am ill and unnerved; trifles startle me.'' He stopped, and shrank away, under the anxious scrutiny of Allan's eyes. ''If you *will* have it,'' he burst out, abruptly, ''the horror of that night on board the Wreck has got me again; there's a dreadful oppression on my head; there's a dreadful sinking at my heart. I am afraid of something happening to us, if we don't part before the day is out. I can't break my promise to you; for God's sake, release me from it, and let me go back!''

Remonstrance, to any one who knew Midwinter, was plainly useless at that moment. Allan humored him. ''Come out of this dark, airless place,'' he said, ''and we will talk about it. The water and the open sky are within a stone's throw of us. I hate a wood in the evening; it even gives *me* the horrors. You have been working too hard over the steward's books. Come and breathe freely in the blessed open air.''

Midwinter stopped, considered for a moment, and suddenly submitted.

"You're right," he said, "and I'm wrong, as usual. I'm wasting time and distressing you to no purpose. What folly to ask you to let me go back! Suppose you had said yes?"

"Well?" asked Allan.

"Well," repeated Midwinter, "something would have happened at the first step to stop me, that's all. Come on."

They walked together in silence on the way to the Mere.

At the last turn in the path Allan's cigar went out. While he stopped to light it again, Midwinter walked on before him, and was the first to come in sight of the open ground.

Allan had just kindled the match, when, to his surprise, his friend came back to him round the turn in the path. There was light enough to show objects more clearly in this part of the plantation. The match, as Midwinter faced him, dropped on the instant from Allan's hand.

"Good God!" he cried, starting back, "you look as you looked on board the Wreck!"

Midwinter held up his hand for silence. He spoke with his wild eyes riveted on Allan's face, with his white lips close at Allan's ear.

"You remember how I *looked*," he answered, in a whisper. "Do you remember what I *said* when you and the doctor were talking of the Dream?"

"I have forgotten the Dream," said Allan.

As he made that answer, Midwinter took his

hand, and led him round the last turn in the path.

"Do you remember it now?" he asked, and pointed to the Mere.

The sun was sinking in the cloudless westward heaven. The waters of the Mere lay beneath, tinged red by the dying light. The open country stretched away, darkening drearily already on the right hand and the left. And on the near margin of the pool, where all had been solitude before, there now stood, fronting the sunset, the figure of a woman.

The two Armadales stood together in silence, and looked at the lonely figure and the dreary view.

Midwinter was the first to speak.

"Your own eyes have seen it," he said. "Now look at your own words."

He opened the narrative of the Dream, and held it under Allan's eyes. His finger pointed to the lines which recorded the first Vision; his voice, sinking lower and lower, repeated the words:

"The sense came to me of being left alone in the darkness.

"I waited.

"The darkness opened, and showed me the vision—as in a picture—of a broad, lonely pool, surrounded by open ground. Above the further margin of the pool I saw the cloudless western sky, red with the light of sunset.

"On the near margin of the pool there stood the Shadow of a Woman."

He ceased, and let the hand which held the manuscript drop to his side. The other hand pointed to the lonely figure, standing with its back turned on them, fronting the setting sun.

"There," he said, "stands the living Woman, in the Shadow's place! There speaks the first of the dream warnings to you and to me! Let the future time find us still together, and the second figure that stands in the Shadow's place will be Mine."

Even Allan was silenced by the terrible certainty of conviction with which he spoke.

In the pause that followed, the figure at the pool moved, and walked slowly away round the margin of the shore. Allan stepped out beyond the last of the trees, and gained a wider view of the open ground. The first object that met his eyes was the pony-chaise from Thorpe Ambrose.

He turned back to Midwinter with a laugh of relief. "What nonsense have you been talking!" he said. "And what nonsense have I been listening to! It's the governess at last."

Midwinter made no reply. Allan took him by the arm, and tried to lead him on. He released himself suddenly, and seized Allan with both hands, holding him back from the figure at the pool, as he had held him back from the cabin door on the deck of the timber ship. Once again the effort was in vain. Once again Allan broke away as easily as he had broken away in the past time.

"One of us must speak to her," he said. "And if you won't, I will."

He had only advanced a few steps toward the Mere, when he heard, or thought he heard, a voice faintly calling after him, once and once only, the word Farewell. He stopped, with a feeling of uneasy surprise, and looked round.

"Was that you, Midwinter?" he asked.

There was no answer. After hesitating a moment more, Allan returned to the plantation. Midwinter was gone.

He looked back at the pool, doubtful in the new emergency what to do next. The lonely figure had altered its course in the interval; it had turned, and was advancing toward the trees. Allan had been evidently either heard or seen. It was impossible to leave a woman unbefriended, in that helpless position and in that solitary place. For the second time Allan went out from the trees to meet her.

As he came within sight of her face, he stopped in ungovernable astonishment. The sudden revelation of her beauty, as she smiled and looked at him inquiringly, suspended the movement in his limbs and the words on his lips. A vague doubt beset him whether it was the governess, after all.

He roused himself, and, advancing a few paces, mentioned his name. "May I ask," he added, "if I have the pleasure—?"

The lady met him easily and gracefully half-way. "Major Milroy's governess," she said. "Miss Gwilt."

# CHAPTER X.

### THE HOUSE-MAID'S FACE.

ALL was quiet at Thorpe Ambrose. The hall was solitary, the rooms were dark. The servants, waiting for the supper hour in the garden at the back of the house, looked up at the clear heaven and the rising moon, and agreed that there was little prospect of the return of the picnic party until later in the night. The general opinion, led by the high authority of the cook, predicted that they might all sit down to supper without the least fear of being disturbed by the bell. Having arrived at this conclusion, the servants assembled round the table, and exactly at the moment when they sat down the bell rang.

The footman, wondering, went up stairs to open the door, and found to his astonishment Midwinter waiting alone on the threshold, and looking (in the servant's opinion) miserably ill. He asked for a light, and, saying he wanted nothing else, withdrew at once to his room. The footman went back to his fellow-servants, and reported that something had certainly happened to his master's friend.

On entering his room, Midwinter closed the door, and hurriedly filled a bag with the necessaries for traveling. This done, he took from a locked drawer, and placed in the breast pocket of his coat, some little presents which Allan had given him—a cigar case, a purse, and a set of studs in plain gold. Having possessed himself of these memorials, he snatched up the bag and laid his hand on the door. There, for the first time, he paused. There, the headlong haste of all his actions thus far suddenly ceased, and the hard despair in his face began to soften: he waited, with the door in his hand.

Up to that moment he had been conscious of but one motive that animated him, but one purpose that he was resolute to achieve. "For Allan's sake!" he had said to himself, when he looked back toward the fatal landscape and saw his friend leaving him to meet the woman at the pool. "For Allan's sake!" he had said again, when he crossed the open country beyond the wood, and saw afar, in the gray twilight, the long line of embankment and the distant glimmer of the railway lamps beckoning him away already to the iron road.

It was only when he now paused before he closed the door behind him—it was only when his own impetuous rapidity of action came for the first time to a check, that the nobler nature of the man rose in protest against the superstitious despair which was hurrying him from all that he held dear. His conviction of the terrible necessity of leaving Allan for Allan's good had not been shaken for an instant since he had seen the first Vision of the Dream realized on the shores of the Mere. But now, for the first time, his own heart rose against him in unanswerable rebuke. "Go, if you must and will! but remember the time when you were ill, and he sat by your bedside; friendless, and he opened his heart to you—and write, if you fear to speak; write and ask him to forgive you, before you leave him forever!"

The half-opened door closed again softly. Midwinter sat down at the writing-table and took up the pen.

He tried again and again, and yet again, to write the farewell words; he tried, till the floor all round him was littered with torn sheets of paper. Turn from them which way he would, the old times still came back and faced him reproachfully. The spacious bed-chamber in which he sat, narrowed, in spite of him, to the sick usher's garret at the west-country inn. The kind hand that had once patted him on the shoulder touched him again; the kind voice that had cheered him spoke unchangeably in the old friendly tones. He flung his arms on the table and dropped his head on them in tearless despair. The parting words that his tongue was powerless to utter his pen was powerless to write. Mercilessly in earnest, his superstition pointed to him to go while the time was his own. Mercilessly in earnest, his love for Allan held him back till the farewell plea for pardon and pity was written.

He rose with a sudden resolution, and rang for the servant, "When Mr. Armadale returns," he said, "ask him to excuse my coming downstairs, and say that I am trying to get to sleep." He locked the door and put out the light, and sat down alone in the darkness. "The night will keep us apart," he said; "and time may help me to write. I may go in the early morning; I may go while—" The thought died in him uncompleted; and the sharp agony of the struggle forced to his lips the first cry of suffering that had escaped him yet.

He waited in the darkness.

As the time stole on, his senses remained mechanically awake, but his mind began to sink slowly under the heavy strain that had now been laid on it for some hours past. A dull vacancy possessed him; he made no attempt to kindle the light and write once more. He never started; he never moved to the open window, when the first sound of approaching wheels broke in on the silence of the night. He heard the carriages draw up at the door; he heard the horses champing their bits; he heard the voices of Allan and young Pedgift on the steps; and still he sat quiet in the darkness, and still no interest was aroused in him by the sounds that reached his ear from outside.

The voices remained audible after the carriages had been driven away; the two young men were evidently lingering on the steps before they took leave of each other. Every word they said reached Midwinter through the open window. Their one subject of conversation was the new governess. Allan's voice was loud in her praise. He had never passed such an hour of delight in his life as the hour he had spent with Miss Gwilt in the boat, on the way from Hurle Mere to the picnic party waiting at the other Broad. Agreeing, on his side, with all that his client said in praise of the charming stranger, young Pedgift appeared to treat the subject, when it fell into his hands, from a different point of view. Miss Gwilt's attractions had not so entirely absorbed his attention as to prevent him from noticing the impression which the new governess had produced on her employer and her pupil.

"There's a screw loose somewhere, sir, in Major Milroy's family," said the voice of young Pedgift. "Did you notice how the major and his daughter looked when Miss Gwilt made her excuses for being late at the Mere? You don't remember? Do you remember what Miss Gwilt said?"

"Something about Mrs. Milroy, wasn't it?" Allan rejoined.

Young Pedgift's voice dropped mysteriously a note lower.

"Miss Gwilt reached the cottage this afternoon, sir, at the time when I told you she would reach it, and she would have joined us at the time I told you she would come, but for Mrs. Milroy. Mrs. Milroy sent for her upstairs as soon as she entered the house, and kept her upstairs a good half-hour and more. That was Miss Gwilt's excuse, Mr. Armadale, for being late at the Mere."

"Well, and what then?"

"You seem to forget, sir, what the whole neighborhood has heard about Mrs. Milroy ever since the major first settled among us. We have all been told, on the doctor's own authority, that she is too great a sufferer to see strangers. Isn't it a little odd that she should have suddenly turned out well enough to see Miss Gwilt (in her husband's absence) the moment Miss Gwilt entered the house?"

"Not a bit of it! Of course she was anxious to make acquaintance with her daughter's governess."

"Likely enough, Mr. Armadale. But the major and Miss Neelie don't see it in that light, at any rate. I had my eye on them both when the governess told them that Mrs. Milroy had sent for her. If ever I saw a girl look thoroughly frightened, Miss Milroy was that girl; and (if I may be allowed, in the strictest confidence, to libel a gallant soldier) I should say that the major himself was much in the same condition. Take my word for it, sir, there's something wrong upstairs in that pretty cottage of yours; and Miss Gwilt is mixed up in it already!"

There was a minute of silence. When the voices were next heard by Midwinter, they were further away from the house—Allan was probably accompanying young Pedgift a few steps on his way back.

After a while, Allan's voice was audible once more under the portico, making inquiries after his friend; answered by the servant's voice giving Midwinter's message. This brief interruption over, the silence was not broken again till the time came for shutting up the house. The servants' footsteps passing to and fro, the clang

of closing doors, the barking of a disturbed dog
in the stable-yard—these sounds warned Midwinter it was getting late. He rose mechanically
to kindle a light. But his head was giddy, his
hand trembled; he laid aside the match-box, and
returned to his chair. The conversation between
Allan and young Pedgift had ceased to occupy his
attention the instant he ceased to hear it; and
now again, the sense that the precious time was
failing him became a lost sense as soon as the
house noises which had awakened it had passed
away. His energies of body and mind were both
alike worn out; he waited with a stolid resignation for the trouble that was to come to him with
the coming day.

An interval passed, and the silence was once
more disturbed by voices outside; the voices of
a man and a woman this time. The first few
words exchanged between them indicated plainly
enough a meeting of the clandestine kind; and
revealed the man as one of the servants at Thorpe
Ambrose, and the woman as one of the servants
at the cottage.

Here again, after the first greetings were over,
the subject of the new governess became the all-
absorbing subject of conversation.

The major's servant was brimful of forebodings (inspired solely by Miss Gwilt's good looks),
which she poured out irrepressibly on her "sweetheart," try as he might to divert her to other
topics. Sooner or later, let him mark her words,
there would be an awful "upset" at the cottage.
Her master, it might be mentioned in confidence,

led a dreadful life with her mistress. The major was the best of men; he hadn't a thought in his heart beyond his daughter and his everlasting clock. But only let a nice-looking woman come near the place, and Mrs. Milroy was jealous of her—raging jealous, like a woman possessed, on that miserable sick-bed of hers. If Miss Gwilt (who was certainly good-looking, in spite of her hideous hair) didn't blow the fire into a flame before many days more were over their heads, the mistress was the mistress no longer, but somebody else. Whatever happened, the fault, this time, would lie at the door of the major's mother. The old lady and the mistress had had a dreadful quarrel two years since; and the old lady had gone away in a fury, telling her son, before all the servants, that, if he had a spark of spirit in him, he would never submit to his wife's temper as he did. It would be too much, perhaps, to accuse the major's mother of purposely picking out a handsome governess to spite the major's wife. But it might be safely said that the old lady was the last person in the world to humor the mistress's jealousy, by declining to engage a capable and respectable governess for her granddaughter because that governess happened to be blessed with good looks. How it was all to end (except that it was certain to end badly) no human creature could say. Things were looking as black already as things well could. Miss Neelie was crying, after the day's pleasure (which was one bad sign); the mistress had found fault with nobody (which was another);

the master had wished her good-night through the door (which was a third); and the governess had locked herself up in her room (which was the worst sign of all, for it looked as if she distrusted the servants). Thus the stream of the woman's gossip ran on, and thus it reached Midwinter's ears through the window, till the clock in the stable-yard struck, and stopped the talking. When the last vibrations of the bell had died away, the voices were not audible again, and the silence was broken no more.

Another interval passed, and Midwinter made a new effort to rouse himself. This time he kindled the light without hesitation, and took the pen in hand.

He wrote at the first trial with a sudden facility of expression, which, surprising him as he went on, ended in rousing in him some vague suspicion of himself. He left the table, and bathed his head and face in water, and came back to read what he had written. The language was barely intelligible; sentences were left unfinished; words were misplaced one for the other; every line recorded the protest of the weary brain against the merciless will that had forced it into action. Midwinter tore up the sheet of paper as he had torn up the other sheets before it, and, sinking under the struggle at last, laid his weary head on the pillow. Almost on the instant, exhaustion overcame him, and before he could put the light out he fell asleep.

He was roused by a noise at the door. The sunlight was pouring into the room, the candle had burned down into the socket, and the servant was waiting outside with a letter which had come for him by the morning's post.

"I ventured to disturb you, sir," said the man, when Midwinter opened the door, "because the letter is marked 'Immediate,' and I didn't know but it might be of some consequence."

Midwinter thanked him, and looked at the letter. It *was* of some consequence—the handwriting was Mr. Brock's.

He paused to collect his faculties. The torn sheets of paper on the floor recalled to him in a moment the position in which he stood. He locked the door again, in the fear that Allan might rise earlier than usual and come in to make inquiries. Then—feeling strangely little interest in anything that the rector could write to him now—he opened Mr. Brock's letter, and read these lines:

"Tuesday.

"MY DEAR MIDWINTER—It is sometimes best to tell bad news plainly, in few words. Let me tell mine at once, in one sentence. My precautions have all been defeated: the woman has escaped me.

"This misfortune—for it is nothing less—happened yesterday (Monday). Between eleven and twelve in the forenoon of that day, the business which originally brought me to London obliged me to go to Doctors' Commons, and to leave my servant Robert to watch the house opposite our lodging until my return. About an hour and a half after my departure he observed an empty

cab drawn up at the door of the house. Boxes
and bags made their appearance first; they were
followed by the woman herself, in the dress I had
first seen her in. Having previously secured a
cab, Robert traced her to the terminus of the
North-western Railway, saw her pass through
the ticket office, kept her in view till she reached
the platform, and there, in the crowd and confusion caused by the starting of a large mixed
train, lost her. I must do him the justice to
say that he at once took the right course in this
emergency. Instead of wasting time in searching for her on the platform, he looked along the
line of carriages; and he positively declares that
he failed to see her in any one of them. He ad-
mits, at the same time, that his search (conducted
between two o'clock, when he lost sight of her,
and ten minutes past, when the train started)
was, in the confusion of the moment, necessarily
an imperfect one. But this latter circumstance,
in my opinion, matters little. I as firmly disbelieve in the woman's actual departure by that
train as if I had searched every one of the carriages myself; and you, I have no doubt, will
entirely agree with me.

"You now know how the disaster happened.
Let us not waste time and words in lamenting
it. The evil is done, and you and I together
must find the way to remedy it.

"What I have accomplished already, on my
side, may be told in two words. Any hesitation I might have previously felt at trusting this
delicate business in strangers' hands was at an

end the moment I heard Robert's news. I went
back at once to the city, and placed the whole
matter confidentially before my lawyers. The
conference was a long one, and when I left the
office it was past the post hour, or I should have
written to you on Monday instead of writing to-
day. My interview with the lawyers was not
very encouraging. They warn me plainly that
serious difficulties stand in the way of our recovering the lost trace. But they have promised
to do their best, and we have decided on the
course to be taken, excepting one point on which
we totally differ. I must tell you what this
difference is; for, while business keeps me away
from Thorpe Ambrose, you are the only person
whom I can trust to put my convictions to the
test.

"The lawyers are of opinion, then, that the
woman has been aware from the first that I was
watching her; that there is, consequently, no
present hope of her being rash enough to appear
personally at Thorpe Ambrose; that any mischief she may have it in contemplation to do
will be done in the first instance by deputy; and
that the only wise course for Allan's friends and
guardians to take is to wait passively till events
enlighten them. My own idea is diametrically
opposed to this. After what has happened at
the railway, I cannot deny that the woman must
have discovered that I was watching her. But
she has no reason to suppose that she has not
succeeded in deceiving me; and I firmly believe
she is bold enough to take us by surprise, and

to win or force her way into Allan's confidence before we are prepared to prevent her.

"You and you only (while I am detained in London) can decide whether I am right or wrong —and you can do it in this way. Ascertain at once whether any woman who is a stranger in the neighborhood has appeared since Monday last at or near Thorpe Ambrose. If any such person has been observed (and nobody escapes observation in the country), take the first opportunity you can get of seeing her, and ask yourself if her face does or does not answer certain plain questions which I am now about to write down for you. You may depend on my accuracy. I saw the woman unveiled on more than one occasion, and the last time through an excellent glass.

"1. Is her hair light brown, and (apparently) not very plentiful? 2. Is her forehead high, narrow, and sloping backward from the brow? 3. Are her eyebrows very faintly marked, and are her eyes small, and nearer dark than light —either gray or hazel (I have not seen her close enough to be certain which)? 4. Is her nose aquiline? 5. Are her lips thin, and is the upper lip long? 6. Does her complexion look like an originally fair complexion, which has deteriorated into a dull, sickly paleness. 7 (and lastly). Has she a retreating chin, and is there on the left side of it a mark of some kind—a mole or a scar, I can't say which?

"I add nothing about her expression, for you may see her under circumstances which may partially alter it as seen by me.   Test her by her features, which no circumstances can change.   If there is a stranger in the neighborhood, and if her face answers my seven questions, *you have found the woman!*   Go instantly, in that case, to the nearest lawyer, and pledge my name and credit for whatever expenses may be incurred in keeping her under inspection night and day. Having done this, take the speediest means of communicating with me; and whether my business is finished or not, I will start for Norfolk by the first train.

"Always your friend,   DECIMUS BROCK."

Hardened by the fatalist conviction that now possessed him, Midwinter read the rector's confession of defeat, from the first line to the last, without the slightest betrayal either of interest or surprise.   The one part of the letter at which he looked back was the closing part of it.   "I owe much to Mr. Brock's kindness," he thought; "and I shall never see Mr. Brock again.   It is useless and hopeless; but he asks me to do it, and it shall be done.   A moment's look at her will be enough—a moment's look at her with his letter in my hand—and a line to tell him that the woman is here!"

Again he stood hesitating at the half-opened door; again the cruel necessity of writing his farewell to Allan stopped him, and stared him in the face.

He looked aside doubtingly at the rector's letter.   "I will write the two together," he said.

"One may help the other." His face flushed deep as the words escaped him. He was conscious of doing what he had not done yet—of voluntarily putting off the evil hour; of making Mr. Brock the pretext for gaining the last respite left, the respite of time.

The only sound that reached him through the open door was the sound of Allan stirring noisily in the next room. He stepped at once into the empty corridor, and meeting no one on the stairs, made his way out of the house. The dread that his resolution to leave Allan might fail him if he saw Allan again was as vividly present to his mind in the morning as it had been all through the night. He drew a deep breath of relief as he descended the house steps—relief at having escaped the friendly greeting of the morning from the one human creature whom he loved!

He entered the shrubbery with Mr. Brock's letter in his hand, and took the nearest way that led to the major's cottage. Not the slightest recollection was in his mind of the talk which had found its way to his ears during the night. His one reason for determining to see the woman was the reason which the rector had put in his mind. The one remembrance that now guided him to the place in which she lived was the remembrance of Allan's exclamation when he first identified the governess with the figure at the pool.

Arrived at the gate of the cottage, he stopped. The thought struck him that he might defeat his own object if he looked at the rector's questions

in the woman's presence.  Her suspicions would
be probably roused, in the first instance, by his
asking to see her (as he had determined to ask,
with or without an excuse), and the appearance
of the letter in his hand might confirm them.
She might defeat him by instantly leaving the
room.  Determined to fix the description in his
mind first, and then to confront her, he opened
the letter; and, turning away slowly by the side
of the house, read the seven questions which he
felt absolutely assured beforehand the woman's
face would answer.

In the morning quiet of the park slight noises
traveled far.  A slight noise disturbed Midwinter over the letter.

He looked up and found himself on the brink
of a broad grassy trench, having the park on one
side and the high laurel hedge of an inclosure on
the other.  The inclosure evidently surrounded
the back garden of the cottage, and the trench
was intended to protect it from being damaged
by the cattle grazing in the park.

Listening carefully as the slight sound which
had disturbed him grew fainter, he recognized
in it the rustling of women's dresses.  A few
paces ahead, the trench was crossed by a bridge
(closed by a wicket gate) which connected the
garden with the park.  He passed through the
gate, crossed the bridge, and, opening a door at
the other end, found himself in a summer-house,
thickly covered with creepers, and commanding
a full view of the garden from end to end.

He looked, and saw the figures of two ladies

walking slowly away from him toward the cottage. The shorter of the two failed to occupy his attention for an instant; he never stopped to think whether she was or was not the major's daughter. His eyes were riveted on the other figure—the figure that moved over the garden walk with the long, lightly falling dress and the easy, seductive grace. There, presented exactly as he had seen her once already—there, with her back again turned on him, was the Woman at the pool!

There was a chance that they might take another turn in the garden—a turn back toward the summer-house. On that chance Midwinter waited. No consciousness of the intrusion that he was committing had stopped him at the door of the summer-house, and no consciousness of it troubled him even now. Every finer sensibility in his nature, sinking under the cruel laceration of the past night, had ceased to feel. The dogged resolution to do what he had come to do was the one animating influence left alive in him. He acted, he even looked, as the most stolid man living might have acted and looked in his place. He was self-possessed enough, in the interval of expectation before governess and pupil reached the end of the walk, to open Mr. Brock's letter, and to fortify his memory by a last look at the paragraph which described her face.

He was still absorbed over the description when he heard the smooth rustle of the dresses traveling toward him again. Standing in the shadow of the summer-house, he waited while she lessened the distance between them. With her written portrait vividly impressed on his mind, and with the clear light of the morning to help him, his eyes questioned her as she came on; and these were the answers that her face gave him back:

The hair in the rector's description was light brown and not plentiful. This woman's hair, superbly luxuriant in its growth, was of the one unpardonably remarkable shade of color which the prejudice of the Northern nations never entirely forgives—it was *red!* The forehead in the rector's description was high, narrow, and sloping backward from the brow; the eyebrows were faintly marked; and the eyes small, and in color either gray or hazel. This woman's forehead was low, upright, and broad toward the temples; her eyebrows, at once strongly and delicately marked, were a shade darker than her hair; her eyes, large, bright, and well opened, were of that purely blue color, without a tinge in it of gray or green, so often presented to our admiration in pictures and books, so rarely met with in the living face. The nose in the rector's description was aquiline. The line of this woman's nose bent neither outward nor inward: it was the straight, delicately molded nose (with the short upper lip beneath) of the ancient statues and busts. The lips in the rector's description were thin and the upper lip long; the complexion was of a dull, sickly paleness; the chin retreating, and the mark of a mole or a scar on the left side of it. This woman's lips were full, rich, and sensual. Her complexion was the lovely complexion which accompanies such hair as hers—so delicately bright in its rosier tints, so warmly and softly white in its gentler gradations of color on the forehead and the neck. Her chin, round and dimpled, was pure of the slightest blemish in every part of it, and perfectly in line with her forehead to the end. Nearer and nearer, and fairer and fairer she came, in the glow of the morning light—the most startling, the most unanswerable contradiction that eye could see or mind conceive to the description in the rector's letter.

Both governess and pupil were close to the summer - house before they looked that way, and noticed Midwinter standing inside. The governess saw him first.

"A friend of yours, Miss Milroy?" she asked, quietly, without starting or betraying any sign of surprise.

Neelie recognized him instantly. Prejudiced against Midwinter by his conduct when his friend had introduced him at the cottage, she now fairly detested him as the unlucky first cause of her misunderstanding with Allan at the picnic. Her face flushed and she drew back from the summer-house with an expression of merciless surprise.

"He is a friend of Mr. Armadale's," she replied, sharply. "I don't know what he wants, or why he is here."

"A friend of Mr. Armadale's!" The governess's face lighted up with a suddenly roused interest as she repeated the words. She returned

Midwinter's look, still steadily fixed on her, with equal steadiness on her side.

"For my part," pursued Neelie, resenting Midwinter's insensibility to her presence on the scene, "I think it a great liberty to treat papa's garden as if it were the open park!"

The governess turned round, and gently interposed.

"My dear Miss Milroy," she remonstrated, "there are certain distinctions to be observed. This gentleman is a friend of Mr. Armadale's. You could hardly express yourself more strongly if he was a perfect stranger."

"I express my opinion," retorted Neelie, chafing under the satirically indulgent tone in which the governess addressed her. "It's a matter of taste, Miss Gwilt; and tastes differ." She turned away petulantly, and walked back by herself to the cottage.

"She is very young," said Miss Gwilt, appealing with a smile to Midwinter's forbearance; "and, as you must see for yourself, sir, she is a spoiled child." She paused—showed, for an instant only, her surprise at Midwinter's strange silence and strange persistency in keeping his eyes still fixed on her—then set herself, with a charming grace and readiness, to help him out of the false position in which he stood. "As you have extended your walk thus far," she resumed, "perhaps you will kindly favor me, on your return, by taking a message to your friend? Mr. Armadale has been so good as to invite me to see the Thorpe Ambrose gardens this morning. Will you say that Major Milroy permits me to accept the invitation (in company with Miss Milroy) between ten and eleven o'clock?" For a moment her eyes rested, with a renewed look of interest, on Midwinter's face. She waited, still in vain, for an answering word from him—smiled, as if his extraordinary silence amused rather than angered her — and followed her pupil back to the cottage.

It was only when the last trace of her had disappeared that Midwinter roused himself, and attempted to realize the position in which he stood. The revelation of her beauty was in no respect answerable for the breathless astonishment which had held him spell-bound up to this moment. The one clear impression she had produced on him thus far began and ended with his discovery of the astounding contradiction that her face offered, in one feature after another, to the description in Mr. Brock's letter. All beyond this was vague and misty—a dim consciousness of a tall, elegant woman, and of kind words, modestly and gracefully spoken to him, and nothing more.

He advanced a few steps into the garden without knowing why—stopped, glancing hither and thither like a man lost—recognized the summerhouse by an effort, as if years had elapsed since he had seen it—and made his way out again, at last, into the park. Even here, he wandered first in one direction, then in another. His mind was still reeling under the shock that had fallen on it; his perceptions were all confused. Something kept him mechanically in action, walking eagerly without a motive, walking he knew not where.

A far less sensitively organized man might have been overwhelmed, as he was overwhelmed now, by the immense, the instantaneous revulsion of feeling which the event of the last few minutes had wrought in his mind.

At the memorable instant when he had opened the door of the summer-house, no confusing influence troubled his faculties. In all that related to his position toward his friend, he had reached an absolutely definite conclusion by an absolutely definite process of thought. The whole strength of the motive which had driven him into the resolution to part from Allan rooted itself in the belief that he had seen at Hurle Mere the fatal fulfillment of the first Vision of the Dream. And this belief, in its turn, rested, necessarily, on the conviction that the woman who was the one survivor of the tragedy in Madeira must be also inevitably the woman whom he had seen standing in the Shadow's place at the pool. Firm in that persuasion, he had himself compared the object of his distrust and of the rector's distrust with the description written by the rector himself—a description, carefully minute, by a man entirely trustworthy — and his own eyes had informed him that the woman whom he had seen at the Mere, and the woman whom Mr. Brock had identified in London, were not one, but Two. In the place of the Dream Shadow, there had stood, on the evidence of the rector's letter, not the instrument of the Fatality—but a stranger!

No such doubts as might have troubled a less superstitious man were started in *his* mind by the discovery that had now opened on him.

It never occurred to him to ask himself whether a stranger might not be the appointed instrument of the Fatality, now when the letter had persuaded him that a stranger had been revealed as the figure in the dream landscape. No such idea entered or could enter his mind. The one woman whom *his* superstition dreaded was the woman who had entwined herself with the lives of the two Armadales in the first generation, and with the fortunes of the two Armadales in the second —who was at once the marked object of his father's death-bed warning, and the first cause of the family calamities which had opened Allan's way to the Thorpe Ambrose estate—the woman, in a word, whom he would have known instinctively, but for Mr. Brock's letter, to be the woman whom he had now actually seen.

Looking at events as they had just happened, under the influence of the misapprehension into which the rector had innocently misled him, his mind saw and seized its new conclusion instantaneously, acting precisely as it had acted in the past time of his interview with Mr. Brock at the Isle of Man.

Exactly as he had once declared it to be an all-sufficient refutation of the idea of the Fatality, that he had never met with the timber ship in any of his voyages at sea, so he now seized on the similarly derived conclusion, that the whole claim of the Dream to a supernatural origin stood self-refuted by the disclosure of a stranger in the Shadow's place. Once started from this point—once encouraged to let his love for Allan influence him undividedly again, his mind hurried along the whole resulting chain of thought at lightning speed. If the Dream was proved to be no longer a warning from the other world, it followed inevitably that accident and not fate had led the way to the night on the Wreck, and that all the events which had happened since Allan and he had parted from Mr. Brock were events in themselves harmless, which his superstition had distorted from their proper shape. In less than a moment his mobile imagination had taken him back to the morning at Castletown when he had revealed to the rector the secret of his name; when he had declared to the rector, with his father's letter before his eyes, the better faith that was in him. Now once more he felt his heart holding firmly by the bond of brotherhood between Allan and himself; now once more he could say with the eager sincerity of the old time, "If the thought of leaving him breaks my heart, the thought of leaving him is wrong!" As that nobler conviction possessed itself again of his mind — quieting the tumult, clearing the confusion within him—the house at Thorpe Ambrose, with Allan on the steps, waiting and looking for him, opened on his eyes through the trees. A sense of illimitable relief lifted his eager spirit high above the cares, and doubts, and fears that had oppressed it so long, and showed him once more the better and brighter future of his early dreams. His eyes filled with tears, and he pressed the rector's letter, in his wild, passionate way, to his lips, as he looked at Allan through the vista of the trees. "But for this morsel of paper," he thought, "my life might have been one long sorrow to me, and my father's crime might have parted us forever!"

Such was the result of the stratagem which had shown the house-maid's face to Mr. Brock as the face of Miss Gwilt. And so—by shaking Midwinter's trust in his own superstition, in the one case in which that superstition pointed to the truth—did Mother Oldershaw's cunning triumph over difficulties and dangers which had never been contemplated by Mother Oldershaw herself.

---

## CHAPTER XI.

### MISS GWILT AMONG THE QUICKSANDS.

1. *From the Rev. Decimus Brock to Ozias Midwinter.*

"Thursday.

"MY DEAR MIDWINTER—No words can tell what a relief it was to me to get your letter this morning, and what a happiness I honestly feel in having been thus far proved to be in the wrong. The precautions you have taken in case the woman should still confirm my apprehensions by venturing herself at Thorpe Ambrose seem to me to be all that can be desired. You are no doubt sure to hear of her from one or other of the people in the lawyer's office, whom you have asked to inform you of the appearance of a stranger in the town.

"I am the more pleased at finding how entirely I can trust you in this matter; for I am likely to be obliged to leave Allan's interests longer than I supposed solely in your hands. My visit to Thorpe Ambrose must, I regret to say, be deferred for two months. The only one of my brother-clergymen in London who is able to take my duty for me cannot make it convenient to remove with his family to Somersetshire before that time. I have no alternative but to finish my business here, and be back at my rectory on Saturday next. If anything happens, you will, of course, instantly communicate with me; and, in that case, be the inconvenience what it may, I must leave home for Thorpe Ambrose. If, on the other hand, all goes more smoothly than my own obstinate apprehensions will allow me to suppose, then Allan (to whom I have written) must not expect to see me till this day two months.

"No result has, up to this time, rewarded our exertions to recover the trace lost at the railway. I will keep my letter open, however, until post time, in case the next few hours bring any news.

"Always truly yours,      DECIMUS BROCK.

"P. S.—I have just heard from the lawyers. They have found out the name the woman passed by in London. If this discovery (not a very important one, I am afraid) suggests any new course of proceeding to you, pray act on it at once. The name is—Miss Gwilt."

## 2. *From Miss Gwilt to Mrs. Oldershaw.*

"The Cottage, Thorpe Ambrose, Saturday, June 28.

"IF you will promise not to be alarmed, Mamma Oldershaw, I will begin this letter in a very odd way, by copying a page of a letter written by somebody else. You have an excellent memory, and you may not have forgotten that I received a note from Major Milroy's mother (after she had engaged me as governess) on Monday last. It was dated and signed; and here it is, as far as the first page: 'June 23d, 1851. Dear Madam —Pray excuse my troubling you, before you go to Thorpe Ambrose, with a word more about the habits observed in my son's household. When I had the pleasure of seeing you at two o'clock to-day, in Kingsdown Crescent, I had another appointment in a distant part of London at three; and, in the hurry of the moment, one or two little matters escaped me which I think I ought to impress on your attention.' The rest of the letter is not of the slightest importance, but the lines that I have just copied are well worthy of all the attention you can bestow on them. They have saved me from discovery, my dear, before I have been a week in Major Milroy's service!

"It happened no later than yesterday evening, and it began and ended in this manner:

"There is a gentleman here (of whom I shall have more to say presently) who is an intimate friend of young Armadale's, and who bears the strange name of Midwinter. He contrived yesterday to speak to me alone in the park. Almost as soon as he opened his lips, I found that my name had been discovered in London (no doubt by the Somersetshire clergyman); and that Mr. Midwinter had been chosen (evidently by the same person) to identify the Miss Gwilt who had vanished from Brompton with the Miss Gwilt who had appeared at Thorpe Ambrose. You foresaw this danger, I remember; but you could scarcely have imagined that the exposure would threaten me so soon.

"I spare you the details of our conversation to come to the end. Mr. Midwinter put the matter very delicately, declaring, to my great surprise, that he felt quite certain himself that I was not the Miss Gwilt of whom his friend was in search; and that he only acted as he did out of regard to the anxiety of a person whose wishes he was bound to respect. Would I assist him in setting that anxiety completely at rest, as far as I was concerned, by kindly answering one plain question—which he had no other right to ask me than the right my indulgence might give him? The lost 'Miss Gwilt' had been missed on Monday last, at two o'clock, in the crowd on the platform of the North-western Railway, in Euston Square. Would I authorize him to say that on that day, and at that hour, the Miss Gwilt who was Major Milroy's governess had never been near the place?

"I need hardly tell you that I seized the fine

opportunity he had given me of disarming all future suspicion. I took a high tone on the spot, and met him with the old lady's letter. He politely refused to look at it. I insisted on his looking at it. 'I don't choose to be mistaken,' I said, 'for a woman who may be a bad character, because she happens to bear, or to have assumed, the same name as mine. I insist on your reading the first part of this letter for my satisfaction, if not for your own.' He was obliged to comply; and there was the proof, in the old lady's handwriting, that, at two o'clock on Monday last, she and I were together in Kingsdown Crescent, which any directory would tell him is a 'crescent' in Bayswater! I leave you to imagine his apologies, and the perfect sweetness with which I received them.

"I might, of course, if I had not preserved the letter, have referred him to you, or to the major's mother, with similar results. As it is, the object has been gained without trouble or delay. *I have been proved not to be myself;* and one of the many dangers that threatened me at Thorpe Ambrose is a danger blown over from this moment. Your house-maid's face may not be a very handsome one; but there is no denying that it has done us excellent service.

"So much for the past; now for the future. You shall hear how I get on with the people about me; and you shall judge for yourself what the chances are for and against my becoming mistress of Thorpe Ambrose.

"Let me begin with young Armadale — because it is beginning with good news. I have produced the right impression on him already, and Heaven knows *that* is nothing to boast of! Any moderately good-looking woman who chose to take the trouble could make him fall in love with her. He is a rattle-pated young fool—one of those noisy, rosy, light-haired, good-tempered men whom I particularly detest. I had a whole hour alone with him in a boat, the first day I came here, and I have made good use of my time, I can tell you, from that day to this. The only difficulty with him is the difficulty of concealing my own feelings, especially when he turns my dislike of him into downright hatred by sometimes reminding me of his mother. I really never saw a man whom I could use so ill, if I had the opportunity. He will give me the opportunity, I believe, if no accident happens, sooner than we calculated on. I have just returned from a party at the great house, in celebration of the rent-day dinner, and the squire's attentions to me, and my modest reluctance to receive them, have already excited general remark.

"My pupil, Miss Milroy, comes next. She, too, is rosy and foolish; and, what is more, awkward and squat and freckled, and ill-tempered and ill-dressed. No fear of *her*, though she hates me like poison, which is a great comfort, for I get rid of her out of lesson time and walking time. It is perfectly easy to see that she has made the most of her opportunities with young Armadale (opportunities, by-the-by, which we never calculated on), and that she has been stupid enough to let him slip through her fingers. When I tell you that she is obliged, for the sake of appearances, to go with her father and me to the little entertainments at Thorpe Ambrose, and to see how young Armadale admires me, you will understand the kind of place I hold in her affections. She would try me past all endurance if I didn't see that I aggravate her by keeping my temper, so, of course, I keep it. If I do break out, it will be over our lessons—not over our French, our grammar, history, and globes—but over our music. No words can say how I feel for her poor piano. Half the musical girls in England ought to have their fingers chopped off in the interests of society, and, if I had my way, Miss Milroy's fingers should be executed first.

"As for the major, I can hardly stand higher in his estimation than I stand already. I am always ready to make his breakfast, and his daughter is not. I can always find things for him when he loses them, and his daughter can't. I never yawn when he proses, and his daughter does. I like the poor dear harmless old gentleman, so I won't say a word more about him.

"Well, here is a fair prospect for the future surely? My good Oldershaw, there never was a prospect yet without an ugly place in it. *My* prospect has two ugly places in it. The name of one of them is Mrs. Milroy, and the name of the other is Mr. Midwinter.

"Mrs. Milroy first. Before I had been five

minutes in the cottage, on the day of my arrival, what do you think she did? She sent downstairs and asked to see me. The message startled me a little, after hearing from the old lady, in London, that her daughter-in-law was too great a sufferer to see anybody; but, of course, when I got her message, I had no choice but to go upstairs to the sick-room. I found her bedridden with an incurable spinal complaint, and a really horrible object to look at, but with all her wits about her; and, if I am not greatly mistaken, as deceitful a woman, with as vile a temper, as you could find anywhere in all your long experience. Her excessive politeness, and her keeping her own face in the shade of the bed-curtains while she contrived to keep mine in the light, put me on my guard the moment I entered the room. We were more than half an hour together, without my stepping into any one of the many clever little traps she laid for me. The only mystery in her behavior, which I failed to see through at the time, was her perpetually asking me to bring her things (things she evidently did not want) from different parts of the room.

"Since then events have enlightened me. My first suspicions were raised by overhearing some of the servants' gossip; and I have been confirmed in my opinion by the conduct of Mrs. Milroy's nurse.

"On the few occasions when I have happened to be alone with the major, the nurse has also happened to want something of her master, and has invariably forgotten to announce her appear-

ance by knocking at the door. Do you understand now why Mrs. Milroy sent for me the moment I got into the house, and what she wanted
when she kept me going backward and forward,
first for one thing and then for another? There
is hardly an attractive light in which my face
and figure can be seen, in which that woman's
jealous eyes have not studied them already. I
am no longer puzzled to know why the father
and daughter started, and looked at each other,
when I was first presented to them; or why the
servants still stare at me with a mischievous expectation in their eyes when I ring the bell and
ask them to do anything. It is useless to disguise the truth, Mother Oldershaw, between you
and me. When I went upstairs into that sick-
room, I marched blindfold into the clutches of
a jealous woman. If Mrs. Milroy *can* turn me
out of the house, Mrs. Milroy *will;* and, morning and night, she has nothing else to do in that
bed prison of hers but to find out the way.

"In this awkward position, my own cautious
conduct is admirably seconded by the dear old
major's perfect insensibility. His wife's jealousy of him is as monstrous a delusion as any
that could be found in a mad-house; it is the
growth of her own vile temper, under the aggravation of an incurable illness. The poor man
hasn't a thought beyond his mechanical pursuits;
and I don't believe he knows at this moment
whether I am a handsome woman or not. With
this chance to help me, I may hope to set the
nurse's intrusions and the mistress's contrivances

at defiance—for a time, at any rate. But you
know what a jealous woman is, and I think I
know what Mrs. Milroy is; and I own I shall
breathe more freely on the day when young Armadale opens his foolish lips to some purpose, and
sets the major advertising for a new governess.

"Armadale's name reminds me of Armadale's
friend. There is more danger threatening in
that quarter; and, what is worse, I don't feel
half as well armed beforehand against Mr. Midwinter as I do against Mrs. Milroy.

"Everything about this man is more or less
mysterious, which I don't like, to begin with.
How does he come to be in the confidence of the
Somersetshire clergyman? How much has that
clergyman told him? How is it that he was so
firmly persuaded, when he spoke to me in the
park, that I was not the Miss Gwilt of whom his
friend was in search? I haven't the ghost of an
answer to give to any of those three questions. I
can't even discover who he is, or how he and
young Armadale first became acquainted. I hate
him. No, I don't; I only want to find out about
him. He is very young, little and lean, and active and dark, with bright black eyes which say
to me plainly, 'We belong to a man with brains
in his head and a will of his own; a man who
hasn't always been hanging about a country
house, in attendance on a fool.' Yes; I am
positively certain Mr. Midwinter has done something or suffered something in his past life, young
as he is; and I would give I don't know what
to get at it. Don't resent my taking up so much

space in my writing about him. He has influence enough over young Armadale to be a very awkward obstacle in my way, unless I can secure his good opinion at starting.

"Well, you may ask, and what is to prevent your securing his good opinion? I am sadly afraid, Mother Oldershaw, I have got it on terms I never bargained for. I am sadly afraid the man is in love with me already.

"Don't toss your head and say, 'Just like her vanity!' After the horrors I have gone through, I have no vanity left; and a man who admires me is a man who makes me shudder. There was a time, I own— Pooh! what am I writing? Sentiment, I declare! Sentiment to *you!* Laugh away, my dear. As for me, I neither laugh nor cry; I mend my pen, and get on with my—what do the men call it?—my report.

"The only thing worth inquiring is, whether I am right or wrong in my idea of the impression I have made on him.

"Let me see; I have been four times in his company. The first time was in the major's garden, where we met unexpectedly, face to face. He stood looking at me, like a man petrified, without speaking a word. The effect of my horrid red hair, perhaps? Quite likely; let us lay it on my hair. The second time was in going over the Thorpe Ambrose grounds, with young Armadale on one side of me, and my pupil (in the sulks) on the other. Out comes Mr. Midwinter to join us, though he had work to do in the steward's office, which he had never been known to neglect on any other occasion. Laziness, possibly? or an attachment to Miss Milroy? I can't say; we will lay it on Miss Milroy, if you like; I only know he did nothing but look at *me*. The third time was at the private interview in the park, which I have told you of already. I never saw a man so agitated at putting a delicate question to a woman in my life. But *that* might have been only awkwardness; and his perpetually looking back after me when we had parted might have been only looking back at the view. Lay it on the view; by all means, lay it on the view! The fourth time was this very evening, at the little party. They made me play; and, as the piano was a good one, I did my best. All the company crowded round me, and paid me their compliments (my charming pupil paid hers, with a face like a cat's just before she spits), except Mr. Midwinter. *He* waited till it was time to go, and then he caught me alone for a moment in the hall. There was just time for him to take my hand, and say two words. Shall I tell you *how* he took my hand, and what his voice sounded like when he spoke? Quite needless! You have always told me that the late Mr. Oldershaw doted on you. Just recall the first time he took your hand, and whispered a word or two addressed to your private ear. To what did you attribute his behavior on that occasion? I have no doubt, if you had been playing on the piano in the course of the evening, you would have attributed it entirely to the music!

"No! you may take my word for it, the harm

is done. *This* man is no rattle-pated fool, who changes his fancies as readily as he changes his clothes. The fire that lights those big black eyes of his is not an easy fire, when a woman has once kindled it, for that woman to put out. I don't wish to discourage you; I don't say the changes are against us. But with Mrs. Milroy threatening me on one side, and Mr. Midwinter on the other, the worst of all risks to run is the risk of losing time. Young Armadale has hinted already, as well as such a lout can hint, at a private interview! Miss Milroy's eyes are sharp, and the nurse's eyes are sharper; and I shall lose my place if either of them find me out. No matter! I must take my chance, and give him the interview. Only let me get him alone, only let me escape the prying eyes of the women, and— if his friend doesn't come between us—I answer for the result!

"In the meantime, have I anything more to tell you? Are there any other people in our way at Thorpe Ambrose? Not another creature! None of the resident families call here, young Armadale being, most fortunately, in bad odor in the neighborhood. There are no handsome highly-bred women to come to the house, and no persons of consequence to protest against his attentions to a governess. The only guests he could collect at his party to-night were the lawyer and his family (a wife, a son, and two daughters), and a deaf old woman and *her* son—all perfectly unimportant people, and all obedient humble servants of the stupid young squire.

"Talking of obedient humble servants, there
is one other person established here, who is
employed in the steward's office—a miserable,
shabby, dilapidated old man, named Bashwood.
He is a perfect stranger to me, and I am evidently a perfect stranger to him, for he has been
asking the house-maid at the cottage who I am.
It is paying no great compliment to myself to confess it, but it is not the less true that I produced
the most extraordinary impression on this feeble
old creature the first time he saw me.   He turned
all manner of colors, and stood trembling and
staring at me, as if there was something perfectly
frightful in my face.   I felt quite startled for the
moment, for, of all the ways in which men have
looked at me, no man ever looked at me in that
way before.   Did you ever see the boa-constrictor
fed at the Zoological Gardens?   They put a live
rabbit into his cage, and there is a moment when
the two creatures look at each other.   I declare
Mr. Bashwood reminded me of the rabbit!

"Why do I mention this?   I don't know why.
Perhaps I have been writing too long, and my
head is beginning to fail me.   Perhaps Mr. Bashwood's manner of admiring me strikes my fancy
by its novelty.   Absurd!   I am exciting myself,
and troubling you about nothing.   Oh, what a
weary, long letter I have written! and how brightly the stars look at me through the window, and
how awfully quiet the night is!   Send me some
more of those sleeping drops, and write me one
of your nice, wicked, amusing letters   You
shall hear from me again as soon as I know a

little better how it is all likely to end. Good-
night, and keep a corner in your stony old heart
for                                              L. G."

### 3. *From Mrs. Oldershaw to Miss Gwilt.*

"Diana Street, Pimlico, Monday.

'MY DEAR LYDIA—I am in no state of mind
to write you an amusing letter. Your news is
very discouraging, and the recklessness of your
tone quite alarms me. Consider the money I
have already advanced, and the interests we both
have at stake. Whatever else you are, don't be
reckless, for Heaven's sake!

"What can I do? I ask myself, as a woman
of business, what can I do to help you? I can't
give you advice, for I am not on the spot, and I
don't know how circumstances may alter from
one day to another. Situated as we are now, I
can only be useful in one way. I can discover
a new obstacle that threatens you, and I think I
can remove it.

"You say, with great truth, that there never
was a prospect yet without an ugly place in it,
and that there are two ugly places in your prospect. My dear, there may be *three* ugly places,
if I don't bestir myself to prevent it; and the
name of the third place will be—Brock! Is it
possible you can refer, as you have done, to the
Somersetshire clergyman, and not see that the
progress you make with young Armadale will
be, sooner or later, reported to him by young
Armadale's friend? Why, now I think of it,
you are doubly at the parson's mercy! You are

at the mercy of any fresh suspicion which may
bring him into the neighborhood himself at a
day's notice; and you are at the mercy of his
interference the moment he hears that the squire
is committing himself with a neighbor's governess. If I can do nothing else, I can keep this
additional difficulty out of your way. And oh,
Lydia, with what alacrity I shall exert myself,
after the manner in which the old wretch insulted me when I told him that pitiable story
in the street! I declare I tingle with pleasure
at this new prospect of making a fool of Mr.
Brock.

"And how is it to be done? Just as we have
done it already, to be sure. He has lost 'Miss
Gwilt' (otherwise my house-maid), hasn't he?
Very well. He shall find her again, wherever
he is now, suddenly settled within easy reach of
him. As long as *she* stops in the place, *he* will
stop in it; and as we know he is not at Thorpe
Ambrose, there you are free of him! The old gentleman's suspicions have given us a great deal
of trouble so far. Let us turn them to some
profitable account at last; let us tie him, by his
suspicions, to my house-maid's apron - string.
Most refreshing. Quite a moral retribution,
isn't it?

"The only help I need trouble you for is help
you can easily give. Find out from Mr. Midwinter where the parson is now, and let me know
by return of post. If he is in London, I will personally assist my house-maid in the necessary
mystification of him. If he is anywhere else, I

will send her after him, accompanied by a person on whose discretion I can implicitly rely.

"You shall have the sleeping drops to-morrow. In the meantime, I say at the end what I said at the beginning—no recklessness. Don't encourage poetical feelings by looking at the stars; and don't talk about the night being awfully quiet. There are people (in observatories) paid to look at the stars for you; leave it to them. And as for the night, do what Providence intended you to do with the night when Providence provided you with eyelids—go to sleep in it.          Affectionately yours,

"MARIA OLDERSHAW."

### 4. *From the Reverend Decimus Brock to Ozias Midwinter.*

"Boscombe Rectory, West Somerset, Thursday, July 3.

"MY DEAR MIDWINTER—One line before the post goes out, to relieve you of all sense of responsibility at Thorpe Ambrose, and to make my apologies to the lady who lives as governess in Major Milroy's family.

"*The* Miss Gwilt—or perhaps I ought to say, the woman calling herself by that name—has, to my unspeakable astonishment, openly made her appearance here, in my own parish! She is staying at the inn, accompanied by a plausible-looking man, who passes as her brother. What this audacious proceeding really means—unless it marks a new step in the conspiracy against Allan, taken under new advice—is, of course, more than I can yet find out.

"My own idea is, that they have recognized the impossibility of getting at Allan, without finding me (or you) as an obstacle in their way; and that they are going to make a virtue of necessity by boldly trying to open their communications through me. The man looks capable of any stretch of audacity; and both he and the woman had the impudence to bow when I met them in the village half an hour since. They have been making inquiries already about Allan's mother here, where her exemplary life may set their closest scrutiny at defiance. If they will only attempt to extort money, as the price of the woman's silence on the subject of poor Mrs. Armadale's conduct in Madeira at the time of her marriage, they will find me well prepared for them beforehand. I have written by this post to my lawyers to send a competent man to assist me, and he will stay at the rectory, in any character which he thinks it safest to assume under present circumstances.

"You shall hear what happens in the next day or two.

"Always truly yours,   DECIMUS BROCK."

## CHAPTER XII.

### THE CLOUDING OF THE SKY.

NINE days had passed, and the tenth day was nearly at an end, since Miss Gwilt and her pupil had taken their morning walk in the cottage garden.

The night was overcast. Since sunset, there had been signs in the sky from which the popular forecast had predicted rain. The reception-rooms at the great house were all empty and dark. Allan was away, passing the evening with the Milroys; and Midwinter was waiting his return—not where Midwinter usually waited, among the books in the library, but in the little back room which Allan's mother had inhabited in the last days of her residence at Thorpe Ambrose.

Nothing had been taken away, but much had been added to the room, since Midwinter had first seen it. The books which Mrs. Armadale had left behind her, the furniture, the old matting on the—floor, the old paper on the walls, were all undisturbed. The statuette of Niobe still stood on its bracket, and the French window still opened on the garden. But now, to the relics left by the mother, were added the personal possessions belonging to the son. The wall, bare hitherto, was decorated with water-color drawings—with a portrait of Mrs. Armadale, supported on one side by a view of the old house in Somersetshire, and on the other by a picture of the yacht. Among the books which bore in faded ink Mrs. Armadale's inscriptions, "From my father," were other books inscribed in the same handwriting, in brighter ink, "To my son." Hanging to the wall, ranged on the chimney-piece, scattered over the table, were a host of little objects, some associated with Allan's past life, others necessary to his daily pleasures and pursuits, and all plainly testifying that the room which he habitually occupied at Thorpe Ambrose was the very room which had once recalled to Midwinter the second vision of the dream. Here, strangely unmoved by the scene around him, so lately the object of his superstitious distrust, Allan's friend now waited composedly for Allan's return; and here, more strangely still, he looked on a change in the household arrangements, due in the first instance entirely to himself. His own lips had revealed the discovery which he had made on the first morning in the new house; his own voluntary act had induced the son to establish himself in the mother's room.

Under what motives had he spoken the words? Under no motives which were not the natural growth of the new interests and the new hopes that now animated him.

The entire change wrought in his convictions by the memorable event that had brought him face to face with Miss Gwilt was a change which it was not in his nature to hide from Allan's knowledge. He had spoken openly, and had spoken as it was in his character to speak. The merit of conquering his superstition was a merit which he shrank from claiming, until he had first unsparingly exposed that superstition in its worst and weakest aspects to view.

It was only after he had unreservedly acknowledged the impulse under which he had left

Allan at the Mere, that he had taken credit to
himself for the new point of view from which
he could now look at the Dream.   Then, and not
till then, he had spoken of the fulfillment of the
first Vision as the doctor at the Isle of Man
might have spoken of it.   He had asked, as the
doctor might have asked, Where was the wonder
of their seeing a pool at sunset, when they had
a whole network of pools within a few hours'
drive of them? and what was there extraordinary
in discovering a woman at the Mere, when there
were roads that led to it, and villages in its neighborhood, and boats employed on it, and pleasure
parties visiting it?   So again, he had waited to
vindicate the firmer resolution with which he
looked to the future, until he had first revealed
all that he now saw himself of the errors of the
past.   The abandonment of his friend's interests,
the unworthiness of the confidence that had given
him the steward's place, the forgetfulness of the
trust that Mr. Brock had reposed in him all implied in the one idea of leaving Allan—were all
pointed out.   The glaring self-contradictions betrayed in accepting the Dream as the revelation
of a fatality, and in attempting to escape that
fatality by an exertion of free-will—in toiling
to store up knowledge of the steward's duties
for the future, and in shrinking from letting
the future find him in Allan's house—were, in
their turn, unsparingly exposed.   To every
error, to every inconsistency, he resolutely confessed, before he ventured on the last simple
appeal which closed all, "Will you trust me in

the future? Will you forgive and forget the past?"

A man who could thus open his whole heart, without one lurking reserve inspired by consideration for himself, was not a man to forget any minor act of concealment of which his weakness might have led him to be guilty toward his friend. It lay heavy on Midwinter's conscience that he had kept secret from Allan a discovery which he ought in Allan's dearest interests to have revealed—the discovery of his mother's room.

But one doubt still closed his lips—the doubt whether Mrs. Armadale's conduct in Madeira had been kept secret on her return to England.

Careful inquiry, first among the servants, then among the tenantry, careful consideration of the few reports current at the time, as repeated to him by the few persons left who remembered them, convinced him at last that the family secret had been successfully kept within the family limits. Once satisfied that whatever inquiries the son might make would lead to no disclosure which could shake his respect for his mother's memory, Midwinter had hesitated no longer. He had taken Allan into the room, and had shown him the books on the shelves, and all that the writing in the books disclosed. He had said plainly, "My one motive for not telling you this before sprang from my dread of interesting you in the room which I looked at with horror as the second of the scenes pointed at in the Dream. Forgive me this also, and you will have forgiven me all."

With Allan's love for his mother's memory,
but one result could follow such an avowal as
this. He had liked the little room from the
first, as a pleasant contrast to the oppressive
grandeur of the other rooms at Thorpe Ambrose,
and, now that he knew what associations were
connected with it, his resolution was at once
taken to make it especially his own. The same
day, all his personal possessions were collected
and arranged in his mother's room—in Midwinter's presence, and with Midwinter's assistance
given to the work.

Under those circumstances had the change
now wrought in the household arrangements
been produced; and in this way had Midwinter's victory over his own fatalism—by making
Allan the daily occupant of a room which he
might otherwise hardly ever have entered—actually favored the fulfillment of the Second Vision
of the Dream.

The hour wore on quietly as Allan's friend sat
waiting for Allan's return. Sometimes reading,
sometimes thinking placidly, he whiled away
the time. No vexing cares, no boding doubts,
troubled him now. The rent-day, which he had
once dreaded, had come and gone harmlessly. A
friendlier understanding had been established between Allan and his tenants; Mr. Bashwood had
proved himself to be worthy of the confidence reposed in him; the Pedgifts, father and son, had
amply justified their client's good opinion of
them. Wherever Midwinter looked, the pros-

pect was bright, the future was without a cloud.

He trimmed the lamp on the table beside him and looked out at the night. The stable clock was chiming the half-hour past eleven as he walked to the window, and the first rain-drops were beginning to fall. He had his hand on the bell to summon the servant, and send him over to the cottage with an umbrella, when he was stopped by hearing the familiar footstep on the walk outside.

"How late you are!" said Midwinter, as Allan entered through the open French window. "Was there a party at the cottage?"

"No! only ourselves. The time slipped away somehow." He answered in lower tones than usual, and sighed as he took his chair.

"You seem to be out of spirits?" pursued Midwinter. "What's the matter?"

Allan hesitated. "I may as well tell you," he said, after a moment. "It's nothing to be ashamed of; I only wonder you haven't noticed it before! There's a woman in it, as usual—I'm in love."

Midwinter laughed. "Has Miss Milroy been more charming to-night than ever?" he asked, gayly.

"Miss Milroy!" repeated Allan. "What are you thinking of! I'm not in love with Miss Milroy."

"Who is it, then?"

"Who is it! What a question to ask! Who *can* it be but Miss Gwilt?"

There was a sudden silence. Allan sat listlessly, with his hands in his pockets, looking out through the open window at the falling rain. If he had turned toward his friend when he mentioned Miss Gwilt's name he might possibly have been a little startled by the change he would have seen in Midwinter's face.

"I suppose you don't approve of it?" he said, after waiting a little.

There was no answer.

"It's too late to make objections," proceeded Allan. "I really mean it when I tell you I'm in love with her."

"A fortnight since you were in love with Miss Milroy," said the other, in quiet, measured tones.

"Pooh! a mere flirtation. It's different this time. I'm in earnest about Miss Gwilt."

He looked round as he spoke. Midwinter turned his face aside on the instant, and bent it over a book.

"I see you don't approve of the thing," Allan went on. "Do you object to her being only a governess? You can't do that, I'm sure. If you were in my place, her being only a governess wouldn't stand in the way with *you?*"

"No," said Midwinter; "I can't honestly say it would stand in the way with me." He gave the answer reluctantly, and pushed his chair back out of the light of the lamp.

"A governess is a lady who is not rich," said Allan, in an oracular manner; "and a duchess is a lady who is not poor. And that's all the difference I acknowledge between them. Miss

Gwilt is older than I am—I don't deny that. What age do you guess her at, Midwinter? I say, seven or eight and twenty. What do you say?"

"Nothing. I agree with you."

"Do you think seven or eight and twenty is too old for me? If you were in love with a woman yourself, you wouldn't think seven or eight and twenty too old—would you?"

"I can't say I should think it too old, if—"

"If you were really fond of her?"

Once more there was no answer.

"Well," resumed Allan, "if there's no harm in her being only a governess, and no harm in her being a little older than I am, what's the objection to Miss Gwilt?"

"I have made no objection."

"I don't say you have. But you don't seem to like the notion of it, for all that."

There was another pause. Midwinter was the first to break the silence this time.

"Are you sure of yourself, Allan?" he asked, with his face bent once more over the book. "Are you really attached to this lady? Have you thought seriously already of asking her to be your wife?"

"I am thinking seriously of it at this moment," said Allan. "I can't be happy—I can't live without her. Upon my soul, I worship the very ground she treads on!"

"How long—" His voice faltered, and he stopped. "How long," he reiterated, "have you worshiped the very ground she treads on?"

"Longer than you think for. I know I can trust you with all my secrets—"

"Don't trust me!"

"Nonsense! I *will* trust you. There is a little difficulty in the way which I haven't mentioned yet. It's a matter of some delicacy, and I want to consult you about it. Between ourselves, I have had private opportunities with Miss Gwilt—"

Midwinter suddenly started to his feet, and opened the door.

"We'll talk of this to-morrow," he said. "Good-night."

Allan looked round in astonishment. The door was closed again, and he was alone in the room.

"He has never shaken hands with me!" exclaimed Allan, looking bewildered at the empty chair.

As the words passed his lips the door opened, and Midwinter appeared again.

"We haven't shaken hands," he said, abruptly. "God bless you, Allan! We'll talk of it to-morrow. Good-night."

Allan stood alone at the window, looking out at the pouring rain. He felt ill at ease, without knowing why. "Midwinter's ways get stranger and stranger," he thought. "What can he mean by putting me off till to-morrow, when I wanted to speak to him to-night?" He took up his bedroom candle a little impatiently, put it down again, and, walking back to the open window, stood looking out in the direction of the cottage. "I wonder if she's thinking of me?" he said to himself softly.

She *was* thinking of him.   She had just opened her desk to write to Mrs. Oldershaw; and her pen had that moment traced the opening line: "Make your mind easy.   I have got him!"

---

## CHAPTER XIII.

### EXIT.

It rained all through the night, and when the morning came it was raining still.

Contrary to his ordinary habit, Midwinter was waiting in the breakfast-room when Allan entered it.   He looked worn and weary, but his smile was gentler and his manner more composed than usual.   To Allan's surprise he approached the subject of the previous night's conversation of his own accord as soon as the servant was out of the room.

"I am afraid you thought me very impatient and very abrupt with you last night," he said. "I will try to make amends for it this morning. I will hear everything you wish to say to me on the subject of Miss Gwilt."

"I hardly like to worry you," said Allan. "You look as if you had had a bad night's rest."

"I have not slept well for some time past," replied Midwinter, quietly.   "Something has been wrong with me. But I believe I have found out the way to put myself right again without troubling the doctors. Late in the morning I shall have something to say to you about this. Let us get back first to what you were talking of last night. You were speaking of some difficulty—" He hesitated, and finished the sentence in a tone so low that Allan failed to hear him. "Perhaps it would be better," he went on, "if, instead of speaking to me, you spoke to Mr. Brock?"

"I would rather speak to *you*," said Allan. "But tell me first, was I right or wrong last night in thinking you disapproved of my falling in love with Miss Gwilt?"

Midwinter's lean, nervous fingers began to crumble the bread in his plate. His eyes looked away from Allan for the first time.

"If you have any objection," persisted Allan, "I should like to hear it."

Midwinter suddenly looked up again, his cheeks turning ashy pale, and his glittering black eyes fixed full on Allan's face.

"You love her," he said. "Does *she* love *you?*"

"You won't think me vain?" returned Allan. "I told you yesterday I had had private opportunities with her—"

Midwinter's eyes dropped again to the crumbs on his plate. "I understand," he interposed, quickly. "You were wrong last night. I had no objections to make."

"Don't you congratulate me?" asked Allan,

a little uneasily. "Such a beautiful woman! such a clever woman!"

Midwinter held out his hand. "I owe you more than mere congratulations," he said. "In anything which is for your happiness I owe you help." He took Allan's hand, and wrung it hard. "Can I help you?" he asked, growing paler and paler as he spoke.

"My dear fellow," exclaimed Allan, "what *is* the matter with you? Your hand is as cold as ice."

Midwinter smiled faintly. "I am always in extremes," he said; "my hand was as hot as fire the first time you took it at the old west-country inn. Come to that difficulty which you have not come to yet. You are young, rich, your own master—and she loves you. What difficulty can there be?"

Allan hesitated. "I hardly know how to put it," he replied. "As you said just now, I love her, and she loves me; and yet there is a sort of strangeness between us. One talks a good deal about one's self when one is in love, at least I do. I've told her all about myself and my mother, and how I came in for this place, and the rest of it. Well—though it doesn't strike me when we are together—it comes across me now and then, when I'm away from her, that she doesn't say much on her side. In fact, I know no more about her than you do."

"Do you mean that you know nothing about Miss Gwilt's family and friends?"

"That's it, exactly."

"Have you never asked her about them?"

"I said something of the sort the other day," returned Allan: "and I'm afraid, as usual, I said it in the wrong way. She looked—I can't quite tell you how; not exactly displeased, but —oh, what things words are! I'd give the world, Midwinter, if I could only find the right word when I want it as well as you do."

"Did Miss Gwilt say anything to you in the way of a reply?"

"That's just what I was coming to. She said, 'I shall have a melancholy story to tell you one of these days, Mr. Armadale, about myself and my family; but you look so happy, and the circumstances are so distressing, that I have hardly the heart to speak of it now.' Ah, *she* can express herself—with the tears in her eyes, my dear fellow, with the tears in her eyes! Of course, I changed the subject directly. And now the difficulty is how to get back to it, delicately, without making her cry again. We *must* get back to it, you know. Not on my account; I am quite content to marry her first and hear of her family misfortunes, poor thing, afterward. But I know Mr. Brock. If I can't satisfy him about her family when I write to tell him of this (which, of course, I must do), he will be dead against the whole thing. I'm my own master, of course, and I can do as I like about it. But dear old Brock was such a good friend to my poor mother, and he has been such a good friend to me—you see what I mean, don't you?"

"Certainly, Allan; Mr. Brock has been your

second father. Any disagreement between you about such a serious matter as this would be the saddest thing that could happen. You ought to satisfy him that Miss Gwilt is (what I am sure Miss Gwilt will prove to be) worthy, in every way worthy—'' His voice sank in spite of him, and he left the sentence unfinished.

"Just my feeling in the matter!" Allan struck in, glibly. "Now we can come to what I particularly wanted to consult you about. If this was your case, Midwinter, you would be able to say the right words to her—you would put it delicately, even though you were putting it quite in the dark. I can't do that. I'm a blundering sort of fellow; and I'm horribly afraid, if I can't get some hint at the truth to help me at starting, of saying something to distress her. Family misfortunes are such tender subjects to touch on, especially with such a refined woman, such a tender-hearted woman, as Miss Gwilt. There may have been some dreadful death in the family—some relation who has disgraced himself—some infernal cruelty which has forced the poor thing out on the world as a governess. Well, turning it over in my mind, it struck me that the major might be able to put me on the right tack. It is quite possible that he might have been informed of Miss Gwilt's family circumstances before he engaged her, isn't it?"

"It is possible, Allan, certainly."

"Just my feeling again! My notion is to speak to the major. If I could only get the story from him first, I should know so much better how to speak to Miss Gwilt about it afterward. You advise me to try the major, don't you?"

There was a pause before Midwinter replied. When he did answer, it was a little reluctantly.

"I hardly know how to advise you, Allan," he said. "This is a very delicate matter."

"I believe you would try the major, if you were in my place," returned Allan, reverting to his inveterately personal way of putting the question.

"Perhaps I might," said Midwinter, more and more unwillingly. "But if I did speak to the major, I should be very careful, in your place, not to put myself in a false position. I should be very careful to let no one suspect me of the meanness of prying into a woman's secrets behind her back."

Allan's face flushed. "Good heavens, Midwinter," he exclaimed, "who could suspect me of that?"

"Nobody, Allan, who really knows you."

"The major knows me. The major is the last man in the world to misunderstand me. All I want him to do is to help me (if he can) to speak about a delicate subject to Miss Gwilt, without hurting her feelings. Can anything be simpler between two gentlemen?"

Instead of replying, Midwinter, still speaking as constrainedly as ever, asked a question on his side. "Do you mean to tell Major Milroy," he said, "what your intentions really are toward Miss Gwilt?"

Allan's manner altered. He hesitated, and looked confused.

"I have been thinking of that," he replied; "and I mean to feel my way first, and then tell him or not afterward, as matters turn out?"

A proceeding so cautious as this was too strikingly inconsistent with Allan's character not to surprise any one who knew him. Midwinter showed his surprise plainly.

"You forget that foolish flirtation of mine with Miss Milroy," Allan went on, more and more confusedly. "The major may have noticed it, and may have thought I meant—well, what I didn't mean. It might be rather awkward, mightn't it, to propose to his face for his governess instead of his daughter?"

He waited for a word of answer, but none came. Midwinter opened his lips to speak, and suddenly checked himself. Allan, uneasy at his silence, doubly uneasy under certain recollections of the major's daughter which the conversation had called up, rose from the table and shortened the interview a little impatiently.

"Come! come!" he said, "don't sit there looking unutterable things; don't make mountains out of mole-hills. You have such an old, old head, Midwinter, on those young shoulders of yours! Let's have done with all these *pros* and *cons*. Do you mean to tell me in plain words that it won't do to speak to the major?"

"I can't take the responsibility, Allan, of tell-

ing you that. To be plainer still, I can't feel
confident of the soundness of any advice I may
give you in—in our present position toward each
other. All I am sure of is that I cannot possibly
be wrong in entreating you to do two things."

"What are they?"

"If you speak to Major Milroy, pray remember the caution I have given you! Pray think
of what you say before you say it!"

"I'll think, never fear! What next?"

"Before you take any serious step in this matter, write and tell Mr. Brock. Will you promise
me to do that?"

"With all my heart. Anything more?"

"Nothing more. I have said my last words."

Allan led the way to the door. "Come into
my room," he said, "and I'll give you a cigar.
The servants will be in here directly to clear
away, and I want to go on talking about Miss
Gwilt."

"Don't wait for me," said Midwinter; "I'll
follow you in a minute or two."

He remained seated until Allan had closed the
door, then rose, and took from a corner of the
room, where it lay hidden behind one of the curtains, a knapsack ready packed for traveling.
As he stood at the window thinking, with the
knapsack in his hand, a strangely old, care-worn
look stole over his face: he seemed to lose the
last of his youth in an instant.

What the woman's quicker insight had discovered days since, the man's slower perception had

only realized in the past night. The pang that had wrung him when he heard Allan's avowal had set the truth self-revealed before Midwinter for the first time. He had been conscious of looking at Miss Gwilt with new eyes and a new mind, on the next occasion when they met after the memorable interview in Major Milroy's garden; but he had never until now known the passion that she had roused in him for what it really was. Knowing it at last, feeling it consciously in full possession of him, he had the courage which no man with a happier experience of life would have possessed — the courage to recall what Allan had confided to him, and to look resolutely at the future through his own grateful remembrances of the past.

Steadfastly, through the sleepless hours of the night, he had bent his mind to the conviction that he must conquer the passion which had taken possession of him, for Allan's sake; and that the one way to conquer it was—to go. No after-doubt as to the sacrifice had troubled him when morning came; and no after-doubt troubled him now. The one question that kept him hesitating was the question of leaving Thorpe Ambrose. Though Mr. Brock's letter relieved him from all necessity of keeping watch in Norfolk for a woman who was known to be in Somersetshire; though the duties of the steward's office were duties which might be safely left in Mr. Bashwood's tried and trustworthy hands—still, admitting these considerations, his mind was not easy at the thought of leaving Allan, at

a time when a crisis was approaching in Allan's
life.

He slung the knapsack loosely over his shoulder
and put the question to his conscience for the
last time. "Can you trust yourself to see her,
day by day, as you must see her—can you trust
yourself to hear him talk of her, hour by hour,
as you must hear him—if you stay in this house?"
Again the answer came, as it had come all through
the night. Again his heart warned him, in the
very interests of the friendship that he held
sacred, to go while the time was his own; to
go before the woman who had possessed herself
of his love had possessed herself of his power of
self-sacrifice and his sense of gratitude as well.

He looked round the room mechanically before
he turned to leave it. Every remembrance of
the conversation that had just taken place between Allan and himself pointed to the same
conclusion, and warned him, as his own conscience had warned him, to go.

Had he honestly mentioned any one of the
objections which he, or any man, must have
seen to Allan's attachment? Had he — as his
knowledge of his friend's facile character bound
him to do—warned Allan to distrust his own
hasty impulses, and to test himself by time and
absence, before he made sure that the happiness
of his whole life was bound up in Miss Gwilt?
No. The bare doubt whether, in speaking of
these things, he could feel that he was speaking
disinterestedly, had closed his lips, and would
close his lips for the future, till the time for

speaking had gone by. Was the right man to restrain Allan the man who would have given the world, if he had it, to stand in Allan's place? There was but one plain course of action that an honest man and a grateful man could follow in the position in which he stood. Far removed from all chance of seeing her, and from all chance of hearing of her—alone with his own faithful recollection of what he owed to his friend—he might hope to fight it down, as he had fought down the tears in his childhood under his gypsy master's stick; as he had fought down the misery of his lonely youth time in the country bookseller's shop. "I must go," he said, as he turned wearily from the window, "before she comes to the house again. I must go before another hour is over my head."

With that resolution he left the room; and, in leaving it, took the irrevocable step from Present to Future.

The rain was still falling. The sullen sky, all round the horizon, still lowered watery and dark, when Midwinter, equipped for traveling, appeared in Allan's room.

"Good heavens!" cried Allan, pointing to the knapsack, "what does *that* mean?"

"Nothing very extraordinary," said Midwinter. "It only means—good-by."

"Good-by!" repeated Allan, starting to his feet in astonishment.

Midwinter put him back gently into his chair, and drew a seat near to it for himself.

"When you noticed that I looked ill this morning," he said, "I told you that I had been thinking of a way to recover my health, and that I meant to speak to you about it later in the day. That latter time has come. I have been out of sorts, as the phrase is, for some time past. You have remarked it yourself, Allan, more than once; and, with your usual kindness, you have allowed it to excuse many things in my conduct which would have been otherwise unpardonable, even in your friendly eyes."

"My dear fellow," interposed Allan, "you don't mean to say you are going out on a walking tour in this pouring rain!"

"Never mind the rain," rejoined Midwinter. "The rain and I are old friends. You know something, Allan, of the life I led before you met with me. From the time when I was a child, I have been used to hardship and exposure. Night and day, sometimes for months together, I never had my head under a roof. For years and years, the life of a wild animal—perhaps I ought to say, the life of a savage—was the life I led, while you were at home and happy. I have the leaven of the vagabond—the vagabond animal, or the vagabond man, I hardly know which—in me still. Does it distress you to hear me talk of myself in this way? I won't distress you. . I will only say that the comfort and the luxury of our life here are, at times, I think, a little too much for a man to whom comforts and luxuries come as strange things. I want nothing to put me right again but more air and exercise; fewer good breakfasts and dinners, my dear friend, than I get here. Let me go back to some of the hardships which this comfortable house is expressly made to shut out. Let me meet the wind and weather as I used to meet them when I was a boy; let me feel weary again for a little while, without a carriage near to pick me up; and hungry when the night falls, with miles of walking between my supper and me. Give me a week or two away, Allan—up northward, on foot, to the Yorkshire moors— and I promise to return to Thorpe Ambrose, better company for you and for your friends. I shall be back before you have time to miss me. Mr. Bashwood will take care of the business in the office; it is only for a fortnight, and it is for my own good—let me go!''

"I don't like it,'' said Allan. "I don't like your leaving me in this sudden manner. There's something so strange and dreary about it. Why not try riding, if you want more exercise; all the horses in the stables are at your disposal. At all events, you can't possibly go to-day. Look at the rain!''

Midwinter looked toward the window, and gently shook his head.

"I thought nothing of the rain,'' he said, "when. I was a mere child, getting my living with the dancing dogs—why should I think anything of it now? *My* getting wet, and *your* getting wet, Allan, are two very different things. When I was a fisherman's boy in the Hebrides, I hadn't a dry thread on me for weeks together.''

"But you're not in the Hebrides now," persisted Allan; "and I expect our friends from the cottage to-morrow evening. You can't start till after to-morrow. Miss Gwilt is going to give us some more music, and you know you like Miss Gwilt's playing."

Midwinter turned aside to buckle the straps of his knapsack. "Give me another chance of hearing Miss Gwilt when I come back," he said, with his head down, and his fingers busy at the straps.

"You have one fault, my dear fellow, and it grows on you," remonstrated Allan; "when you have once taken a thing into your head, you're the most obstinate man alive. There's no persuading you to listen to reason. If you *will* go," added Allan, suddenly rising, as Midwinter took up his hat and stick in silence, "I have half a mind to go with you, and try a little roughing it too!"

"Go with *me!*" repeated Midwinter, with a momentary bitterness in his tone, "and leave Miss Gwilt!"

Allan sat down again, and admitted the force of the objection in significant silence. Without a word more on his side, Midwinter held out his hand to take leave. They were both deeply moved, and each was anxious to hide his agitation from the other. Allan took the last refuge which his friend's firmness left to him: he tried to lighten the farewell moment by a joke.

"I'll tell you what," he said, "I begin to doubt if you're quite cured yet of your belief in the

Dream. I suspect you're running away from me, after all!''

Midwinter looked at him, uncertain whether he was in jest or earnest. ''What do you mean?'' he asked.

''What did you tell me,'' retorted Allan, ''when you took me in here the other day, and made a clean breast of it? What did you say about this room, and the second vision of the dream? By Jupiter!'' he exclaimed, starting to his feet once more, ''now I look again, here *is* the Second Vision! There's the rain pattering against the window—there's the lawn and the garden outside — here am I where I stood in the Dream—and there are you where the Shadow stood. The whole scene complete, out-of-doors and in; and *I've* discovered it this time!''

A moment's life stirred again in the dead remains of Midwinter's superstition. His color changed; and he eagerly, almost fiercely, disputed Allan's conclusion.

''No!'' he said, pointing to the little marble figure on the bracket, ''the scene is *not* complete —you have forgotten something, as usual. The Dream is wrong this time, thank God—utterly wrong! In the vision you saw, the statue was lying in fragments on the floor, and you were stooping over them with a troubled and an angry mind. There stands the statue safe and sound! and you haven't the vestige of an angry feeling in your mind, have you?'' He seized Allan impulsively by the hand. At the same moment the consciousness came to him that he was speaking and acting as earnestly as if he still believed in the Dream. The color rushed back over his face, and he turned away in confused silence.

"What did I tell you?" said Allan, laughing, a little uneasily. "That night on the Wreck is hanging on your mind as heavily as ever."

"Nothing hangs ·heavy on me," retorted Midwinter, with a sudden outburst of impatience, "but the knapsack on my back, and the time I'm wasting here. I'll go out, and see if it's likely to clear up."

"You'll come back?" interposed Allan.

Midwinter opened the French window, and stepped out into the garden.

"Yes," he said, answering with all his former gentleness of manner; "I'll come back in a fortnight. Good - by, Allan; and good luck with Miss Gwilt!"

He pushed the window to, and was away across the garden before his friend could open it again and follow him.

Allan rose, and took one step into the garden; then checked himself at the window, and returned to his chair. He knew Midwinter well enough to feel the total uselessness of attempting to follow him or to call him back. He was gone, and for two weeks to come there was no hope of seeing him again. An hour or more passed, the rain still fell, and the sky still threatened. A heavier and heavier sense of loneliness and despondency—the sense of all others which his previous life had least fitted him to understand and endure — possessed itself of Allan's mind. In sheer horror of his own uninhabitably solitary house, he rang for his hat and umbrella, and resolved to take refuge in the major's cottage.

"I might have gone a little way with him," thought Allan, his mind still running on Midwinter as he put on his hat.· "I should like to have seen the dear old fellow fairly started on his journey."

He took his umbrella. If he had noticed the face of the servant who gave it to him, he might possibly have asked some questions, and might have heard some news to interest him in his present frame of mind. As it was, he went out without looking at the man, and without suspecting that his servants knew more of Midwinter's last moments at Thorpe Ambrose than he knew himself. Not ten minutes since, the grocer and butcher had called in to receive payment of their bills, and the grocer and the butcher had seen how Midwinter started on his journey.

The grocer had met him first, not far from the house, stopping on his way, in the pouring rain, to speak to a little ragged imp of a boy, the pest of the neighborhood. The boy's customary impudence had broken out even more unrestrainedly than usual at the sight of the gentleman's knapsack. And what had the gentleman done in return? He had stopped and looked distressed, and had put his two hands gently on the boy's shoulders. The grocer's own eyes had seen that; and the grocer's own ears had heard him say, "Poor little chap! I know how the wind gnaws and the rain wets through a ragged jacket, better than most people who have got a good coat on their backs." And with those words he had put his hand in his pocket, and had rewarded the boy's impudence with a present of a shilling. "Wrong hereabouts," said the grocer, touching his forehead. "That's my opinion of Mr. Armadale's friend!"

The butcher had seen him further on in the journey, at the other end of the town. He had stopped—again in the pouring rain—and this time to look at nothing more remarkable than a half-starved cur, shivering on a doorstep. "I had my eye on him," said the butcher; "and what do you think he did? He crossed the road over to my shop, and bought a bit of meat fit for a Christian. Very well. He says good-morning, and crosses back again; and, on the word of a man, down he goes on his knees on the wet doorstep, and out he takes his knife, and cuts up the meat, and gives it to the dog. Meat, I tell you again, fit for a Christian! I'm not a hard man, ma'am," concluded the butcher, addressing the cook, "but meat's meat; and it will serve your master's friend right if he lives to want it."

With those old unforgotten sympathies of the old unforgotten time to keep him company on his lonely road, he had left the town behind him, and had been lost to view in the misty rain. The grocer and the butcher had seen the last of him, and had judged a great nature, as all natures *are* judged from the grocer and the butcher point of view.

THE END OF THE SECOND BOOK.

---

## BOOK THE THIRD.

---

## CHAPTER I.

### MRS. MILROY.

TWO days after Midwinter's departure from Thorpe Ambrose, Mrs. Milroy, having completed her morning toilet, and having dismissed her nurse, rang the bell again five minutes afterward, and on the woman's re-appearance asked impatiently if the post had come in.

"Post?" echoed the nurse. "Haven't you got your watch? Don't you know that it's a good half-hour too soon to ask for your letters?" She spoke with the confident insolence of a servant long accustomed to presume on her mistress's weakness and her mistress's necessities. Mrs. Milroy, on her side, appeared to be well used to her nurse's manner; she gave her orders composedly, without noticing it.

"When the postman does come," she said,

"see him yourself. I am expecting a letter which I ought to have had two days since. I don't understand it. I'm beginning to suspect the servants."

The nurse smiled contemptuously. "Whom will you suspect next?" she asked. "There! don't put yourself out. I'll answer the gate-bell this morning; and we'll see if I can't bring you a letter when the postman comes." Saying those words, with the tone and manner of a woman who is quieting a fractious child, the nurse, without waiting to be dismissed, left the room.

Mrs. Milroy turned slowly and wearily on her bed, when she was left by herself again, and let the light from the window fall on her face. It was the face of a woman who had once been handsome, and who was still, so far as years went, in the prime of her life. Long-continued suffering of body and long-continued irritation of mind had worn her away—in the roughly expressive popular phrase—to skin and bone. The utter wreck of her beauty was made a wreck horrible to behold, by her desperate efforts to conceal the sight of it from her own eyes, from the eyes of her husband and her child, from the eyes even of the doctor who attended her, and whose business it was to penetrate to the truth. Her head, from which the greater part of the hair had fallen off, would have been less shocking to see than the hideously youthful wig by which she tried to hide the loss. No deterioration of her complexion, no wrinkling of her skin, could

have been so dreadful to look at as the rouge
that lay thick on her cheeks, and the white
enamel plastered on her forehead. The delicate
lace, and the bright trimming on her dressing-
gown, the ribbons in her cap, and the rings on
her bony fingers, all intended to draw the eye
away from the change that had passed over her,
directed the eye to it, on the contrary; empha-
sized it; made it by sheer force of contrast more
hopeless and more horrible than it really was.
An illustrated book of the fashions, in which
women were represented exhibiting their finery
by means of the free use of their limbs, lay on
the bed, from which she had not moved for years
without being lifted by her nurse. A hand-glass
was placed with the book so that she could reach
it easily. She took up the glass after her attendant had left the room, and looked at her face
with an unblushing interest and attention which
she would have been ashamed of herself at the
age of eighteen.

"Older and older, and thinner and thinner!"
she said. "The major will soon be a free man;
but I'll have that red-haired hussy out of the
house first!"

She dropped the looking-glass on the counterpane, and clinched the hand that held it. Her
eyes suddenly riveted themselves on a little
crayon portrait of her husband hanging on the
opposite wall; they looked at the likeness with
the hard and cruel brightness of the eyes of a
bird of prey. "Red is your taste in your old
age, is it?" she said to the portrait. "Red

hair, and a scrofulous complexion, and a padded figure, a ballet-girl's walk, and a pickpocket's light fingers. *Miss* Gwilt! *Miss*, with those eyes, and that walk!" She turned her head suddenly on the pillow, and burst into a harsh, jeering laugh. "*Miss!*" she repeated over and over again, with the venomously pointed emphasis of the most merciless of all human forms of contempt—the contempt of one woman for another.

The age we live in is an age which finds no human creature inexcusable. Is there an excuse for Mrs. Milroy? Let the story of her life answer the question.

She had married the major at an unusually early age; and, in marrying him, had taken a man for her husband who was old enough to be her father—a man who, at that time, had the reputation, and not unjustly, of having made the freest use of his social gifts and his advantages of personal appearance in the society of women. Indifferently educated, and below her husband in station, she had begun by accepting his addresses under the influence of her own flattered vanity, and had ended by feeling the fascination which Major Milroy had exercised over women infinitely her mental superiors in his earlier life. He had been touched, on his side, by her devotion, and had felt, in his turn, the attraction of her beauty, her freshness, and her youth. Up to the time when their little daughter and only child had reached the age of eight years, their married life had been an unusually happy one. At that period the double misfortune fell on the household, of the failure of the wife's health, and the almost total loss of the husband's fortune; and from that moment the domestic happiness of the married pair was virtually at an end.

Having reached the age when men in general are readier, under the pressure of calamity, to resign themselves than to resist, the major had secured the little relics of his property, had retired into the country, and had patiently taken refuge in his mechanical pursuits. A woman nearer to him in age, or a woman with a better training and more patience of disposition than his wife possessed, would have understood the major's conduct, and have found consolation in the major's submission. Mrs. Milroy found consolation in nothing. Neither nature nor training helped her to meet resignedly the cruel calamity which had struck at her in the bloom of womanhood and the prime of beauty. The curse of incurable sickness blighted her at once and for life.

Suffering can, and does, develop the latent evil that there is in humanity, as well as the latent good. The good that was in Mrs. Milroy's nature shrank up, under that subtly deteriorating influence in which the evil grew and flourished. Month by month, as she became the weaker woman physically, she became the worse woman morally. All that was mean, cruel, and false in her expanded in steady proportion to the contraction of all that had once been generous, gentle, and true. Old suspicions of her husband's

readiness to relapse into the irregularities of his
bachelor life, which, in her healthier days of
mind and body, she had openly confessed to him
—which she had always sooner or later seen to
be suspicions that he had not deserved—came
back, now that sickness had divorced her from
him, in the form of that baser conjugal distrust
which keeps itself cunningly secret; which
gathers together its inflammatory particles
atom by atom into a heap, and sets the slowly
burning frenzy of jealousy alight in the mind.
No proof of her husband's blameless and patient
life that could now be shown to Mrs. Milroy; no
appeal that could be made to her respect for herself, or for her child growing up to womanhood,
availed to dissipate the terrible delusion born of
her hopeless illness, and growing steadily with
its growth.   Like all other madness, it had its
ebb and flow, its time of spasmodic outburst,
and its time of deceitful repose; but, active or
passive, it was always in her.   It had injured innocent servants, and insulted blameless strangers.
It had brought the first tears of shame and sorrow into her daughter's eyes, and had set the
deepest lines that scored it in her husband's
face.   It had made the secret misery of the little household for years; and it was now to pass
beyond the family limits, and to influence coming events at Thorpe Ambrose, in which the
future interests of Allan and Allan's friend were
vitally concerned.

A moment's glance at the posture of domestic
affairs in the cottage, prior to the engagement of

the new governess, is necessary to the due appreciation of the serious consequences that followed Miss Gwilt's appearance on the scene.

On the marriage of the governess who had lived in his service for many years (a woman of an age and an appearance to set even Mrs. Milroy's jealousy at defiance), the major had considered the question of sending his daughter away from home far more seriously than his wife supposed. He was conscious that scenes took place in the house at which no young girl should be present; but he felt an invincible reluctance to apply the one efficient remedy—the keeping his daughter away from home in school time and holiday time alike. The struggle thus raised in his mind once set at rest, by the resolution to advertise for a new governess, Major Milroy's natural tendency to avoid trouble rather than to meet it had declared itself in its customary manner. He had closed his eyes again on his home anxieties as quietly as usual, and had gone back, as he had gone back on hundreds of previous occasions, to the consoling society of his old friend the clock.

It was far otherwise with the major's wife. The chance which her husband had entirely overlooked, that the new governess who was to come might be a younger and a more attractive woman than the old governess who had gone, was the first chance that presented itself as possible to Mrs. Milroy's mind. She had said nothing. Secretly waiting, and secretly nursing her inveterate distrust, she had encouraged her husband and her daughter to leave her on the occasion of the picnic, with the express purpose of making an opportunity for seeing the new governess alone. The governess had shown herself; and the smoldering fire of Mrs. Milroy's jealousy had burst into flame in the moment when she and the handsome stranger first set eyes on each other.

The interview over, Mrs. Milroy's suspicions fastened at once and immovably on her husband's mother.

She was well aware that there was no one else in London on whom the major could depend to make the necessary inquiries; she was well aware that Miss Gwilt had applied for the situation, in the first instance, as a stranger answering an advertisement published in a newspaper. Yet knowing this, she had obstinately closed her eyes, with the blind frenzy of the blindest of all the passions, to the facts straight before her; and, looking back to the last of many quarrels between them which had ended in separating the elder lady and herself, had seized on the conclusion that Miss Gwilt's engagement was due to her mother-in-law's vindictive enjoyment of making mischief in her household. The inference which the very servants themselves, witnesses of the family scandal, had correctly drawn—that the major's mother, in securing the services of a well-recommended governess for her son, had thought it no part of her duty to consider that governess's looks in the purely fanciful interests of the major's wife—was an inference which it was simply impossible to convey into Mrs. Milroy's mind. Miss Gwilt had barely closed the sick-room door when the whispered words hissed out of Mrs. Milroy's lips, "Before another week is over your head, my lady, you go!"

From that moment, through the wakeful night and the weary day, the one object of the bedridden woman's life was to procure the new governess's dismissal from the house. .

The assistance of the nurse, in the capacity of spy, was secured—as Mrs. Milroy had been accustomed to secure other extra services which her attendant was not bound to render her—by a present of a dress from the mistress's wardrobe. One after another articles of wearing apparel which were now useless to Mrs. Milroy had ministered in this way to feed the nurse's greed—the insatiable greed of an ugly woman for fine clothes. Bribed with the smartest dress she had secured yet, the household spy took her secret orders, and applied herself with a vile enjoyment of it to her secret work.

The days passed, the work went on; but nothing had come of it. Mistress and servant had a woman to deal with who was a match for both of them.

Repeated intrusions on the major, when the governess happened to be in the same room with him, failed to discover the slightest impropriety of word, look, or action, on either side. Stealthy watching and listening at the governess's bedroom door detected that she kept a light in her room at late hours of the night, and that she groaned and ground her teeth in her sleep—and detected nothing more. Careful superintendence in the day-time proved that she regularly posted her own letters, instead of giving them to the servant; and that on certain occasions, when the occupation of her hours out of lesson time and walking time was left at her own disposal, she had been suddenly missed from the garden, and then caught coming back alone to it from the park. Once and once only, the nurse had found an opportunity of following her out of the garden, had been detected immediately in the park, and had been asked with the most exasperating politeness if she wished to join Miss Gwilt in a walk. Small circumstances of this kind, which were sufficiently suspicious to the mind of a jealous woman, were discovered in abundance. But circumstances, on which to found a valid ground of complaint that might be laid before the major, proved to be utterly wanting. Day followed day, and Miss Gwilt remained persistently correct in her conduct, and persistently irreproachable in her relations toward her employer and her pupil.

Foiled in this direction, Mrs. Milroy tried next to find an assailable place in the statement which the governess's reference had made on the subject of the governess's character.

Obtaining from the major the minutely careful report which his mother had addressed to him on this topic, Mrs. Milroy read and re-read it, and failed to find the weak point of which she was in search in any part of the letter. All the customary questions on such occasions had been asked, and all had been scrupulously and plainly answered. The one sole opening for an attack which it was possible to discover was an opening which showed itself, after more practical matters had been all disposed of, in the closing sentences of the letter.

"I was so struck," the passage ran, "by the grace and distinction of Miss Gwilt's manners that I took an opportunity, when she was out of the room, of asking how she first came to be governess. 'In the usual way,' I was told. 'A sad family misfortune, in which she behaved nobly. She is a very sensitive person, and shrinks from speaking of it among strangers— a natural reluctance which I have always felt it a matter of delicacy to respect.' Hearing this, of course, I felt the same delicacy on my side. It was no part of my duty to intrude on the poor thing's private sorrows; my only business was to do what I have now done, to make sure that I was engaging a capable and respectable governess to instruct my grandchild."

After careful consideration of these lines, Mrs. Milroy, having a strong desire to find circumstances suspicious, found them suspicious accordingly. She determined to sift the mystery of Miss Gwilt's family misfortunes to the bottom, on the chance of extracting from it something useful to her purpose. There were two ways of doing this. She might begin by questioning the governess herself, or she might begin by questioning the governess's reference. Experience

of Miss Gwilt's quickness of resource in dealing
with awkward questions at their introductory
interview decided her on taking the latter course.
"I'll get the particulars from the reference first,"
thought Mrs. Milroy, "and then question the
creature herself, and see if the two stories
agree."

The letter of inquiry was short, and scrupulously to the point.

Mrs. Milroy began by informing her correspondent that the state of her health necessitated
leaving her daughter entirely under the governess's influence and control. On that account
she was more anxious than most mothers to be
thoroughly informed in every respect about the
person to whom she confided the entire charge
of an only child; and feeling this anxiety, she
might perhaps be excused for putting what might
be thought, after the excellent character Miss
Gwilt had received, a somewhat unnecessary
question. With that preface, Mrs. Milroy came
to the point, and requested to be informed of the
circumstances which had obliged Miss Gwilt to
go out as a governess.

The letter, expressed in these terms, was posted
the same day. On the morning when the answer was due, no answer appeared. The next
morning arrived, and still there was no reply.
When the third morning came, Mrs. Milroy's
impatience had broken loose from all restraint.
She had rung for the nurse in the manner which
has been already recorded, and had ordered the
woman to be in waiting to receive the letters of

the morning with her own hands.  In this position matters now stood; and in these domestic circumstances the new series of events at Thorpe Ambrose took their rise.

Mrs. Milroy had just looked at her watch, and had just put her hand once more to the bell-pull, when the door opened and the nurse entered the room.

"Has the postman come?" asked Mrs. Milroy.

The nurse laid a letter on the bed without answering, and waited, with unconcealed curiosity, to watch the effect which it produced on her mistress.

Mrs. Milroy tore open the envelope the instant it was in her hand.  A printed paper appeared (which she threw aside), surrounding a letter (which she looked at) in her own handwriting! She snatched up the printed paper.  It was the customary Post - office circular, informing her that her letter had been duly presented at the right address, and that the person whom she had written to was not to be found.

"Something wrong?" asked the nurse, detecting a change in her mistress's face.

The question passed unheeded.  Mrs. Milroy's writing-desk was on the table at the bedside. She took from it the letter which the major's mother had written to her son, and turned to the page containing the name and address of Miss Gwilt's reference.  "Mrs. Mandeville, 18 Kingsdown Crescent, Bayswater," she read, eagerly, to herself, and then looked at the ad-

MRS. MILROY TORE OPEN THE ENVELOPE.

—Armadale, Vol. Eight, page 584.

dress on her own returned letter. No error had been committed: the directions were identically the same.

"Something wrong?" reiterated the nurse, advancing a step nearer to the bed

"Thank God—yes!" cried Mrs. Milroy, with a sudden outburst of exultation. She tossed the Post-office circular to the nurse, and beat her bony hands on the bedclothes in an ecstasy of anticipated triumph. "Miss Gwilt's an impostor! Miss Gwilt's an impostor! If I die for it, Rachel, I'll be carried to the window to see the police take her away!"

"It's one thing to say she's an impostor behind her back, and another thing to prove it to her face," remarked the nurse. She put her hand as she spoke into her apron pocket, and, with a significant look at her mistress, silently produced a second letter.

"For me?" asked Mrs. Milroy.

"No!" said the nurse; "for Miss Gwilt."

The two women eyed each other, and understood each other without another word.

"Where is she?" said Mrs. Milroy.

The nurse pointed in the direction of the park. "Out again, for another walk before breakfast—by herself."

Mrs. Milroy beckoned to the nurse to stoop close over her. "Can you open it, Rachel?" she whispered.

Rachel nodded.

"Can you close it again, so that nobody would know?"

"Can you spare the scarf that matches your pearl gray dress?" asked Rachel.

"Take it!" said Mrs. Milroy, impatiently.

The nurse opened the wardrobe in silence, took the scarf in silence, and left the room in silence. In less than five minutes she came back with the envelope of Miss Gwilt's letter open in her hand.

"Thank you, ma'am, for the scarf," said Rachel, putting the open letter composedly on the counterpane of the bed.

Mrs. Milroy looked at the envelope. It had been closed as usual by means of adhesive gum, which had been made to give way by the application of steam. As Mrs. Milroy took out the letter, her hand trembled violently, and the white enamel parted into cracks over the wrinkles on her forehead.

Rachel withdrew to the window to keep watch on the park. "Don't hurry," she said. "No signs of her yet."

Mrs. Milroy still paused, keeping the all-important morsel of paper folded in her hand. She could have taken Miss Gwilt's life, but she hesitated at reading Miss Gwilt's letter.

"Are you troubled with scruples?" asked the nurse, with a sneer. "Consider it a duty you owe to your daughter."

"You wretch!" said Mrs. Milroy. With that expression of opinion, she opened the letter.

It was evidently written in great haste, was undated, and was signed in initials only. Thus it ran:

"Diana Street.

"MY DEAR LYDIA—The cab is waiting at the door, and I have only a moment to tell you that I am obliged to leave London, on business, for three or four days, or a week at longest. My letters will be forwarded if you write. I got yours yesterday, and I agree with you that it is very important to put him off the awkward subject of yourself and your family as long as you safely can. The better you know him, the better you will be able to make up the sort of story that will do. Once told, you will have to stick to it; and, *having* to stick to it, beware of making it complicated, and beware of making it in a hurry. I will write again about this, and give you my own ideas. In the meantime, don't risk meeting him too often in the park.

"Yours, M. O."

"Well?" asked the nurse, returning to the bedside. "Have you done with it?"

"Meeting him in the park!" repeated Mrs. Milroy, with her eyes still fastened on the letter. "*Him!* Rachel, where is the major?"

"In his own room."

"I don't believe it!"

"Have your own way. I want the letter and the envelope."

"Can you close it again so that she won't know?"

"What I can open I can shut. Anything more?"

"Nothing more."

Mrs. Milroy was left alone again, to review her plan of attack by the new light that had now been thrown on Miss Gwilt.

The information that had been gained by opening the governess's letter pointed plainly to the conclusion that an adventuress had stolen her way into the house by means of a false reference. But having been obtained by an act of treachery which it was impossible to acknowledge, it was not information that could be used either for warning the major or for exposing Miss Gwilt. The one available weapon in Mrs. Milroy's hands was the weapon furnished by her own returned letter, and the one question to decide was how to make the best and speediest use of it.

The longer she turned the matter over in her mind, the more hasty and premature seemed the exultation which she had felt at the first sight of the Post-office circular. That a lady acting as reference to a governess should have quitted her residence without leaving any trace behind her, and without even mentioning an address to which her letters could be forwarded, was a circumstance in itself sufficiently suspicious to be mentioned to the major. But Mrs. Milroy, however perverted her estimate of her husband might be in some respects, knew enough of his character to be assured that, if she told him what had happened, he would frankly appeal to the governess herself for an explanation. Miss Gwilt's quickness and cunning would, in that case, produce some plausible answer on the spot, which the major's partiality would be only too ready to accept; and she would at the same time, no doubt, place matters in train, by means of the post, for the due arrival of all needful confirmation on the part of her accomplice in London. To keep strict silence for the present, and to institute (without the governess's knowledge) such inquiries as might be necessary to the discovery of undeniable evidence, was plainly the only safe course to take with such a man as the major, and with such a woman as Miss Gwilt. Helpless herself, to whom could Mrs. Milroy commit the difficult and dangerous task of investigation? The nurse, even if she was to be trusted, could not be spared at a day's notice, and could not be sent away without the risk of exciting remark. Was there any other competent and reliable person to employ, either at Thorpe Ambrose or in London? Mrs. Milroy turned from side to side of the bed, searching every corner of her mind for the needful discovery, and searching in vain. "Oh, if I could only lay my hand on some man I could trust!" she thought, despairingly. "If I only knew where to look for somebody to help me!"

As the idea passed through her mind, the sound of her daughter's voice startled her from the other side of the door.

"May I come in?" asked Neelie.

"What do you want?" returned Mrs. Milroy, impatiently.

"I have brought up your breakfast, mamma."

"My breakfast?" repeated Mrs. Milroy, in surprise. "Why doesn't Rachel bring it up as usual?" She considered a moment, and then called out, sharply, "Come in!"

---

## CHAPTER II.

### THE MAN IS FOUND.

NEELIE entered the room, carrying the tray with the tea, the dry toast, and the pat of butter which composed the invalid's invariable breakfast.

"What does this mean?" asked Mrs. Milroy, speaking and looking as she might have spoken and looked if the wrong servant had come into the room.

Neelie put the tray down on the bedside table. "I thought I should like to bring you up your breakfast, mamma, for once in a way," she replied, "and I asked Rachel to let me."

"Come here," said Mrs. Milroy, "and wish me good-morning."

Neelie obeyed. As she stooped to kiss her mother, Mrs. Milroy caught her by the arm, and turned her roughly to the light. There were plain signs of disturbance and distress in her daughter's face. A deadly thrill of terror ran through Mrs. Milroy on the instant. She suspected that the opening of the letter had been discovered by Miss Gwilt, and that the nurse was keeping out of the way in consequence.

"Let me go, mamma," said Neelie, shrinking under her mother's grasp. "You hurt me."

"Tell me why you have brought up my breakfast this morning," persisted Mrs. Milroy.

"I have told you, mamma."

"You have *not!* You have made an excuse; I see it in your face. Come! what is it?"

Neelie's resolution gave way before her mother's. She looked aside uneasily at the things in the tray. "I have been vexed," she said, with an effort; "and I didn't want to stop in the breakfast-room. I wanted to come up here, and to speak to you."

"Vexed? Who has vexed you? What has happened? Has Miss Gwilt anything to do with it?"

Neelie looked round again at her mother in sudden curiosity and alarm. "Mamma!" she said, "you read my thoughts. I declare you frighten me. It *was* Miss Gwilt."

Before Mrs. Milroy could say a word more on her side, the door opened and the nurse looked in.

"Have you got what you want?" she asked, as composedly as usual. "Miss, there, insisted on taking your tray up this morning. Has she broken anything?"

"Go to the window. I want to speak to Rachel," said Mrs. Milroy.

As soon as her daughter's back was turned, she beckoned eagerly to the nurse. "Anything wrong?" she asked, in a whisper. "Do you think she suspects us?"

The nurse turned away, with her hard, sneering smile. "I told you it should be done," she said, "and it *has* been done. She hasn't the ghost of a suspicion.  I waited in the room; and I saw her take up the letter and open it."

Mrs. Milroy drew a deep breath of relief. "Thank you," she said, loud enough for her daughter to hear.  "I want nothing more."

The nurse withdrew; and Neelie came back from the window.  Mrs. Milroy took her by the hand, and looked at her more attentively and more kindly than usual.  Her daughter inter-ested her that morning; for her daughter had something to say on the subject of Miss Gwilt.

"I used to think that you promised to be pretty, child," she said, cautiously resuming the interrupted conversation in the least direct way.  "But you don't seem to be keeping your promise.  You look out of health and out of spirits.  What is the matter with you?"

If there had been any sympathy between mother and child, Neelie might have owned the truth.  She might have said frankly: "I am looking ill, because my life is miserable to me.  I am fond of Mr. Armadale, and Mr. Armadale was once fond of me.  We had one little disagreement, only one, in which I was to blame.  I wanted to tell him so at the time, and I have wanted to tell him so ever since; and Miss Gwilt stands between us and prevents me.  She has made us like strangers; she has altered him, and taken him away from me.  He doesn't look at me as he did; he doesn't speak to me as he did; he is never alone with me as he used to be; I can't say the words to him that I long to say; and I can't write to him, for it would look as if

I wanted to get him back. It is all over between me and Mr. Armadale; and it is that woman's fault. There is ill-blood between Miss Gwilt and me the whole day long; and say what I may, and do what I may, she always gets the better of me, and always puts me in the wrong. Everything I saw at Thorpe Ambrose pleased me, everything I did at Thorpe Ambrose made me happy, before she came. Nothing pleases me, and nothing makes me happy now!" If Neelie had ever been accustomed to ask her mother's advice and to trust herself to her mother's love, she might have said such words as these. As it was, the tears came into her eyes, and she hung her head in silence.

"Come!" said Mrs. Milroy, beginning to lose patience. "You have something to say to me about Miss Gwilt. What is it?"

Neelie forced back her tears, and made an effort to answer.

"She aggravates me beyond endurance, mamma; I can't bear her; I shall do something—" Neelie stopped, and stamped her foot angrily on the floor. "I shall throw something at her head if we go on much longer like this! I should have thrown something this morning if I hadn't left the room. Oh, do speak to papa about it! Do find out some reason for sending her away! I'll go to school—I'll do anything in the world to get rid of Miss Gwilt!"

To get rid of Miss Gwilt! At those words—at that echo from her daughter's lips of the one dominant desire kept secret in her own heart—

Mrs. Milroy slowly raised herself in bed. What did it mean? Was the help she wanted coming from the very last of all quarters in which she could have thought of looking for it?

"Why do you want to get rid of Miss Gwilt?" she asked. "What have you got to complain of?"

"Nothing!" said Neelie. "That's the aggravation of it. Miss Gwilt won't let me have anything to complain of. She is perfectly detestable; she is driving me mad; and she is the pink of propriety all the time. I dare say it's wrong, but I don't care—I hate her!"

Mrs. Milroy's eyes questioned her daughter's face as they had never questioned it yet. There was something under the surface, evidently—something which it might be of vital importance to her own purpose to discover—which had not risen into view. She went on probing her way deeper and deeper into Neelie's mind, with a warmer and warmer interest in Neelie's secret.

"Pour me out a cup of tea," she said; "and don't excite yourself, my dear. Why do you speak to *me* about this? Why don't you speak to your father?"

"I have tried to speak to papa," said Neelie. "But it's no use; he is too good to know what a wretch she is. She is always on her best behavior with him; she is always contriving to be useful to him. I can't make him understand why I dislike Miss Gwilt; I can't make *you* understand—I only understand it myself." She tried to pour out the tea, and in trying upset the cup. "I'll go downstairs again!" exclaimed Neelie, with a burst of tears "I'm not fit for anything; I can't even pour out a cup of tea!"

Mrs. Milroy seized her hand and stopped her. Trifling as it was, Neelie's reference to the relations between the major and Miss Gwilt had roused her mother's ready jealousy. The restraints which Mrs. Milroy had laid on herself thus far vanished in a moment—vanished even in the presence of a girl of sixteen, and that girl her own child!

"Wait here!" she said, eagerly. "You have come to the right place and the right person. Go on abusing Miss Gwilt. I like to hear you—I hate her, too!"

"You, mamma!" exclaimed Neelie, looking at her mother in astonishment.

For a moment Mrs. Milroy hesitated before she said more. Some last-left instinct of her married life in its earlier and happier time pleaded hard with her to respect the youth and the sex of her child. But jealousy respects nothing; in the heaven above and on the earth beneath, nothing but itself. The slow fire of self-torment, burning night and day in the miserable woman's breast, flashed its deadly light into her eyes, as the next words dropped slowly and venomously from her lips.

"If you had had eyes in your head, you would never have gone to your father," she said. "Your father has reasons of his own for hearing nothing that you can say, or that anybody can say, against Miss Gwilt."

Many girls at Neelie's age would have failed to see the meaning hidden under those words. It was the daughter's misfortune, in this instance, to have had experience enough of the mother to understand her. Neelie started back from the bedside, with her face in a glow. "Mamma!" she said, "you are talking horribly! Papa is the best, and dearest, and kindest—oh, I won't hear it! I won't hear it!"

Mrs. Milroy's fierce temper broke out in an instant—broke out all the more violently from her feeling herself, in spite of herself, to have been in the wrong.

"You impudent little fool!" she retorted, furiously. "Do you think I want *you* to remind me of what I owe to your father? Am I to learn how to speak of your father, and how to think of your father, and how to love and honor your father, from a froward little minx like you! I was finely disappointed, I can tell you, when you were born—I wished for a boy, you impudent hussy! If you ever find a man who is fool enough to marry you, he will be a lucky man if you only love him half as well, a quarter as well, a hundred-thousandth part as well, as I loved your father. Ah, you can cry when it's too late; you can come creeping back to beg your mother's pardon after you have insulted her. You little dowdy, half-grown creature! I was handsomer than ever you will be when I married your father. I would have gone through fire and water to serve your father! If he had asked me to cut off one of my arms, I would have done it

—I would have done it to please him!" She turned suddenly with her face to the wall, forgetting her daughter, forgetting her husband, forgetting everything but the torturing remembrance of her lost beauty. "My arms!" she repeated to herself, faintly. "What arms I had when I was young!" She snatched up the sleeve of her dressing-gown furtively, with a shudder. "Oh, look at it now! look at it now!"

Neelie fell on her knees at the bedside and hid her face. In sheer despair of finding comfort and help anywhere else, she had cast herself impulsively on her mother's mercy; and this was how it had ended! "Oh, mamma," she pleaded, "you know I didn't mean to offend you! I couldn't help it when you spoke so of my father. Oh, do, do forgive me!"

Mrs. Milroy turned again on her pillow, and looked at her daughter vacantly. "Forgive you?" she repeated, with her mind still in the past, groping its way back darkly to the present.

"I beg your pardon, mamma—I beg your pardon on my knees. I am so unhappy; I do so want a little kindness! Won't you forgive me?"

"Wait a little," rejoined Mrs. Milroy. "Ah," she said, after an interval, "now I know! Forgive you? Yes; I'll forgive you on one condition." She lifted Neelie's head, and looked her searchingly in the face. "Tell me why you hate Miss Gwilt! You've a reason of your own for hating her, and you haven't confessed it yet."

Neelie's head dropped again. The burning

color that she was hiding by hiding her face showed itself on her neck. Her mother saw it, and gave her time.

"Tell me," reiterated Mrs. Milroy, more gently, "why do you hate her?"

The answer came reluctantly, a word at a time, in fragments.

"Because she is trying—"

"Trying what?"

"Trying to make somebody who is much—"

"Much what?"

"Much too young for her—"

"Marry her?"

"Yes, mamma."

Breathlessly interested, Mrs. Milroy leaned forward, and twined her hand caressingly in her daughter's hair.

"Who is it, Neelie?" she asked, in a whisper.

"You will never say I told you, mamma?"

"Never! Who is it?"

"Mr. Armadale."

Mrs. Milroy leaned back on her pillow in dead silence. The plain betrayal of her daughter's first love, by her daughter's own lips, which would have absorbed the whole attention of other mothers, failed to occupy her for a moment. Her jealousy, distorting all things to fit its own conclusions, was busied in distorting what she had just heard. "A blind," she thought, "which has deceived my girl. It doesn't deceive *me*. Is Miss Gwilt likely to succeed?" she asked, aloud. "Does Mr. Armadale show any sort of interest in her?"

Neelie looked up at her mother for the first time. The hardest part of the confession was over now. She had revealed the truth about Miss Gwilt, and she had openly mentioned Allan's name.

"He shows the most unaccountable interest," she said. "It's impossible to understand it. It's downright infatuation. I haven't patience to talk about it!"

"How do *you* come to be in Mr. Armadale's secrets?" inquired Mrs. Milroy. "Has he informed *you*, of all the people in the world, of his interest in Miss Gwilt?"

"Me!" exclaimed Neelie, indignantly. "It's quite bad enough that he should have told papa."

At the re-appearance of the major in the narrative, Mrs. Milroy's interest in the conversation rose to its climax. She raised herself again from the pillow. "Get a chair," she said. "Sit down, child, and tell me all about it. Every word, mind—every word!"

"I can only tell you, mamma, what papa told me."

"When?"

"Saturday. I went in with papa's lunch to the workshop, and he said, 'I have just had a visit from Mr. Armadale; and I want to give you a caution while I think of it.' I didn't say anything, mamma; I only waited. Papa went on, and told me that Mr. Armadale had been speaking to him on the subject of Miss Gwilt, and that he had been asking a question about her which nobody in his position had a right to ask.

Papa said he had been obliged, good-humoredly, to warn Mr. Armadale to be a little more delicate, and a little more careful next time. I didn't feel much interested, mamma; it didn't matter to *me* what Mr. Armadale said or did. Why should I care about it?"

"Never mind yourself," interposed Mrs. Milroy, sharply. "Go on with what your father said. What was he doing when he was talking about Miss Gwilt? How did he look?"

"Much as usual, mamma. He was walking up and down the workshop; and I took his arm and walked up and down with him."

"I don't care what *you* were doing," said Mrs. Milroy, more and more irritably. "Did your father tell you what Mr. Armadale's question was, or did he not?"

"Yes, mamma. He said Mr. Armadale began by mentioning that he was very much interested in Miss Gwilt, and he then went on to ask whether papa could tell him anything about her family misfortunes—"

"What!" cried Mrs. Milroy. The word burst from her almost in a scream, and the white enamel on her face cracked in all directions. "Mr. Armadale said *that?*" she went on, leaning out further and further over the side of the bed.

Neelie started up, and tried to put her mother back on the pillow.

"Mamma!" she exclaimed, "are you in pain? Are you ill? You frighten me!"

"Nothing, nothing, nothing," said Mrs. Milroy. She was too violently agitated to make any other than the commonest excuse. "My nerves are bad this morning; don't notice it. I'll try the other side of the pillow. Go on! go on! I'm listening, though I'm not looking at you." She turned her face to the wall, and clinched her trembling hands convulsively beneath the bedclothes. "I've got her!" she whispered to herself, under her breath. "I've got her at last!"

"I'm afraid I've been talking too much," said Neelie. "I'm afraid I've been stopping here too long. Shall I go downstairs, mamma, and come back later in the day?"

"Go on," repeated Mrs. Milroy, mechanically. "What did your father say next? Anything more about Mr. Armadale?"

"Nothing more, except how papa answered him," replied Neelie. "Papa repeated his own words when he told me about it. He said, 'In the absence of any confidence volunteered by the lady herself, Mr. Armadale, all I know or wish to know—and you must excuse me for saying, all any one else need know or wish to know—is that Miss Gwilt gave me a perfectly satisfactory reference before she entered my house.' Severe, mamma, wasn't it? I don't pity him in the least; he richly deserved it. The next thing was papa's caution to *me*. He told me to check Mr. Armadale's curiosity if he applied to me next. As if he was likely to apply to me! And as if I should listen to him if he did! That's all, mamma. You won't suppose, will you, that I

have told you this because I want to hinder Mr.
Armadale from marrying Miss Gwilt?   Let him
marry her if he pleases; I don't care!" said
Neelie, in a voice that faltered a little, and with
a face which was hardly composed enough to be
in perfect harmony with a declaration of indifference.   "All I want is to be relieved from the
misery of having Miss Gwilt for my governess.
I'd rather go to school.   I should like to go to
school.   My mind's quite changed about all that,
only I haven't the heart to tell papa.   I don't
know what's come to me, I don't seem to have
heart enough for anything now; and when papa
takes me on his knee in the evening, and says,
'Let's have a talk, Neelie,' he makes me cry.
Would you mind breaking it to him, mamma,
that I've changed my mind, and I want to go
to school?"   The tears rose thickly in her eyes,
and she failed to see that her mother never even
turned on the pillow to look round at her.

"Yes, yes," said Mrs. Milroy, vacantly.
"You're a good girl; you shall go to school."

The cruel brevity of the reply, and the tone
in which it was spoken, told Neelie plainly
that her mother's attention had been wandering far away from her, and that it was useless and needless to prolong the interview.
She turned aside quietly, without a word of remonstrance.   It was nothing new in her experience to find herself shut out from her mother's
sympathies.   She looked at her eyes in the glass,
and, pouring out some cold water, bathed her
face.   "Miss Gwilt shan't see I've been crying!"

thought Neelie, as she went back to the bedside
to take her leave. "I've tired you out," mamma," she said, gently. "Let me go now; and
let me come back a little later when you have
had some rest."

"Yes," repeated her mother, as mechanically
as ever; "a little later when I have had some
rest."

Neelie left the room. The minute after the
door had closed on her, Mrs. Milroy rang the
bell for her nurse. In the face of the narrative
she had just heard. in the face of every reasonable estimate of probabilities, she held to her
own jealous conclusions as firmly as ever. "Mr.
Armadale may believe her, and my daughter
may believe her," thought the furious woman.
"But I know the major; and she can't deceive
*me!*"

The nurse came in. "Prop me up," said Mrs.
Milroy. "And give me my desk. I want to write."

"You're excited," replied the nurse. "You're
not fit to write."

"Give me the desk," reiterated Mrs. Milroy.

"Anything more?" asked Rachel, repeating
her invariable formula as she placed the desk on
the bed.

"Yes. Come back in half an hour. I shall
want you to take a letter to the great house."

The nurse's sardonic composure deserted her
for once. "Mercy on us!" she exclaimed, with
an accent of genuine surprise. "What next?
You don't mean to say you're going to write—?"

"I am going to write to Mr. Armadale," inter-

posed Mrs. Milroy; "and you are going to take
the letter to him, and wait for an answer; and,
mind this, not a living soul but our two selves
must know of it in the house."

"Why are you writing to Mr. Armadale?"
asked Rachel. "And why is nobody to know
of it but our two selves?"

"Wait," rejoined Mrs. Milroy, "and you will
see."

The nurse's curiosity, being a woman's curiosity, declined to wait.

"I'll help you with my eyes open," she said;
"but I won't help you blindfold."

"Oh, if I only had the use of my limbs!"
groaned Mrs. Milroy. "You wretch, if I could
only do without you!"

"You have the use of your head," retorted
the impenetrable nurse. "And you ought to
know better than to trust me by halves, at this
time of day."

It was brutally put; but it was true—doubly
true, after the opening of Miss Gwilt's letter.
Mrs. Milroy gave way.

"What do you want to know?" she asked.
"Tell me, and leave me."

"I want to know what you are writing to Mr.
Armadale about?"

"About Miss Gwilt."

"What has Mr. Armadale to do with you and
Miss Gwilt?"

Mrs. Milroy held up the letter that had been
returned to her by the authorities at the Post-
office.

"Stoop," she said. "Miss Gwilt may be listening at the door. I'll whisper."

The nurse stooped, with her eye on the door.

"You know that the postman went with this letter to Kingsdown Crescent?" said Mrs. Milroy. "And you know that he found Mrs. Mandeville gone away, nobody could tell where?"

"Well," whispered Rachel, "what next?"

"This, next. When Mr. Armadale gets the letter that I am going to write to him, he will follow the same road as the postman; and we'll see what happens when he knocks at Mrs. Mandeville's door."

"How do you get him to the door?"

"I tell him to go to Miss Gwilt's reference."

"Is he sweet on Miss Gwilt?"

"Yes."

"Ah!" said the nurse. "I see!"

## CHAPTER III.

### THE BRINK OF DISCOVERY.

THE morning of the interview between Mrs. Milroy and her daughter at the cottage was a morning of serious reflection for the squire at the great house.

Even Allan's easy-tempered nature had not been proof against the disturbing influences exercised on it by the events of the last three days. Midwinter's abrupt departure had vexed him; and Major Milroy's reception of his in-

quiries relating to Miss Gwilt weighed unpleas-
antly on his mind. Since his visit to the cottage, he had felt impatient and ill at ease, for
the first time in his life, with everybody who
came near him. Impatient with Pedgift Junior,
who had called on the previous evening to announce his departure for London, on business,
the next day, and to place his services at the disposal of his client; ill at ease with Miss Gwilt,
at a secret meeting with her in the park that
morning; and ill at ease in his own company,
as he now sat moodily smoking in the solitude of
his room. "I can't live this sort of life much
longer," thought Allan. "If nobody will help
me to put the awkward question to Miss Gwilt,
I must stumble on some way of putting it for
myself."

What way? The answer to that question was
as hard to find as ever. Allan tried to stimulate
his sluggish invention by walking up and down
the room, and was disturbed by the appearance
of the footman at the first turn.

"Now then! what is it?" he asked, impatiently.

"A letter, sir; and the person waits for an
answer."

Allan looked at the address. It was in a
strange handwriting. He opened the letter,
and a little note inclosed in it dropped to the
ground. The note was directed, still in the
strange handwriting, to "Mrs. Mandeville, 18
Kingsdown Crescent, Bayswater. Favored by
Mr. Armadale." More and more surprised,

Allan turned for information to the signature at the end of the letter. It was "Anne Milroy."

"Anne Milroy?" he repeated. "It must be the major's wife. What can she possibly want with me?" By way of discovering what she wanted, Allan did at last what he might more wisely have done at first. He sat down to read the letter.

["Private."]                    "The Cottage, Monday.

"DEAR SIR—The name at the end of these lines will, I fear, recall to you a very rude return made on my part, some time since, for an act of neighborly kindness on yours. I can only say in excuse that I am a great sufferer, and that, if I was ill-tempered enough, in a moment of irritation under severe pain, to send back your present of fruit, I have regretted doing so ever since. Attribute this letter, if you please, to my desire to make some atonement, and to my wish to be of service to our good friend and landlord, if I possibly can.

"I have been informed of the question which you addressed to my husband, the day before yesterday, on the subject of Miss Gwilt. From all I have heard of you, I am quite sure that your anxiety to know more of this charming person than you know now is an anxiety proceeding from the most honorable motives. Believing this, I feel a woman's interest—incurable invalid as I am—in assisting you. If you are desirous of becoming acquainted with Miss Gwilt's family circumstances without directly appealing to Miss Gwilt herself, it rests with you to make the discovery; and I will tell you how.

"It so happens that, some few days since, I wrote privately to Miss Gwilt's reference on this very subject. I had long observed that my governess was singularly reluctant to speak of her family and her friends; and, without attributing her silence to other than perfectly proper motives, I felt it my duty to my daughter to make some inquiry on the subject. The answer that I have received is satisfactory as far as it goes. My correspondent informs me that Miss Gwilt's story is a very sad one, and that her own conduct throughout has been praiseworthy in the extreme. The circumstances (of a domestic nature, as I gather) are all plainly stated in a collection of letters now in the possession of Miss Gwilt's reference. This lady is perfectly willing to let me see the letters; but not possessing copies of them, and being personally responsible for their security, she is reluctant, if it can be avoided, to trust them to the post; and she begs me to wait until she or I can find some reliable person who can be employed to transmit the packet from her hands to mine.

"Under these circumstances, it has struck me that you might possibly, with your interest in the matter, be not unwilling to take charge of the papers. If I am wrong in this idea, and if you are not disposed, after what I have told you, to go to the trouble and expense of a journey to London, you have only to burn my letter and inclosure, and to think no more about it. If you decide on becoming my envoy, I gladly provide you with the necessary introduction to Mrs. Mandeville. You have only, on presenting it, to receive the letters in a sealed packet, to send them here on your return to Thorpe Ambrose, and to wait an early communication from me acquainting you with the result.

"In conclusion, I have only to add that I see no impropriety in your taking (if you feel so inclined) the course that I propose to you. Miss Gwilt's manner of receiving such allusions as I have made to her family circumstances has rendered it unpleasant for me (and would render it quite impossible for you) to seek information in the first instance from herself. I am certainly justified in applying to her reference; and you are certainly not to blame for being the medium of safely transmitting a sealed communication with one lady to another. If I find in that communication family secrets which cannot honorably be mentioned to any third person, I shall, of course, be obliged to keep you waiting until I have first appealed to Miss Gwilt. If I find nothing recorded but what is to her honor, and what is sure to raise her still higher in your estimation, I am undeniably doing her a service by taking you into my confidence. This is how I look at the matter; but pray don't allow me to influence *you*.

"In any case, I have one condition to make, which I am sure you will understand to be indispensable. The most innocent actions are liable, in this wicked world, to the worst possible interpretation. I must, therefore, request that you will consider this communication as *strictly private*. I write to you in a confidence which is on no account (until circumstances may, in my opinion, justify the revelation of it) to extend beyond our two selves.

"Believe me, dear sir, truly yours,
                "ANNE MILROY."

In this tempting form the unscrupulous ingenuity of the major's wife had set the trap. Without a moment's hesitation, Allan followed his impulses, as usual, and walked straight into it, writing his answer and pursuing his own reflections simultaneously in a highly characteristic state of mental confusion.

"By Jupiter, this *is* kind of Mrs. Milroy!" ("My dear madam.") "Just the thing I wanted, at the time when I needed it most!" ("I don't know how to express my sense of your kindness, except by saying that I will go to London and fetch the letters with the greatest pleasure.") "She shall have a basket of fruit regularly every day, all through the season." ("I will go at once, dear madam, and be back to-morrow.") "Ah, nothing like the women for helping one when one is in love! This is just what my poor mother would have done in Mrs. Milroy's place." ("On my word of honor as a gentleman, I will take the utmost care of the letters; and keep the thing strictly private, as you request.") "I would have given five hundred pounds to anybody who would have put me up to the right way to speak to Miss Gwilt; and here is this blessed woman does it for nothing." ("Believe me, my dear madam, gratefully yours, Allan Armadale.")

Having sent his reply out to Mrs. Milroy's messenger, Allan paused in a momentary perplexity. He had an appointment with Miss Gwilt in the park for the next morning. It was absolutely necessary to let her know that he would be unable to keep it; she had forbidden him to write, and he had no chance that day of seeing her alone. In this difficulty, he determined to let the necessary intimation reach her through the medium of a message to the major, announcing his departure for London on business, and asking if he could be of service to any member of the family. Having thus removed the only obstacle to his freedom of action, Allan consulted the time-table, and found, to his disappointment, that there was a good hour to spare before it would be necessary to drive to the railway station. In his existing frame of mind he would infinitely have preferred starting for London in a violent hurry.

When the time came at last, Allan, on passing the steward's office, drummed at the door, and called through it to Mr. Bashwood, "I'm going to town; back to-morrow." There was no answer from within; and the servant, interposing, informed his master that Mr. Bashwood, having no business to attend to that day, had locked up the office, and had left some hours since.

On reaching the station, the first person whom

Allan encountered was Pedgift Junior, going to
London on the legal business which he had mentioned on the previous evening at the great
house. The necessary explanations exchanged,
it was decided that the two should travel in the
same carriage. Allan was glad to have a companion; and Pedgift, enchanted as usual to make
himself useful to his client, bustled away to get
the tickets and see to the luggage. Sauntering
to and fro on the platform, until his faithful follower returned, Allan came suddenly upon no
less a person than Mr. Bashwood himself, standing back in a corner with the guard of the train,
and putting a letter (accompanied, to all appearance, by a fee) privately into the man's hand.

"Halloo!" cried Allan, in his hearty way.
"Something important there, Mr. Bashwood, eh?"

If Mr. Bashwood had been caught in the act
of committing murder, he could hardly have
shown greater alarm than he now testified at Allan's sudden discovery of him. Snatching off his
dingy old hat, he bowed bare-headed, in a palsy
of nervous trembling from head to foot. "No,
sir—no, sir; only a little letter, a little letter, a
little letter," said the deputy-steward, taking
refuge in reiteration, and bowing himself swiftly
backward out of his employer's sight.

Allan turned carelessly on his heel. "I wish
I could take to that fellow," he thought, "but I
can't; he's such a sneak! What the deuce was
there to tremble about? Does he think I want
to pry into his secrets?"

Mr. Bashwood's secret on this occasion con-

cerned Allan more nearly than Allan supposed.
The letter which he had just placed in charge of
the guard was nothing less than a word of warning addressed to Mrs. Oldershaw, and written by
Miss Gwilt.

"If you can hurry your business" (wrote the
major's governess) "do so, and come back to
London immediately. Things are going wrong
here, and . Miss Milroy is at the bottom of the
mischief. This morning she insisted on taking
up her mother's breakfast, always on other occasions taken up by the nurse. They had a long
confabulation in private; and half an hour later
I saw the nurse slip out with a letter, and take
the path that leads to the great house. The sending of the letter has been followed by young Armadale's sudden departure for London—in the
face of an appointment which he had with me
for to-morrow morning. This looks serious.
The girl is evidently bold enough to make a
fight of it for the position of Mrs. Armadale of
Thorpe Ambrose, and she has found out some
way of getting her mother to help her. Don't
suppose I am in the least nervous or discouraged,
and don't do anything till you hear from me
again. Only get back to London, for I may
have serious need of your assistance in the
course of the next day or two.

"I send this letter to town (to save a post) by
the midday train, in charge of the guard. As
you insist on knowing every step I take at
Thorpe Ambrose, I may as well tell you that my
messenger (for I can't go to the station myself)

is that curious old creature whom I mentioned
to you in my first letter. Ever since that time
he has been perpetually hanging about here for
a look at me. I am not sure whether I frighten
him or fascinate him; perhaps I do both together. All you need care to know is that I can
trust him with my trifling errands, and possibly,
as time goes on, with something more.    L. G."

Meanwhile the train had started from the
Thorpe Ambrose station, and the squire and his
traveling companion were on their way to London.

Some men, finding themselves in Allan's company under present circumstances, might have
felt curious to know the nature of his business
in the metropolis. Young Pedgift's unerring
instinct as a man of the world penetrated the
secret without the slightest difficulty. "The old
story," thought this wary old head, wagging
privately on its lusty young shoulders. "There's
a woman in the case, as usual. Any other business would have been turned over to *me*." Perfectly satisfied with this conclusion, Mr. Pedgift
the younger proceeded, with an eye to his professional interest, to make himself agreeable to
his client in the capacity of volunteer courier.
He seized on the whole administrative business
of the journey to London, as he had seized on
the whole administrative business of the picnic
at the Broads. On reaching the terminus, Allan
was ready to go to any hotel that might be recommended. His invaluable solicitor straight-
way drove him to a hotel at which the Pedgift

family had been accustomed to put up for three
generations.

"You don't object to vegetables, sir?" said
the cheerful Pedgift, as the cab stopped at a
hotel in Covent Garden Market. "Very good;
you may leave the rest to my grandfather, my
father, and me. I don't know which of the
three is most beloved and respected in this house.
How d'ye do, William? (Our head-waiter, Mr.
Armadale.) Is your wife's rheumatism better,
and does the little boy get on nicely at school?
Your master's out, is he? Never mind, you'll
do. This, William, is Mr. Armadale of Thorpe
Ambrose. I have prevailed on Mr. Armadale
to try our house. Have you got the bedroom I
wrote for? Very good. Let Mr. Armadale
have it instead of me (my grandfather's favorite
bedroom, sir; No. 5, on the second floor); pray
take it; I can sleep anywhere. Will you have
the mattress on the top of the feather-bed? You
hear, William? Tell Matilda, the mattress on
the top of the feather-bed. How is Matilda?
Has she got the toothache, as usual? The
head-chambermaid, Mr. Armadale, and a most
extraordinary woman; she will *not* part with a
hollow tooth in her lower jaw. My grandfather
says, 'Have it out;' my father says, 'Have it
out;' I say, 'Have it out;' and Matilda turns a
deaf ear to all three of us. Yes, William, yes;
if Mr. Armadale approves, this sitting-room will
do. About dinner, sir? Shall we say, in that
case, half-past seven? William, half-past seven.
Not the least need to order anything, Mr. Arma-

dale. The head-waiter has only to give my
compliments to the cook, and the best dinner in
London will be sent up, punctual to the minute,
as a necessary consequence. Say, Mr. Pedgift
Junior, if you please, William; otherwise, sir,
we might get my grandfather's dinner or my
father's dinner, and they *might* turn out a little
too heavy and old-fashioned in their way of feeding for you and me. As to the wine, William.
At dinner, *my* Champagne, and the sherry that
my father thinks nasty. After dinner, the claret
with the blue seal—the wine my innocent grandfather said wasn't worth sixpence a bottle. Ha!
ha! poor old boy! You will send up the evening papers and the play-bills, just as usual, and
—that will do, I think, William, for the present.
An invaluable servant, Mr. Armadale; they're
all invaluable servants in this house. We may
not be fashionable here, sir, but by the Lord
Harry we are snug! A cab? you would like a
cab? Don't stir! I've rung the bell twice—
that means, Cab wanted in a hurry. Might I
ask, Mr. Armadale, which way your business
takes you? Toward Bayswater? Would you
mind dropping me in the park? It's a habit of
mine when I'm in London to air myself among
the aristocracy. Yours truly, sir, has an eye for
a fine woman and a fine horse; and when he's
in Hyde Park he's quite in his native element.''
Thus the all-accomplished Pedgift ran on; and
by these little arts did he recommend himself to
the good opinion of his client.

When the dinner hour united the traveling

companions again in their sitting-room at the hotel, a far less acute observer than young Pedgift must have noticed the marked change that appeared in Allan's manner. He looked vexed and puzzled, and sat drumming with his fingers on the dining-table without uttering a word.

"I'm afraid something has happened to annoy you, sir, since we parted company in the Park?" said Pedgift Junior. "Excuse the question; I only ask it in case I can be of any use."

"Something that I never expected has happened," returned Allan; "I don't know what to make of it. I should like to have your opinion," he added, after a little hesitation; "that is to say, if you will excuse my not entering into any particulars?"

"Certainly!" assented young Pedgift. "Sketch it in outline, sir. The merest hint will do; I wasn't born yesterday." ("Oh, these women!" thought the youthful philosopher, in parenthesis.)

"Well," began Allan, "you know what I said when we got to this hotel; I said I had a place to go to in Bayswater" (Pedgift mentally checked off the first point: Case in the suburbs, Bayswater); "and a person—that is to say—no—as I said before, a person to inquire after." (Pedgift checked off the next point: Person in the case. She-person, or he-person? She-person, unquestionably!) "Well, I went to the house, and when I asked for her—I mean the person—she—that is to say, the person—oh, confound it!" cried Allan, "I shall drive myself mad, and you, too, if I try to tell my story in this round-about way. Here it is in two words. I went to No. 18 Kingsdown Crescent, to see a lady named Mandeville; and, when I asked for her, the servant said Mrs. Mandeville had gone away, without telling anybody where, and without even leaving an address at which letters could be sent to her. There! it's out at last. And what do you think of it now?"

"Tell me first, sir," said the wary Pedgift, "what inquiries you made when you found this lady had vanished?"

"Inquiries!" repeated Allan. "I was utterly staggered; I didn't say anything. What inquiries ought I to have made?"

Pedgift Junior cleared his throat, and crossed his legs in a strictly professional manner.

"I have no wish, Mr. Armadale," he began, "to inquire into your business with Mrs. Mandeville—"

"No," interposed Allan, bluntly; "I hope you won't inquire into that. My business with Mrs. Mandeville must remain a secret."

"But," pursued Pedgift, laying down the law with the forefinger of one hand on the outstretched palm of the other, "I may, perhaps, be allowed to ask generally whether your business with Mrs. Mandeville is of a nature to interest you in tracing her from Kingsdown Crescent to her present residence?"

"Certainly!" said Allan. "I have a very particular reason for wishing to see her."

"In that case, sir," returned Pedgift Junior,

"there were two obvious questions which you ought to have asked, to begin with—namely, on what date Mrs. Mandeville left, and how she left. Having discovered this, you should have ascertained next under what domestic circumstances she went away—whether there was a misunderstanding with anybody; say a difficulty about money matters. Also, whether she went away alone, or with somebody else. Also, whether the house was her own, or whether she only lodged in it. Also, in the latter event—"

"Stop! stop! you're making my head swim," cried Allan. "I don't understand all these ins and outs. I'm not used to this sort of thing."

"I've been used to it myself from my childhood upward, sir," remarked Pedgift. "And if I can be of any assistance, say the word."

"You're very kind," returned Allan. "If you could only help me to find Mrs. Mandeville; and if you wouldn't mind leaving the thing afterward entirely in my hands—?"

"I'll leave it in your hands, sir, with all the pleasure in life," said Pedgift Junior. ("And I'll lay five to one," he added, mentally, "when the time comes, you'll leave it in mine!") "We'll go to Bayswater together, Mr. Armadale, to-morrow morning. In the meantime, here's the soup. The case now before the court is, Pleasure *versus* Business. I don't know what you say, sir; I say, without a moment's hesitation, Verdict for the plaintiff. Let us gather our rosebuds while we may. Excuse my high spirits, Mr. Armadale. Though buried in the country,

I was made for a London life; the very air
of the metropolis intoxicates me." With that
avowal the irresistible Pedgift placed a chair for
his patron, and issued his orders cheerfully to
his viceroy, the head-waiter. "Iced punch,
William, after the soup. I answer for the
punch, Mr. Armadale; it's made after a recipe
of my great-uncle's. He kept a tavern, and
founded the fortunes of the family. I don't
mind telling you the Pedgifts have had a publican among them; there's no false pride about
me. 'Worth makes the man (as Pope says) and
want of it the fellow; the rest is all but leather
and prunella.' I cultivate poetry as well as
music, sir, in my leisure hours; in fact, I'm
more or less on familiar terms with the whole of
the nine Muses. Aha! here's the punch! The
memory of my great-uncle, the publican, Mr.
Armadale—drunk in solemn silence!"

Allan tried hard to emulate his companion's
gayety and good humor, but with very indifferent success. His visit to Kingsdown Crescent
recurred ominously again and again to his
memory all through the dinner, and all through
the public amusements to which he and his legal
adviser repaired at a later hour of the evening.
When Pedgift Junior put out his candle that
night, he shook his wary head, and regretfully
apostrophized "the women" for the second time.

By ten o'clock the next morning the indefatigable Pedgift was on the scene of action. To
Allan's great relief, he proposed making the
necessary inquiries at Kingsdown Crescent in

his own person, while his patron waited near at
hand, in the cab which had brought them from
the hotel. After a delay of little more than five
minutes, he re-appeared, in full possession of all
attainable particulars. His first proceeding was
to request Allan to step out of the cab, and to
pay the driver. Next, he politely offered his
arm, and led the way round the corner of the
crescent, across a square, and into a by-street,
which was rendered exceptionally lively by the
presence of the local cab-stand. Here he stopped,
and asked jocosely whether Mr. Armadale saw
his way now, or whether it would be necessary
to test his patience by making an explanation.

"See my way?" repeated Allan, in bewilderment. "I see nothing but a cab-stand."

Pedgift Junior smiled compassionately, and
entered on his explanation. It was a lodging-
house at Kingsdown Crescent, he begged to state
to begin with. He had insisted on seeing the
landlady. A very nice person, with all the remains of having been a fine girl about fifty years
ago; quite in Pedgift's style—if he had only been
alive at the beginning of the present century—
quite in Pedgift's style. But perhaps Mr. Armadale would prefer hearing about Mrs. Mandeville?
Unfortunately, there was nothing to tell. There
had been no quarreling, and not a farthing left
unpaid: the lodger had gone, and there wasn't
an explanatory circumstance to lay hold of anywhere. It was either Mrs. Mandeville's way to
vanish, or there was something under the rose,
quite undiscoverable so far. Pedgift had got

the date on which she left, and the time of day
at which she left, and the means by which she
left.  The means might help to trace her.  She
had gone away in a cab which the servant had
fetched from the nearest stand.  The stand was
now before their eyes; and the waterman was
the first person to apply to—going to the waterman for information being clearly (if Mr. Armadale would excuse the joke) going to the fountain - head.  Treating the subject in this airy
manner, and telling Allan that he would be back
in a moment, Pedgift Junior sauntered down the
street, and beckoned the waterman confidentially
into the nearest public-house.

In a little while the two re-appeared, the waterman taking Pedgift in succession to the first,
third, fourth, and sixth of the cabmen whose
vehicles were on the stand.  The longest conference was held with the sixth man; and it ended
in the sudden approach of the sixth cab to the
part of the street where Allan was waiting.

"Get in, sir," said Pedgift, opening the door;
"I've found the man.  He remembers the lady;
and, though he has forgotten the name of the
street, he believes he can find the place he drove
her to when he once gets back into the neighborhood.  I am charmed to inform you, Mr. Armadale, that we are in luck's way so far.  I asked
the waterman to show me the regular men on the
stand; and it turns out that one of the regular
men drove Mrs. Mandeville.  The waterman
vouches for him; he's quite an anomaly—a respectable cabman; drives his own horse, and

has never been in any trouble. These are the sort of men, sir, who sustain one's belief in human nature. I've had a look at our friend, and I agree with the waterman; I think we can depend on him."

The investigation required some exercise of patience at the outset. It was not till the cab had traversed the distance between Bayswater and Pimlico that the driver began to slacken his pace and look about him. After once or twice retracing its course, the vehicle entered a quiet by-street, ending in a dead wall, with a door in it; and stopped at the last house on the left-hand side, the house next to the wall.

"Here it is, gentlemen," said the man, opening the cab door.

Allan and Allan's adviser both got out, and both looked at the house, with the same feeling of instinctive distrust.

Buildings have their physiognomy—especially buildings in great cities—and the face of this house was essentially furtive in its expression. The front windows were all shut, and the front blinds were all drawn down. It looked no larger than the other houses in the street, seen in front; but it ran back deceitfully, and gained its greater accommodation by means of its greater depth. It affected to be a shop on the ground-floor; but it exhibited absolutely nothing in the space that intervened between the window and an inner row of red curtains, which hid the interior entirely from view. At one side was the shop door, having more red curtains behind the glazed part of it, and bearing a brass plate on the wooden part of it, inscribed with the name of "Oldershaw." On the other side was the private door, with a bell marked Professional; and another brass plate, indicating a medical occupant on this side of the house, for the name on it was, "Doctor Downward." If ever brick and mortar spoke yet, the brick and mortar here said plainly, "We have got our secrets inside, and we mean to keep them."

"This can't be the place," said Allan; "there must be some mistake."

"You know best, sir," remarked Pedgift Junior, with his sardonic gravity. "You know Mrs. Mandeville's habits."

"I!" exclaimed Allan. "You may be surprised to hear it; but Mrs. Mandeville is a total stranger to me."

"I'm not in the least surprised to hear it, sir; the landlady at Kingsdown Crescent informed me that Mrs. Mandeville was an old woman. Suppose we inquire?" added the impenetrable Pedgift, looking at the red curtains in the shop window with a strong suspicion that Mrs. Mandeville's granddaughter might possibly be behind them.

They tried the shop door first. It was locked. They rang. A lean and yellow young woman, with a tattered French novel in her hand, opened it.

"Good - morning, miss," said Pedgift. "Is Mrs. Mandeville at home?"

The yellow young woman stared at him in

astonishment. "No person of that name is known here," she answered, sharply, in a foreign accent.

"Perhaps they know her at the private door?" suggested Pedgift Junior.

"Perhaps they do," said the yellow young woman, and shut the door in his face.

"Rather a quick-tempered young person that, sir," said Pedgift. "I congratulate Mrs. Mandeville on not being acquainted with her." He led the way, as he spoke, to Doctor Downward's side of the premises, and rang the bell.

The door was opened this time by a man in a shabby livery. He, too, stared when Mrs. Mandeville's name was mentioned; and he, too, knew of no such person in the house.

"Very odd," said Pedgift, appealing to Allan.

"What is odd?" asked a softly stepping, softly speaking gentleman in black, suddenly appearing on the threshold of the parlor door.

Pedgift Junior politely explained the circumstances, and begged to know whether he had the pleasure of speaking to Doctor Downward.

The doctor bowed. If the expression may be pardoned, he was one of those carefully constructed physicians in whom the public—especially the female public—implicitly trust. He had the necessary bald head, the necessary double eyeglass, the necessary black clothes, and the necessary blandness of manner, all complete. His voice was soothing, his ways were deliberate, his smile was confidential. What particular branch of his profession Doc-

tor Downward followed was not indicated on
his door-plate; but he had utterly mistaken his
vocation if he was not a ladies' medical man.

"Are you quite sure there is no mistake about
the name?" asked the doctor, with a strong underlying anxiety in his manner. "I have known
very serious inconvenience to arise sometimes
from mistakes about names. No? There is
really no mistake? In that case, gentlemen, I
can only repeat what my servant has already told
you. Don't apologize, pray. Good-morning."
The doctor withdrew as noiselessly as he had
appeared; the man in the shabby livery silently
opened the door; and Allan and his companion
found themselves in the street again.

"Mr. Armadale," said Pedgift, "I don't know
how you feel; I feel puzzled."

"That's awkward," returned Allan. "I was
just going to ask you what we ought to do next."

"I don't like the look of the place, the look of
the shop-woman, or the look of the doctor," pursued the other. "And yet I can't say I think
they are deceiving us; I can't say I think they
really know Mrs. Mandeville's name."

The impressions of Pedgift Junior seldom misled him; and they had not misled him in this
case. The caution which had dictated Mrs.
Oldershaw's private removal from Bayswater
was the caution which frequently overreaches
itself. It had warned her to trust nobody at
Pimlico with the secret of the name she had assumed as Miss Gwilt's reference; but it had entirely failed to prepare her for the emergency

that had really happened. In a word, Mrs.
Oldershaw had provided for everything except
for the one unimaginable contingency of an
after-inquiry into the character of Miss Gwilt.

"We must do something," said Allan; "it
seems useless to stop here."

Nobody had ever yet caught Pedgift Junior
at the end of his resources; and Allan failed to
catch him at the end of them now. "I quite
agree with you, sir," he said; "we must do
something. We'll cross-examine the cabman."

The cabman proved to be immovable. Charged
with mistaking the place, he pointed to the empty
shop window. "I don't know what you may
have seen, gentlemen," he remarked; "but
there's the only shop window I ever saw with
nothing at all inside it. *That* fixed the place
in my mind at the time, and I know it again
when I see it." Charged with mistaking the
person, or the day, or the house at which he had
taken the person up, the cabman proved to be
still unassailable. The servant who fetched him
was marked as a girl well known on the stand.
The day was marked as the unluckiest working-
day he had had since the first of the year; and
the lady was marked as having had her money
ready at the right moment (which not one elderly
lady in a hundred usually had), and having paid
him his fare on demand without disputing it
(which not one elderly lady in a hundred usually
did). "Take my number, gentlemen," concluded
the cabman, "and pay me for my time; and what
I've said to you, I'll swear to anywhere."

Pedgift made a note in his pocket-book of the man's number. Having added to it the name of the street, and the names on the two brass plates, he quietly opened the cab door. "We are quite in the dark, thus far," he said. "Suppose we grope our way back to the hotel?"

He spoke and looked more seriously than usual. The mere fact of "Mrs. Mandeville's" having changed her lodging without telling any one where she was going, and without leaving any address at which letters could be forwarded to her—which the jealous malignity of Mrs. Milroy had interpreted as being undeniably suspicious in itself—had produced no great impression on the more impartial judgment of Allan's solicitor. People frequently left their lodgings in a private manner, with perfectly producible reasons for doing so. But the appearance of the place to which the cabman persisted in declaring that he had driven "Mrs. Mandeville" set the character and proceedings of that mysterious lady before Pedgift Junior in a new light. His personal interest in the inquiry suddenly strengthened, and he began to feel a curiosity to know the real nature of Allan's business which he had not felt yet.

"Our next move, Mr. Armadale, is not a very easy move to see," he said, as they drove back to the hotel. "Do you think you could put me in possession of any further particulars?"

Allan hesitated; and Pedgift Junior saw that he had advanced a little too far. "I mustn't force it," he thought; "I must give it time, and let it come of its own accord." "In the absence of any other information, sir," he resumed, "what do you say to my making some inquiry about that queer shop, and about those two names on the door-plate? My business in London, when I leave you, is of a professional nature; and I am going into the right quarter for getting information, if it is to be got."

"There can't be any harm, I suppose, in making inquiries," replied Allan.

He, too, spoke more seriously than usual; he, too, was beginning to feel an all-mastering curiosity to know more. Some vague connection, not to be distinctly realized or traced out, began to establish itself in his mind between the difficulty of approaching Miss Gwilt's family circumstances and the difficulty of approaching Miss Gwilt's reference. "I'll get down and walk, and leave you to go on to your business," he said. "I want to consider a little about this, and a walk and a cigar will help me."

"My business will be done, sir, between one and two," said Pedgift, when the cab had been stopped, and Allan had got out. "Shall we meet again at two o'clock, at the hotel?"

Allan nodded, and the cab drove off.

(END OF PART ONE OF "ARMADALE.")

END OF VOLUME EIGHT.